Excel

ADVANCED SKILLS

MATHS

YEAR 5

AGES 10–11

ADVANCED MATHEMATICS

Get the Results You Want!

PASCAL PRESS

Allyn Jones

Updated in 2025 for the NSW Curriculum and Australian Curriculum Version 9.0 changes

Reprinted 2025

ISBN 978 1 74125 658 1

Pascal Press
PO Box 250
Glebe NSW 2037
www.pascalpress.com.au

Publisher: Vivienne Joannou
Project editor: Rosemary Peers
Edited and proofread by Rosemary Peers
Answers checked by Peter Little and Melinda Amaral
Cover and page design by Sonia Woo
Typeset by Grizzly Graphics (Leanne Richters)
Printed by Vivar Printing/Green Giant Press

Contents

Introduction 4

The *Excel* step-by-step improvement plan 5

Excel books to help you *get the results you want!* 6

Marking grids 7

Section 1

Units 1A & 1B: **Number and place value** 10

Units 2A & 2B: **Fractions and decimals** 12

Units 3A & 3B: **Money and financial mathematics** 14

Units 4A & 4B: **Patterns and algebra** 16

Units 5A & 5B: **Using units of measurements** 18

Units 6A & 6B: **Shape** 20

Units 7A & 7B: **Location and transformation** 24

Units 8A & 8B: **Geometric reasoning** 28

Units 9A & 9B: **Chance** 30

Units 10A & 10B: **Data representation and interpretation** 32

Section 2

Unit 1 36

Unit 2 38

Unit 3 40

Unit 4 42

Unit 5 44

Unit 6 46

Unit 7 48

Unit 8 50

Unit 9 52

Unit 10 54

Unit 11 56

Unit 12 58

Unit 13 60

Unit 14 62

Unit 15 64

NAPLAN-style Test 1 66

Unit 16 70

Unit 17 72

Unit 18 74

Unit 19 76

Unit 20 78

Unit 21 80

Unit 22 82

Unit 23 84

Unit 24 86

Unit 25 88

Unit 26 90

Unit 27 92

Unit 28 94

Unit 29 96

Unit 30 98

NAPLAN-style Test 2 100

Worked Solutions & Answers 104

Introduction

The aim of the ***Excel*** Advanced Skills: Advanced Mathematics series is to build on and extend students' skills in Mathematics. Each book in the series supports the requirements of the Australian Curriculum (Mathematics) at each year level.

The series consists of six books, one for each year level, from Year 1 to Year 6. The series is supported by other books in the ***Excel*** Mathematics range.

Structure of the book

Level of difficulty key Level ★★★★★

The level of difficulty of each page is shown by a key at the top of the page showing a number of stars, with three stars being the least challenging questions and five stars being the most difficult.

Section 1

This section consists of ten double-page units of teaching and learning activities, each focused on a specific topic from the Number, Algebra, Measurement, Space, Statistics and Probability areas of the syllabus.

- **Unit A** provides work at an advanced four-star level
- **Unit B** provides work at the most advanced five-star level.

Section 2

This section consists of 30 carefully graded double-page units of teaching and learning activities. Each page provides questions from all areas of the syllabus: Number, Algebra, Measurement, Space, Statistics and Probability.

- **Units 1 to 15 A** provide introductory work at a three-star level
- **Units 1 to 15 B** and **16 to 30 A** provide work at an advanced four-star level
- **Units 16 to 30 B** provide work at the book's most advanced five-star level.

NAPLAN-style Tests

There are two mini NAPLAN-style tests. These tests:

- provide practice for the Year 5 NAPLAN Numeracy test
- are graded so that the questions in Test 2 are more challenging than in Test 1.

Worked Solutions & Answers

Worked solutions are provided for every question to support students' learning. Answers are also provided in bold for quick reference.

How to use this book with the *Excel* Advanced Skills English series

For a complete weekly English and Mathematics program use this book in conjunction with the ***Excel* Advanced Skills English Year 6** book. This way a student will have work set for four days a week—two days for English and two days for Mathematics.

How to assess students' progress

The results of the work undertaken in each unit can be recorded on the marking grids. The marking grids on pages 7, 8 and 9 (please see the example on page 5) are easy-to-use diagnostic tools that indicate where students' strengths and weaknesses lie in relation to specific areas of Mathematics. These results can be used to gather extra information about students' progress and their further revision needs.

The *Excel* Advanced and Basic Skills Series

If students are experiencing difficulty, require additional practice or need extension in any area of the course, further books are available to support them in the ***Excel*** Basic Skills and Advanced Skills series. (Please see the comprehensive list of ***Excel*** books on page 6.)

The *Excel* step-by-step improvement plan

Step 1

Read the introduction on page 4.

Step 2

The results of the work undertaken in each unit can be recorded on the marking grids.

These are easy-to-use diagnostic tools that indicate both where each student's strengths and weaknesses are in relation to specific areas of Mathematics as well as their ability to work at different levels of difficulty.

These results can be used to gather extra information about each student's progress and their further revision needs.

When marking answers on the grid, simply mark incorrect answers with 'X' in the appropriate box. This will result in a graphical representation of areas needing further work.

Section 1 Marking grid

See the sample Section 1 marking grid below:

Questions	1	2	3	4	5	6
Unit 1A ★★★★☆						
Unit 1B ★★★★★		X	X	X	X	
Unit 2A ★★★★☆						
Unit 2B ★★★★★						
Unit 3A ★★★★☆						
Unit 3B ★★★★★						
Unit 4A ★★★★☆						
Unit 4B ★★★★★						

This grid indicates that the student needs extra help and practice with the most advanced five-star level questions in Unit 1 (Number and Place Value).

If a student has only a few crosses marked in Unit 1A but a lot in Unit 1B, they are finding the more advanced questions in this topic challenging. This topic will therefore require more practice.

Section 2 Marking grid

See the sample Section 2 marking grid below.

If a student is consistently getting more than one in five questions wrong in any topic they need help in this area.

An example for the first five units is shown below. If a question has several parts, it should be counted as wrong if one or more mistakes are made.

		Factors & multiples	Estimation, addition and subtraction	Multiplication	Division	Mental strategies
	Questions	1	2	3	4	5
Unit 1A	★★★☆☆					
Unit 1B	★★★★☆					X
Unit 2A	★★★☆☆					
Unit 2B	★★★★☆					X
Unit 3A	★★★☆☆					
Unit 3B	★★★★☆					X
Unit 4A	★★★☆☆					
Unit 4B	★★★★☆					X
Unit 5A	★★★☆☆					
Unit 5B	★★★★☆					X

This grid indicates that the student needs extra help and practice with advanced four-star level mental strategies questions.

Step 3

Refer to page 6: *Excel* books to help you get the results you want!

Under each topic there is a comprehensive list of books in our range to help students practise the topic they are having difficulty with.

For example, if a student wants more practice with fractions questions, the books shown will help them. Each ***Excel*** book has a comprehensive contents page that will identify the appropriate pages in the book to target the specific topic area that is causing problems.

Excel books to help you *get the results you want!*

NUMBER AND ALGEBRA

Number, place value, fractions and decimals

Excel Basic Skills

9781741255904

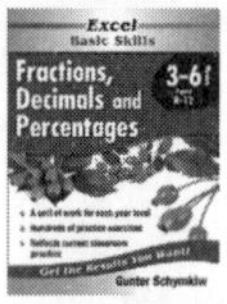

9781864412901

9781741257281

Excel Advanced Skills

9781741252620

Excel NAPLAN-style Tests

9781741253603

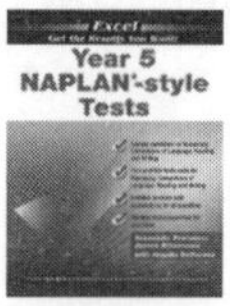

9781741251739

9781741252088

Money and financial mathematics

Excel Basic Skills

9781741255904

9781864412901

9781741257281

Excel Advanced Skills

9781741252620

Excel NAPLAN-style Tests

9781741253603

9781741251739

9781741252088

Patterns and algebra

Excel Basic Skills

9781741257281

Excel Advanced Skills

9781741252620

Excel NAPLAN-style Tests

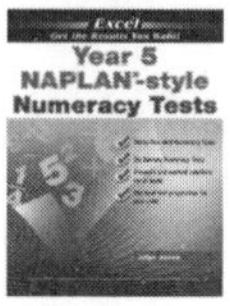

9781741253603

Excel NAPLAN-style Tests

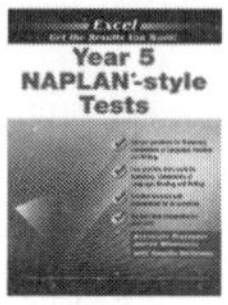

9781741251739

Excel NAPLAN-style Tests

9781741252088

MEASUREMENT AND SPACE

Using units of measurement

Excel Basic Skills

9781741257281

Excel Advanced Skills

9781741252620

Excel NAPLAN-style Tests

9781741253603

Excel NAPLAN-style Tests

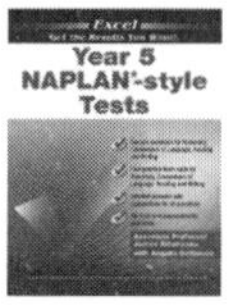

9781741251739

Excel NAPLAN-style Tests

9781741252088

Shape

Excel Basic Skills

9781741257281

Excel Advanced Skills

9781741252620

Excel NAPLAN-style Tests

9781741253603

Excel NAPLAN-style Tests

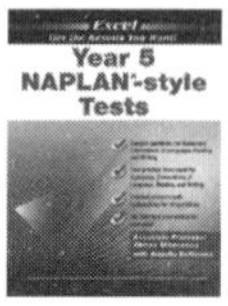

9781741251739

Excel NAPLAN-style Tests

9781741252088

Location, transformation and geometric reasoning

Excel Basic Skills

9781741257281

Excel Advanced Skills

9781741252620

Excel NAPLAN-style Tests

9781741253603

Excel NAPLAN-style Tests

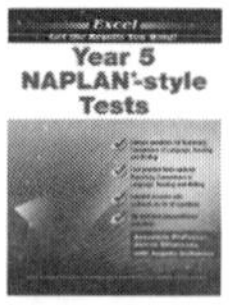

9781741251739

Excel NAPLAN-style Tests

9781741252088

STATISTICS AND PROBABILITY

Chance and data representation and interpretation

Excel Basic Skills

9781741257281

Excel Advanced Skills

9781741252620

Excel NAPLAN-style Tests

9781741253603

Excel NAPLAN-style Tests

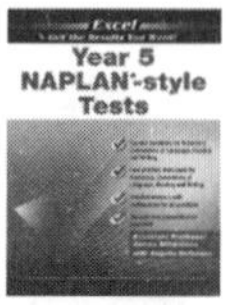

9781741251739

Excel NAPLAN-style Tests

9781741252088

Section 1 Marking grid

Number and Algebra
Units 1A & 1B: Number and place value
Units 2A & 2B: Fractions and decimals
Units 3A & 3B: Money and financial mathematics
Units 4A & 4B: Patterns and algebra

Measurement and Space
Units 5A & 5B: Using units of measurement
Units 6A & 6B: Shape
Units 7A & 7B: Location and transformation
Units 8A & 8B: Geometric reasoning

Statistics and Probability
Units 9A & 9B: Chance
Units 10A & 10B: Data representation and interpretation

Questions	1	2	3	4	5	6	7	8	9	10	11	12	13	14	15	16	17	18	19	20	21	22	23	24	25	26	27	28
Unit 1A ★★★★☆																												
Unit 1B ★★★★★																												
Unit 2A ★★★★☆																												
Unit 2B ★★★★★																												
Unit 3A ★★★★☆																												
Unit 3B ★★★★★																												
Unit 4A ★★★★☆																												
Unit 4B ★★★★★																												
Unit 5A ★★★★☆																												
Unit 5B ★★★★★																												
Unit 6A* ★★★★☆																												
Unit 6B* ★★★★★																												
Unit 7A ★★★★☆																												
Unit 7B ★★★★★																												
Unit 8A ★★★★☆																												
Unit 8B ★★★★★																												
Unit 9A ★★★★☆																												
Unit 9B ★★★★★																												
Unit 10A ★★★★☆																												
Unit 10B ★★★★★																												
Questions	1	2	3	4	5	6	7	8	9	10	11	12	13	14	15	16	17	18	19	20	21	22	23	24	25	26	27	28

Section 2 Marking grid

		Number and Algebra											Measurement and Space					Statistics and Probability	
		Factors & multiples	Estimation, addition and subtraction	Multiplication	Division	Mental strategies	Fractions: Comparing and ordering	Fractions: Adding and subtracting	Decimals: Ordering and operations	Financial mathematics	Patterns	Number sentences	Units, perimeter and area	Time	Shapes	Direction, symmetry and transformations	Angles	Probability	Statistics
	Questions	1	2	3	4	5	6	7	8	9	10	11	12	13	14	15	16	17	18
Unit 1A	★★★☆☆																		
Unit 1B	★★★★☆																		
Unit 2A	★★★☆☆																		
Unit 2B	★★★★☆																		
Unit 3A	★★★☆☆																		
Unit 3B	★★★★☆																		
Unit 4A	★★★☆☆																		
Unit 4B	★★★★☆																		
Unit 5A	★★★☆☆																		
Unit 5B	★★★★☆																		
Unit 6A	★★★☆☆																		
Unit 6B	★★★★☆																		
Unit 7A	★★★☆☆																		
Unit 7B	★★★★☆																		
Unit 8A	★★★☆☆																		
Unit 8B	★★★★☆																		
Unit 9A	★★★☆☆																		
Unit 9B	★★★★☆																		
Unit 10A	★★★☆☆																		
Unit 10B	★★★★☆																		
Unit 11A	★★★☆☆																		
Unit 11B	★★★★☆																		
Unit 12A	★★★☆☆																		
Unit 12B	★★★★☆																		
Unit 13A	★★★☆☆																		
Unit 13B	★★★★☆																		
Unit 14A	★★★☆☆																		
Unit 14B	★★★★☆																		
Unit 15A	★★★☆☆																		
Unit 15B	★★★★☆																		
	Questions	1	2	3	4	5	6	7	8	9	10	11	12	13	14	15	16	17	18

Section 2 Marking grid

		Number and Algebra											Measurement and Space					Statistics and Probability	
		Factors & multiples	Estimation, mixed operations	Mixed operations	Mixed operations	Mixed strategies	Fractions: Comparing and ordering	Fractions: Adding and subtracting	Decimals: Ordering and operations	Financial mathematics	Patterns	Number sentences	Units, perimeter and area	Time	Shapes	Direction, symmetry and transformations	Angles	Probability	Statistics
	Questions	1	2	3	4	5	6	7	8	9	10	11	12	13	14	15	16	17	18
Unit 16A	★★★★☆																		
Unit 16B	★★★★★																		
Unit 17A	★★★★☆																		
Unit 17B	★★★★★																		
Unit 18A	★★★★☆																		
Unit 18B	★★★★★																		
Unit 19A	★★★★☆																		
Unit 19B	★★★★★																		
Unit 20A	★★★★☆																		
Unit 20B	★★★★★																		
Unit 21A	★★★★☆																		
Unit 21B	★★★★★																		
Unit 22A	★★★★☆																		
Unit 22B	★★★★★																		
Unit 23A	★★★★☆																		
Unit 23B	★★★★★																		
Unit 24A	★★★★☆																		
Unit 24B	★★★★★																		
Unit 25A	★★★★☆																		
Unit 25B	★★★★★																		
Unit 26A	★★★★☆																		
Unit 26B	★★★★★																		
Unit 27A	★★★★☆																		
Unit 27B	★★★★★																		
Unit 28A	★★★★☆																		
Unit 28B	★★★★★																		
Unit 29A	★★★★☆																		
Unit 29B	★★★★★																		
Unit 30A	★★★★☆																		
Unit 30B	★★★★★																		
	Questions	1	2	3	4	5	6	7	8	9	10	11	12	13	14	15	16	17	18

FOCUS ON NUMBER AND PLACE VALUE

1 For the number 16 043, what is the value of the 6?

2 In the number 386 009, what is the value of the 8?

3 The number 67 452 is multiplied by 10.
What is the new place value of the 4?

4 How many zeros are in the number eighty thousand, four hundred and two?

5 Circle the numbers that are multiples of 6.

24, 26, 36, 40, 46

6 Circle the numbers that are divisible by 7.

17, 63, 71, 49, 7

7 How many multiples of 4 are between 30 and 50?

8 A book has 314 pages. Judi has read 186 pages. How many more pages does she need to read?

9 Before Janay left on her trip, her car's odometer showed 37 658 km. During her holiday she drove 3128 km. What did the odometer show at the end of her holiday?

10 Isla, Eloise and Cora are comparing the number of friends they have on a social media platform. Isla has 71, Eloise has 48 and Cora has 57. Estimate the total number of friends the three girls have, to the nearest ten.

11 712 – 293 = ☐
Circle the number closest to the answer.

300 400 500

12 Which of these rounds to 14 000, to the nearest thousand?

140 13 498 13 583 135

13 Tobias is walking on a pilgrimage through Spain. He plans to walk 28 km each day. How far will he walk in a week?

14
$$\begin{array}{r} 9736 \\ \times \quad 7 \\ \hline \end{array}$$

15 What is 579 multiplied by 90?

16 A British band played eight Australian concerts and the average attendance per concert was 27 974.
What was the total attendance?

17 What is 25 × 2 × 7?

18 Jasper has a collection of matchbox cars. He arranges the cars in 14 rows of 12 cars. How many cars are in Jasper's collection?

19 Share 425 marbles evenly between five boys.

20 What is one-third of 369?

21 One thousand, four hundred and twenty oranges are to be placed into bags of 10 oranges.
How many bags are required?

22 What is the remainder when 37 is divided by 5?

23 Mark thinks of a number. He multiplies it by 4 and the answer is 316.
What number did Mark think of?

24 Brielle baked 115 cakes to sell at the school market day. She sold the cakes in small boxes of four.
How many boxes did she fill?

25 Complete: 320 ÷ 16 = ☐ ÷ 8

26 Add 747 + 99.

27 What is 99 × 39?

28 Complete: 14 × 41 + 6 × 41 = ☐

FOCUS ON NUMBER AND PLACE VALUE

1 What is the sum of the values of the 3s in the numbers 1398 and 23 891?

2 What is the difference between the values of the 9s in the numbers 190 231 and 128 970?

3 Herman entered the digits 1, 2, 3, 4, 5, 6, 7, 8 and 9 in order into a calculator. Herman read the number. What is the place value of the 5 in his number?

4 How many zeros are in the number seventy million, three hundred and sixty thousand, and nine?

5 Circle the numbers that are divisible by 2, 3 and 5.

30, 50, 60, 90, 100

6 The number 536 is divisible by 8. How many numbers between 510 and 550 are divisible by 8?

7 Jordan wrote a list of the first 30 numbers that were divisible by 2. Maria wrote a list of the first 30 numbers that were divisible by 3. How many numbers were common to both lists?

8 By road the distance from Dubbo to Perth is 3556 km. From Dubbo to Brisbane is 836 km. What is the difference between the distances?

9 In 2011 the population of a city was 187 693. In the following 10 years the population increased by 19 879. What was the population of the city in 2021?

10 Four blocks of land in a new housing estate have areas of 517 m^2, 587 m^2, 595 m^2 and 613 m^2. Estimate the total area of the four blocks, to the nearest 100 m^2.

11 56 191 − 33 894 = ☐

Circle the number closest to the answer.

21 000   22 000   23 000

12 Which of these is closest to 250 000?

238 563   261 445

13 The Supporters Club organised 18 buses to drive from Newcastle to Sydney for a Knights NRL Grand Final game. If each bus has a capacity of 53 passengers, find the total number of potential passengers.

14 A garden centre has 42 packets of daffodil bulbs for sale. Each packet contains 24 bulbs. What is the total number of bulbs for sale?

15 What is 730 multiplied by 230?

16 Last Monday an airport had 86 aircraft landings. The average number of passengers per flight was 210. What was the total number of passengers?

17 Nolan rides 19 km to work each morning and rides the same route home in the evening. He rides four days every week. What is the total distance he rides?

18 Josephine has 15 jigsaw boxes in her cupboard. Six of the jigsaws have 750 pieces, seven have 1000 pieces and the remainder have 1500 pieces. What is the total number of jigsaw pieces?

19 2178 bales of hay are to be transported on nine trucks. If each truck will have the same number of bales, how many will be on each truck?

20 Heidi has a casual job and is paid $19 per hour. One week she works for 16 hours and the next week she works for 14 hours. What is her total pay for the two weeks?

21 What is the remainder when 83 is divided by 4?

22 Chockybars are produced in packets of 8. How many packets would be needed for 29 016 Chockybars?

23 A winery sells gift packs of four bottles of wine. If the winery had a total of 7375 bottles, how many gift packs could they make?

24 Complete 1218 ÷ 21 = ☐ ÷ 7

FOCUS ON FRACTIONS AND DECIMALS

1 The shape is divided into three equal sections.

Shade $\frac{2}{3}$ of the shape.

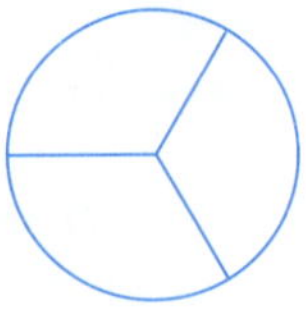

2 Circle the fraction that is the smallest.

$\frac{1}{5}$ $\frac{1}{3}$ $\frac{1}{10}$

3 Circle the fractions that are the same as one whole.

$\frac{6}{6}$ $\frac{1}{2}$ $\frac{10}{5}$ $\frac{3}{3}$

4 Rewrite $2\frac{3}{4}$ as an improper fraction.

5 Three rectangles are shown below.

Shade squares to represent the improper fraction $\frac{3}{2}$.

6 Part of a square is shaded.

What fraction is not shaded?

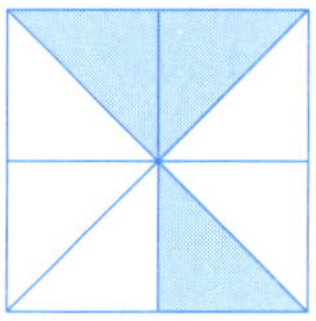

7 A number line is shown.

Which letter represents $\frac{5}{8}$?

8 What is $\frac{3}{10} + \frac{4}{10}$?

9 What is $1 - \frac{4}{15}$?

10 Naveen has a bucket of water. He pours $\frac{3}{5}$ of the bucket around a shrub. What fraction of the original water remains in the bucket?

11 What is the missing fraction?

$1 - \square = \frac{7}{10}$

12 What is $\frac{3}{4} + \frac{3}{4} + \frac{3}{4}$?

13 What is $1\frac{7}{8} - \frac{4}{8}$?

14 What is $\frac{413}{1000}$ written as a decimal?

15 How many thousandths are in 4 hundredths?

16 Which of these is closest to 30?

13.29 29.31 29.7 30.21

17 What is added to 3.872 to make 3.875? Circle the correct answer.

3 tenths 3 hundredths 3 thousandths

18 Choose from the following cards to make a number with two decimal places between 4.39 and 4.56.

7 5 3 4 8 .

19 What decimal is represented by the answer to $\frac{14}{100} + \frac{37}{100}$?

20 What decimal is halfway between 7.8 and 7.81?

21 Here are three decimals: 4.38, 4.309, 4.379.

Rewrite the decimals from smallest to largest.

22 Here is a number line.

Which letter is closest to 2.75?

23 What is the sum of 87.4 and 5?

24 Round 13.426 to two decimal places.

25 What is the sum of 1.6 and 0.34?

26 Rewrite 0.007 as a fraction.

FOCUS ON FRACTIONS AND DECIMALS

1 The shape is divided into six equal sections.
Shade $\frac{2}{3}$ of the shape.

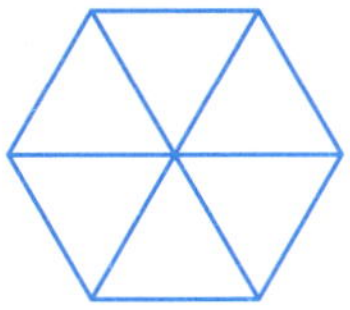

2 Rearrange these fractions from smallest to largest.

$\frac{1}{10}$ $\frac{1}{3}$ $\frac{1}{5}$ $\frac{1}{8}$

3 Circle the fraction(s) that are smaller than 1.

$\frac{3}{5}$ $\frac{6}{6}$ $\frac{11}{1}$ $\frac{3}{4}$

4 For half-time at a football match, oranges are cut into quarters. How many quarters can be cut from $4\frac{1}{2}$ oranges?

5 Three rectangles are shown below.

Shade squares to represent the improper fraction $\frac{7}{3}$.

6 Part of a square is shaded.
What fraction is not shaded?

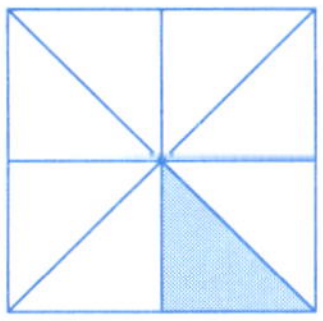

7 Here are four points located on a number line.

Which letter represents the improper fraction $\frac{18}{5}$?

8 What is $\frac{7}{8} + \frac{6}{8}$ as a mixed numeral?

9 What is the missing fraction?
$1 - \frac{417}{1000} = \square$

10 Last week Tacoma started reading a new novel. She has already read $\frac{7}{20}$ of the book and tonight she plans to read $\frac{4}{20}$ of the entire book.
What fraction will she have remaining?

11 What is the missing fraction?
$1 - \square = \frac{28}{45}$

12 Every morning for five days Chloe walks $\frac{3}{4}$ km around her block. What is the total distance walked?

13 Logan had a $4\frac{1}{5}$ metre length of stormwater pipe. He removed a $\frac{3}{5}$ metre long section from one end of the pipe. What was the remaining length of pipe?

14 What is $5\frac{9}{1000}$ written as a decimal?

15 How many thousandths are in 51 tenths?

16 Which of these is closest to 23?

23.4 23.087 22.92 22.908

17 What is subtracted from 18.699 to make 18.674? Circle the correct answer.

2 hundredths 25 hundredths
25 thousandths 5 hundredths

18 Choose from the following cards to make a number with three decimal places between 7.9 and 8.346.

7 5 3 4 8 .

19 What decimal is represented by the answer to $\frac{5}{10} + \frac{21}{1000} + \frac{3}{100}$?

20 What decimal is halfway between 14.63 and 14.64?

21 Four friends ran a 100-metre race and recorded their times in seconds. Erica: 13.41, Heidi: 13.38, Lana: 13.357 and Suzy: 13.408.
Who came third?

22 Here is a number line, where a is 2.96 and b is 2.98.

Which decimal is represented by c?

23 What is 3.697, correct to two decimal places?

24 Multiply 3.76 by 100.

FOCUS ON MONEY AND FINANCIAL MATHEMATICS

1 Eva saved $7.80 each week for 8 weeks. What was her total savings?

2 Layla had a $20 note. She spends $9.15 in a shop. How much change does she receive?

3 Leon bought two loaves of bread for $9.80. What was the cost of one loaf?

4 Molly bought the following items: a 4-L tin of paint for $78.90, a set of paintbrushes for $24.55, a roller for $9.20 and a packet of sandpaper for $6.75. What was the total cost?

5 Hayden buys a dartboard which costs $49 and a soccer ball for $24. How much change will he receive from $100?

6 A pair of running shoes are discounted by $54.05 to a price of $135.95. What was the original price of the shoes?

7 A bookshop was selling paperbacks for $15 each or 3 for $35. Thea wanted to buy four paperbacks. How much did she spend?

8 A three-person tent was originally priced at $825 but has been reduced in price by $145. What is the new price?

9 Entry tickets to a zoo cost $44.50 for adults and $26.80 for children. What would be the cost for Daisy and her 9-year-old son?

10 Owen bought a pair of shoes for $90 and two T-shirts for $40 each. How much did Owen pay in total?

11 Jasper and Aurora took their son Blake to the movies. An adult ticket cost $19 and a child ticket cost $12. What was the total cost of their tickets?

12 A supermarket sells a 2-L container of milk for $4 and a 500-g packet of mince for $9.50. How much will Felix pay in total if he buys two containers of milk and two packets of mince?

13 Frankie's uncle gave her $70 for her birthday. She bought two T-shirts for $29 each. How much did she have left?

14 An electrician charges $75 per hour. If a job took him 5 hours, what was the total cost of the job?

15 The entry prices for a circus are $35 for adults and $25 for children. What would be the total cost of entry for two adults and three children?

16 Xavier has saved $65. His grandmother gives him $80 for his birthday and he spends $110 on a new fishing rod and reel. How much does he have left?

17 Wilhelmina purchased 40 L of petrol at $1.49 per litre. What was the total cost?

18 Aiden bought a tray of sausages for $6.90, a packet of bread rolls for $2.80, a small bag of onions for $3.75 and a bottle of sauce for $2.65. What was the total cost?

19 A Laser Tag centre charges $18.50 per person per game. What will be the total cost for four people playing two games each?

20 For school, Max bought two notebooks at $2.48 each and a pencil case for $3.78. What was the total cost, to the nearest 5 cents?

21 The usual price of a necklace is $56. At a sale, the price is reduced by $18.45. What is the new price?

22 When Michael works as a service station attendant, he is paid $18.65 per hour. What is he paid for working 5 hours?

23 Ryan receives 10 cents for each bottle he deposits in a recycling machine. On Saturday he deposited 96 bottles and on Monday another 127 bottles.

How much did he receive in total?

24 Sienna buys a beach bag for $29.90, a pair of swimmers for $48.95 and a bodyboard for $50.

What is the total amount she spent?

FOCUS ON MONEY AND FINANCIAL MATHEMATICS

1 Justin and Maria buy lunch for their friends from the same shop. Justin orders a wrap and a hamburger and pays $11.50. Maria orders three wraps for $14.10. What is the price of the hamburger?

2 A street vendor sells fruit. Apples cost 80 cents each and mandarins cost 60 cents each. Hank buys two apples, three mandarins and four bananas. He hands the vendor $10 and gets $3 in change. What is the cost of a banana?

3 At a footy game, Archer bought a pie and two soft drinks for $10 and Kai bought two pies and a soft drink for $11. What is the total cost of a pie and a soft drink?

4 A game of golf costs $28 per person and the hire of a golf cart for two people is a total of $42. What will Sofia and Isabelle pay for a game of golf and golf cart hire?

5 The ticket prices for a concert are $32.50 for adults and $18.50 for children. However, a family ticket is available for a price of $85. How much is saved by Mr and Mrs Brady and their two children if they buy a family ticket?

6 Three baseballs cost the same as two cricket balls. If a baseball costs $12, what is the price of a cricket ball?

7 Petrol is priced at $2.04 per litre. Mila fills her car with 41.5 L of petrol. She uses her loyalty card to receive a discount of 4 cents per litre. How much will Mila pay?

8 Bars of chocolate are on sale for 2 for $5. Piper spends $20 on chocolate bars. How many did she buy?

9 A drive-in cinema's ticket prices are $13 for adults and $9 for children. The cost for Finn and his family was $40. If there was only one adult, how many children went to the cinema?

10 A company is holding a training day at a local club. There is a hiring fee of $50 plus a cost per person. If 10 people attend, the total cost will be $200. What will the total cost be if 16 people attend?

11 A school bought 15 tables and 30 chairs. A table costs twice as much as a chair. If chairs cost $20 each, what was the total amount spent by the school?

12 Mackenzie's parents give her a weekly allowance of $12 every Wednesday. If 1 October is a Monday, how much will Mackenzie be paid in October?

13 Kate won a lottery prize of 5.3 million dollars. She decided to give $875 000 to charity. How much did she have left?

14 Adrian runs a small business from home. In September his expenses totalled $6782 and his income was $10 558. What was his profit for September?

15 Leilani babysits for her parents' friends. She charges $15 plus $7.50 for every hour of babysitting. How much will she charge for babysitting from 6 pm to 10 pm?

16 Last week Naomi worked for 12 hours in her casual job and was paid $216. This week she worked for 19 hours at the same pay rate. What will she be paid for this week's work?

17 As a hobby, Skye makes children's clothes to sell at markets. She paid $65 for a stall at a Saturday market and throughout the day sold 18 dresses at $45 each. If each dress cost $16 to make, how much profit did she make?

18 For every kilogram cherries cost $8.90, lychees cost $7.50 and dates cost $18.40. Leah bought half a kilogram of each of the three fruits. What was her change from a $20 note?

19 Elke bought a skirt for $32.50 and a top for $24.95. She also bought a coat that was four times the price of the skirt. What was the total amount she spent?

20 Theodore won a $2890 lotto prize. He decided to give $290 to charity, $640 to his sister and half the remainder to his son. What amount does Theodore keep?

21 Each week Hayley earns $1640. She pays $425 rent and budgets $240 for food, $85 for transport, $70 for entertainment and $260 for other expenses. The remainder is saved. How much money will Hayley save in two weeks?

FOCUS ON PATTERNS AND ALGEBRA

1 Here is a sequence of numbers: 14, 26, 38 …
What are the next three numbers?

2 Here is a sequence with two missing numbers.
45, ……, 33, 27, ……, 15, 9
What are the missing numbers?

3 Here is a pattern of numbers: 17, 30, 43 …
What are the next two numbers?

4 Here is a pattern of decimals: 2.1, 3.3, 4.5 …
What are the next two decimals?

5 Here is a pattern of numbers.
……, ……, 37, 41, 45, 49
What are the first two numbers?

6 Here is a pattern of decimals.
……, 8.6, 9, 9.4, ……
What are the two missing decimals?

7 Here is a pattern of fractions: $\frac{1}{4}$, $\frac{3}{4}$, $1\frac{1}{4}$, ……, ……
What are the next two numbers in the pattern, written as mixed numerals?

8 Here is a pattern of decimals.
……, 4.25, 4.45, 4.65, ……
What are the two missing decimals?

9 Here is a pattern of numbers:
6, 21, ……, 51, 66
Find the missing number.

10 Here is a pattern of fractions.
$\frac{2}{5}$, $\frac{3}{5}$, $\frac{4}{5}$, ……, …… …
What are the two missing numbers?

11 Find the first four numbers in the sequence that starts with 540 and decreases by 30.

12 'The quotient of forty-two and seven is the same as six.' Rewrite this statement as a number sentence.

13 INPUT → × 8 → + 3 → OUTPUT
If the INPUT is 5, what is the OUTPUT?

14 Here is a number sentence.
$96 \div 8 = \square - 5$
What is the missing number?

15 Here is a number sentence.
$9 \times 7 = 43 + \square$
What is the missing number?

16 $14.7 + \square = 22.5$
Find the missing number.

17 $15.4 - \square = 8$
Find the missing number.

18 $\square - 8.3 = 12$
Find the missing number.

19 $\square + \frac{2}{5} = 1$
Find the missing number.

20 Here is a number sentence.
$\square + 19 = 41$
Justin thinks the missing number is 22. Is Justin correct?

21 Here is a number sentence.
$4 \times \square = 240$
Rachael thinks the missing number is 80. Is she correct?

22 Here is a number sentence.
$560 \div \square = 8$
Jodie thinks the missing number is 70. Is Jodie correct?

23 $4 - \square = 1.48$
Find the missing number.

24 Use one of these symbols: <, =, or > to make a true number sentence.
$83 - 48 \ \square \ 18 + 15$

FOCUS ON PATTERNS AND ALGEBRA

1 Here is a sequence of fractions: $\frac{3}{8}, \frac{5}{8}, \frac{7}{8} \ldots$

What is the twelfth member of the sequence, as a mixed numeral? [ ]

2 Here are some numbers in a pattern: … 48, 52, 56 …
If 48 is the sixth number in the pattern, what is the first number? [ ]

3 Here are some numbers in a pattern.
… 65, 58, 51 …
If 51 is the eighth number in the pattern, what is the first number? [ ]

4 Here are some numbers in a pattern.
… 36, 44, 52 …
If 36 is the fourth number in the pattern, what is the tenth number? [ ]

5 Simone writes a pattern of numbers.
… 83, 100, 117 …
If 83 is the fifth number in the pattern, what is the twenty-fifth number? [ ]

6 Here is a sequence of mixed numerals.

$4\frac{3}{8}, 6\frac{5}{8}, 8\frac{7}{8} \ldots$

What comes next in the sequence? [ ]

7 Kelly is training for a fun run. Every week she plans to run 1.2 km longer than the previous week. In week 4 she ran 7.6 km. How far does Kelly plan to run in week 10? [ ]

8 Gordon uses the rule 'Start with 36 and increase by 8'. What will be the tenth number in the sequence? [ ]

9 Sam uses the rule 'Start with 310 and decrease by 8'. What will be the nineteenth number in the sequence? [ ]

10 Here is a pattern of decimals.

[ ], 5.883, 5.871, 5.859, [ ]

What are the two missing decimals?

11 Here is a pattern of numbers.

[ ],1087, 1068, 1049, [ ]

What are the two missing numbers?

12 Here is a number sentence: [ ] ÷ 14 = 56

What is the missing number? [ ]

13 INPUT → × 4 → + 5 → OUTPUT

If the OUTPUT is 29, what is the INPUT? [ ]

14 Here is a number sentence.

9 × 8 − [ ] = 48

What is the missing number? [ ]

15 Here is a number sentence.

12 × 7 + [ ] = 110

What is the missing number? [ ]

16 364 + [ ] = 612

Find the missing number. [ ]

17 3.5 + 4.4 = 5.5 + [ ]

Find the missing number. [ ]

18 [ ] + $\frac{2}{5} + \frac{1}{5} = 1$

Find the missing number. [ ]

19 INPUT → ÷ 8 → − 50 → OUTPUT

If the INPUT is 640, what is the OUTPUT? [ ]

20 INPUT → + 14 → × 9 → OUTPUT

If the INPUT is 10, what is the OUTPUT? [ ]

21 Here is a number sentence.

57 + [ ] = 123 − 44

What is the missing number? [ ]

22 Leila thought of a number [?]. The sum of Leila's number and 16 is the same as the difference between 44 and 11. Using Leila's number [?] and symbols, write a number sentence and find her number. [ ]

FOCUS ON USING UNITS OF MEASUREMENT

1 A square has a perimeter of 96 cm. What is the length of each side of the square, in centimetres?

2 Marcus sets out to walk 5 km. After 45 minutes he has walked 4 km 50 m. How much further does Marcus need to walk?

3 A running circuit around a local park has a length of 780 m. Greg runs around the circuit three times. How far does he run, in metres?

4 Find the perimeter of the shape.

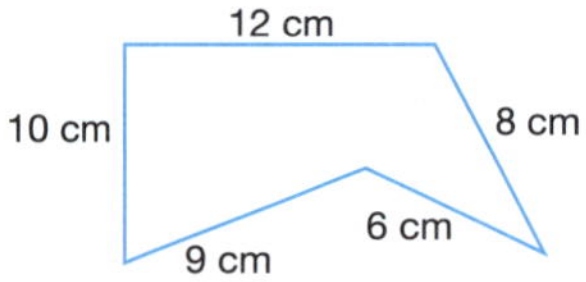

5 Find the perimeter of the shape.

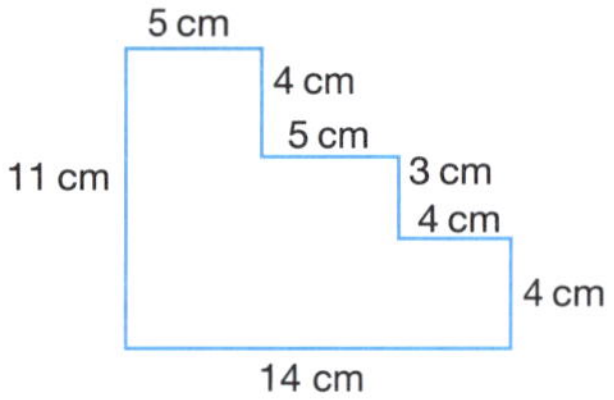

6 The perimeter of an equilateral triangle is 240 cm.

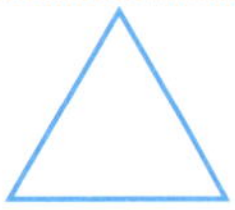

What is the length of each side?

7 The shape has a perimeter of 38 cm. What is the length of the missing side?

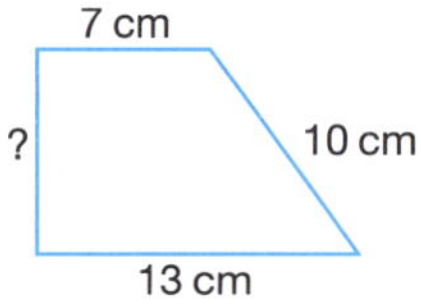

8 Find the area of the rectangle.

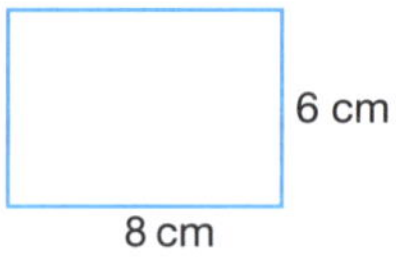

9 A rectangle has an area of 60 cm^2. If the length of the rectangle is 10 cm, what is the width?

10 How many hectares are in 120 000 m^2?

11 A square has a perimeter of 80 cm. What is the area of the square?

12 The area of the square is 20 cm^2.

If the square has been divided into four equal triangles, what is the area of the shaded triangle?

13 A shape is made up of six identical squares. The total area of the shape is 24 cm^2. What is the area of each square?

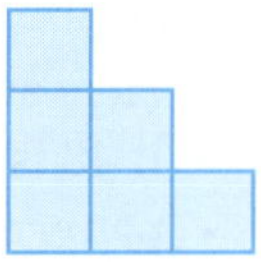

14 The solid is made up of identical cubic-centimetre blocks. What is the volume of the solid, in cubic centimetres?

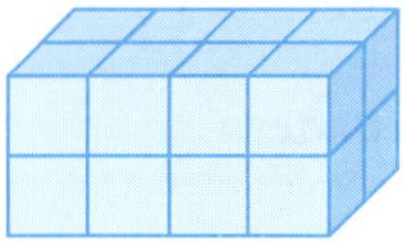

15 The solid is made up of cubic-centimetre blocks. The mass of each block is 4 kilograms.

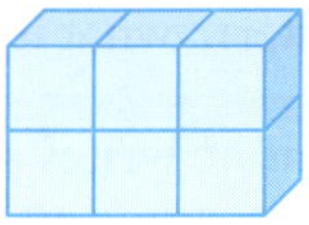

What is the total mass of the solid?

16 A glass contains 180 mL of water. If Graeme drinks half of the water, what amount of water remains in the glass?

17 Henrietta buys a 1.5-litre bottle of iced tea. She pours 250 mL into a glass. What amount is left in the bottle, in millilitres?

18 Last night Luca went to bed at twenty past eight. Write this in 24-hour time.

19 A concert finished at 11:00 pm. What is this in 24-hour time?

20 A game of rugby league is expected to finish at 9:50 pm. What is this time in 24-hour time?

21 Soren's school bell rings at 3:15 pm and one hour later he starts his soccer training. What time, in 24-hour time, does Soren's training start?

22 Last night Clara finished reading at 2148 and turned off her lamp. What is this in 12-hour time?

FOCUS ON USING UNITS OF MEASUREMENT

1 A square has a perimeter of 2 m 20 cm. What is the length of each side of the square, in centimetres?

2 Henry sets out to walk $5\frac{1}{2}$ km. After 20 minutes he has walked $1\frac{3}{4}$ km. How much further does Henry need to walk, in **metres**?

3 A running circuit is marked in a local reserve. Amelia runs around the circuit three times. If she runs a total of 4 km 350 m, how long is the circuit?

4 The perimeter of this shape is 58 cm. What is the length of the missing side?

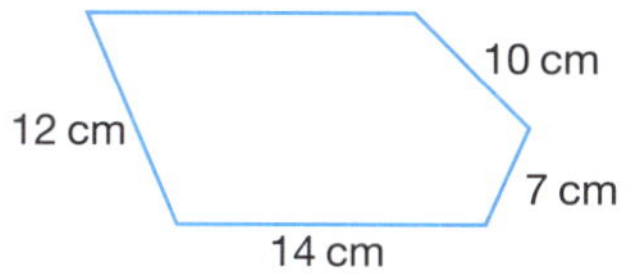

5 Find the perimeter of the shape.

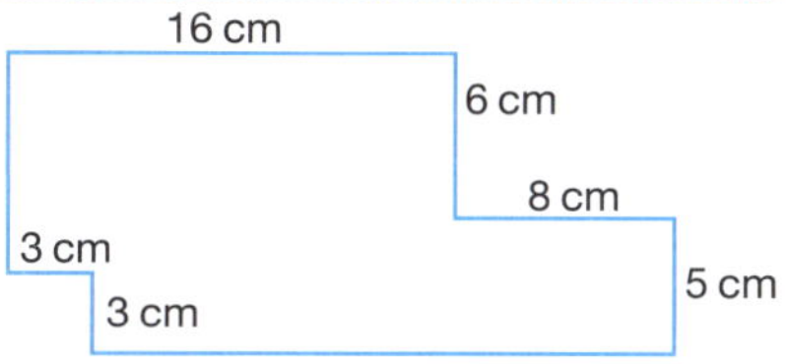

6 The shape shows an isosceles triangle joined to a rectangle. The perimeter of the shape is 42 cm.

What is the length of the rectangle?

7 A regular hexagon has each side of length 320 mm. What is the perimeter in metres and millimetres?

m mm

8 What is the length of a rectangle with a perimeter of 20 cm and an area of 24 cm^2?

9 What is the area, in hectares, of a rectangular park which measures 3.6 km long by 800 m wide?

10 The perimeter of a rectangle is 216 cm. The rectangle is three times as long as it is wide. What is the area of the rectangle?

11 A square paddock is to be fenced. The cost of fencing is $16 per metre. If the total cost of fencing is $3840, what is the area of the paddock?

12 The perimeter of this square is 24 cm. The square has been split into four equal triangles. What is the area of the shaded triangle?

13 A rectangular prism is made of cubic-centimetre blocks. The length is 4 blocks long, the width is 3 blocks wide and the height is 5 blocks high.

What is the volume of the prism?

14 The mass of a box of chocolates is 270 g. There are 12 identical chocolates in the box. When Cynthia eats two chocolates, the box now has a mass of 230 g. What is the mass of the empty box?

15 This cube is made of cubic-centimetre blocks. The mass of each block is 10 g.

What is the total mass of the cube?

16 A bottle contains 2 L of water. Sharon drinks 430 mL of water. How much water remains in the bottle?

17 Ajay has three containers: a 1-litre, a 2-litre and a 3-litre container. Each container is half-filled with milk. What is the total amount of milk, in millilitres?

18 Muhammad leaves his home at 2015 and drives to his holiday unit, arriving 11 hours later. What is the time he arrives, in 12-hour time?

19 Eden and Elliot went to the same party. Eden left the party at 2250 while Elliot stayed for another two and a quarter hours. At what time did Elliot leave the party, in 12-hour time?

20 Alisha attended a concert that started at 7:50 pm. The concert ran for 2 hours 40 minutes. At what 24-hour time did the concert finish?

FOCUS ON SHAPE

1 The net of a cube is drawn below. What letter is on the opposite face to *B*?

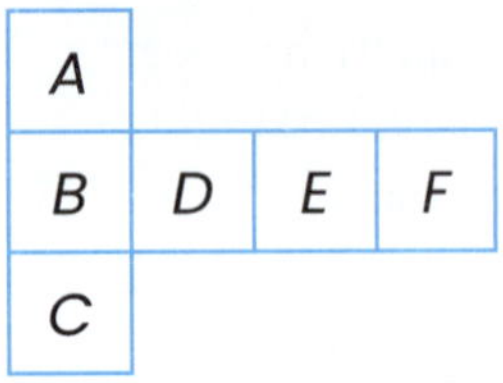

2 The net of a cube is drawn below. What letter is on the opposite face to *E*?

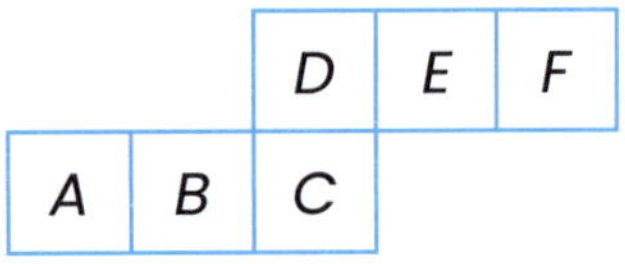

3 The net of a cube is drawn below.

What letter is on the opposite face to *P*?

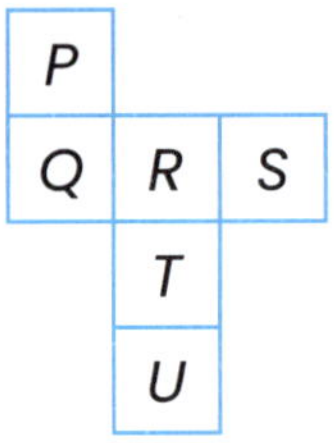

4 The net of a cube is drawn below.

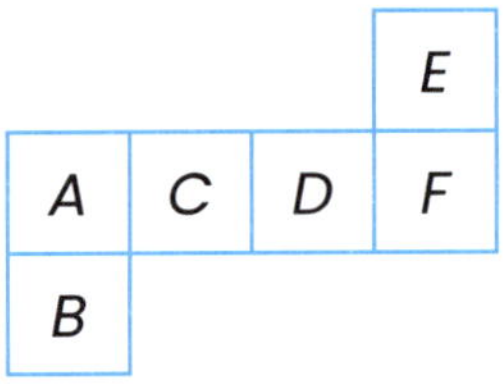

What letter is on the opposite face to *B*?

5 The net of a cube is drawn below.

What symbol is on the opposite face to ♥ ?

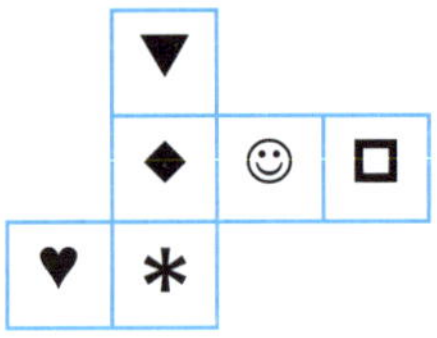

6 The net of a cube is drawn below.

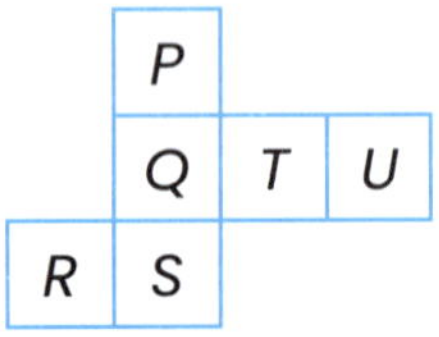

What letter is on the opposite face to *T*?

7 How many pairs of parallel faces does a triangular prism have?

8 Gabriella draws the net of a hexagon-based pyramid. Complete the statement.

The net is made up of ....

and ....

9 The net of a cube is drawn below. The opposite faces add to 7.

Use numbers to label the missing faces.

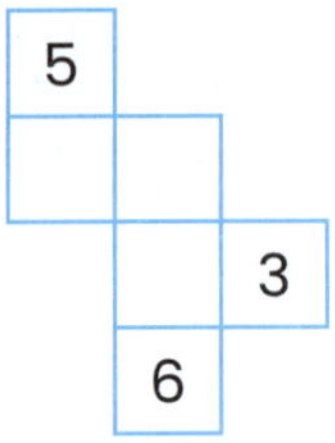

10 The net of a cube is drawn below.

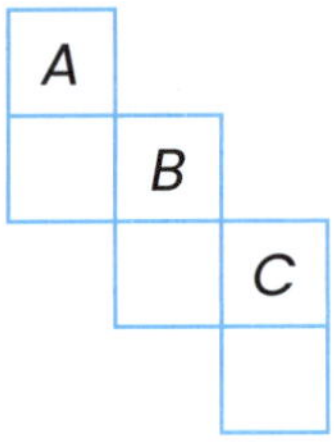

The opposite faces are *B* and *E*, *C* and *D*, and *A* and *F*. Use the letters *D*, *E* and *F* to label the missing faces.

11 The net of a cube is drawn below.

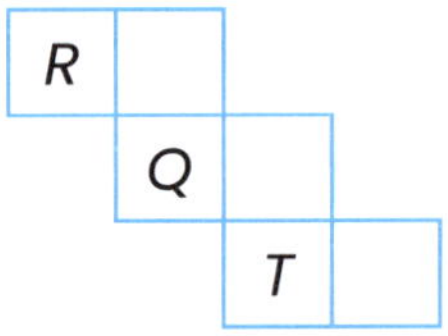

The opposite faces are *P* and *Q*, *R* and *S*, and *T* and *U*. Use the letters *P*, *S* and *U* to label the missing faces.

12 Here are some 3D shapes. Circle the prism(s).

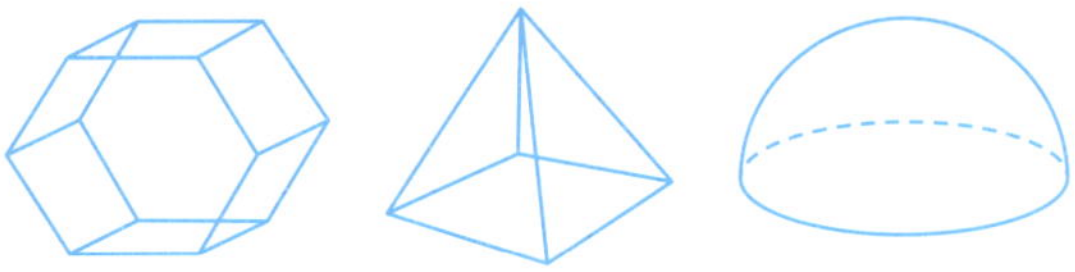

13 Here are some 3D shapes. Circle any solid(s) with five faces.

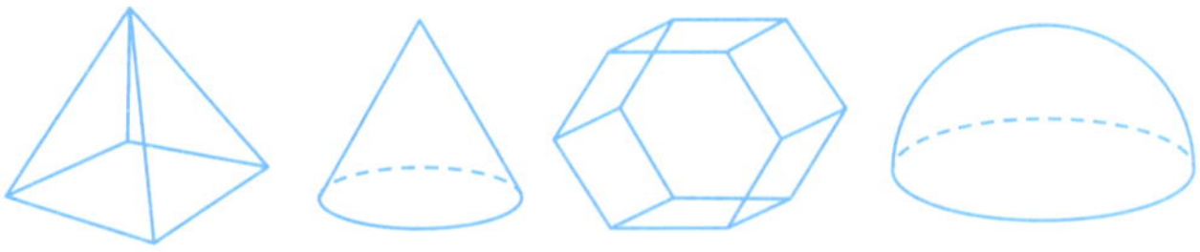

14 Here are some 3D shapes. Circle the solid(s) with more than five edges.

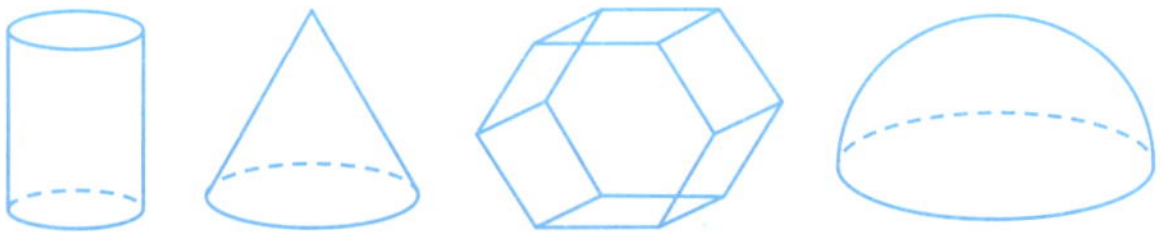

15 Which two 3D shapes were used to construct this shape?

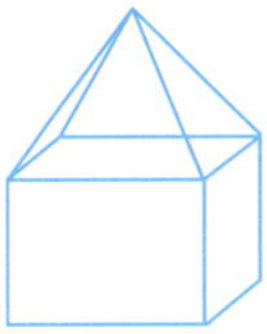

16 How many faces has a hexagonal prism?

17 How many vertices has a pentagonal prism?

18 How many vertices has a square-based pyramid?

19 How many faces has a triangular prism?

20 This solid is cut with a knife, shown by the dotted line.

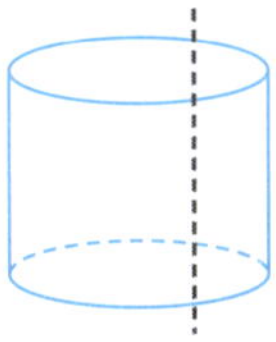

Circle the shape that is the cut face.

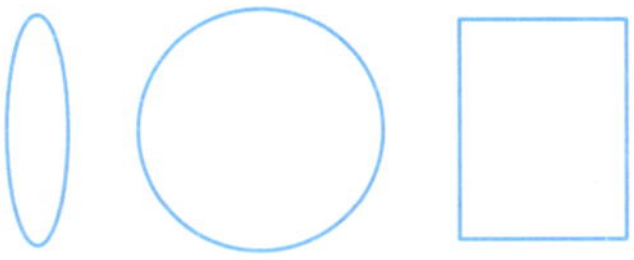

21 This solid is cut with a knifc, shown by the dotted line.

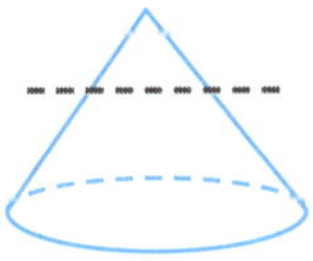

Circle the shape that is the cut face.

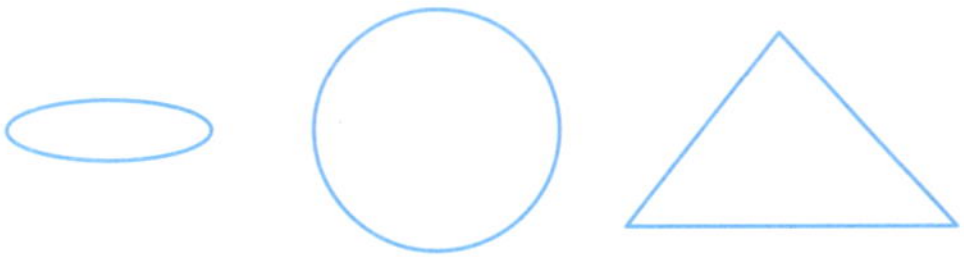

22 Circle the isosceles triangle(s).

23 Circle the scalene triangle(s).

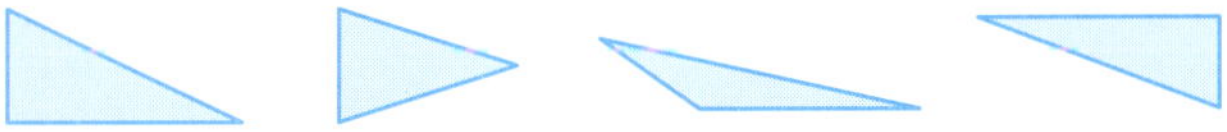

24 Here are the names of some polygons.

hexagon decagon pentagon octagon

Circle the name of the polygon with the most sides.

25 Draw a right-angled isosceles triangle.

26 Chelsea wrote these two statements. Only one of her statements is true.

All rectangles are parallelograms.
All parallelograms are rectangles.

Tick the correct statement.

27 The parallelogram below is not drawn to scale. The length of side AB is 8 cm and the length of BC is 7 cm.

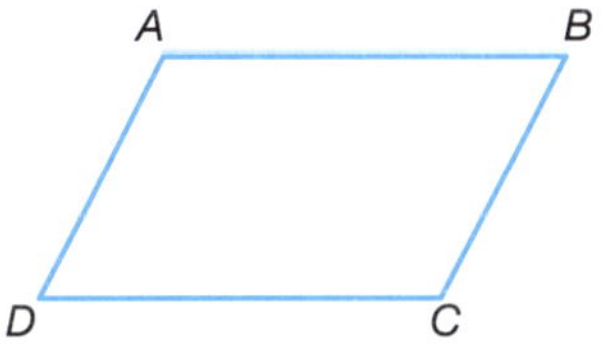

What is the perimeter of the parallelogram?

28 Draw a right-angled scalene triangle.

FOCUS ON **SHAPE**

1 The net of a cube is drawn below.

The numbers on opposite faces add to the same total.

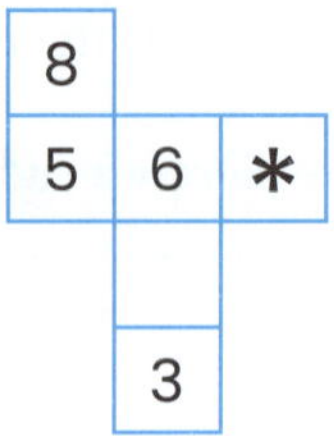

What number is represented by *?

---

2 The net of a cube is drawn below.

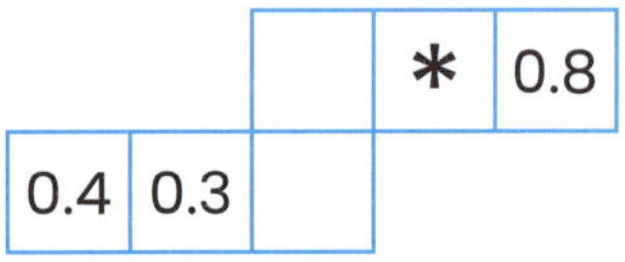

The numbers on opposite faces add to 1.

What number is represented by *?

---

3 The net of a cube is drawn below.

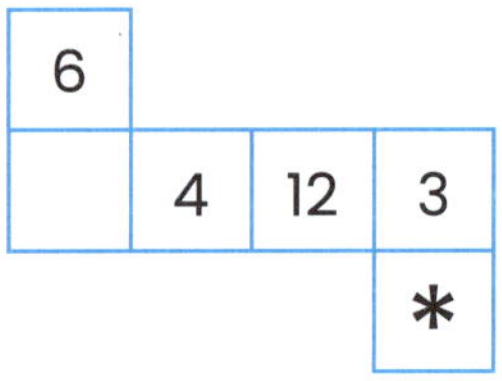

The numbers on opposite faces multiply to the same number.

What number is represented by *?

---

4 The net of a cube is drawn below.

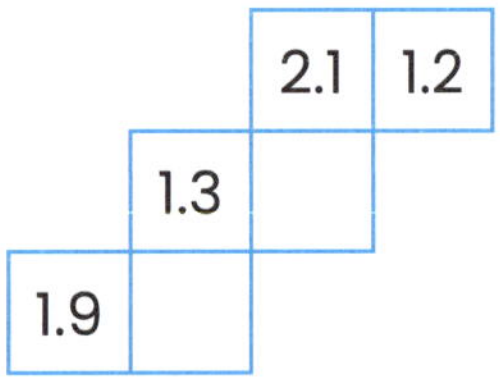

The numbers on opposite faces always add to the same total.

What is the sum of all the faces of the cube?

---

5 The net of a cube is drawn below.

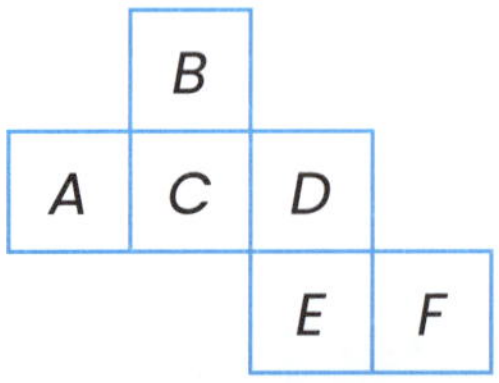

The numbers on opposite faces multiply to the same number.

If $A = 6$, $B = 12$, $C = 24$ and $D = 8$, what is the number represented by E?

---

6 The net of a cube is drawn below.

The numbers on opposite faces add to the same number.

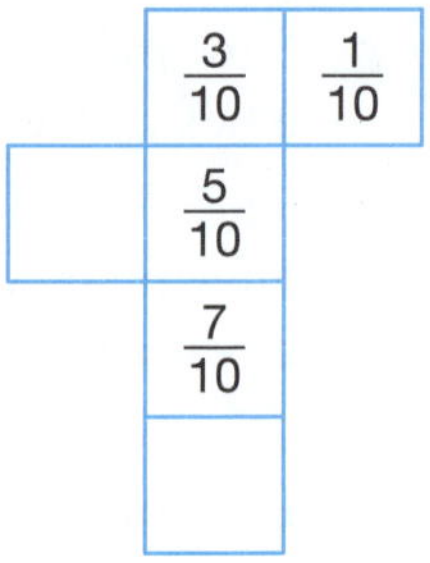

What is the sum of the numbers on all the faces of the cube?

---

7 The net of a cube is drawn below.

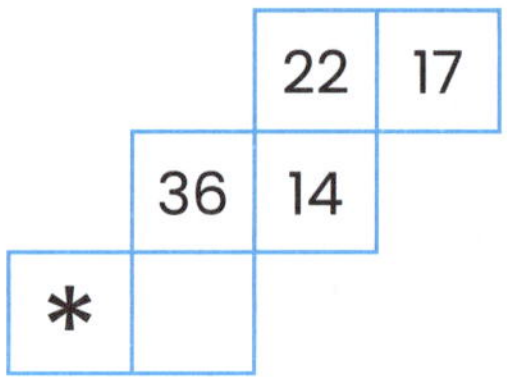

The difference between the numbers on opposite faces is always the same.

What positive number is represented by *?

---

8 Numbers are written on two identical cubes. For the first cube, numbers 1 to 6 are used so that opposite faces add to 7. On the second cube, numbers 5 to 10 are used so that opposite faces add to 15. If the faces with the number 5 are glued together to form a prism, what number is opposite 2?

---

9 How many pairs of parallel faces does a regular hexagonal prism have?

---

10 Ted draws the net of a pentagonal prism. Complete the statement.

The net is made up of ....

and ....

---

11 Here are three solids. Circle the shape(s) with an apex.

---

12 A vertex on a cube is cut off. How many edges has the new solid?

13 The faces of two identical cubes are glued together to form a new solid. How many edges are on the new solid?

14 The top of a square pyramid is removed. How many **more** vertices has the new solid compared to the pyramid?

15 A large cube is made from 27 small identical cubes. The outside of the large cube is painted. Once dry, the cube is pulled apart. How many of the small cubes have one face painted?

16 In a hexagonal prism, what does the number of faces plus the number of vertices minus the number of edges equal?

17 In an octagonal pyramid, what does the number of faces plus the number of vertices minus the number of edges equal?

18 The bases of two identical square-based pyramids are glued together to form a new solid. What does the number of faces plus the number of vertices minus the number of edges equal?

19 An icosahedron is a solid with 20 faces and 12 vertices. If the number of faces plus the number of vertices minus the number of edges equals 2, how many edges has an icosahedron?

20 This solid is cut with a knife, shown by the dotted line.

Circle the shape that is the cut face.

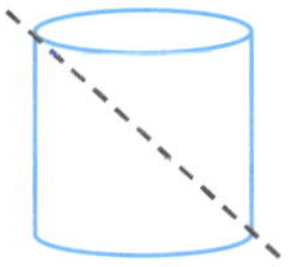

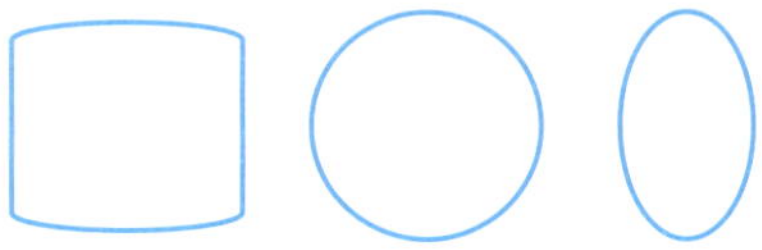

21 This solid is cut with a knife, shown by the dotted line.

Circle the shape that is the cut face.

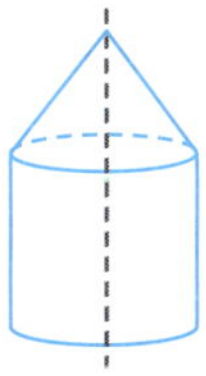

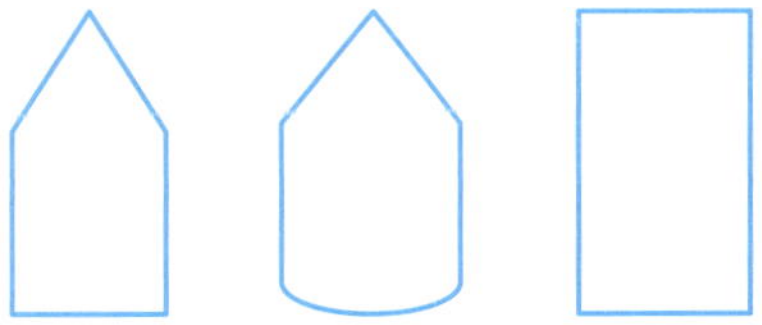

22 Here are three shapes. Circle the regular polygon(s).

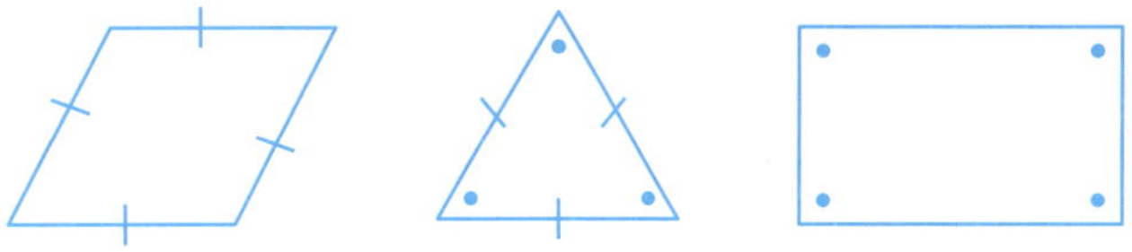

23 All the interior angles in a regular hexagon add to 720°. What is the size of each interior angle?

24 Here are the names of some polygons.

hexagon decagon pentagon octagon

Rewrite the names in order from smallest number of sides to largest.

25 Petra sketched a polygon. It has two pairs of parallel sides. The diagonals are the same length. The diagonals cut each other at right angles. What shape did Petra draw?

26 Greta drew a parallelogram. Her protractor showed one of the interior angles of the parallelogram was 80°. What was the size of the other three angles?

27 The diagram shows a parallelogram named *ABCD*. The two triangles named *ADX* and *BCY* are identical. *CY* is 8 cm long and *AB* is 12 cm long.

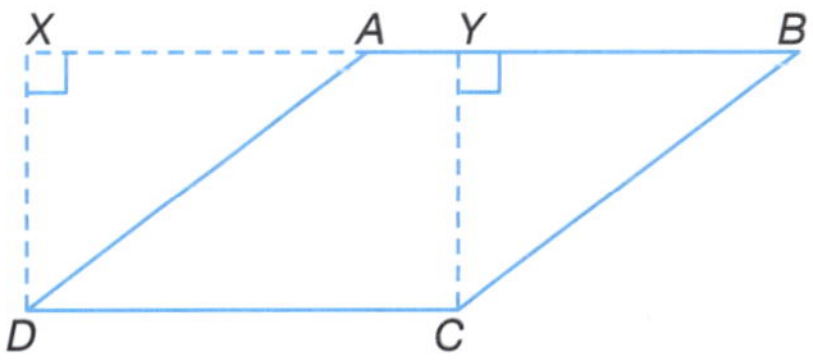

What is the area of the parallelogram?

28 Fiona drew a quadrilateral which has exactly two right angles. Which shape could she have drawn?

Circle the possible shape(s).

rectangle

trapezium

kite

rhombus

FOCUS ON LOCATION AND TRANSFORMATION

1 Draw the line(s) of symmetry on this shape.

2 Here are four letters. Circle the letter(s) with one line of symmetry.

M F T N

3 Draw the line(s) of symmetry on this shape.

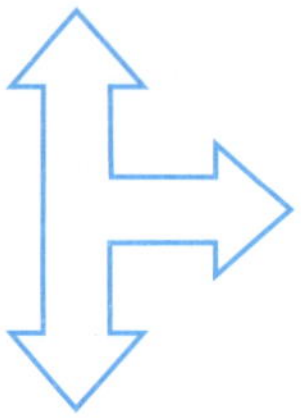

4 Draw the line(s) of symmetry on this shape.

5 Draw the line(s) of symmetry on this shape.

6 Draw the line(s) of symmetry on this shape.

7 Draw the line(s) of symmetry on this shape.

8 How many lines of symmetry has a parallelogram?

9 How many lines of symmetry has a regular octagon?

10 How many lines of symmetry has a circle?

11 How many lines of symmetry has an isosceles triangle?

12 Circle the symbol(s) that have exactly two lines of symmetry.

♥ ♦ ♣ ♠

13 On the grid, mark the location of A4 and D2.

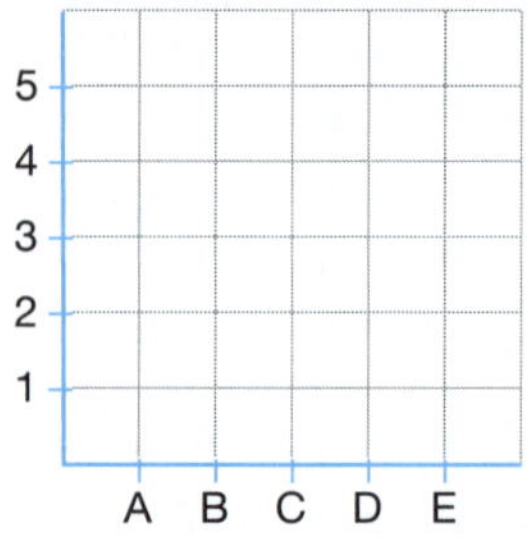

14 The grid shows the points *X* and *Y*.

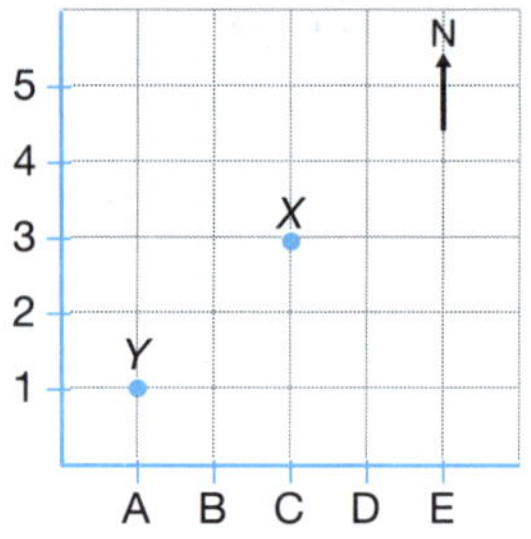

X is .... of *Y*. Circle the correct direction.

south-east   north-east
north-west   south-west

15 On the grid mark *P* at E1. From *P*, move 4 units west and then 3 units north. Mark this location as *Q*.

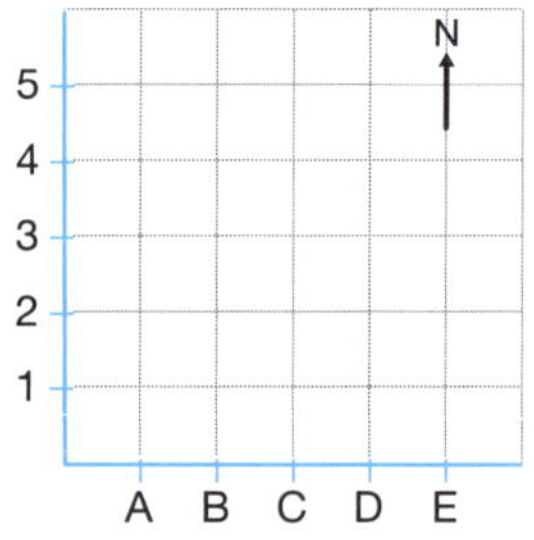

16 The grid represents a map with scale 1 unit = 2 km. Allison leaves *X* and travels south 4 units and then east to *Y*.

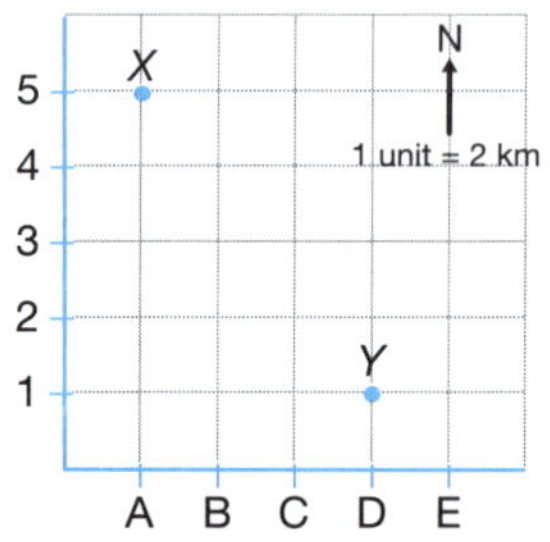

How many kilometres has she travelled?

17 An object is reflected in the mirror line. Draw the image.

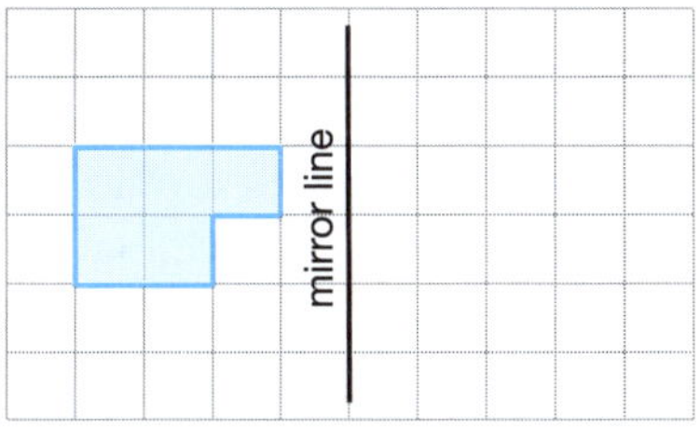

18 Rotate the points P and Q 90° in a clockwise direction about O.

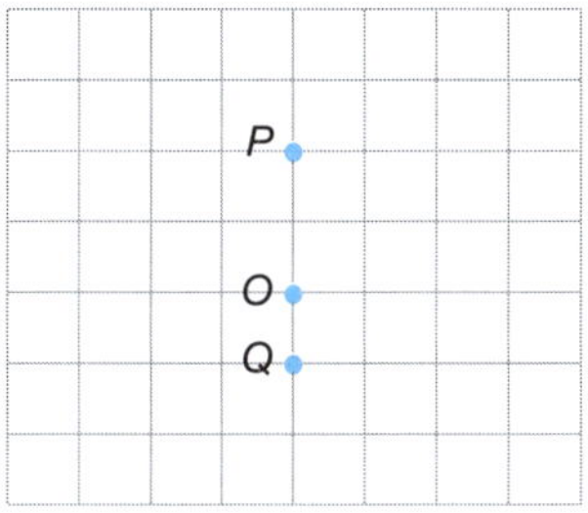

19 Rotate the line AB 90° in a clockwise direction about O.

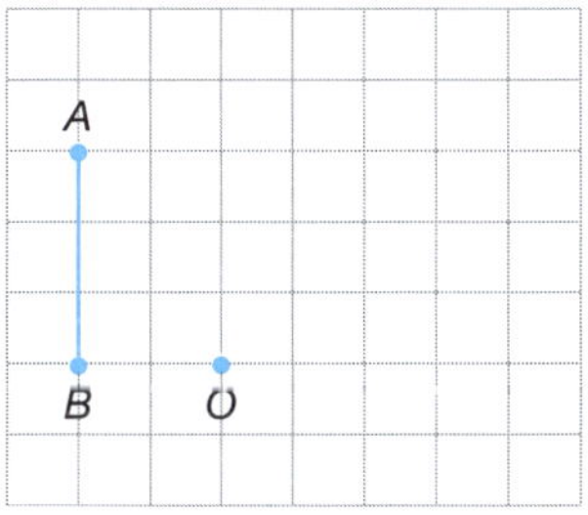

20 Translate the shape 3 units to the right.

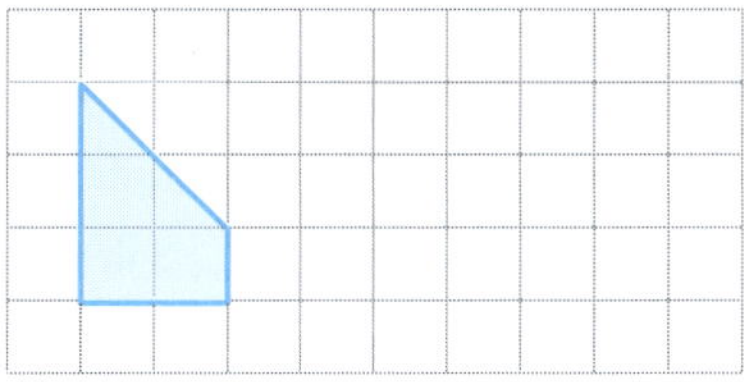

21 Enlarge the shape by a scale factor of 2.

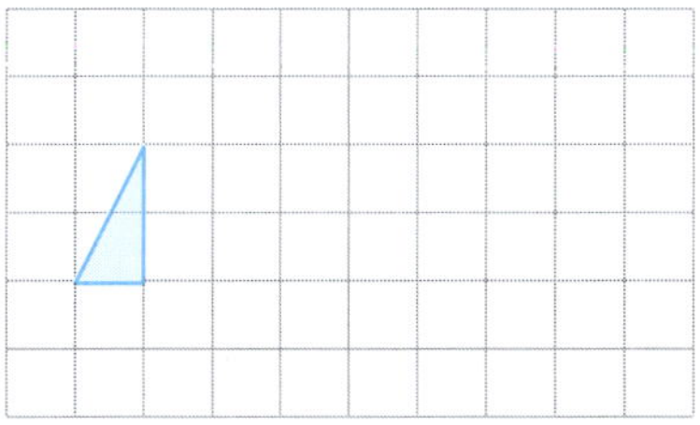

22 Describe the transformation from P to Q.

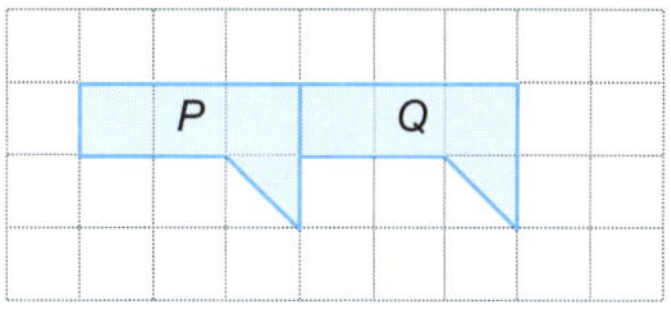

23 Describe the transformation from X to Y.

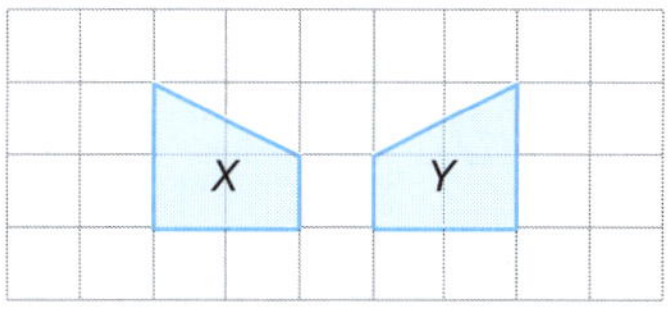

24 A square has a side length of 4 cm. The square is enlarged by a scale factor of 2. What is the perimeter of the new square?

25 The shape is to be enlarged by a factor of 2. Ashlee has started the enlargement by drawing one of the sides. Complete the enlargement.

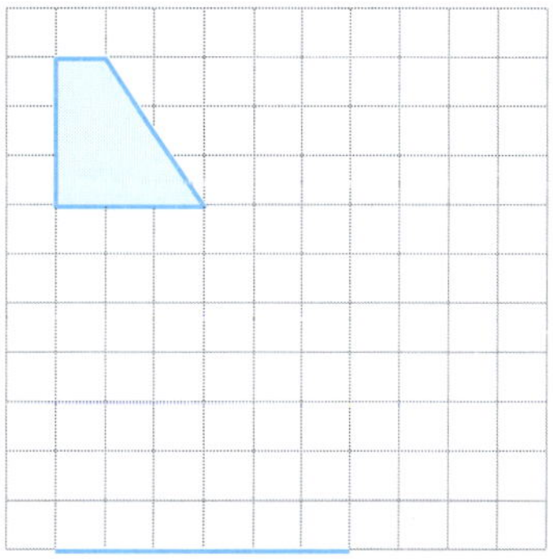

26 Tobias enlarged the square by a factor of 2.

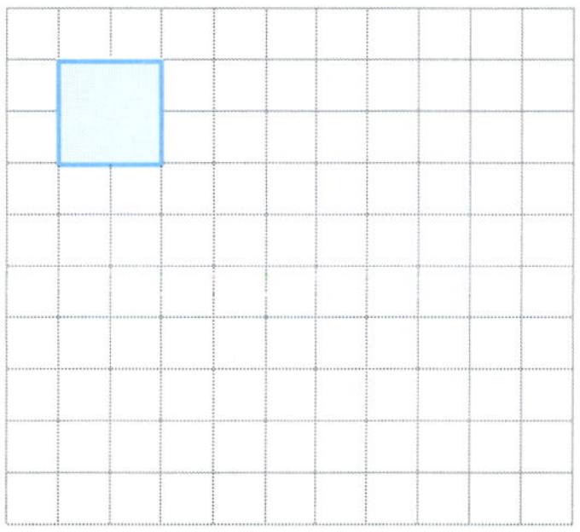

What is the area of the image?

FOCUS ON LOCATION AND TRANSFORMATION

1 Here are three shapes. Circle the shape(s) with a rotational symmetry of order of at least 2.

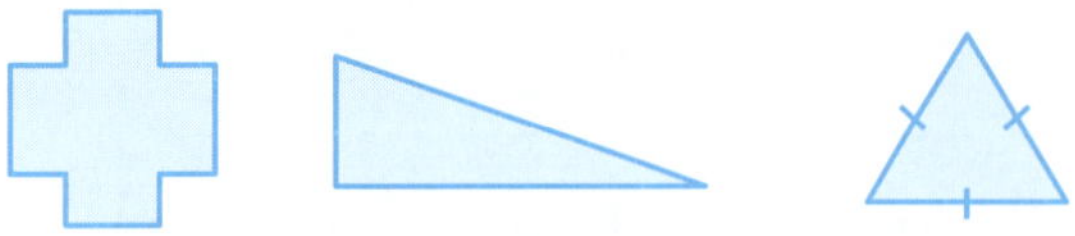

2 Part of a shape with a line of symmetry is shown. Complete the shape.

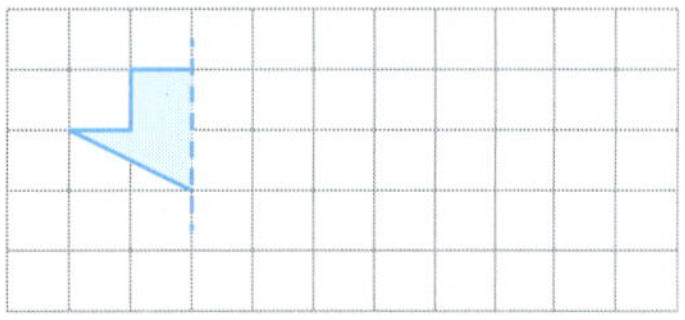

3 Part of a shape with two lines of symmetry is shown. Complete the shape.

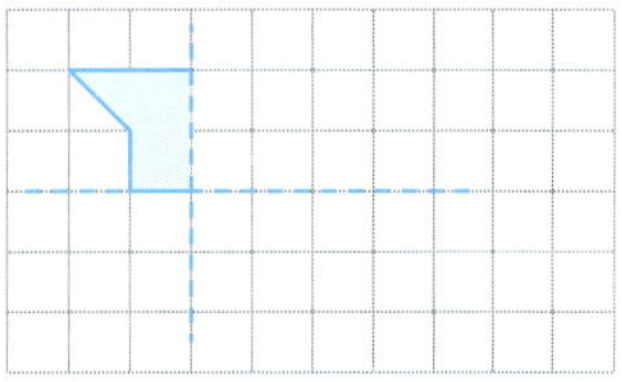

4 Part of a shape with a line of symmetry is shown. Complete the shape.

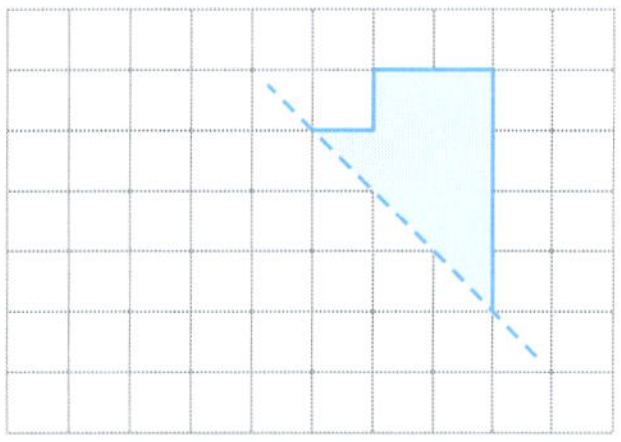

5 What is the order of rotational symmetry for a rectangle?

6 What is the order of rotational symmetry for an isosceles right triangle?

7 What is the order of rotational symmetry for a regular hexagon?

8 What is the order of rotational symmetry for this shape?

9 A shape has rotational symmetry of order 8. Through how many degrees will the shape be rotated until it displays its original shape?

10 Through how many degrees should this shape be rotated before it displays its original shape?

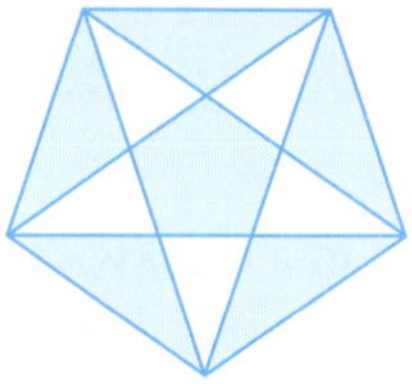

11 A shape is rotated 360°. After every 30° it displays its original shape. What is the order of its rotational symmetry?

12 A regular decagon is rotated around its centre. Through how many degrees should it be rotated before it displays its original shape?

13 On the grid mark *P* at B5. Go to the left 1 unit, down 3 units and to the right 3 units. Mark *Q* at this new location.

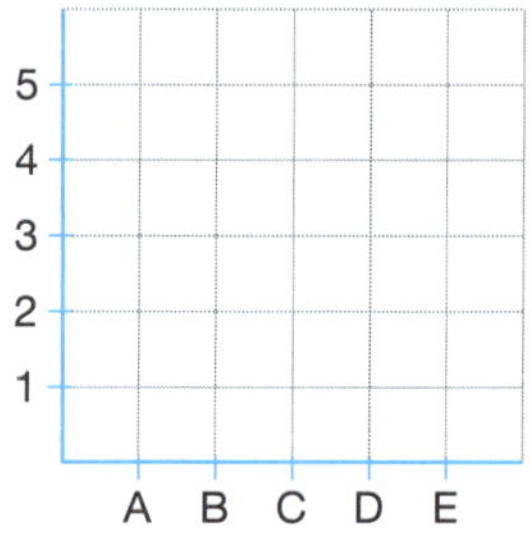

14 *X* is located at D4. From *X* move 3 units west. Now move south to *Y*, which is south-west of *X*.

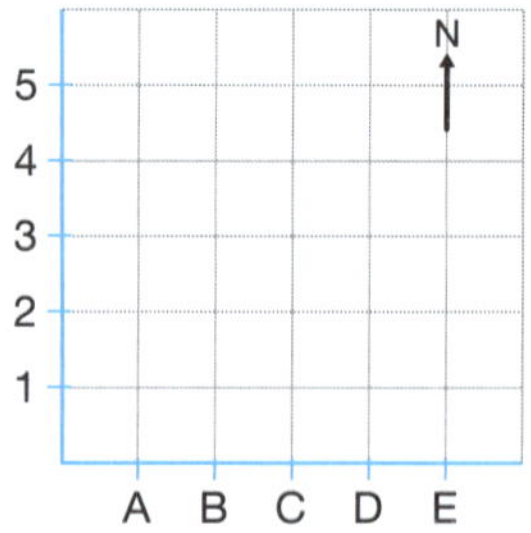

What is the location of *Y*?

15 Start at X, which is at A4. Move east 3 units, south 2 units and then west ☐ unit(s) to Y. Y is south-east of X.

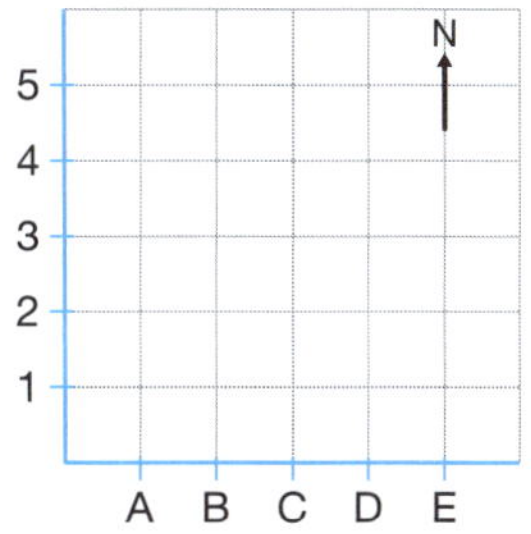

What is the missing number?

16 The grid represents a map. Josh leaves X, travels 15 km south, 20 km east and then 10 km north to Y.

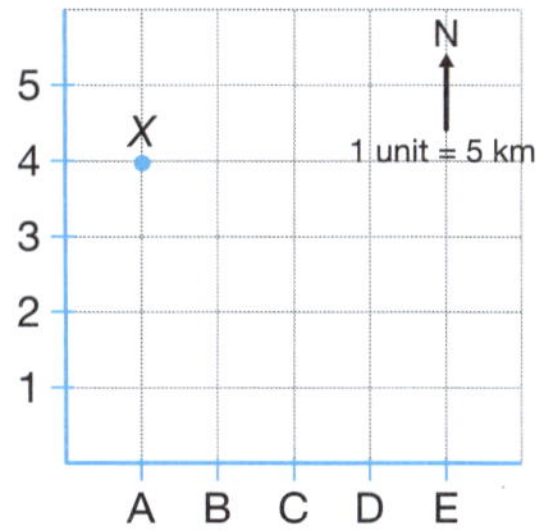

What is the location of Y?

17 An object is reflected in the mirror line. Draw the image.

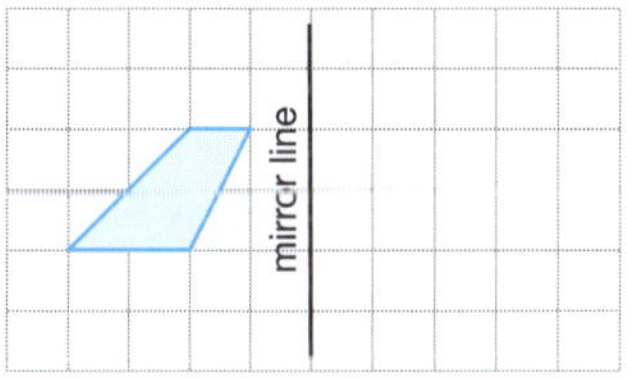

18 Rotate the shape 90° in a clockwise direction about O.

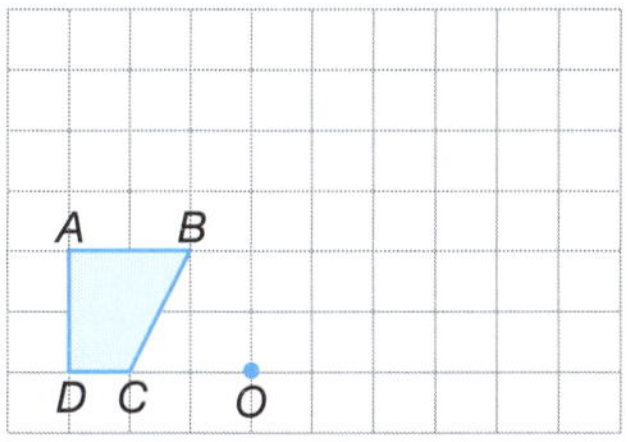

19 Rotate the shape 90° in an anticlockwise direction about O.

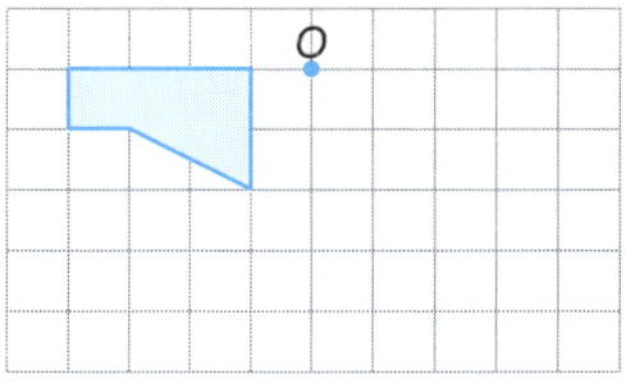

20 Rotate the shape 180° about O.

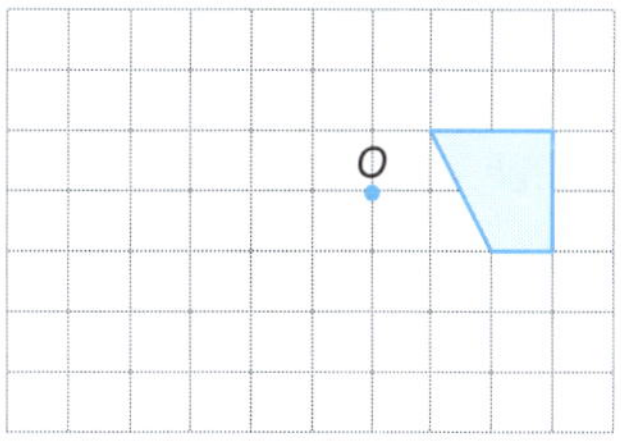

21 The rectangle is enlarged by a scale factor of 3. What is the area of the enlarged shape?

22 Describe the transformation from A to B.

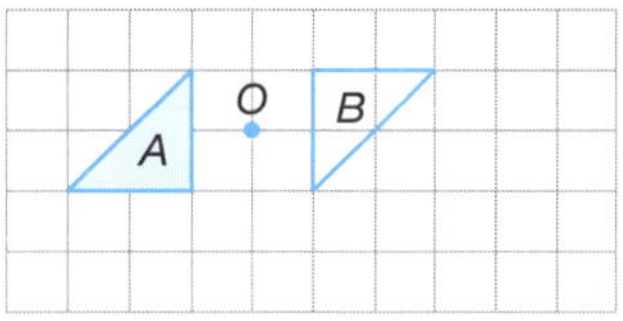

23 Describe the transformation from A to B.

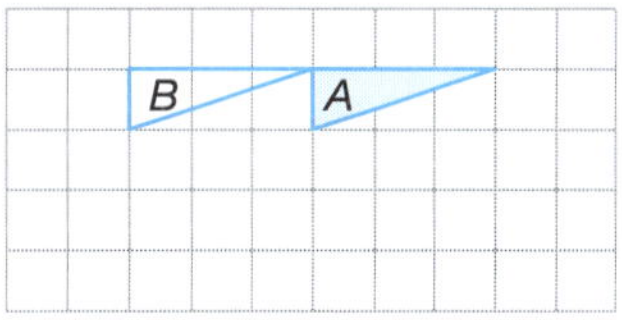

24 A square has an area of 81 cm^2.
The square is to be enlarged by a factor of 3. What is the perimeter of the new square?

25 The shape is to be enlarged by a scale factor of 0.5.

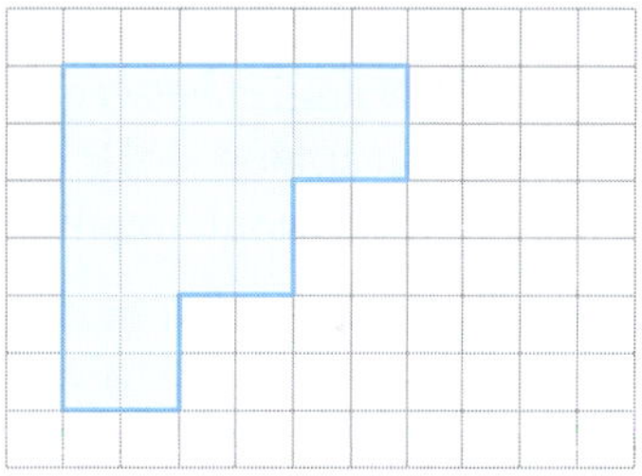

What is the area of the new shape?

FOCUS ON GEOMETRIC REASONING

1 What is the size of the angle?

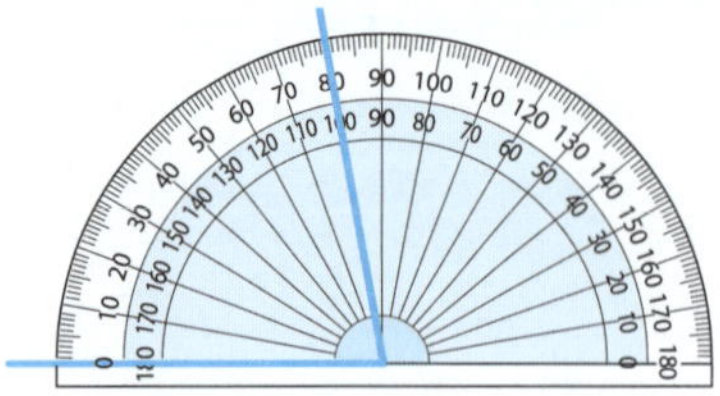

2 Here are four angles. Circle any angles that measure more than 90°.

3 On the diagram, mark with a cross (**X**) the angles that measure less than 90°.

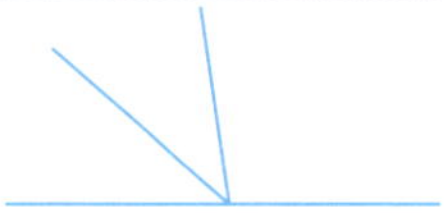

4 Inside the shape, how many angles are more than 90°?

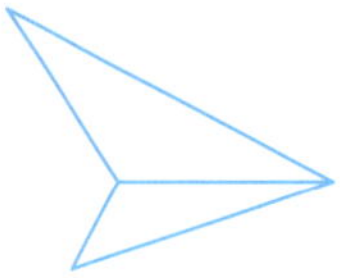

5 Using a cross (**X**), mark any angle inside the shape which measures more than 90° but less than 180°.

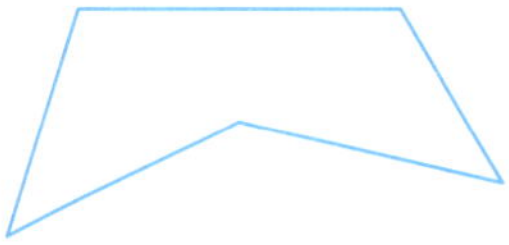

6 Jodie looked at the angles between the hands at different times on an analog clock. Circle the time(s) when the angle would be less than 90°.

half past eight quarter to five
10 o'clock quarter past nine

7 John looked at the angles between the hands at different times on an analog clock. Circle the time(s) when the angle would be 180°.

12 o'clock quarter past three
6 o'clock half past nine

8 Merrill looked at the angles between the hands at different times on an analog clock. Circle the time(s) when the angle would be more than 90° but less than 180°.

5 o'clock half past eight
quarter to seven quarter past ten

9 Triangles have been drawn inside a rectangle. One of the angles that measures less than 90° has been shaded. How many **more** angles measure less than 90°?

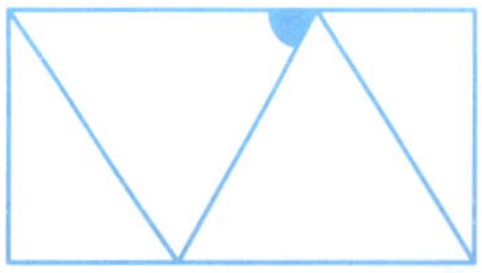

10 Circle the angle that measures about 30°.

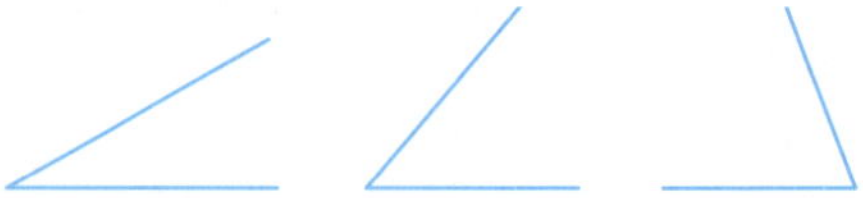

11 Circle the angle that measures about 135°.

12 Circle the angle that measures about 140°.

13 Which of these is the best estimate for the size of the marked angle?

150° 60° 30° 120°

14 On an analog clock the time is half past seven. If the minute hand moves 720°, what is the new time?

15 Draw a shape with two acute angles and two obtuse angles.

16 Draw a shape with two right angles, two obtuse angles and an acute angle.

17 Draw a shape with a right angle, a reflex angle and two acute angles.

18 Here are some angles. Circle the angles that are acute.

61° 114° 193° 83°

19 Here are some angles. Circle the angles that are obtuse.

84° 101° 178° 273°

20 Here are some angles. Circle the angles that are reflex.

69° 305° 168° 199°

21 An analog clock shows 4:30. Christian next checked the time at 5:00. Through what angle has the minute hand moved?

22 How many right angles make up a straight angle?

FOCUS ON

GEOMETRIC REASONING

1 Using a protractor, Marlow measured the angle as 150°. How many degrees is the angle marked as *?

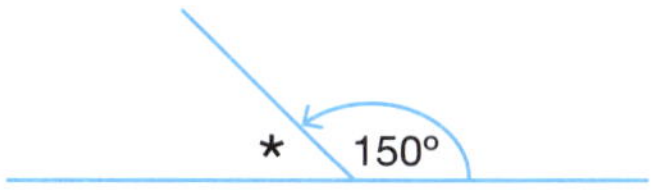

2 Using a protractor, Evie measured an angle as 60°. There is also a right angle shown. How many degrees is the angle marked as *?

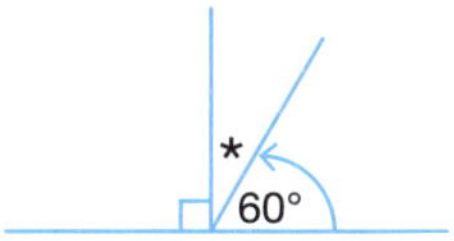

3 Using a protractor, Joss measured an angle as 55°. There is also a right angle shown. How many degrees is the angle marked as *?

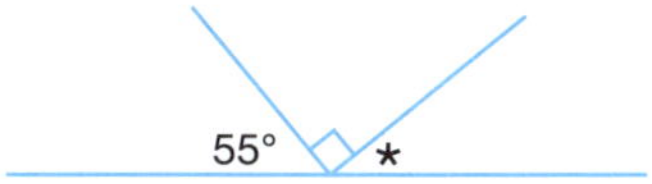

4 Using a protractor, Harriet measured the angle as 115°. How many degrees is the angle marked as *?

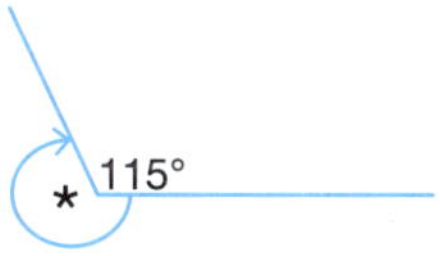

5 The obtuse angle between the hands of an analog clock at 5 o'clock is 150°. At what other 'o'clock' time will the obtuse angle also be 150°?

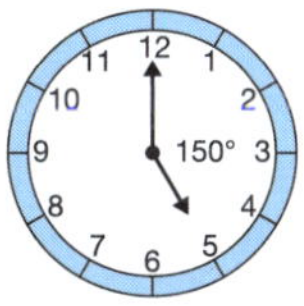

6 Using a protractor, Caleb measured the angle as 62°. How many degrees is the angle marked as *?

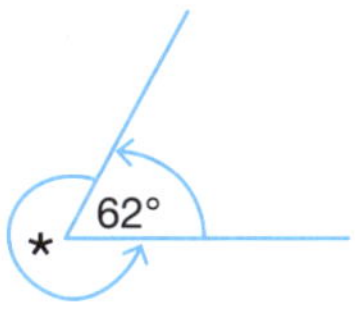

7 Using a protractor, Steve measured the angles as 80° and 70°. How many degrees is the angle marked as *?

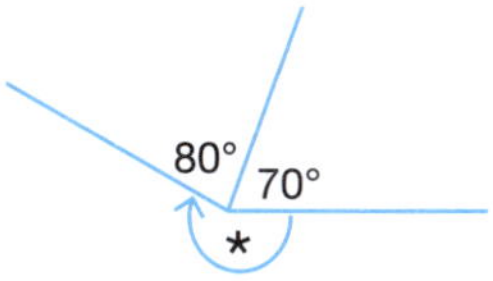

8 On an analog clock the time is 8 o'clock. If the minute hand moves 270°, what is the new time?

9 On an analog clock the time is half past nine. If the minute hand moves 540°, what is the new time?

10 Using a protractor, Brian measured an angle of 40°. The other two angles shown are the same size as each other. How many degrees each are the angles marked as *?

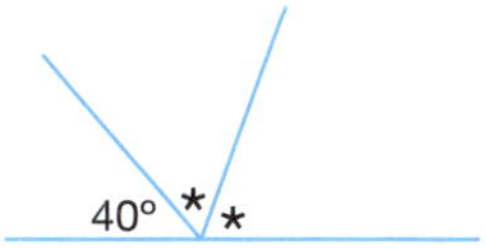

11 Lloyd is giddy after he spun around four times. Through how many degrees did he rotate?

12 Jaanvi uses her protractor to show that the angles in a quadrilateral add to 360°. If one of the angles is a right angle and two of the angles measure 56° and 110°, what is the size of the other angle?

13 Mathieson uses her protractor to show that the angles in a triangle add to 180°. If two of the angles measure 32° and 74°, what type is Mathieson's triangle?

14 An analog clock shows 5:00. Grant next checked the time at 8:00. Through what angle has the hour hand moved?

15 After Neville cooked a large pizza he sliced it into eight equal slices. He measured the angle represented by each slice. What was the measurement?

16 Jeremiah baked an apple pie. He cut the cake into six equal slices. Two slices were removed. He measured the angle represented by the remaining pie.

What was the measurement?

17 Ella faced west. She rotated 315° in a clockwise direction. What direction is she now facing?

18 It is 2 am. If the minute hand on an analog clock moves through 1800°, what is the new time?

FOCUS ON CHANCE

1 The arrow on this spinner is spun. What is the probability it stops on a 2?

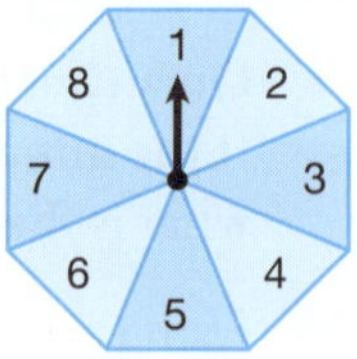

2 The probability of an event occurring is described as impossible. Circle the probability.

$0 \quad \frac{1}{3} \quad \frac{2}{3} \quad 1$

3 A six-sided dice is rolled once. What is the probability of rolling a 4?

4 A box contains red (R), blue (B) and yellow (Y) coloured tokens. A token is chosen at random.

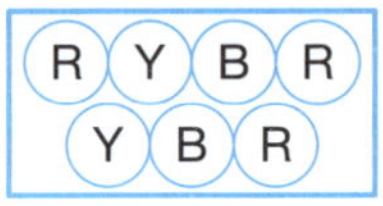

What is the probability that it is blue?

5 A box contains red (R), yellow (Y), green (G) and blue (B) balls. A ball is chosen at random.

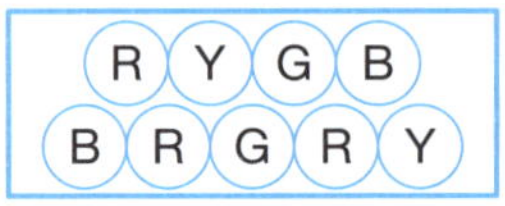

What is the probability that it is yellow?

6 A box contains numbered balls. A ball is chosen at random. What is the probability that the number 4 is chosen?

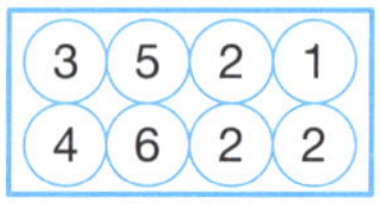

7 A box contains cards which are either black (B) or white (W). A card is chosen at random.

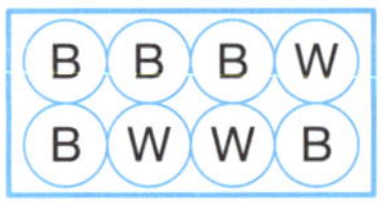

What is the probability that it is black?

8 A box contains numbered counters. A counter is chosen at random. What is the probability that the number is odd?

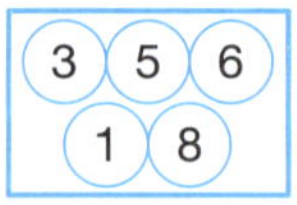

9 A bag contains five green balls, three red balls and two blue balls. A ball is chosen at random. What is the probability that it is green?

10 A normal dice is rolled. What is the probability that it lands on a 3?

11 A bag contains yellow marbles and green marbles. There are five yellow marbles in the bag. A marble is chosen at random. The probability of choosing a yellow marble is $\frac{5}{8}$. How many green marbles are in the bag?

12 A spinner has four sections which are numbered.

What is the probability of spinning a number less than 9?

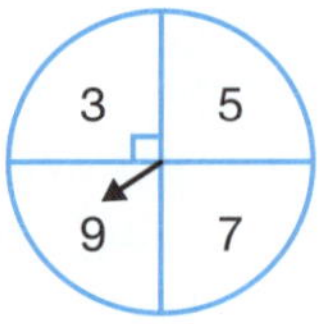

13 A regular hexagon is made into a spinner. Different sections of the spinner have been coloured red (R), blue (B) or green (G). The arrow on this spinner is spun. What is the probability it stops on red?

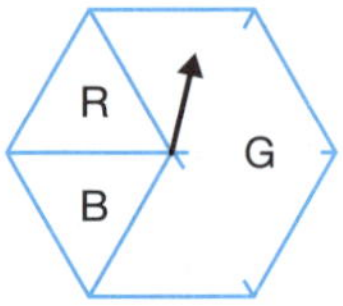

14 There are 12 identical discs in a bag. The discs are either black or white. The probability of randomly selecting a black disc from the bag is $\frac{1}{2}$.

How many black discs are in the bag?

15 A spinner has sections which are coloured red (R), blue (B), yellow (Y) or green (G). Jonah wins a game if he spins blue.

What is the probability that Jonah wins?

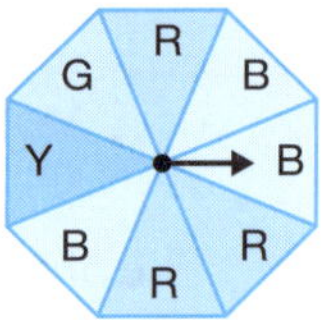

16 A box contains three green balls, two purple balls and some orange balls. If the probability of selecting a green ball is $\frac{3}{8}$, how many orange balls are in the box?

17 There is an equal number of boys and girls in a classroom. A child is chosen at random. What is the probability of selecting a girl?

18 The faces on a normal dice have been renumbered as 1, 1, 2, 3, 3 and 4. The dice is rolled. What is the probability that the number on the uppermost face is a 1?

19 Which of these could be the probability of an event happening? Circle the correct answer(s).

$\frac{3}{8} \quad 1\frac{1}{4} \quad \frac{4}{7} \quad \frac{5}{3}$

FOCUS ON CHANCE

1 The arrow on this spinner is spun. What is the probability it stops on a multiple of 2?

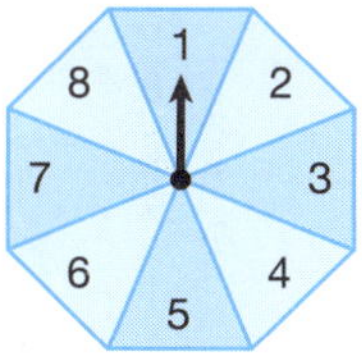

2 The probability of an event occurring is described as 'likely, but not certain'. Which of these is closest to the probability of the event happening?

0 $\frac{1}{3}$ $\frac{2}{3}$ 1

3 A six-sided dice is rolled once. What is the probability of rolling a number greater than 2?

4 A box contains red (R), yellow (Y), green (G) and blue (B) balls. A ball is chosen at random.

What is the probability that it is **not** red?

5 A box contains numbered balls. A ball is chosen at random. What is the probability of choosing an odd number?

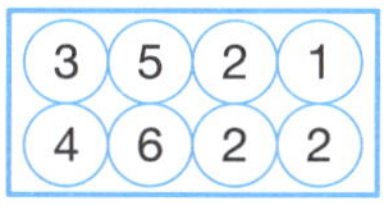

6 A box contains cards which are either black (B) or white (W). Another two white cards are placed in the box. A card is chosen at random.

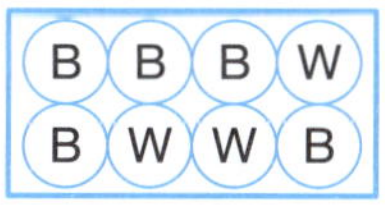

What is the probability that it is white?

7 A box contains numbered counters. A counter is chosen at random.

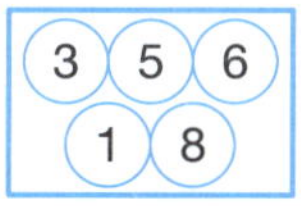

What is the probability that the number is a factor of 24?

8 A bag contains three white balls, five blue balls and two green balls. A ball is chosen at random. What is the probability that it is **not** green?

9 A bag contains red marbles and blue marbles. There are 10 red marbles in the bag. A marble is chosen at random. The probability of choosing a red marble is $\frac{2}{5}$. How many blue marbles are in the bag?

10 A regular octagon is made into a spinner. Different sections of the spinner have been numbered. The arrow on this spinner is spun.

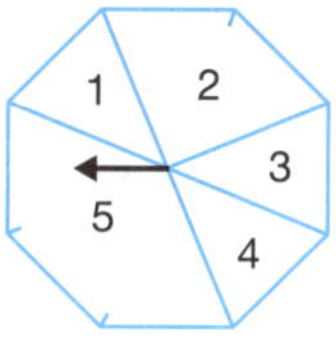

What is the probability it stops on an odd number?

11 This spinner has sections coloured red (R) or blue (B). The arrow is spun and it stops on blue.

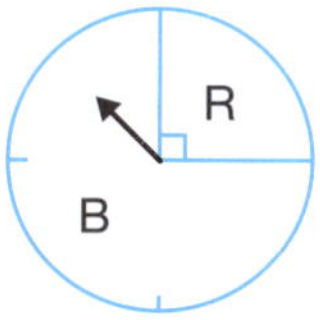

The arrow is spun again and stops on red. When the arrow is spun a third time, what is the probability it stops on blue?

12 A normal dice is rolled. What is the probability that it lands on a number more than 3?

13 There are five identical discs in a bag. The discs are either red, blue or yellow. There are twice as many blue discs in the bag as red discs. The probability of randomly selecting a red disc from the bag is $\frac{1}{5}$.

What is the probability of selecting a yellow disc?

14 A spinner has sections which are coloured red (R), blue (B), yellow (Y) or green (G). Bridget wins a game if she spins red or blue.

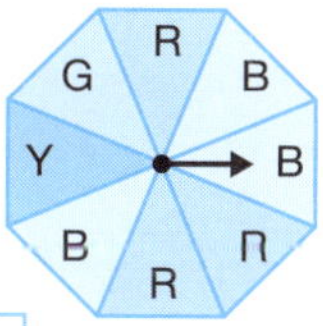

What is the probability that Bridget wins?

15 A box contains seven red balls, four green balls and some blue balls. If the probability of selecting a red ball is $\frac{1}{2}$, what is the probability of selecting a blue ball?

16 There are three times as many red discs in a box as blue discs. A disc is chosen at random. What is the probability of selecting a red disc?

17 The faces on a normal dice have been renumbered as 2, 3, 3, 3, 5 and 6. The dice is rolled. What is the probability that the number facedown on the table is at least 3?

18 Which of these could **not** be the probability of an event happening? Circle the correct answer(s).

$\frac{49}{50}$ 100% $1\frac{1}{2}$ 0.3 –0.8

FOCUS ON DATA REPRESENTATION AND INTERPRETATION

1 The results of 20 students in a maths competition are shown.

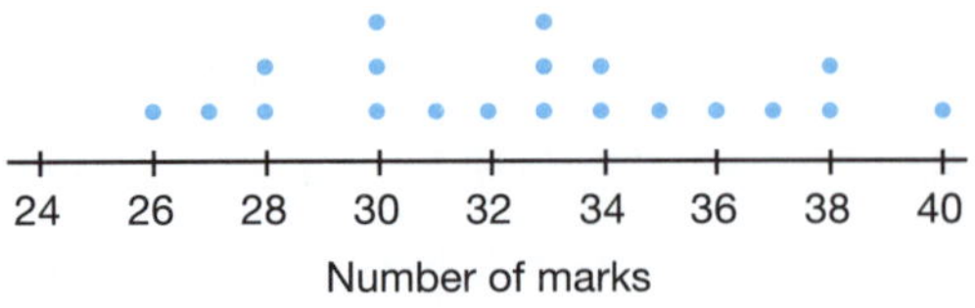

What fraction of the students received a score less than 31?

2 The dot plot shows the ages of children at a party.

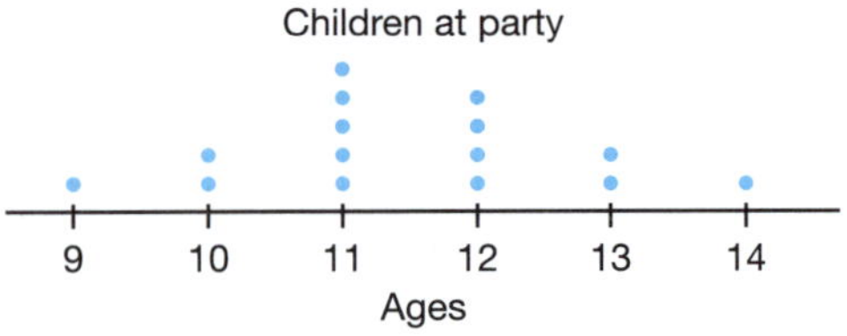

How many 12- and 13-year-old children were at the party?

3 A group of students were asked for the number of their siblings.

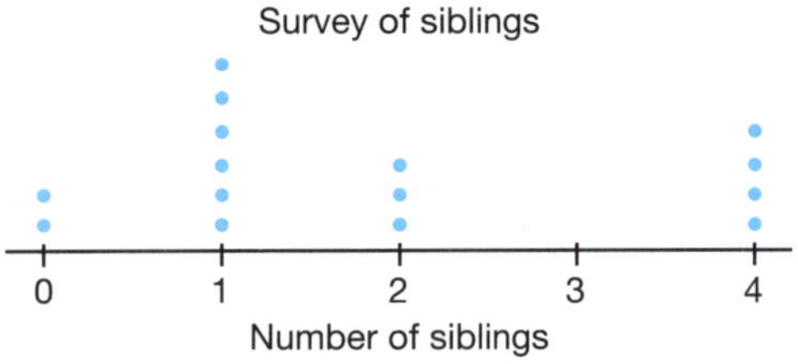

How many students were the only child in their family?

4 A survey was conducted to find the number of home-cooked nightly meals consumed by students in a week.

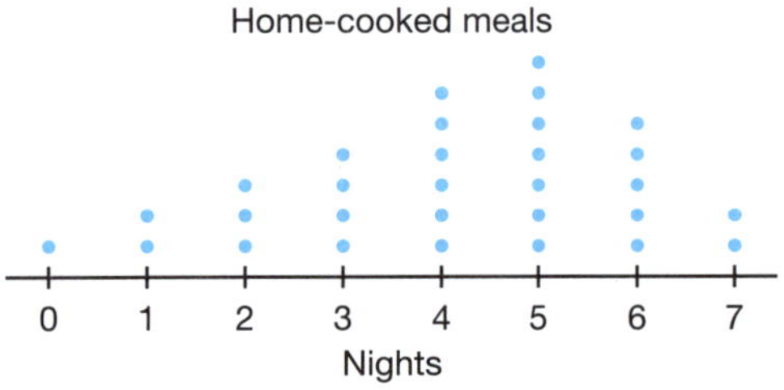

How many students had more than five home-cooked meals?

5 Mr Jacobson drew this table representing the different fruits in his students' lunchboxes.

What was the total number of bananas and oranges?

6 The results of a quiz are shown.

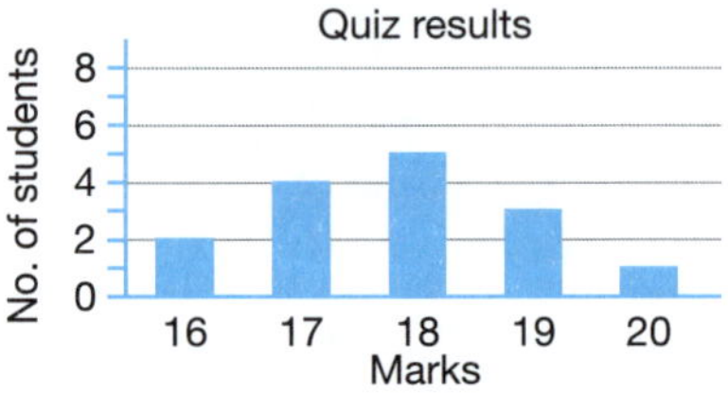

What was the most common mark?

7 The number of goals scored by a team in each of four games of soccer are shown in the graph.

In how many games were at least two goals scored?

8 The graph shows the results of a survey of gym members who attended fitness classes.

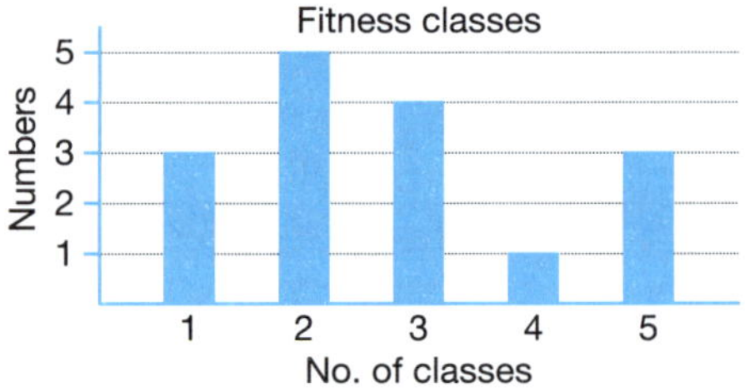

How many classes were attended by four members?

9 The favourite sports of a group of students in a class were recorded.

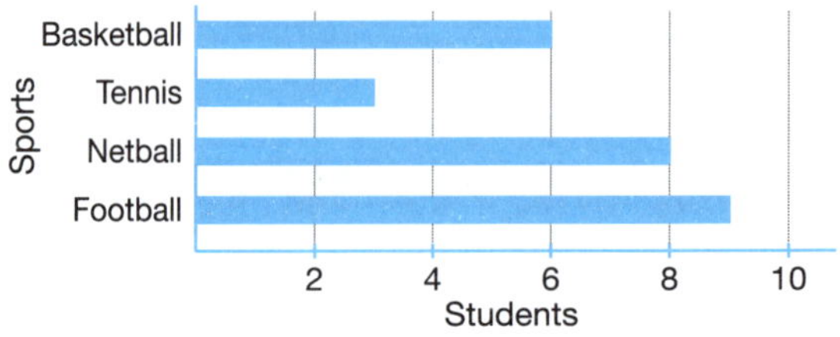

What was the total number of students who liked tennis and netball?

10 Sidney has recorded the number of laps he ran on 5 days.

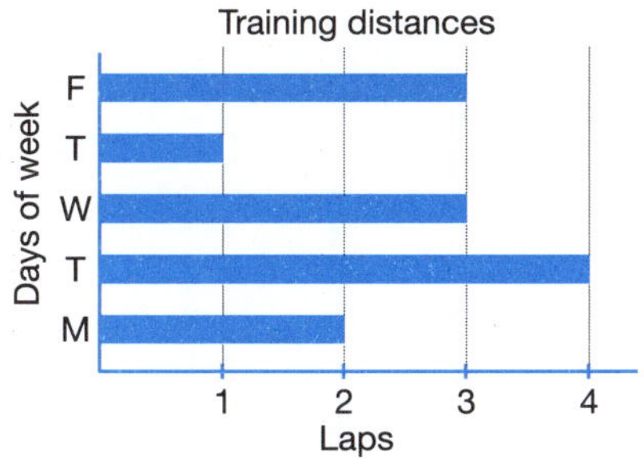

How many laps altogether did Sidney run?

11 Charlotte recorded her pulse rate for 10 minutes after completing a race.

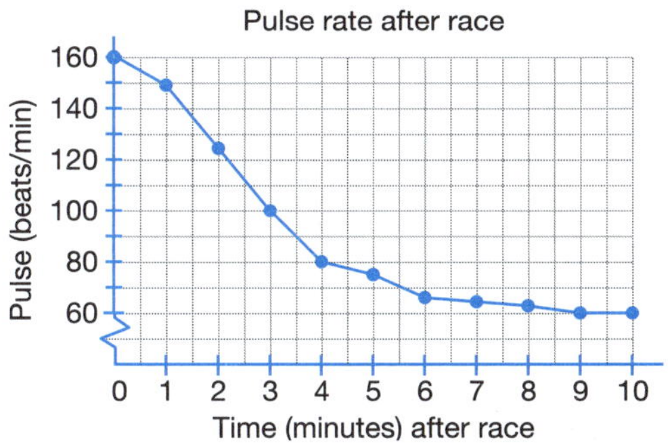

How much did the pulse rate drop in the first 3 minutes after the race?

12 Here is Logan's growth chart. What was his height (in cm) when he was 4 years old?

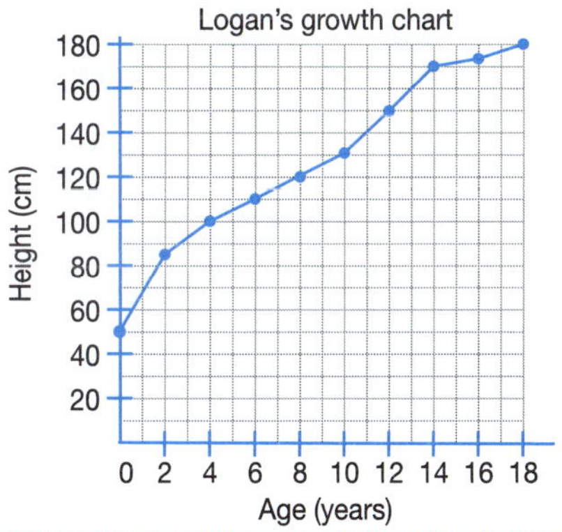

13 The temperatures in Geelong on one spring day were graphed.

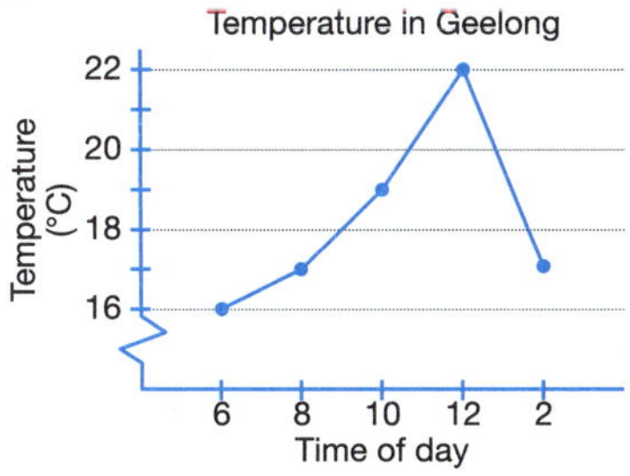

Which of these is the best estimate for the temperature at 1300?

16° 17° 19° 22°

14 A survey found the number of devices in students' homes that connected to the internet.

Connected devices	
Number	**Students**
less than 5	3
5–10	8
11–15	11
more than 15	4

How many students had more than 10 devices in their home?

15 The table shows the result of a survey of students' favourite colours.

Favourite colours	
Colour	**Tally**
Blue	|||
Yellow	𝍸 ||
Green	𝍸 ||||
Red	𝍸 𝍸 |

What was the total number of students who chose green or red?

16 The number of tickets sold for a movie is listed.

Tickets sold	
Category	**Number**
Adult	16
Child	31
Senior	13

Circle the phrase that best describes the number of child tickets sold compared to total sales?

less than half

exactly half

more than half

FOCUS ON DATA REPRESENTATION AND INTERPRETATION

1 The results of students in a maths competition are shown. Any student who gained at least 36 marks received a money prize.

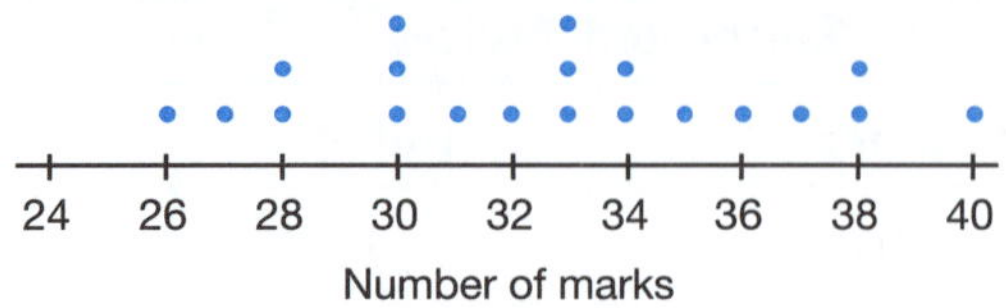

What fraction of the students did **not** win a money prize?

2 The eye colour of 20 students was recorded. The number of students with hazel eyes is shown in the dot plot.

Seven more students have brown eyes than blue eyes. How many students have blue eyes?

3 The dot plot shows the ages of children at a party.

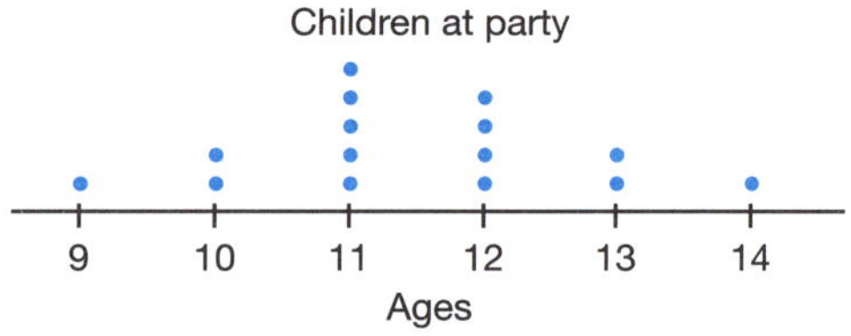

Thirteen-year-old Pablo and his 9-year-old sister Eleni left the party early. How many children remained at the party?

4 A survey was conducted to find the number of home-cooked nightly meals consumed by students in a week.

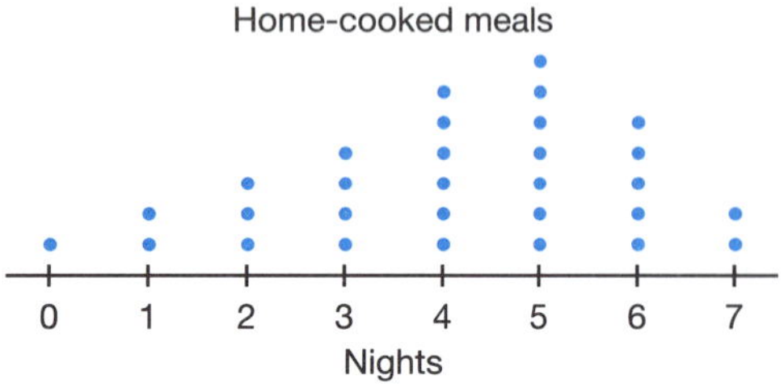

A student is chosen at random. What is the probability that the student's family ate five home-cooked meals?

5 The number of credit cards used by a group of people is recorded.

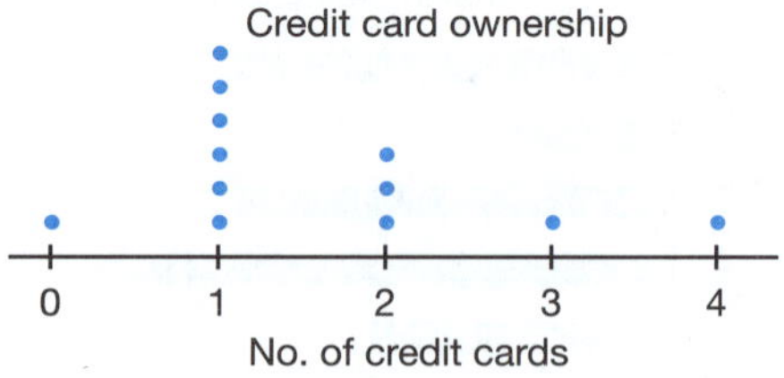

A person is chosen at random. What is the probability they use only one credit card?

6 The number of home streaming subscriptions of a group of people is graphed.

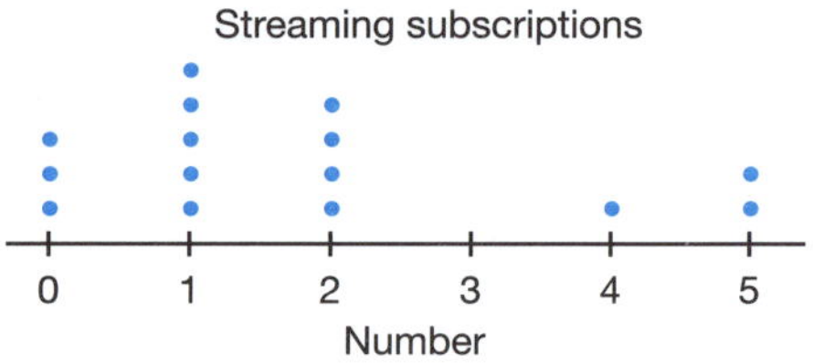

How many people have at least two streaming subscriptions in their home?

7 The number of boys and girls in two classes, 5P and 5R, is recorded.

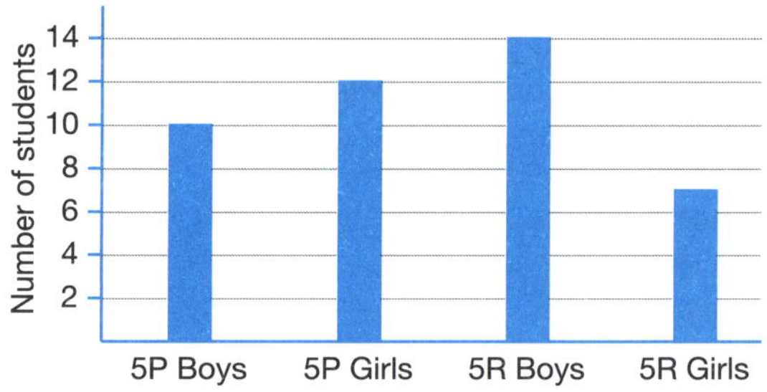

How many more boys are in the classes than girls?

8 The results of a quiz are shown.

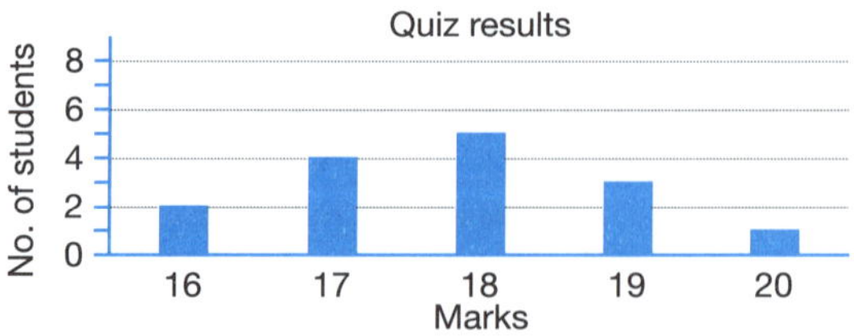

A student is chosen at random. What is the probability that they scored at least 18?

9 The number of goals scored by Ella's team in each of four games of soccer is shown.

After six games, Ella's team had scored a total of 16 goals. If they scored two goals in game E, how many were scored in game F?

10 The favourite sports of a group of students in a class are recorded.

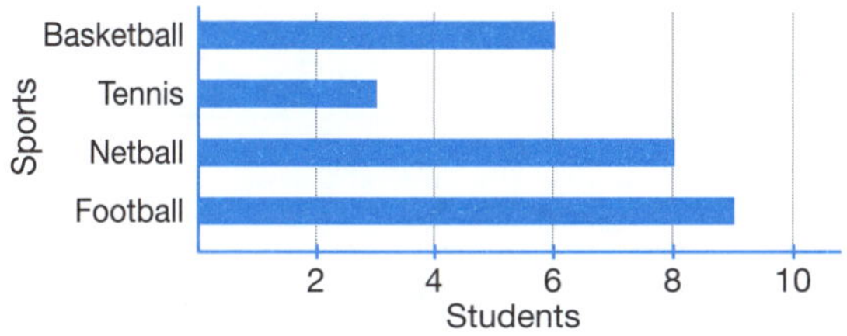

A student is chosen at random. What is the probability that their favourite sport is football?

11 Eleanor has recorded the number of laps she ran on 5 days. On Saturday Eleanor ran twice as far as she had on Thursday and Friday combined.

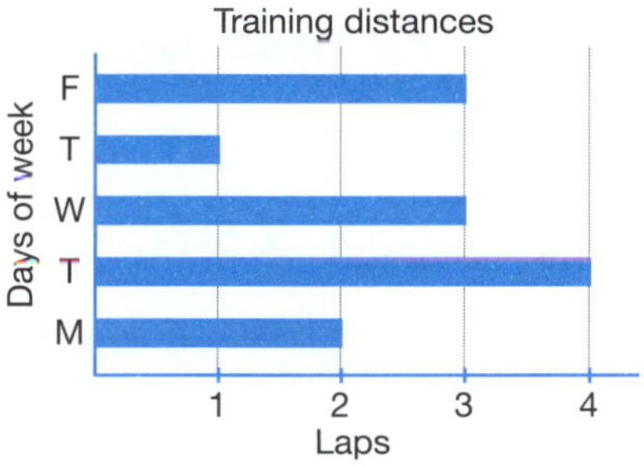

What was the total number of laps in the 6 days?

12 Charlotte recorded her pulse rate for 10 minutes after completing a race.

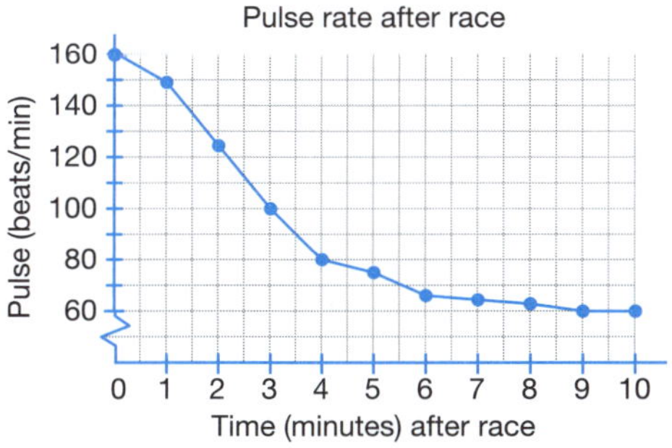

If she finished the race at 10:00, when was the first time her pulse was 80 beats per minute?

13 Here is Logan's growth chart.

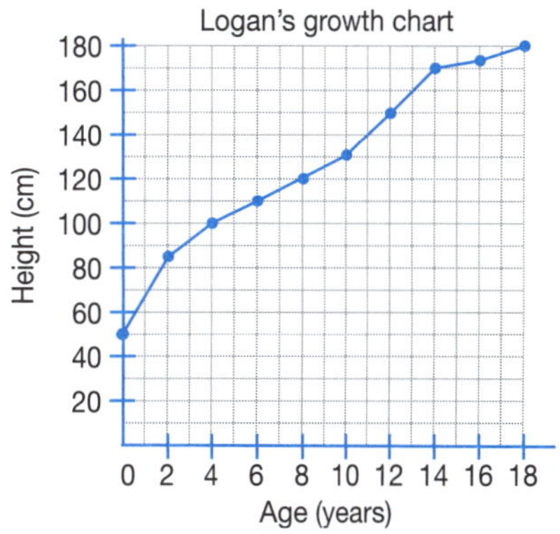

How many years did it take for Logan's birth height to triple?

14 A survey found the number of devices in students' homes that connected to the internet.

Connected devices	
Number	**Students**
less than 5	3
5–10	8
11–15	11
more than 15	4

Alex and Juan were absent from class on the survey day. When they returned, Alex said she had 14 devices and Juan had 10 devices.

How many students now have at least five devices?

15 The table shows some of the results of a survey of students' favourite colours.

Favourite colours	
Colour	**Tally**
Blue	||||
Yellow	
Green	𝍸 ||||
Red	

Three times as many students chose green than yellow and four times as many chose red than blue. How many students were surveyed?

NUMBER AND ALGEBRA

1 Circle the numbers that are multiples of 5.

25, 30, 56, 55, 302

2 What is 293 plus 421 to the nearest hundred?

3 For a school excursion, 45 students are loaded on to each of four buses. How many students travelled by bus?

4 Mrs Scott organised her 28 students into groups of five. How many students were left over?

5 What is $7 \times 5 \times 10$?

6 The shape is divided into six equal sections.

Shade $\frac{2}{3}$ of the shape.

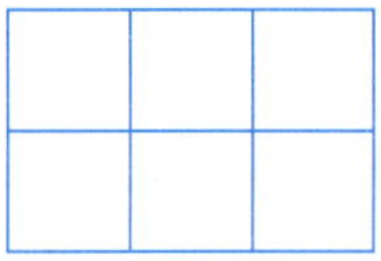

7 Erica pours $\frac{2}{3}$ of a bucket of water around a shrub. What fraction of the original water remains in the bucket?

8 What is $\frac{79}{1000}$ written as a decimal?

9 Bread rolls are sold in packets of eight for $4. Ethan needed to buy 24 bread rolls for a family barbecue. How much did the bread rolls cost?

10 Find the missing number in the pattern.

$\frac{1}{8}, \frac{3}{8}, \frac{5}{8},$ ☐

11 Here is a number sentence. ☐ $\times 6 = 420$

What is the missing number?

MEASUREMENT AND SPACE

12 Find the area of the shaded figure.

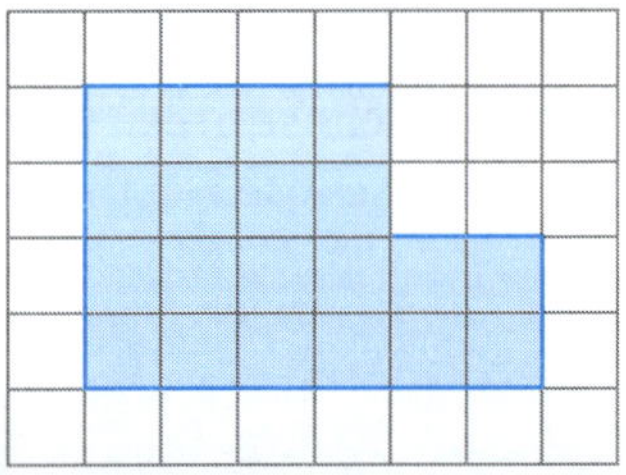

13 What is 9:20 pm in 24-hour time?

14 The net of a cube is drawn below.

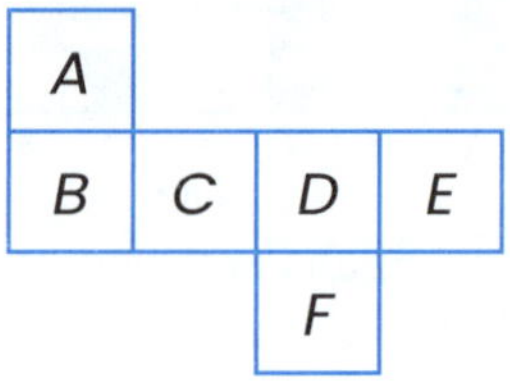

What letter is on the opposite face to *A*?

15 Draw the line(s) of symmetry on this shape:

16

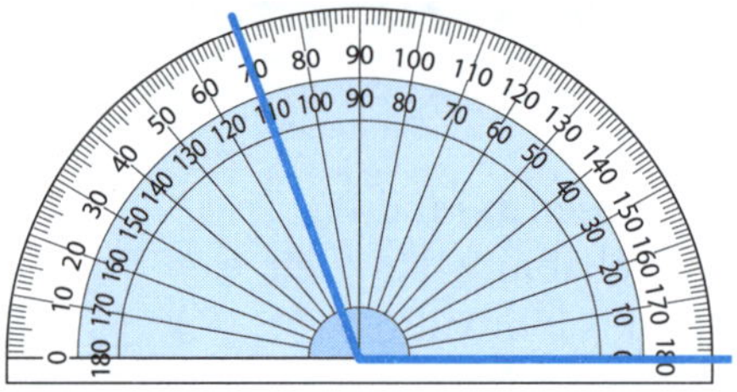

What is the size of the angle?

STATISTICS AND PROBABILITY

17 The arrow on this spinner is spun.

What is the probability it stops on a 5?

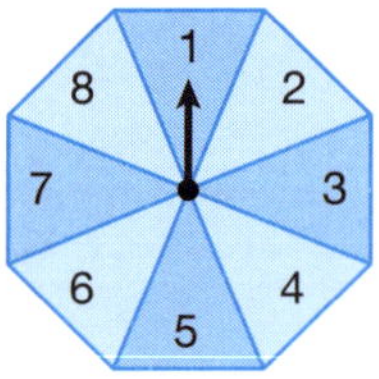

18 The results of 20 students in a maths competition are shown.

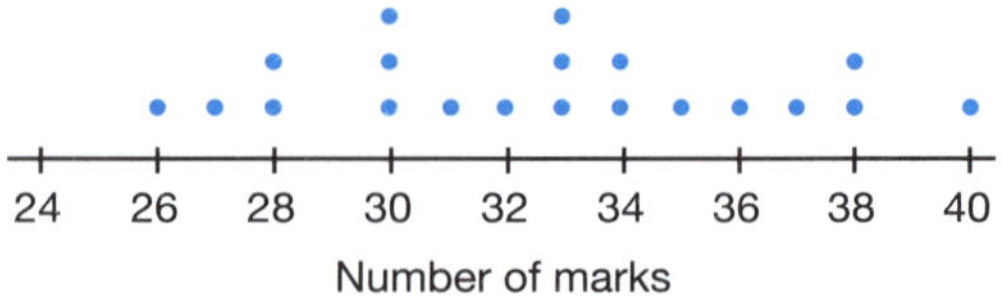

How many students received a score of more than 30?

NUMBER AND ALGEBRA

1 Circle the numbers that are multiples of 3.

26, 30, 73, 93, 301, 1800

2 Sid bought a hard drive for $79.90, an ink cartridge for $48.35, a packet of pens for $17.95 and a desk chair for $112.95.
Estimate the total cost, to the nearest $10.

3 Every day a bakery produces 240 pies. What was the total number of pies produced in 15 days?

4 Eight buses have been ordered to transport the 448 students attending a high school. What is the average number of students on each bus?

5 Find the answer: $16 \times 4 + 16 \times 6$.

6 The shape is divided into six equal sections.

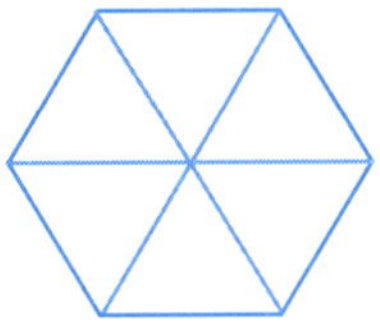

Shade $\frac{2}{3}$ of the shape.

7 Alex takes a bottle of water to school. At recess she drinks $\frac{3}{10}$ of the bottle. She drinks the same amount at lunch.
What fraction remains?

8 What decimal is represented by the answer to

$\frac{3}{10} + \frac{43}{1000} + \frac{7}{100}$?

9 Five oranges cost the same as three avocados. If one orange costs 60 cents, what is the cost of an avocado?

10 Find the missing number in the pattern.

$2, 1\frac{2}{5}, \square, \frac{1}{5}$

11 What is the missing number in the number sentence?

$8 \times \square + 42 = 98$

MEASUREMENT AND SPACE

12 The shaded rectangle has an area of 120 cm^2.

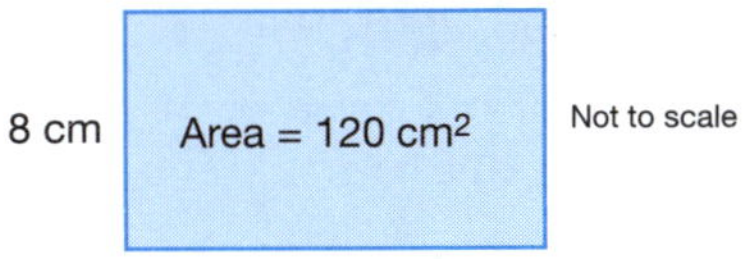

What is the length of the rectangle?

13 A movie starts at 1530 and runs for two-and-a-half hours. At what time will the movie finish, in 12-hour time?

14 The net of a cube is shown below.

The numbers on the opposite faces always add to the same total.

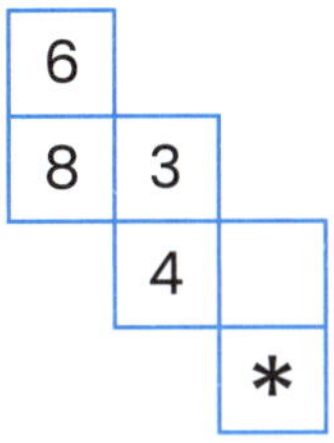

What number is represented by *?

15 Here are three shapes. Circle the shape(s) with a rotational symmetry of order of at least 2.

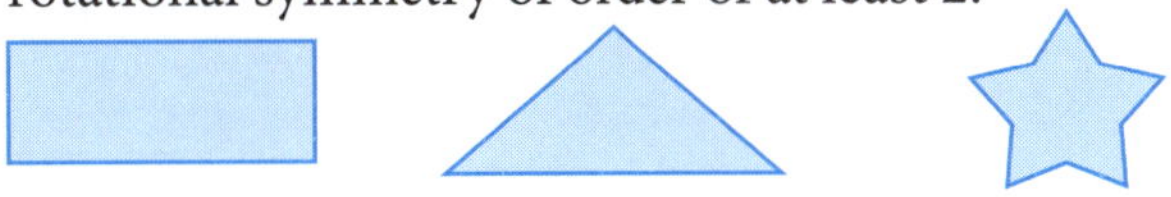

16 Bob used a protractor to draw an angle of 50°.

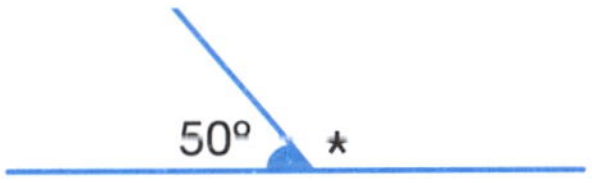

What is the size of the angle marked by *?

STATISTICS AND PROBABILITY

17 The arrow on this spinner is spun.

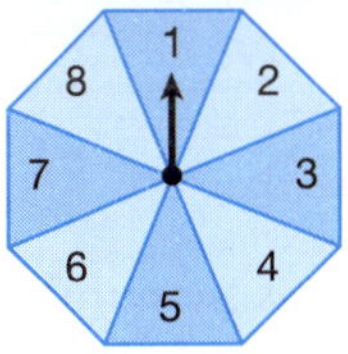

What is the probability it stops on a factor of 24?

18 The results of students in a maths competition are shown. Any student who gained at least 34 marks received a money prize.

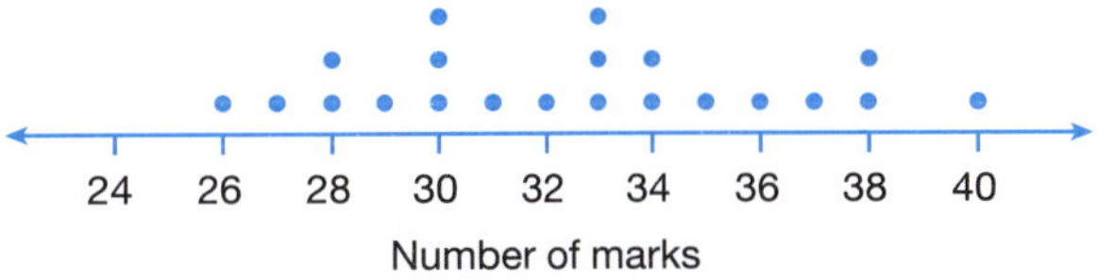

How many students were **less than** 5 marks from gaining a money prize?

NUMBER AND ALGEBRA

1 Circle the numbers that are multiples of 10.

302, 105, 6000, 2001, 980

2 What is 714 and 479 to the nearest hundred?

3 Every morning Layla cycles 34 km around a circuit near her home. What is the total distance Layla cycles in 5 days?

4 Share 126 marbles evenly between three boys.

5 $32 \times 50 = \square \times 100$

6 Circle the fraction that is the smallest.

$\frac{1}{5}$ $\frac{1}{3}$ $\frac{1}{10}$

7 What is the missing fraction?

$1 - \square = \frac{7}{10}$

8 What is $\frac{413}{1000}$ written as a decimal?

9 What is the total of $11.85, $110 and $9.35?

10 Here is a pattern of decimals. Write the next two numbers.

5.30, 5.33, 5.36, ☐, ☐

11 $\square \div 4 = 16$

Find the missing number.

MEASUREMENT AND SPACE

12 A shape is drawn on grid paper. What is the perimeter of the shape?

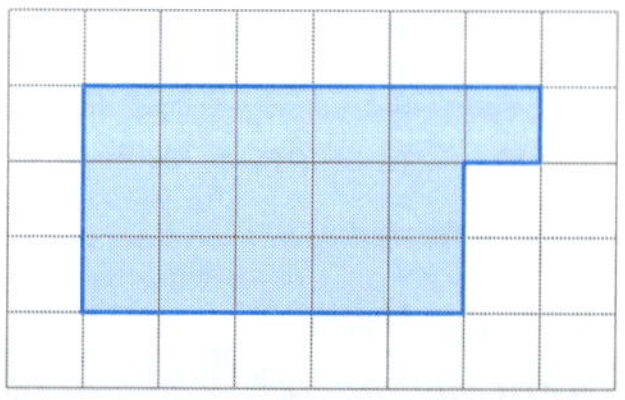

13 What is 5:55 pm in 24-hour time?

14 Circle any triangles that are isosceles.

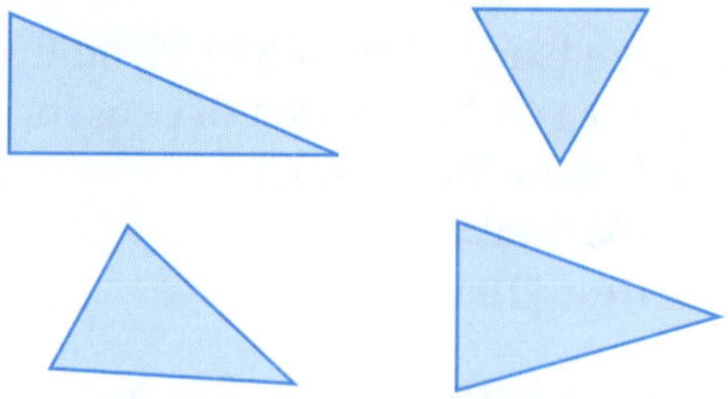

15 Here are four letters. Circle the letter(s) with two lines of symmetry.

E O S M

16 A triangle has been drawn inside a rectangle. One of the angles that measure less than 90° has been shaded. Mark with a cross (**x**) the other angles that measure less than 90°.

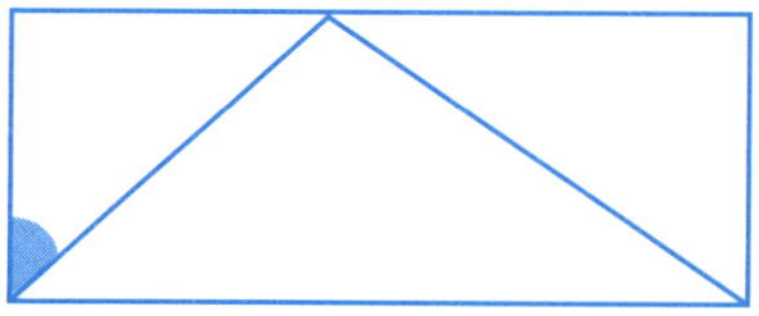

STATISTICS AND PROBABILITY

17 The probability of an event occurring is described as certain. Circle the probability.

0 $\frac{1}{3}$ $\frac{2}{3}$ 1

18 A group of students were surveyed to find the number of their siblings.

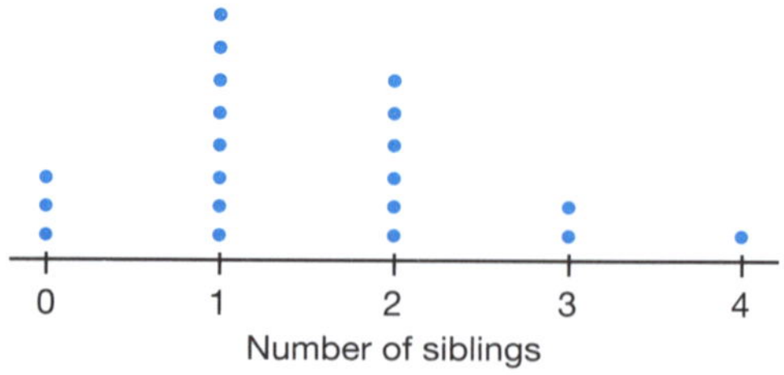

How many students were surveyed?

NUMBER AND ALGEBRA

1 Jolene thinks of a number which has factors of both 2 and 5. Which of these could be Jolene's number?

35, 16, 25, 40

2 What is the sum of 35 768, 29 190 and 16 398 to the nearest ten thousand?

3 Mr Masters placed 16 rows of 14 seats in the library for a parent information evening. What was the total number of seats?

4 1230 bales of hay are to be transported on six trucks. If each truck will have the same number, how many bales will be on each truck?

5 Aditi's teacher wanted her to calculate 376 × 16 but she calculated 376 × 18. How much higher is Aditi's answer than the correct answer?

6 Rearrange these fractions from smallest to largest.

$\frac{2}{5}$ $\frac{2}{4}$ $\frac{2}{6}$ $\frac{2}{3}$

7 What is the missing fraction?

$1 - \square = \frac{28}{45}$

8 What is $5\frac{9}{1000}$ written as a decimal?

9 The entry fees for a wildlife park are $18 for adults and $12 for children. Sarah bought tickets for herself and her children. The total cost was $54. How many children did Sarah take to the wildlife park?

10 Here is a pattern of numbers.

13, 35, 57 …

What is the sixth number in the pattern?

11 $\square + 0.79 = 1$

Find the missing number.

MEASUREMENT AND SPACE

12 A shape is drawn on grid paper. What is the area of the shape?

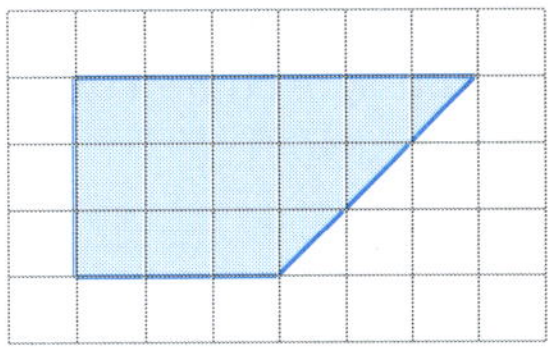

13 How much time is there between 1420 and 1750?

14 The net of a cube is shown to the right.

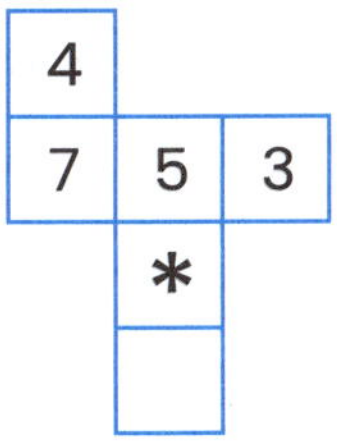

The numbers on opposite faces always add to the same total.

What number is represented by *?

15 How many lines of symmetry has a kite?

16

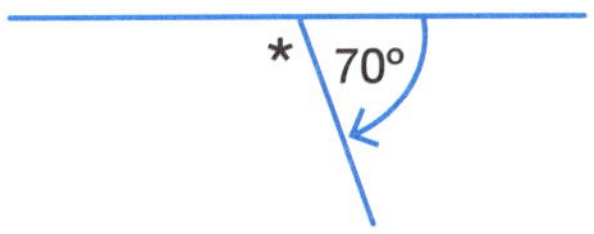

Using a protractor, Emilee measured the angle as 70°. How many degrees is the angle marked as *?

STATISTICS AND PROBABILITY

17 The probability of an event occurring is described as 'possible but not likely'. Which of these could be the probability of the event happening?

0 $\frac{1}{3}$ $\frac{2}{3}$ 1

18 A group of students were surveyed to find the number of their siblings.

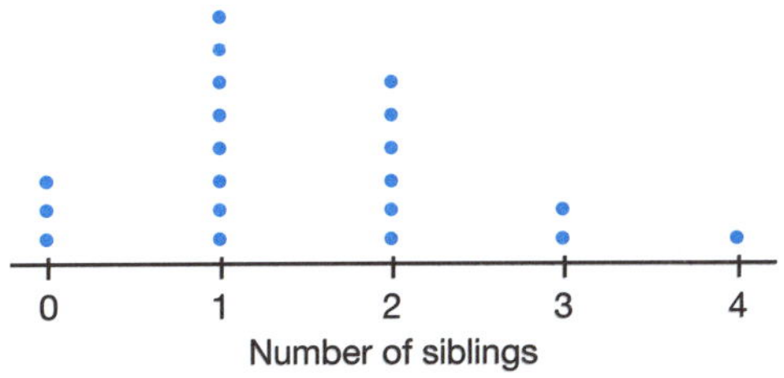

What was the total number of siblings?

NUMBER AND ALGEBRA

1 Circle the numbers that are factors of 20.

2, 15, 8, 10, 3, 20

2 In three cricket innings Brett scored 85 runs, 38 runs and 110 runs. What is the total number of runs scored?

3 A tile warehouse ordered 125 boxes of wall tiles. Each box contained six tiles. How many tiles were in the order?

4 Circle the numbers that can be the remainder when a number is divided by 4.

2 5 8 1

5 $25 \times 12 = 50 \times \square$

6 Circle the fractions that are the same as one whole.

$\frac{6}{6}$ $\frac{1}{2}$ $\frac{10}{5}$ $\frac{3}{3}$

7 What is $\frac{3}{4} + \frac{3}{4} + \frac{3}{4}$?

8 How many thousandths are in 4 hundredths?

9 What is $40 – $12.85?

10 Here is a pattern of decimals.

12.871, 12.877, 12.883, $\square$, $\square$

Write the next two decimals.

11 $5 \times \square = 125$

Find the missing number.

MEASUREMENT AND SPACE

12 A shape is drawn on grid paper. What is the perimeter of the shape?

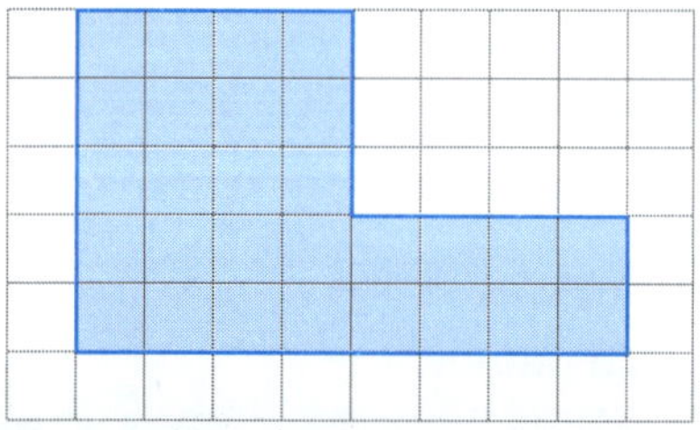

13 A movie starts at 11 am and runs for 2 hours 18 minutes. What time will it finish in 12-hour time?

14 Circle any triangles that are scalene.

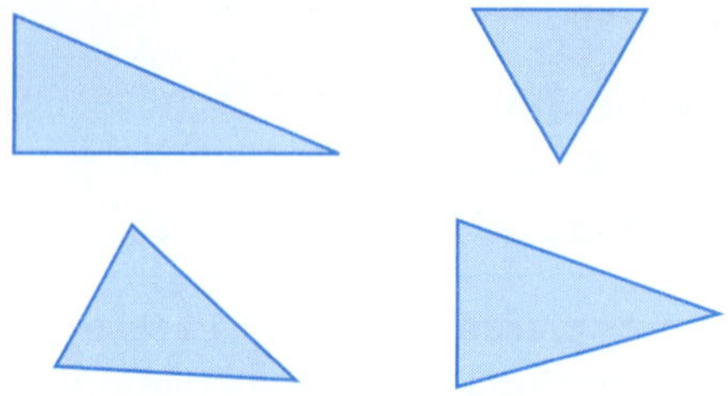

15 Draw the line(s) of symmetry on this shape.

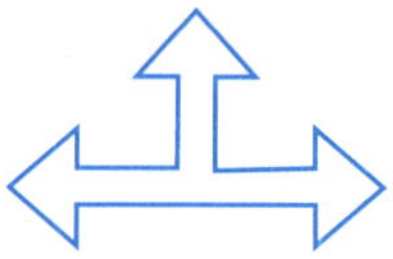

16 On the diagram, mark with a cross (**x**) the angles that measure more than 90°.

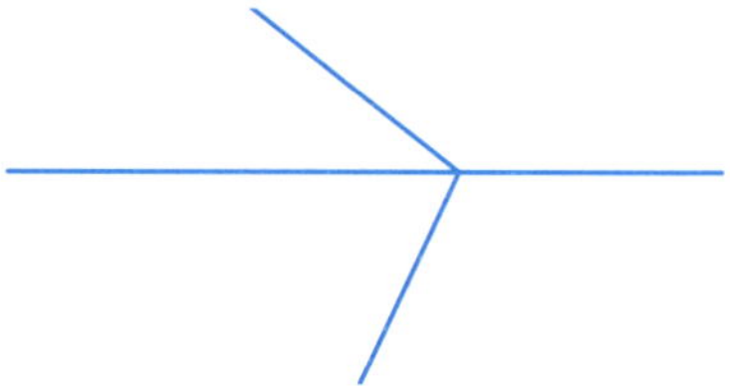

STATISTICS AND PROBABILITY

17 A six-sided dice is rolled once. What is the probability of rolling a 4?

18 Grayson counted the number of vehicles passing his school in 15 minutes.

Vehicle	Number
Car	𝍸 𝍸 𝍸 ||
Van	𝍸 |
Truck	𝍸 𝍸 |
Motorbike	|

How many vehicles did Grayson count?

NUMBER AND ALGEBRA

1 Which of these has the highest number of factors?

15, 18, 24, 28

2 The capacity of three AFL stadiums are listed: Docklands 56 347; Adelaide Oval 53 583; MCG 100 024. What is the total attendance at the three stadiums?

3 The rows of seats in a theatre are named from A to Z. There are 38 seats in each row. How many seats are in the theatre?

4 Four golfers share golf balls equally. They each receive the same number of balls and there are three left over. Which of these is a possible number of balls shared? Circle the correct answer(s).

53 36 39 51

5 Complete 225 ÷ 25 = ☐ ÷ 100.

6 Circle the fractions that are smaller than 1.

$\frac{3}{5}$ $\frac{6}{6}$ $\frac{11}{1}$ $\frac{3}{4}$

7 Every morning for five days Chloe walked $\frac{3}{4}$ km around her block. What is the total distance walked?

8 How many thousandths are in 51 tenths?

9 Brooklyn bought three bananas for $2.40. Zoe bought a banana and two apples for $2.20. What was the cost of each apple?

10 Here is a pattern of numbers.

18, 25, 32 …

What is the first number greater than 50?

11 $\frac{2}{5} = 1 -$ ☐

Find the missing number.

MEASUREMENT AND SPACE

12 A shape is drawn on grid paper.

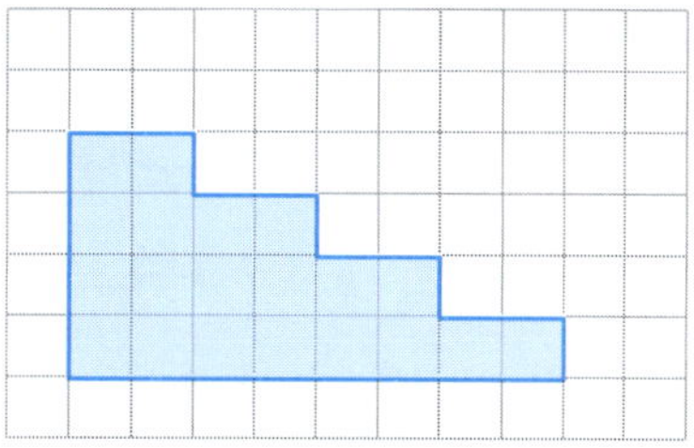

What is the perimeter of the shape?

13 Scouts starts at 6:30 on a Tuesday night and runs for two hours. What 24-hour time does Scouts finish?

14 The net of a cube is shown on the right.

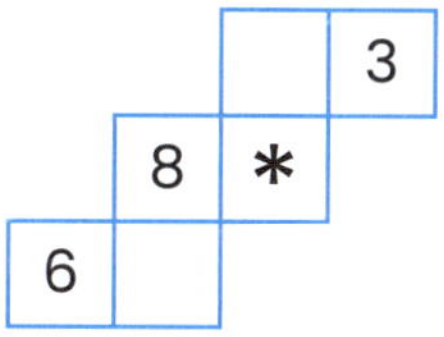

The numbers on opposite faces always multiply to the same number.

What number is represented by *?

15 How many lines of symmetry has a regular pentagon?

16 Using a protractor, Lincoln measured the angle as 60°. How many degrees is the angle marked as *?

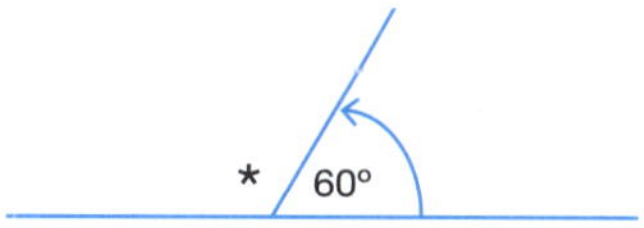

STATISTICS AND PROBABILITY

17 A six-sided dice is rolled once. What is the probability of rolling a number less than 4?

18 Grayson counted the number of vehicles passing his school in 15 minutes.

Vehicle	Number
Car	𝍸 𝍸 𝍸 ||
Van	𝍸 |
Truck	𝍸 𝍸 |
Motorbike	|

How many more cars were there than the total number of vans and motorbikes?

NUMBER AND ALGEBRA

1 Circle the numbers that are multiples of 8.

18, 50, 28, 32, 48

2 Jasper is 136 cm tall and his sister Posie is 145 cm tall. What is the total of their heights?

3 Every team in a junior soccer club has 13 registered players. If the club has 11 teams, what is the total number of players in the club?

4 Divide 435 by 5.

5 What is 1000 less than 13 478?

6 Rewrite $2\frac{3}{4}$ as an improper fraction.

7 What is $1\frac{7}{8} - \frac{4}{8}$?

8 Which of these is closest to 30?

13.29 29.31 30.4 30.21

9 Rory bought four pens for $3.65 each. What was the total cost?

10 Here is a pattern of decimals.

532.8, 532.76, 532.72, ____, ____

Write the next two numbers.

11 84 ÷ ____ = 4

Find the missing number.

MEASUREMENT AND SPACE

12 Complete: 'half' km = ____ m

13 Logan's digital clock shows the time as 1145. What is this time in 12-hour time?

14 The net of a cube is shown below.

What letter is on the opposite face to *P*?

15 Draw the line(s) of symmetry on this shape.

16 In the triangle, how many angles are less than 90°?

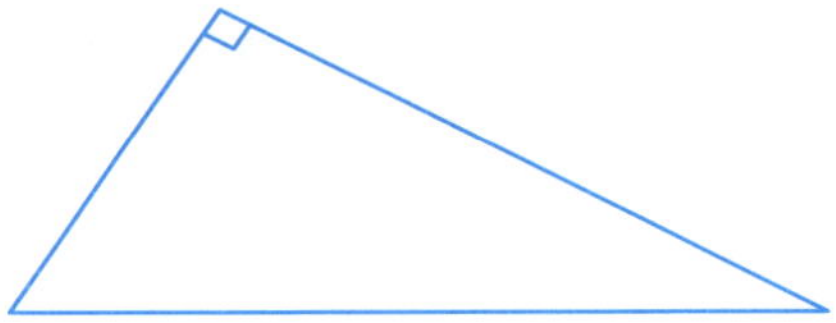

STATISTICS AND PROBABILITY

17 A box contains red (R), blue (B) and yellow (Y) coloured tokens. A token is chosen at random.

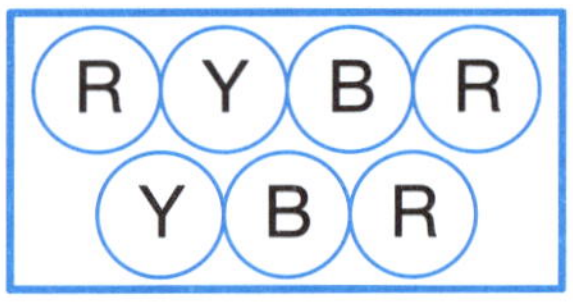

What is the probability that it is red?

18 Ms Freeman drew this table representing the different fruits in her students' lunchboxes.

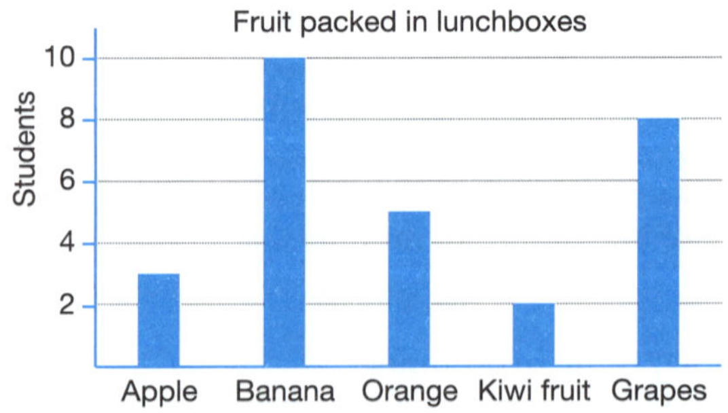

What was the total number of apples and oranges?

NUMBER AND ALGEBRA

1 Which of these are divisible by 3, 4 and 5? Circle the numbers.

30, 40, 60, 80, 120

2 Jackson is 162 cm tall, his father's height is 181 cm and his grandfather is 176 cm tall. What is the total height of the three males?

3 Each school nominates 17 players for a rugby league gala day. If there are 16 schools playing, what is the total number of players?

4 There are 203 students enrolled in a primary school. An equal number of students were allocated to each of four buses for transport to a park, with the remaining students travelling by car. How many students needed to travel in the car?

5 What is the difference between 63 781 and 10 000?

6 For half time in a soccer match, oranges are cut into quarters. How many quarters can be cut from $4\frac{1}{2}$ oranges?

7 Logan had a $4\frac{1}{5}$ metre length of stormwater pipe. He removed a $\frac{3}{5}$ metre long section from one end of the pipe. What was the remaining length of pipe?

8 Which of these is closest to 23?

23.4 23.087 22.92 22.908

9 Austin bought a game console for $499 and two games at $39 each. How much did Austin pay in total?

10 Here is a pattern of numbers.

64, 55, 46 …

What is the first number less than 20?

11 Here is a number sentence.

15 + 12 – 9 = ☐

What is the missing number?

MEASUREMENT AND SPACE

12 A square has a perimeter of 24 cm. What is the area of the square?

13 Late on New Year's Eve, Violet checks that the time is 2345. How much time will she have to wait until midnight?

14 The net of a cube is shown below. The numbers on opposite faces always add to the same total.

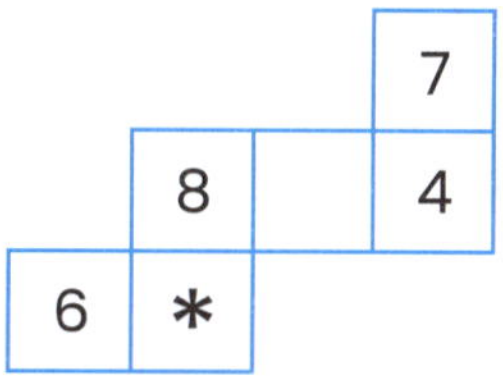

What number is represented by *?

15 How many lines of symmetry has a regular hexagon?

16

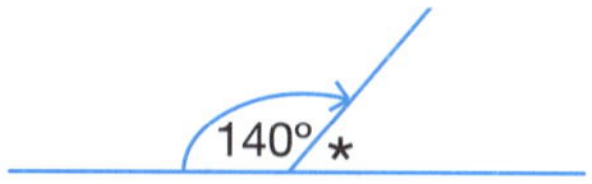

Using a protractor, Lincoln measured the angle as 140°. How many degrees is the angle marked as *?

STATISTICS AND PROBABILITY

17 A box contains red (R), blue (B) and yellow (Y) coloured tokens. A token is chosen at random.

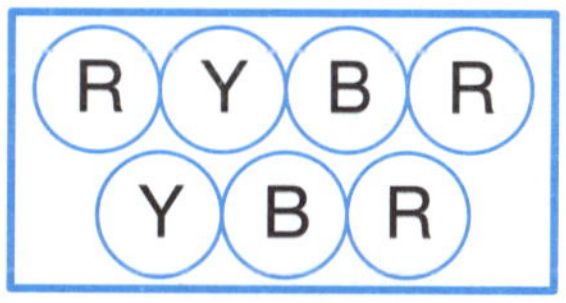

What is the probability that it is red or blue?

18 Ms Freeman drew this table representing the different fruits in her students' lunchboxes.

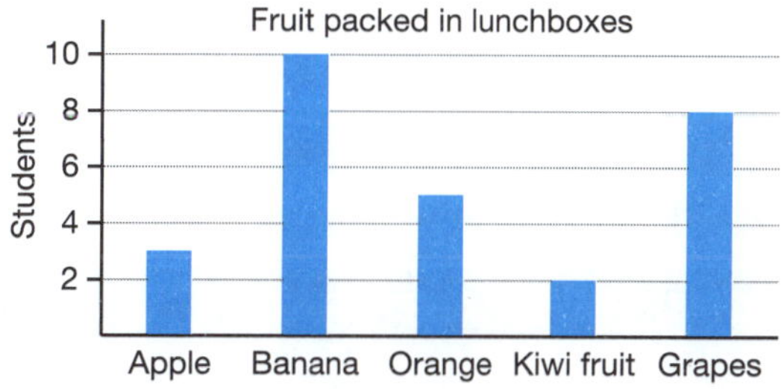

What fraction of the students brought an orange to school?

NUMBER AND ALGEBRA

1 Here are some numbers:

502, 45, 290, 15, 53.

Circle the numbers that are multiples of 5.

2 A town has two primary schools. At Ringtree Public School there are 568 students and St Patrick's School has 387 students. What is the total number of students at both schools?

3 At a market a bag of oranges costs $4. How much will be paid for nine bags of oranges?

4 48 ÷ ☐ = 12

What is the missing number?

5 What is 456 739 – 100 000?

6 Shown below are three rectangles.

Shade squares to represent the improper fraction $\frac{3}{2}$.

7 What is $\frac{2}{5} + \frac{1}{5}$?

8 What is added to 3.872 to make 3.875? Circle the correct answer.

3 tenth 3 hundredths 3 thousandths

9 Grandma wants to give a total of $235 to her five grandchildren. If each is given an equal share, what will each child receive?

10 Fill in the two missing numbers in the sequence.

☐, 5, 9, 13, 17, ☐

11 ☐ × 8 = 120

Find the missing number.

MEASUREMENT AND SPACE

12 Which of these units (cm, kg, L, t, km) would be used to measure the distance from Sydney to Melbourne?

13 Avery got to the beach at 1415. She left 2 hours later. At what time did Avery leave the beach?

14 The net of a cube is drawn .

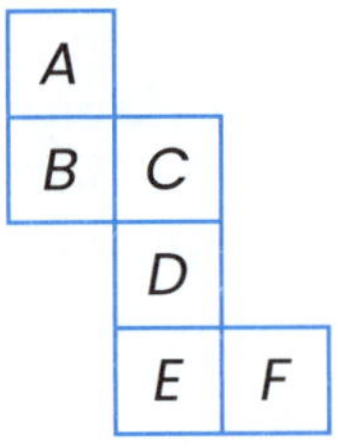

What letter is on the opposite face to *B*?

15 Draw the line(s) of symmetry on this shape.

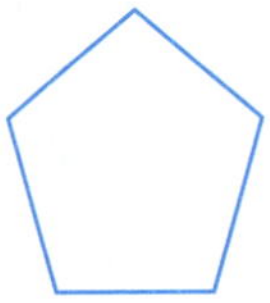

16 Using a cross (**X**) mark any angle inside the shape which measures more than 90° but less than 180°.

STATISTICS AND PROBABILITY

17 A box contains black (B) and white (W) balls. A ball is chosen at random.

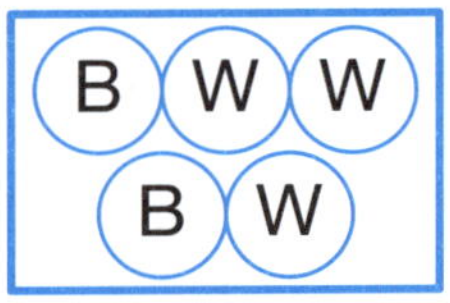

What is the probability that it is black?

18 The favourite sports of a group of students in a class are recorded.

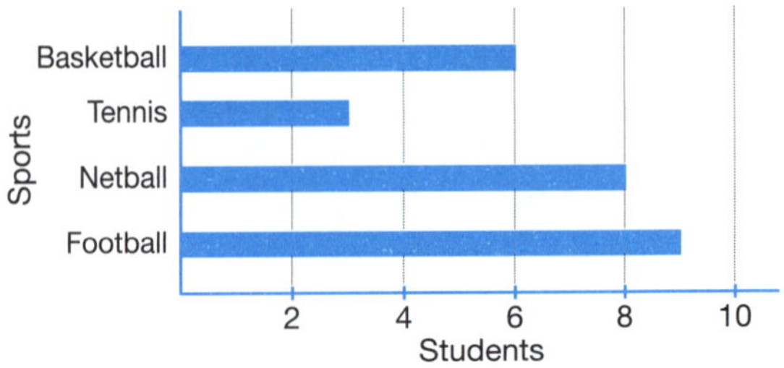

What was the total number of students who liked basketball and football?

NUMBER AND ALGEBRA

1 What is the smallest number that is a multiple of both 8 and 12?

2 The student populations of three universities are 48 088, 50 749 and 84 267. What is the total population of the universities?

3 A company makes widgets which each have a mass of 35 grams. What is the total mass of 65 widgets?

4 What is the missing number?

5424 ÷ ☐ = 6

5 What is 11 876 083 – 1 000 000?

6 Shown below are three rectangles.

Shade squares to represent the improper fraction $\frac{7}{3}$.

7 What is $\frac{2}{5} + \frac{1}{5} + \frac{1}{5}$?

8 What is subtracted from 18.699 to make 18.674? Circle the correct answer.

2 hundredths 25 hundredths
25 thousandths 5 hundredths

9 The price of an adult ticket to a theme park is $42. A child's ticket is half the price of an adult ticket. What is the cost of two adults and two children?

10 Here is a pattern of decimals. Write the next two numbers.

39.29, 39.17, 39.05, ☐, ☐

11 Here is a number sentence.

116 – ☐ = 53 + 37

What is the missing number?

MEASUREMENT AND SPACE

12 A square has an area of 16 cm^2. What is the perimeter of the square?

13 Jared fell asleep at 2100 and woke at 0700 the next morning. How long was he asleep?

14 The net of a cube is shown below.

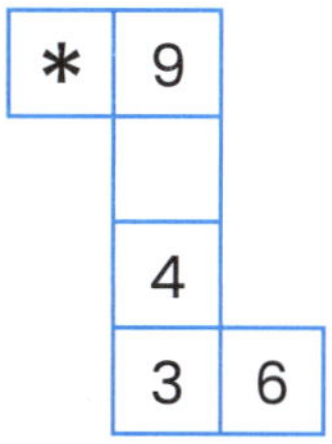

The numbers on opposite faces always multiply to the same number.

What number is represented by ∗?

15 What is the order of rotational symmetry for a scalene triangle?

16 Using a protractor, Harper measured the angle as 150°. How many degrees is the angle marked as *?

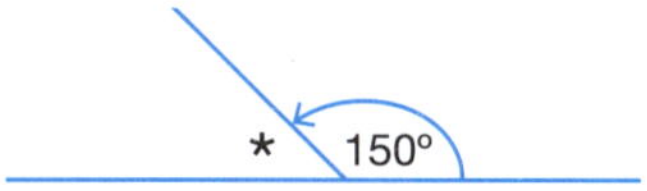

STATISTICS AND PROBABILITY

17 A box contains black (B) and white (W) balls. A ball is chosen at random.

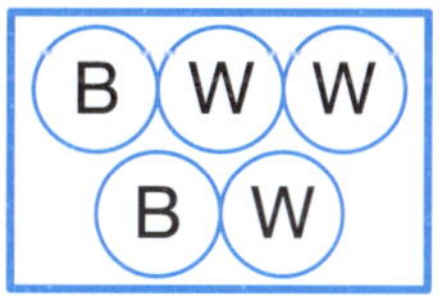

What is the probability that it is green?

18 The favourite sports of a group of students in a class are recorded.

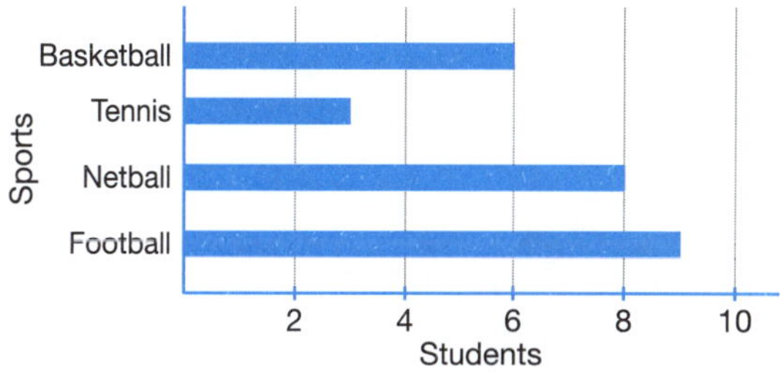

Four students whose favourite sport was netball were absent and the graph was adjusted when they returned to class. What is the total number of students?

NUMBER AND ALGEBRA

1 Which of these are factors of 32? Circle all the correct numbers.

8, 12, 4, 3, 16

2 A book has 538 pages. Meghan has read 379 pages. How many pages remain to be read?

3 Henry is walking across a desert. He plans to walk 24 km each day. How far will he walk in a week?

4 What is one-sixth of 1254?

5 Complete 840 ÷ 14 = ☐ ÷ 7

6 Part of a square is shaded.

What fraction is not shaded?

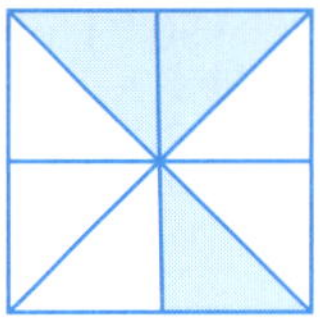

7 What is $\frac{1}{4} + \frac{2}{4}$?

8 Choose from the following cards to make a number with two decimal places between 8.28 and 8.35.

6 | 2 | 7 | 8 | 3 | .

9 If each pizza cost $6.95, what was the total cost of five pizzas?

10 Here is a pattern.

$\frac{5}{10}, \frac{8}{10}, 1\frac{1}{10}$, ☐ , ☐

What are the next two numbers?

11 4 × ☐ = 124

Find the missing number.

MEASUREMENT AND SPACE

12 Which of these units (cm, kg, L, t, km) would be used to measure the capacity of a car's petrol tank?

13 What is 3:47 pm in 24-hour time?

14 The net of a cube is shown below.

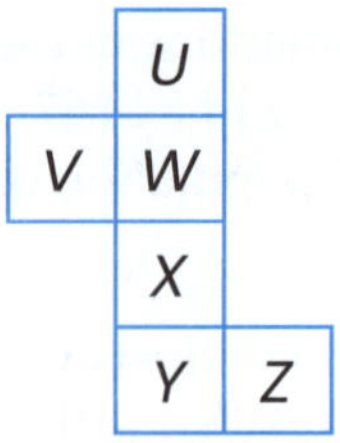

What letter is on the opposite face to *Z*?

15 Draw the line(s) of symmetry on this shape.

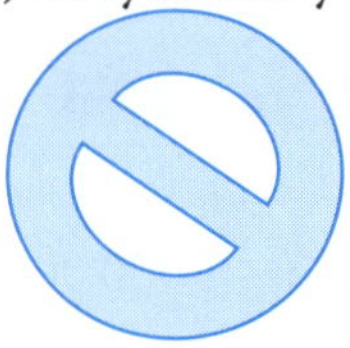

16 Hannah looked at the angles between the hands at different times on an analog clock. Circle the times when the angle would be less than 90°.

4 o'clock | 11 o'clock
half past seven | quarter past ten

STATISTICS AND PROBABILITY

17 A box contains red (R), yellow (Y), green (G) and blue (B) balls. A ball is chosen at random.

What is the probability that it is green?

18 The numbers of boys and girls in two classes, 5P and 5R, are recorded.

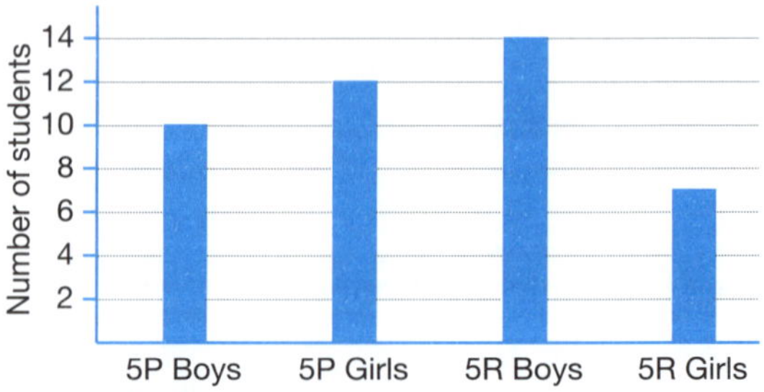

What is the total number of girls in the two classes?

NUMBER AND ALGEBRA

1 Circle the numbers that are multiples of 9.

45, 65, 135, 307, 432

2 By road the distance from Darwin to Brisbane is 3424 km. From Melbourne to Adelaide is 726 km. What is the difference between the distances?

3 A Supporters Club organised 27 buses to drive from Adelaide to Melbourne for a Crows AFL game. If each bus has a capacity of 54 passengers, find the total number of potential passengers.

4 What is one-eighth of 1672?

5 Complete: 4480 ÷ 28 = ______ ÷ 7

6 Part of a square is shaded.

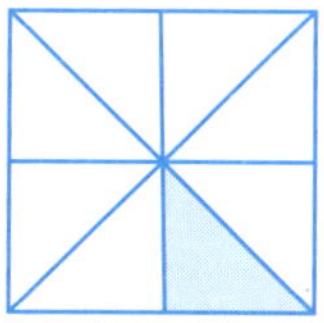

What fraction is **not** shaded?

7 What is $\frac{2}{3} + \frac{2}{3}$ as a mixed numeral?

8 Choose from the following cards to make a number with three decimal places between 7.9 and 8.028.

8 | 4 | 9 | 2 | 0 | .

9 A supermarket sells a tray of mince for $8.90 and a 2-L container of milk for $4.10. How much will Deidre pay for three trays of mince and a container of milk?

10 Here is a sequence of numbers: 1.24, 1.17, 1.1 …

What are the next three numbers?

11 ______ + 0.53 = 1

Find the missing number.

MEASUREMENT AND SPACE

12 Annie stores cardboard boxes in a storage room. Each box is in the shape of a cube of side length 80 cm. The room can fit exactly 10 boxes along its length, five boxes along its width and three boxes along its height. What are the dimensions of the storage room?

13 One afternoon, an analog clock shows the time as twenty past two. Isabella rings her sister and speaks for 10 minutes. What is the 24-hour time when she finishes the call?

14 The net of a cube is shown on the right.

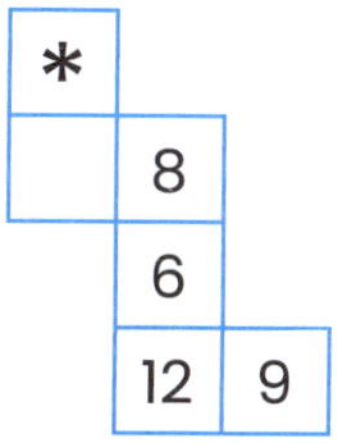

The numbers on opposite faces always add to the same total.

What number is represented by *?

15 What is the order of rotational symmetry for an isosceles triangle?

16

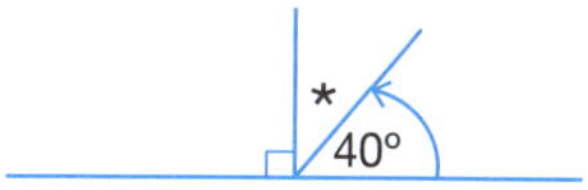

Using a protractor, Harper measured an angle as 40°. There is also a right angle shown. How many degrees is the angle marked as *?

STATISTICS AND PROBABILITY

17 A box contains red (R), yellow (Y), green (G) and blue (B) balls. A ball is chosen at random.

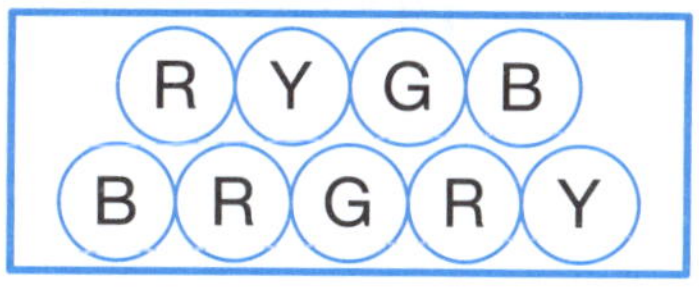

What is the probability that it is **not** blue?

18 The number of boys and girls in two classes, 5P and 5R, is recorded.

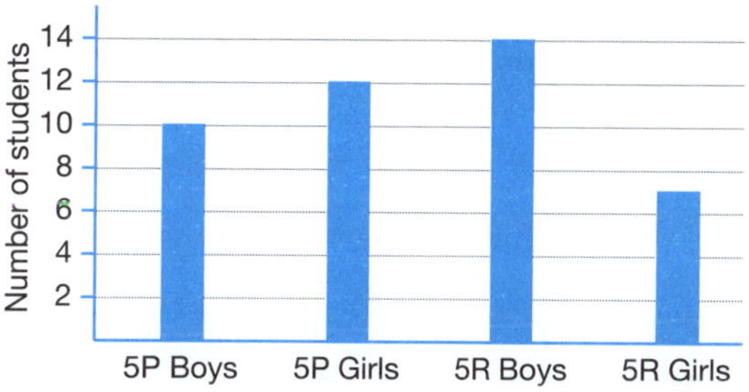

A new boy is enrolled in the school and is placed in 5R. How many more boys are in the classes than girls?

NUMBER AND ALGEBRA

1 Circle the numbers that are **not** multiples of 4.

14, 28, 44, 38, 80

2

$$\begin{array}{r} 29\,276 \\ -\ 16\,135 \\ \hline \end{array}$$

3 Chloe reads 16 pages of her novel every night. How many pages will she read in six nights?

4 Six hundred and thirty potatoes are to be placed into bags of 10 potatoes. How many bags are required?

5 What is 35 + 65 + 28 + 72?

6 A number line is shown.

Which letter represents $\frac{7}{8}$?

7 What is $\frac{3}{10} + \frac{4}{10}$?

8 What decimal is represented by the answer to $\frac{14}{100} + \frac{37}{100}$?

9 Erica saved $8.50 each week for 6 weeks. What was her total savings?

10 Here is a pattern.

$1\frac{1}{4}$, $2\frac{1}{4}$, $3\frac{1}{4}$, ☐, ☐

What are the next two numbers?

11 345 ÷ ☐ = 5

Find the missing number.

MEASUREMENT AND SPACE

12 How much remains when 35 cm is removed from a 1-metre-long length of ribbon?

13 Last night Isaac went to bed at a quarter to nine. Write this in 24-hour time.

14 The net of a cube is drawn below.

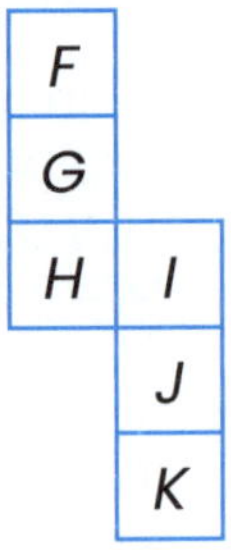

What letter is on the opposite face to G?

15 Draw the line(s) of symmetry on this shape.

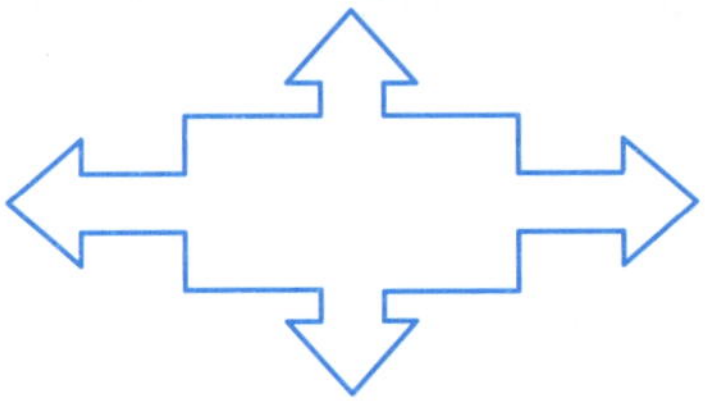

16 Aiden looked at the angles between the hands at different times on an analog clock. Circle the times when the angle would be 90°.

5 o'clock 9 o'clock
half past four 3 o'clock

STATISTICS AND PROBABILITY

17 A box contains numbered balls. A ball is chosen at random.

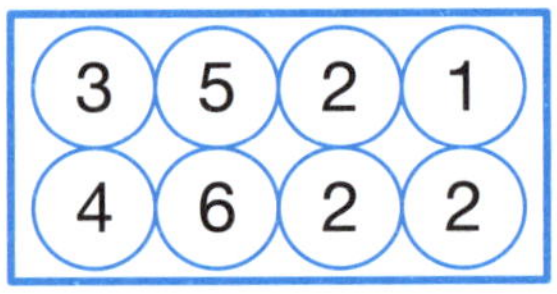

What is the probability that the number 2 is chosen?

18 Mario's Pizzas recorded the number of pizzas sold between 6 pm and 7 pm across 6 days.

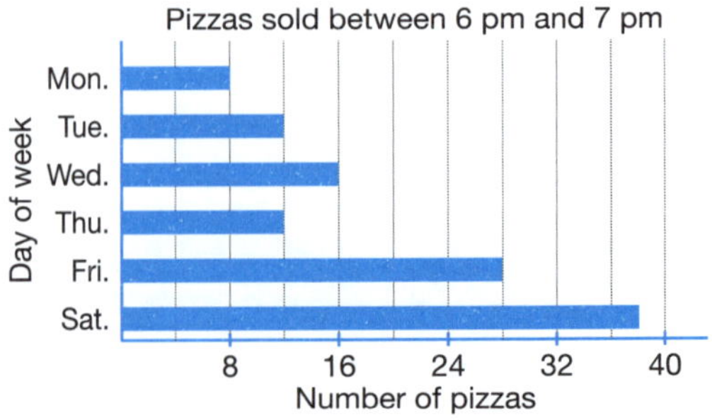

How many more pizzas were sold on Saturday compared to Tuesday?

NUMBER AND ALGEBRA

1 Which of these is divisible by both 2 and 5? Circle the numbers.

320, 125, 400, 2502

2 The attendance at a Collingwood game was given as 78 294. Ten minutes after full time there were still 11 890 people remaining in the stands. How many people had left the stadium, to the nearest thousand?

3 There are 31 days in August. Nathan plans to complete 25 sit-ups each night. What will be the total number of sit-ups he hopes to complete?

4 Find the missing number:

$23\,400 \div \square = 234$

5 What is 123 + 64 + 77 + 436?

6 Here are four points located on a number line.

Which letter represents the improper fraction $\frac{18}{5}$?

7 What is $\frac{7}{8} + \frac{6}{8}$ as a mixed numeral?

8 What decimal is represented by the answer to

$\frac{5}{10} + \frac{21}{1000} + \frac{3}{100}$?

9 Lydia bought three notebooks at $1.70 each, a box of pens at $9.20 and a packet of glue sticks for $4.90. How much change did Lydia receive from a $20 note?

10 Here is a sequence of numbers.

14, 27, 40 …

Circle the number that is a member of the sequence: 54 66 75.

11 $\frac{2}{5} = 1 - \square$

Find the missing number.

MEASUREMENT AND SPACE

12 Peter bent wire to form squares of area 64 cm^2. He made 10 squares. What is the total length of wire used in metres?

13 Joshua leaves his home at 2230 and drives to his holiday unit, arriving 10 hours later. What is the time he arrives, in 12-hour time?

14 The net of a cube is drawn below.

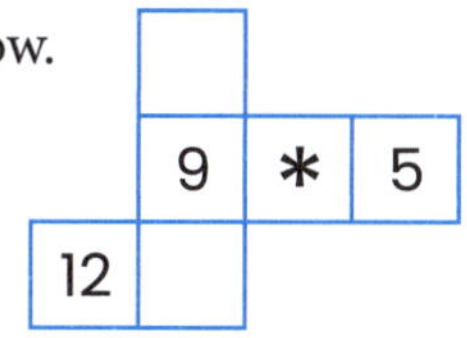

The difference between the numbers on opposite faces is always the same.

What one-digit number is represented by *?

15 What is the order of rotational symmetry for an equilateral triangle?

16 The acute angle between the hands of an analog clock at 10 o'clock is 60°. At what other 'o'clock' time will the acute angle also be 60°?

STATISTICS AND PROBABILITY

17 A box contains numbered balls. A ball is chosen at random.

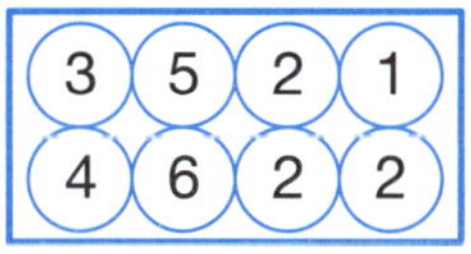

What is the probability of choosing an even number?

18 Mario's Pizzas recorded the number of pizzas sold between 6 pm and 7 pm across 6 days.

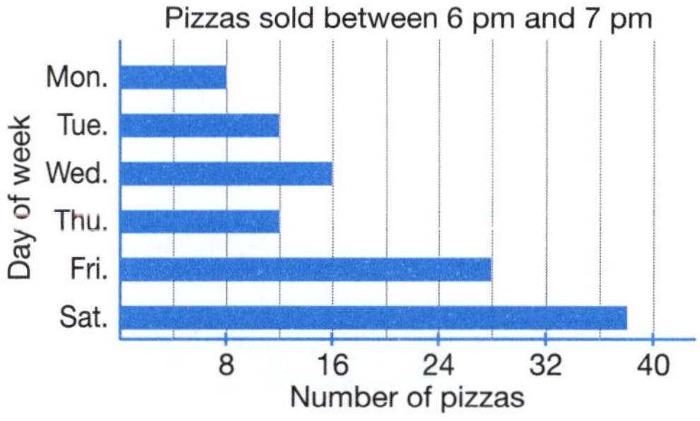

What was the total number of pizzas sold in the six days between 6 pm and 7 pm?

NUMBER AND ALGEBRA

1. Circle the multiples of 3 in this list.

   60, 61, 62, 63, 64, 65, 66

2. Recently the population of Mount Gambier was 26 341 and Whyalla's was 21 997. Estimate the total population of the two cities, to the nearest thousand.

3. 3762 × 4

4. A farmer ordered 1260 bales of hay. The hay is to be delivered to his property in three equal shipments. How many bales are in each shipment?

5. What is 87 – 15 – 5 – 10?

6. Rewrite $\frac{15}{4}$ as a mixed numeral.

7. Find the missing fraction:

   $\frac{2}{10} + \frac{5}{10} = \square$

8. What decimal is halfway between 7.8 and 7.9?

9. Corrie has a $20 note. She spends $8.45 in a shop. How much change does she receive?

10. Here is a pattern of numbers.

    1080, 1050, 1020, ☐, ☐

    What are the next two numbers?

11. ☐ ÷ 6 = 18

    Find the missing number.

MEASUREMENT AND SPACE

12. How much remains when 65 mL is removed from a 1-L bottle of milk?

13. A concert finished at 10:30 pm. What is this in 24-hour time?

14. The net of a cube is drawn below.

    What letter is on the opposite face to *A*?

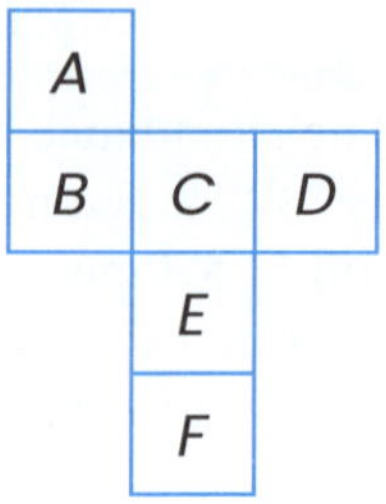

15. How many lines of symmetry has a semicircle?

16. Carter looked at the angles between the hands at different times on an analog clock. Circle the times when the angle would be more than 90° but less than 180°.

    2 o'clock — half past two
    quarter to eleven — quarter past seven

STATISTICS AND PROBABILITY

17. A box contains numbered balls. A ball is chosen at random.

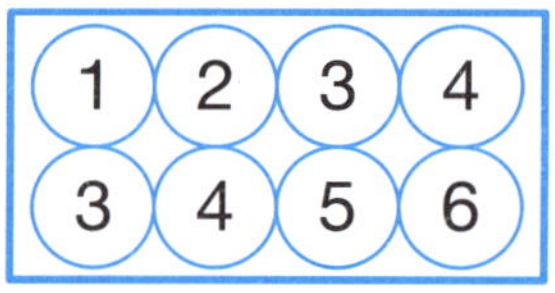

    What is the probability that a 5 is chosen?

18. A group of students were asked the name of their favourite subject.

Subject	Students
Maths	7
English	6
Science	5
Music	4
PE	3

    What fraction of the students chose PE?

NUMBER AND ALGEBRA

1 What are the two numbers that are factors of 6, 8 and 12?

2 The populations of two cities were 168 719 and 350 189. Estimate the total population to the nearest ten thousand.

3 What is the product of 376 and 43?

4 A fundraising concert raised $75 000 to be equally distributed between five charities. How much money will each charity receive?

5 What is 200 – 16 – 14 – 20 – 30?

6 Here are four points located on a number line.

Which letter represents the improper fraction $\frac{15}{4}$?

7 What is $\frac{3}{5} + \frac{4}{5} + \frac{2}{5}$, as a mixed numeral?

8 What decimal is halfway between 14.63 and 14.844?

9 The cost of snacks at a movie complex include: drinks $4.50, chips $3.50, popcorn $4.10 and ice cream $3.90. A family bought three drinks, a packet of chips, two popcorn and two ice creams. To pay for the snacks they used a voucher for $40. How much money was left on the voucher after the purchases?

10 Here is a sequence of numbers.

33, 51, 69 …

Circle the number that is a member of the sequence: 101 103 105.

11 Here is a number sentence.

15 + 12 – 9 = ☐

What is the missing number?

MEASUREMENT AND SPACE

12 Rick purchases a 25-metre ball of string. He cuts five 80-cm lengths of string from the ball. What length of string remains on the ball?

13 Stella leaves home at 11:30 am to go swimming at her local pool. She arrives back home two and a half hours later. At what time does she get home, in 24-hour time?

14 Numbers are written on two identical cubes. For the first cube, numbers 1 to 6 are used so that opposite faces add to 7. On the second cube, numbers 3 to 8 are used so that opposite faces add to 11. If the faces with the number 3 are glued together to form a prism, what number is opposite 8?

15 What is the order of rotational symmetry for a square?

16 The obtuse angle between the hands of an analog clock at 4 o'clock is 120°. At what other 'o'clock' time will the obtuse angle also be 120°?

STATISTICS AND PROBABILITY

17 A box contains numbered balls. A ball is chosen at random.

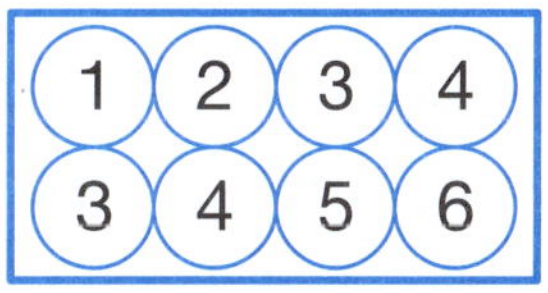

What is the probability the number is a factor of 6?

18 A group of students were asked for the name of their favourite subject.

Subject	Students
Maths	7
English	6
Science	5
Music	4
PE	3

How many more students chose Maths or Science than chose English or Music?

NUMBER AND ALGEBRA

1 Louisa has written a set of numbers.

16, 30, 42, 50, 60

Circle the numbers that have a factor of 6.

2 Before Allison left on her trip, her car's odometer showed 58 659 km. During her holiday she drove 2728 km. What will the odometer now show?

3
$$\begin{array}{r} 4182 \\ \times \quad 5 \\ \hline \end{array}$$

4 Jack drives 240 km in 4 hours. At this speed, how far would he drive in one hour?

5 What is 6 + 200 + 50?

6 Which of these is the largest?

$\frac{1}{2}, \frac{1}{5}, \frac{1}{8}$

7 Raj's dog had a litter of eight puppies.

$\frac{3}{8}$ were females. What fraction were males?

8 Here are three decimals: 4.38, 4.309, 4.379

Write the decimals in order from smallest to largest.

9 Lionel bought three cans of beans for $3.90. What was the cost of one can?

10 Here is a pattern of numbers.

20 000, 20 025, 20 050, ____, ____

What are the next two numbers?

11 'The sum of eight and twelve is equal to twenty.'

Rewrite the statement as a number sentence.

MEASUREMENT AND SPACE

12 How many millimetres are in 3 m 48 mm?

13 What is 5:13 pm in 24-hour time?

14 How many pairs of parallel faces has a rectangular prism?

15 How many lines of symmetry has a square?

16 Circle the angle that measures about 60°.

STATISTICS AND PROBABILITY

17 A box contains numbered balls. A ball is chosen at random.

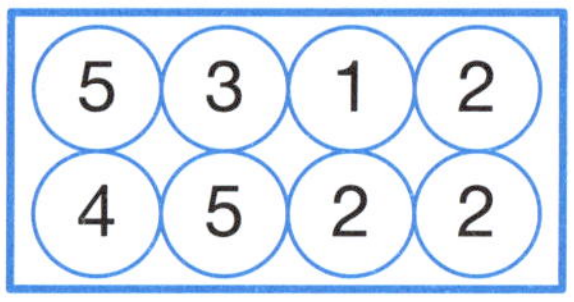

What is the probability that a 2 is chosen?

18 A group of 50 people were asked for their plans for a holiday Monday.

Activity	Votes
Beach	
Movies	13
Shopping	15
Sport	10

How many people nominated the beach?

NUMBER AND ALGEBRA

1. How many factors has 60?

2. In 2011 the population of a city was 167 549. Over the following 10 years the population increased by 12 273. What was the population of the city in 2021?

3. A rollercoaster has a capacity of 24 passengers. In one day there are 165 rides with full capacity. How many passengers rode the rollercoaster?

4. A factory fills 4480 boxes of cereal in 4 hours. How many boxes were filled each hour?

5. What is 32 + 600 + 2100 + 7 + 150?

6. Arrange these fractions in ascending order.
$\frac{3}{5}, \frac{3}{8}, \frac{3}{4}, \frac{3}{10}$

7. What is $\frac{7}{10} + \frac{8}{10} + \frac{6}{10}$ as a mixed numeral?

8. Four friends compared the distance, in metres, they threw in a shot-put event: Jarryd 8.52, Oliver 8.09, Luke 8.37 and Lincoln 8.4. Who came second?

9. Ryan bought two toy cars and three toy trucks for $78. Aaron bought one toy car and two toy trucks for $48. What is the cost of a toy truck?

10. Here is a sequence of numbers.

5, 9, 13, 17 …

One of these numbers is a member of the sequence: 399 400 401.
Circle the correct number.

11. Here is a number sentence.

116 – ☐ = 53 + 37

What is the missing number?

MEASUREMENT AND SPACE

12. How many millimetres are in 18 km 25 m 192 mm?

13. Hala arrived at a shopping centre at 1430. She left the centre 2 hours 20 minutes later. Write the time she left in 12-hour time.

14. How many pairs of parallel faces has a regular pentagonal prism?

15. A shape has a rotational symmetry of order 4. Through how many degrees will the shape be rotated until it displays its original shape?

16.

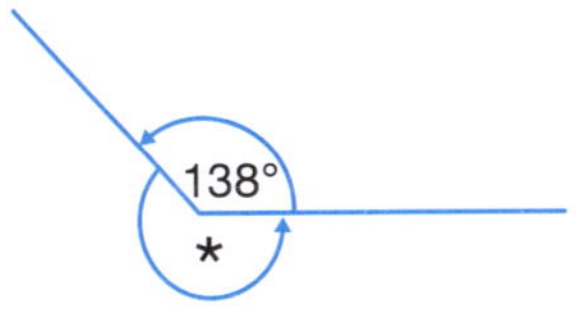

With a protractor Ellie measured the angle as 138°. How many degrees is the angle marked as *?

STATISTICS AND PROBABILITY

17. A box contains numbered balls. A ball is chosen at random.

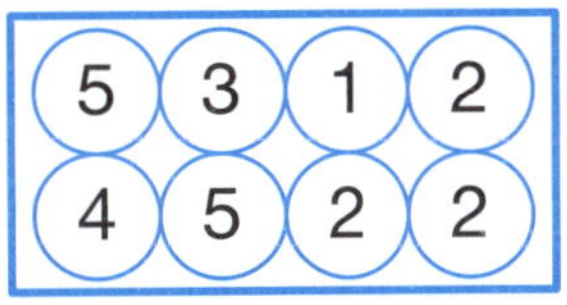

What is the probability of choosing at least a 3?

18. A group of people were asked for their plans for a holiday Monday.

Activity	Votes
Beach	
Movies	13
Shopping	15
Sport	12

One-third of the people surveyed nominated the beach. How many people were surveyed?

NUMBER AND ALGEBRA

1 The number 8 has four factors.

True or false?

2 Increase 337 by 175.

3

$$\begin{array}{r} 1864 \\ \times \quad 6 \\ \hline \end{array}$$

4 $96 \div \square = 4$

What is the missing number?

5 What is the answer to 357×200?

6 Circle the shape(s) that show $\frac{5}{8}$ shaded.

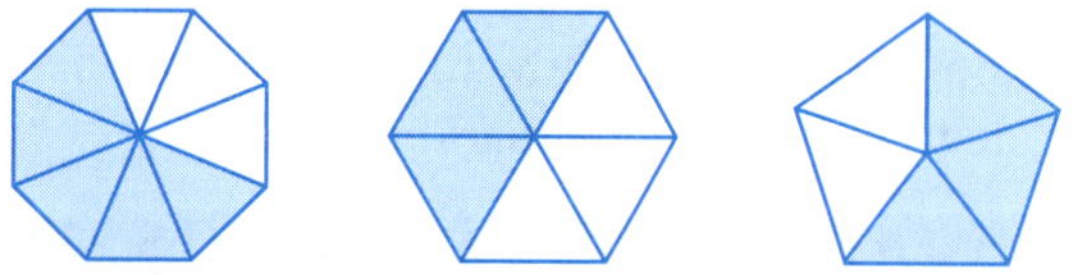

7 What is $1 - \frac{4}{15}$?

8 Here is a number line.

Which letter is closest to 2.75?

9 George bought the following items: wheelbarrow for \$89, hammer for \$18.95, drill for \$119 and fertiliser for \$16.75.
What was the total cost?

10 Find the first five numbers in the sequence that starts with 10 and increases by 6.

11 'The product of ten and nine is greater than sixty-five.'

Write the statement as a number sentence.

MEASUREMENT AND SPACE

12 How many millilitres are in 2 L 85 mL?

13 Oliver's footy training starts at 1600.
What time is this in 12-hour time?

14 Changying draws the net of a square-based pyramid. Complete the statement.

The net is made up of 1 ....

and ....

15 How many lines of symmetry has an equilateral triangle?

16 Circle the angle that measures about 45°.

STATISTICS AND PROBABILITY

17 A box contains balls which are either black (B) or white (W). A ball is chosen at random.

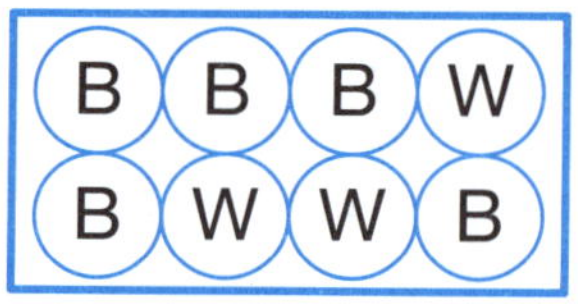

What is the probability that it is white?

18 The daily ticket sales for a school concert are recorded in the table.

Concert ticket sales	
Day	**Number**
Monday	64
Tuesday	49
Wednesday	51
Thursday	36

What was the total number of sales across the four days?

NUMBER AND ALGEBRA

1 How many numbers between 30 and 40 have more than two factors? ☐

2 A high school has 478 boys and 539 girls. What is the total population of the school? ☐

3 A common species of ladybird has 28 spots. How many spots are on 75 ladybirds? ☐

4 335 ÷ ☐ = 5

What is the missing number? ☐

5 Complete: $153 \times 4000 =$ ☐ ☐

6 Shown below are three rectangles.

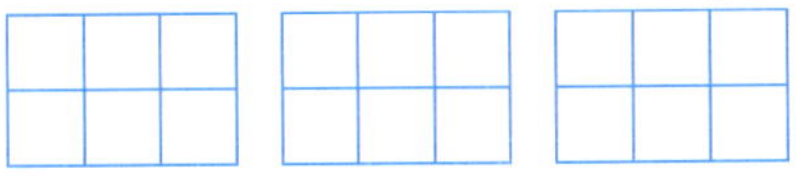

Shade squares to represent the improper fraction $\frac{11}{6}$.

7 What is the missing fraction?

$1 - \frac{417}{1000} =$ ☐ ☐

8 Here is a number line, where a is 2.96 and b is 2.98.

Which decimal is represented by c? ☐

9 A game of golf costs $32 per person and the hire of a golf cart for two people is a total of $36. What will Adam and Kaiden pay in total for a game of golf and the golf cart hire? ☐

10 Here is a sequence of numbers.

11, 17, 23, 29, …

Circle the number that is a member of the sequence: 65 67 69.

11 Here is a number sentence.

☐ ÷ 5 = 315

What is the missing number? ☐

MEASUREMENT AND SPACE

12 How many millilitres are in 10 kL 620 L 16 mL? ☐

13 Michael started watching a YouTube clip at 2050 and it finished at 2115. How long was the video? ☐

14 Robert draws the net of an octagonal prism. Complete the statement.

The net is made up of ………………………………
and ……………………………………….

15 An equilateral triangle is rotated around its centre. Through how many degrees should it be rotated before it displays its original shape? ☐

16 The reflex angle on the diagram measures 237°. How many degrees is the angle marked as *?

☐

STATISTICS AND PROBABILITY

17 A box contains balls which are either black (B) or white (W).

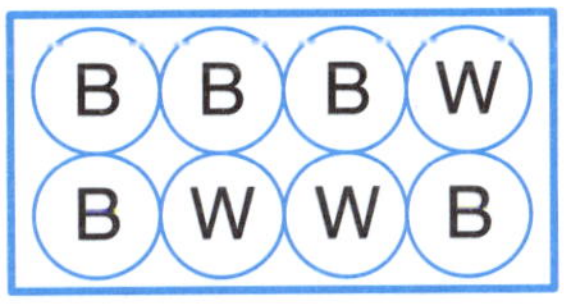

Another two black balls are placed in the box. A ball is chosen at random. What is the probability that it is black? ☐

18 The daily ticket sales for a school concert are recorded in the table.

Concert ticket sales	
Day	**Number**
Monday	64
Tuesday	49
Wednesday	51
Thursday	36

How many more tickets were sold in the first two days than on the last two days of sales? ☐

NUMBER AND ALGEBRA

1 Which of these has a factor of 3? Circle all the correct numbers.

15, 13, 30, 18, 26

2 Three weeks before Easter a store had 5000 boxes of Easter eggs for sale. On Easter Sunday the store still had 167 boxes unsold. How many boxes had been sold?

3

$$\begin{array}{r} 7825 \\ \times \quad 4 \\ \hline \end{array}$$

4 When 147 students are divided into groups of six there are some students left over. How many groups of six can be formed?

5 Add 587 + 99.

6 Circle the shape that shows $\frac{1}{2}$ shaded.

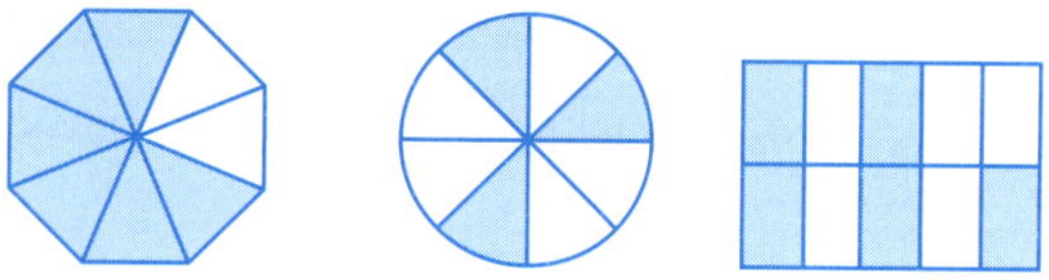

7 What is $\frac{2}{5} + \frac{3}{5}$?

8 Write the number 4 units, 6 tenths, 8 hundredths and 2 thousandths in digits.

9 Harper buys a netball which costs $23 and a pair of shoes costing $85. How much change will she receive from $120?

10 Find the first five numbers in the sequence that starts with 44 and decreases by 8.

11 'The quotient of thirty-five and seven is the same as five.'

Rewrite the statement as a number sentence.

MEASUREMENT AND SPACE

12 Lincoln has four jars that have a mass of 600 g each. What is the total mass in kilograms and grams?

13 What is 2:50 pm in 24-hour time?

14 The net of a cube is drawn below.

What letter is on the opposite face to *P*?

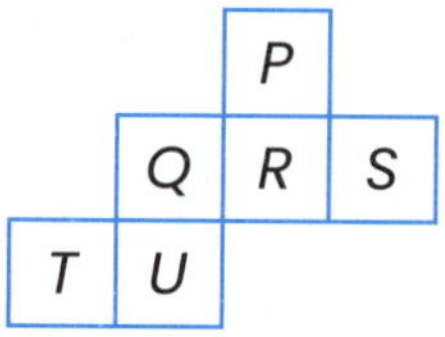

15 How many lines of symmetry has a rectangle?

16 Circle the angle that measures about 120°.

STATISTICS AND PROBABILITY

17 A box contains numbered counters. A counter is chosen at random.

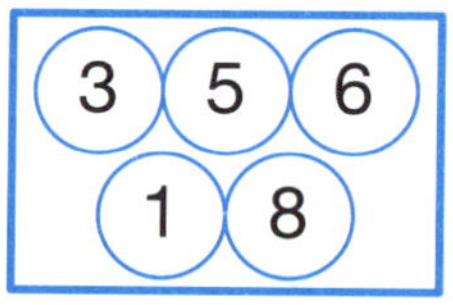

What is the probability that the number is even?

18 A survey found the number of devices in students' homes that connected to the internet.

Connected devices	
Number	**Students**
fewer than 5	3
5–10	8
11–15	11
more than 15	4

How many students had at least five devices in their home?

NUMBER AND ALGEBRA

1 Which of these is divisible by 2 and 3? Circle the number(s).

60, 66, 606, 616

2 Kelsey is playing a game. She needs 12 000 points to move to Level 5. If she currently has 7563 points, how many more points does she need to progress to Level 5?

3 A hardware store has 28 bags of nails for sale. Each bag contains 48 nails. What is the total number of nails for sale?

4 When 367 students are divided into eight equal groups there are some students left over. How many students are left over?

5 Find the sum of 2682 and 990.

6 Shown below are three rectangles.

Shade squares to represent the improper fraction $\frac{5}{3}$.

7 Find the missing fraction:

$\frac{3}{7} + \square = \frac{5}{7}$

8 Write the number seventeen-thousandths in digits.

9 The entry prices for a zoo are adults $29.50 and children $16.50. However, Mr and Mrs Lacy and their two children buy a family ticket which is $75. How much do they save?

10 Here is a sequence of numbers.

123, 112, 101, 90 …

One of these numbers is a member of the sequence: 53 55 57. Circle the correct number.

11 Here is a number sentence.

$\square \div 23 = 460$

What is the missing number?

MEASUREMENT AND SPACE

12 Ruth uses canes to support plants in her garden. She has six lengths of 120 cm and five lengths of 80 cm. What is the total length in metres and centimetres?

13 Riley arrived at the gym at 0615. He spent 1 hour 20 minutes at the gym. What time did he leave, in 12-hour time?

14 Here are three shapes. Circle the regular pentagon(s).

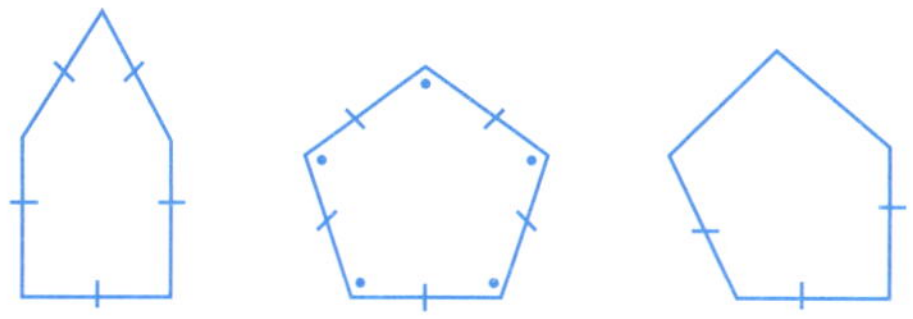

15 A regular pentagon is rotated around its centre. Through how many degrees should it be rotated before it displays its original shape?

16 With a protractor Priya measured the angle as 140°.

How many degrees is the angle marked as *?

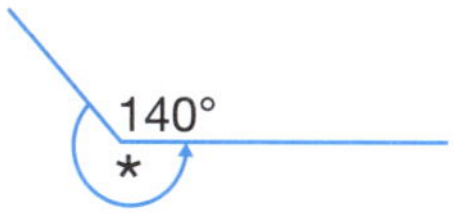

STATISTICS AND PROBABILITY

17 A box contains numbered counters. A counter is chosen at random.

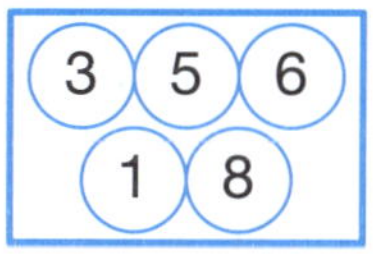

What is the probability that the number is **not** a multiple of 3?

18 A survey found the number of devices in students' homes that connected to the internet.

Connected devices	
Number	**Students**
fewer than 5	3
5–10	8
11–15	11
more than 15	4

One student realised he had miscounted. Instead of nine devices he had 12. How many students now have at least 11 devices?

NUMBER AND ALGEBRA

1 Here are some numbers.

14, 20, 27, 35, 42

Which numbers are divisible by 7?

2 In 2020 the closest the moon was to Earth was 356 906 km. The greatest distance the moon was from Earth was 406 692 km.

What is the difference between the two distances?

3 The 265 students at a primary school paid $6 each for transport to the athletics carnival. How much did they pay altogether?

4 There are 33 students to be transported in cars to the Town Hall. All cars can only transport a maximum of four students.

What is the smallest number of cars required?

5 Complete: $14 \times 25 \times 4 =$

6 Circle the fraction that is the smallest.

$\frac{2}{3}$ $\frac{2}{9}$ $\frac{2}{5}$

7 What is $\frac{3}{10} + \frac{7}{10}$?

8 Here are three decimals: 3.09, 3.2, 3.113, 3.14.

Which of the decimals is the largest?

9 A lawnmower is discounted by $65.50 to a price of $384.40.

What was the original price of the lawnmower?

10 Find the first five numbers in the sequence that starts with 2 and increases by $\frac{1}{3}$.

11 INPUT → × 6 → + 5 → OUTPUT

If the INPUT is 4, what is the OUTPUT?

MEASUREMENT AND SPACE

12 How many metres are in $3\frac{1}{2}$ km?

13 The clock on Charlotte's wall oven shows the time as 1820. What is this in 12-hour time?

14 The net of a cube is drawn below.

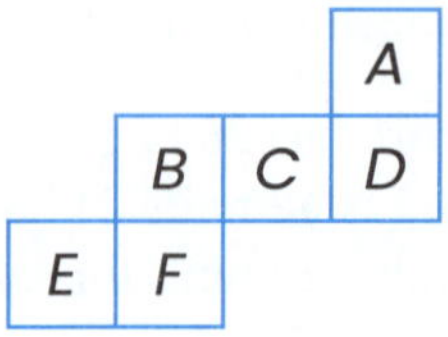

What letter is on the opposite face to *A*?

15 How many lines of symmetry has the shape?

16 Circle the angle that measures about 70°.

STATISTICS AND PROBABILITY

17 A box contains red (R), yellow (Y), green (G) and blue (B) marbles. A marble is chosen at random.

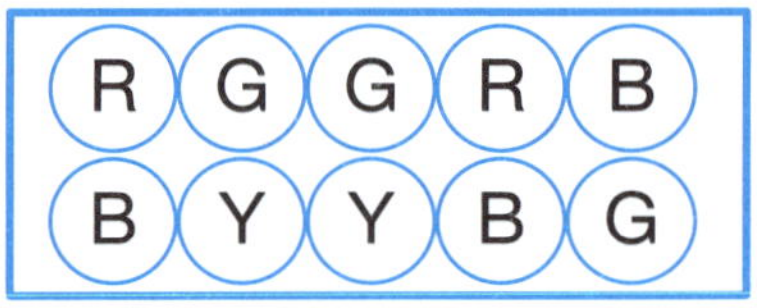

What is the probability that it is green?

18 The table records the number of phones owned by students in Class 5J.

	Phone	No phone
Girls	12	2
Boys	6	6

How many students do not have a phone in 5J?

NUMBER AND ALGEBRA

1 The number 434 is divisible by 7. How many numbers between 425 and 450 are divisible by 7?

2 What is the difference between 1 million and 437 519?

3 An egg producer sells 6840 cartons of eggs to a supermarket chain each week. Each carton contains 12 eggs. What is the total number of eggs sold?

4 There are 19 boys and 17 girls in Year 6. All the students are attending a camp. Boys and girls sleep in separate dormitories in 4-person rooms. What is the smallest number of rooms required?

5 Complete: $6 \times 25 \times 7 \times 4 = \square$

6 Circle the fractions that are **not** the same as one whole.

$\frac{21}{2}$ $\frac{8}{8}$ $\frac{10}{10}$ $\frac{4}{8}$

7 Find the missing fraction: $\frac{7}{10} - \square = \frac{4}{10}$

8 Rewrite 5.034, 5.34, 5.04, 5.403 and 5.304 in ascending order.

9 Three chocolate bars cost the same as four packets of chips. If a packet of chips costs $3, what is the price of a chocolate bar?

10 Here is a sequence of decimals.

3.27, 3.36, 3.45 …

One of these decimals is a member of the sequence: 3.9 3.94 3.98. Circle the correct decimal.

11 INPUT → × 4 → + 3 → OUTPUT

If the OUTPUT is 15, what is the INPUT?

MEASUREMENT AND SPACE

12 Abigail walked $1\frac{1}{2}$ km on Wednesday and $2\frac{1}{4}$ km on Thursday.
What was the total distance walked in the two days, in metres?

13 Gabriel arrives at a national park to walk a trail that takes 2 hours 20 minutes. If he starts his walk at 1350, what time does he expect to return, in 12-hour time?

14 Here are three shapes. Circle the regular quadrilateral(s).

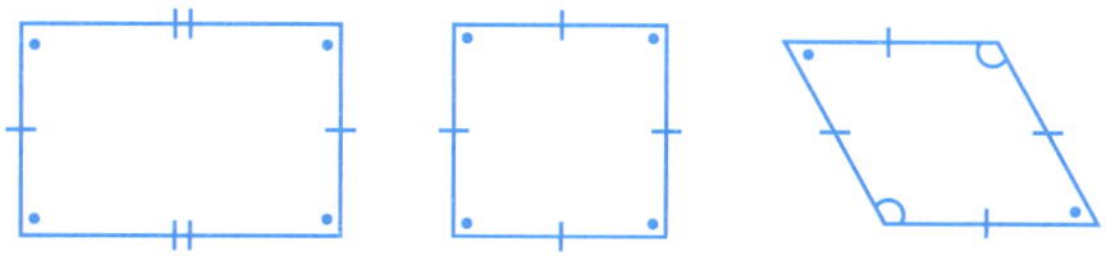

15 A regular hexagon is rotated around its centre. Through how many degrees should it be rotated before it displays its original shape?

16

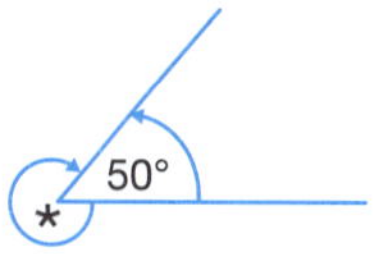

With a protractor, Ryan measured the angle as 50°. How many degrees is the angle marked as *?

STATISTICS AND PROBABILITY

17 A box contains red (R), yellow (Y), green (G) and blue (B) marbles. A marble is chosen at random.

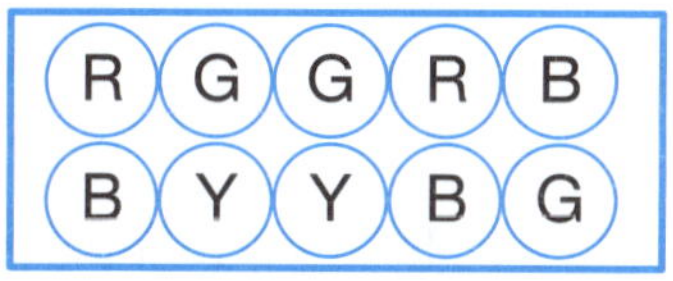

What is the probability that it is either red or green?

18 The table records the number of students with and without a phone in Class 5J. There are twice as many girls as boys who have phones. The same number of boys have a phone as do not have a phone.

	Phone	No phone
Girls	12	
Boys		

If there are 26 students in 5J, how many girls do not have a phone?

NUMBER AND ALGEBRA

1 Seku is learning the multiples of 4. He wrote down some of his answers.

8, 32, 34, 48, 50, 64

Circle Seku's correct numbers.

2 Eloise is reading a book containing 268 pages. At the same time Angus is reading a book which contains 424 pages. How many more pages are in Angus's book?

3 $\square \div 8 = 712$.

What is the missing number?

4 A school has an enrolment of 208. There are eight classes and each class has the same number of students. How many students are in each class?

5 Complete: $20 \times 73 \times 5 = \square$

6 Write $3\frac{4}{5}$ as an improper fraction.

7 What is $\frac{1}{5} + \frac{2}{5} + \frac{2}{5}$?

8 What is the place value of 7 in 31.578?

9 A shop is selling Fight MND fundraising beanies for $20 each or 3 for $50. Anne wants to buy four beanies. How much will she spend?

10 Find the first five numbers in the sequence that starts with $3\frac{1}{2}$ and decreases by $\frac{1}{2}$.

11 INPUT → × 8 → + 3 → OUTPUT

If the INPUT is 6, what is the OUTPUT?

MEASUREMENT AND SPACE

12 A rectangle has a length of 400 mm and a width of 300 mm. What is the perimeter in metres and millimetres?

☐ m ☐ mm

13 A game of basketball is expected to finish at 9:20 pm. What is this time in 24-hour time?

14 The net of a cube is drawn below.

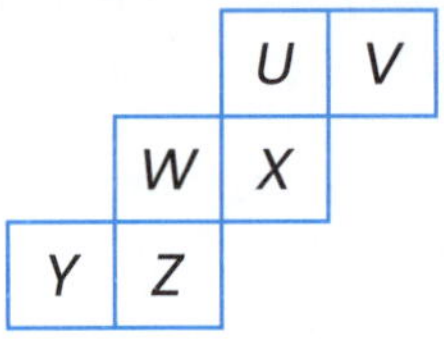

What letter is on the opposite face to *Z*?

15 How many lines of symmetry has a rhombus?

16 Which of these is the best estimate for the size of the marked angle?

100° 150° 180° 120°

STATISTICS AND PROBABILITY

17 A bag contains five green balls, three red balls and two blue balls. A ball is chosen at random.

What is the probability that it is red?

18 Mr Thompson recorded the number of students in his class who play weekend sport.

Weekend sport players		
	Sport	**No sport**
Girls	4	8
Boys	10	5

How many students are in Mr Thompson's class?

NUMBER AND ALGEBRA

1 What number am I? I am divisible by 3 and 5. I am odd. My digits multiply to give 15. I am between 100 and 200.

2 Subtract 23 456 918 from 27 287 115.

3 ☐ ÷ 24 = 387.

What is the missing number?

4 A car park has 380 spaces. If there are 20 rows of car spaces, how many cars can park in each row?

5 Complete: 20 × 32 × 5 × 3 = ☐

6 Find the missing number.

$5\frac{7}{12} = \frac{\square}{12}$

7 A bucket is full of water. Three-quarters of the water is poured out. What fraction of water remains?

8 What is the place value of 2 in 9.0052?

9 Petrol is priced at $1.53/L. Selena fills her car with 36 L of petrol. She uses her loyalty card to receive a discount of 4 cents per litre. How much does Selena pay?

10 Here is a sequence of decimals.

14.3, 14.15, 14 …

One of these decimals is NOT a member of the sequence: 13.85 13.75 13.7. Circle the decimal.

11 INPUT → × 5 → + 4 → OUTPUT

If the OUTPUT is 19, what is the INPUT?

MEASUREMENT AND SPACE

12 A rectangle has a length of 2 m and a width of 65 cm. What is the perimeter in metres and centimetres?

☐ m ☐ cm

13 Ellie's father drops her off at a party at 1930 and plans to pick her up at 2200. How long will Ellie spend at the party?

14 The diagram shows a pyramid. Circle the letter that represents the apex of the pyramid.

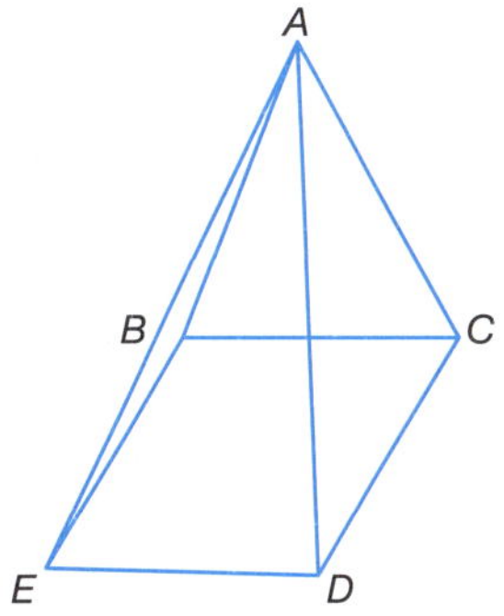

15 A regular octagon is rotated around its centre. Through how many degrees should it be rotated before it displays its original shape?

16

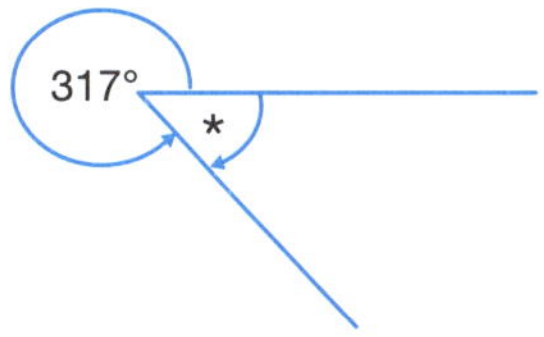

The reflex angle on the diagram measures 317°. How many degrees is the angle marked as *?

STATISTICS AND PROBABILITY

17 A bag contains five green balls, three red balls and two blue balls. A ball is chosen at random.

What is the probability that it is **not** red?

18 Mr Thompson recorded the number of students in his class who play weekend sport.

Weekend sport players		
	Sport	**No sport**
Girls	4	8
Boys	10	5

What fraction of the students who do not play sport are girls?

NUMBER AND ALGEBRA

1 How many multiples of 5 are between 12 and 28?

2 There are two small parks near Lydia's home. In one park there are 236 trees. The other park has a number that is 87 greater. How many trees are growing in the second park?

3 What is the product of 12 345 and 6?

4 Ella has 85 blocks. She builds towers using five blocks each. How many towers can Ella build?

5 Complete: $56 \times 4 \times 250 =$

6 Plot and label $\frac{3}{4}$ on the number line.

7 A rectangle has been split into eighths.

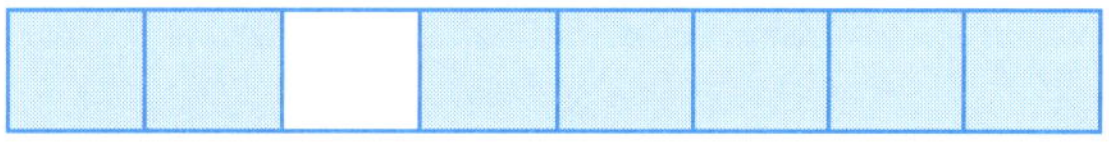

Use the shape to answer

$\frac{2}{8} + \frac{5}{8} =$

8 Use either *greater* or *less* to make this statement correct: 32.761 is .... than 32.8.

9 A wetsuit was originally priced at \$165 but was reduced in price by \$28.75. What is the new price?

10 Find the first five numbers in the sequence that starts with 2.85 and increases by 0.1.

11 Here is a number sentence.

$12 \times 6 = \square \times 9$

What is the missing number?

MEASUREMENT AND SPACE

12 A square has a perimeter of 88 cm. What is the length of each side of the square, in centimetres?

13 Eleanor has set her alarm for half past six in the morning to go for a jog. What is this in 12-hour time?

14 Here are some 3D shapes. Circle any solid that is a pyramid.

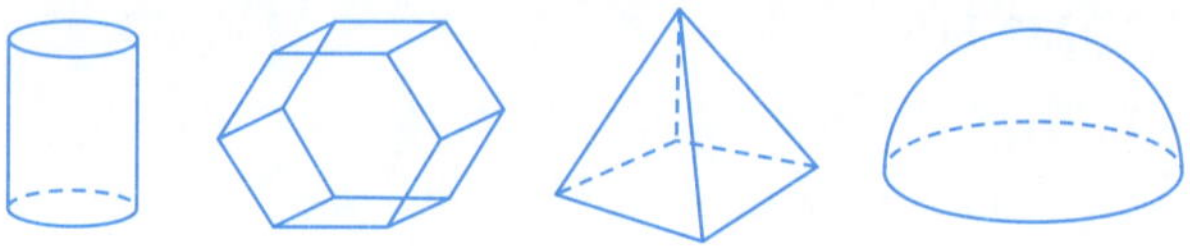

15 On the grid, mark the locations of E4 and B1.

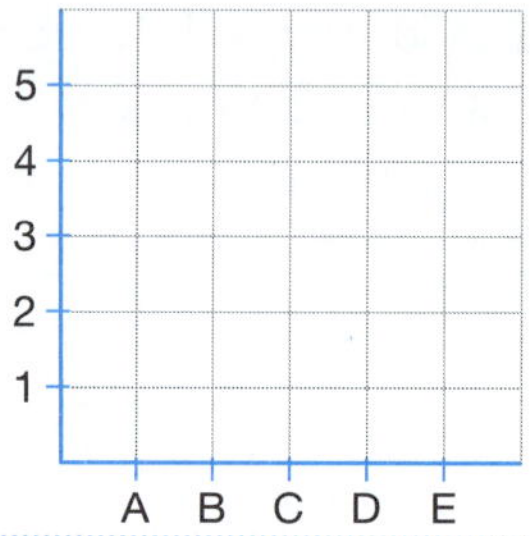

16 Complete the statement.

An acute angle measures less than ....°.

STATISTICS AND PROBABILITY

17 A bag contains red marbles and blue marbles. There are three red marbles in the bag. A marble is chosen at random. The probability of choosing a red marble is $\frac{3}{8}$. How many blue marbles are in the bag?

18 The graph shows the temperature in Bondi one afternoon in March.

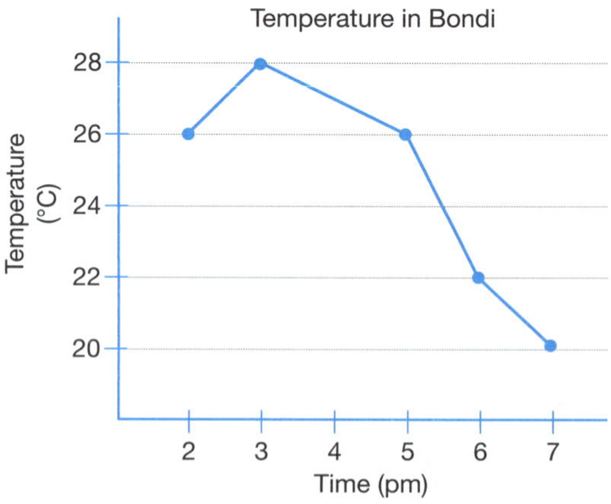

How many degrees did the temperature drop between 3 pm and 6 pm?

NUMBER AND ALGEBRA

1 Here is a list of numbers: 34, 23, 25, 28, 51

Cross out the multiples of 2, 3 or 5. How many numbers remain?

2 Two Year 5 students were estimating the number of hours they had been alive. Zoey calculated she had been alive for 98 232. Levi said he had been alive for 3048 more hours than Zoey. How many hours had Levi been alive?

3 What is the product of 56 and 57?

4 A train has six carriages and seating for 288 passengers. If all carriages have the same seating pattern, how many seats are in each carriage?

5 Complete: $18 \times 4 \times 3 \times 250 =$

6 Here are four points located on a number line.

Which letter represents the improper fraction $\frac{7}{2}$?

7 A car's petrol tank is filled. After driving to Melbourne, the petrol gauge shows three-eighths full. What fraction of the petrol has been used?

8 Use either *greater* or *less* to make this statement correct: 294.1 is .... than 294.098.

9 Kiwi fruit is sold at a price of 3 for $1.75. What will Agnes pay for two dozen kiwi fruit?

10 Here is a sequence of mixed numerals. $4\frac{1}{5}, 4\frac{4}{5}, 5\frac{2}{5} \ldots$

What is the fifth number of the sequence?

11 What is the missing number in the number sentence?

$\square \times 25 + 31 = 231$

MEASUREMENT AND SPACE

12 A square has a perimeter of 2 m 60 cm. What is the length of each side of the square, in centimetres?

13 A timetable shows a train leaves Bellview at 1540 and arrives at Carliste at 1920. How long is the trip?

14 The diagram shows a cone. Circle the letter that represents the apex of the cone.

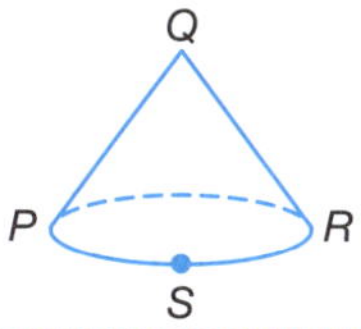

15 On the grid, locate mark *X* at E3. Go to the left three units, go up 2 units and to the left 1 unit. Mark *Y* at this new location.

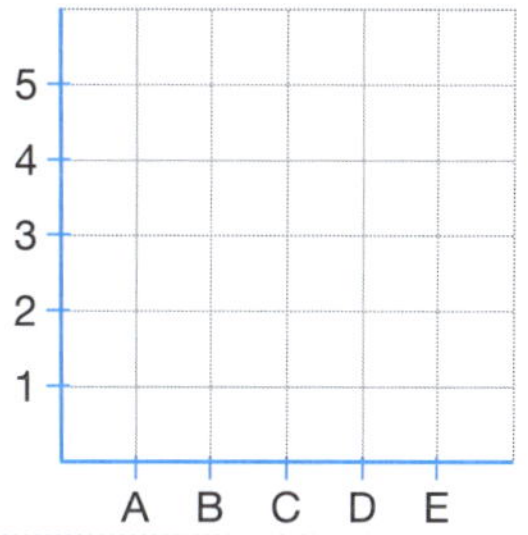

16 The reflex angle on the diagram measures 208°. How many degrees is the angle marked as *?

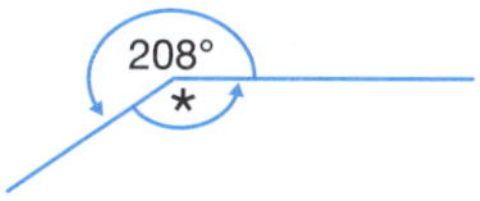

STATISTICS AND PROBABILITY

17 A bag contains red marbles and blue marbles. There are six red marbles in the bag. A marble is chosen at random. The probability of choosing a red marble is $\frac{2}{3}$. How many blue marbles are in the bag?

18 The graph shows the temperature in Bondi one afternoon in March.

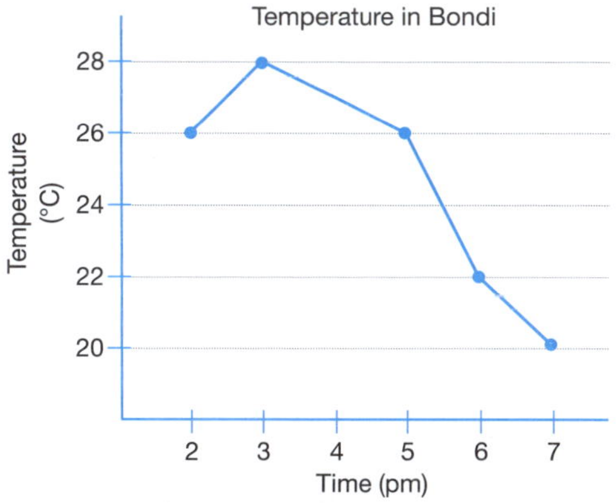

After reaching its highest temperature, how long did it take to drop 8°?

NUMBER AND ALGEBRA

1 Here is a list of numbers.

105, 2900, 2107, 40

Circle the numbers that are multiples of 10.

2 Samantha, Zoe and Georgia are comparing the number of friends they have on a social media platform. Samantha has 87, Zoe has 52 and Georgia has 68. Estimate the total number of friends the three girls have, to the nearest ten.

3 What is 673 multiplied by 40?

4 Isabella swims at her local pool. This morning she swam eight laps and calculated that she had swum a total of 400 metres. What is the length of the pool?

5 Complete: 32 000 ÷ 100 = ☐

6 Plot and label $\frac{1}{3}$ on the number line.

7 A rectangle has been split into eighths.

Use the shape to answer $\frac{3}{8} + \frac{2}{8} =$

8 Here is a number line.

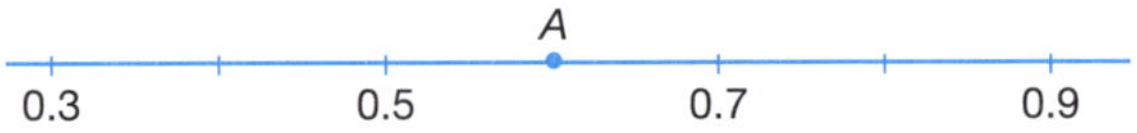

What decimal is represented by *A*?

9 The entry fees for a wildlife park are $18 for adults and $12 for children. What would be the cost for John and Martha and their 8-year-old son?

10 Find the first five numbers in the sequence that starts with 1.3 and decreases by 0.2.

11 Here is a number sentence. What is the missing number?

34 + 8 = ☐ × 7

MEASUREMENT AND SPACE

12 Aaron sets out to walk 3 km. After 30 minutes he has walked 2 km 150 m. How much further does Aaron need to walk?

13 Dylan is late to school and arrives at quarter to ten. What is the 24-hour time?

14 Here are some 3D shapes. Circle any solid that is a cone.

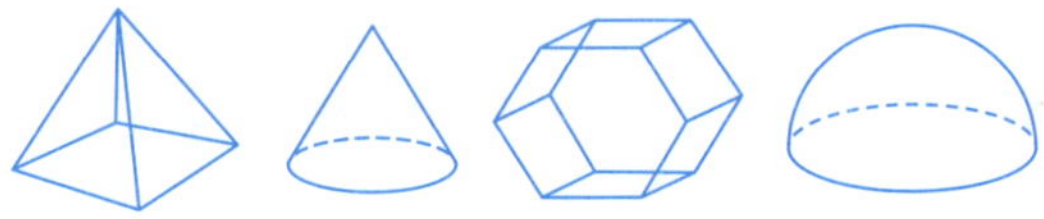

15

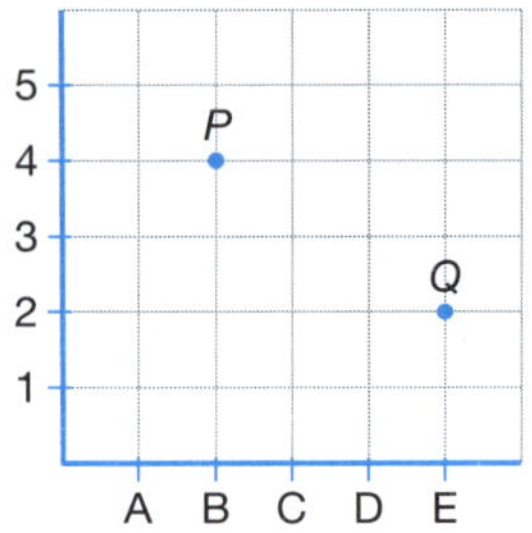

Write the locations of *P* and *Q*.

P = ...

Q = ...

16 On an analog clock the time is 10 o'clock. If the minute hand moves 180°, what is the new time?

STATISTICS AND PROBABILITY

17 A spinner has sections which are coloured red (R), blue (B), yellow (Y) or green (G). The arrow on this spinner is spun.

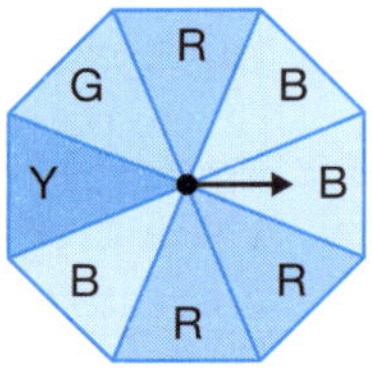

What is the probability it stops on blue?

18 The graph shows the temperature in Hobart one day in September.

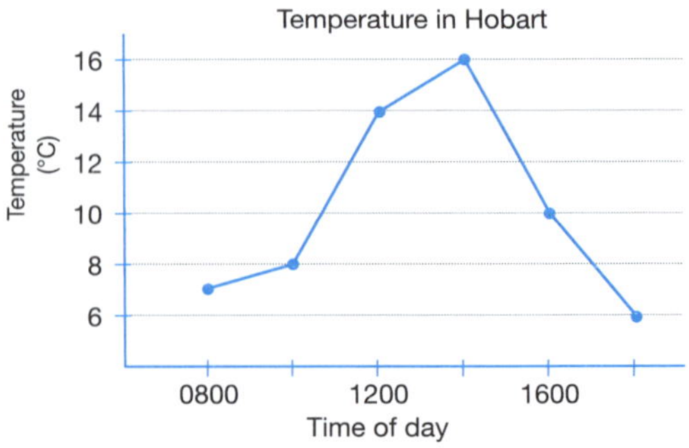

At what time did the temperature **drop** to 10°?

NUMBER AND ALGEBRA

1 A red light flashes every 4 seconds. A blue light flashes every 6 seconds. If they flash together, how many **more** times will they flash together in the next 30 seconds?

2 Four blocks of land in a new housing estate have areas of 688 m^2, 706 m^2, 598 m^2 and 604 m^2. Estimate the total area of the four blocks, to the nearest 100 m^2.

3 What is 2400 multiplied by 150?

4 A company makes 5200 small chocolate eggs. The eggs are to be sold in boxes of eight. How many boxes can be filled?

5 Complete: 940 000 ÷ 10 000 =

6 Here are four points located on a number line.

Which letter represents the improper fraction $\frac{23}{3}$?

7 Priyanka fills a bucket to three-quarters of its capacity. She pours two-quarters of the bucket out to water some plants. What fraction of the bucket's capacity remains?

8 Here is a number line.

What decimal is represented by X?

9 Jonah's family plan to go ice-skating on Sunday afternoon. The ice-skating rink charges adults $15 and children $12. The total cost will be $63. If there is only one adult, how many children are going?

10 Here is a sequence of mixed numerals.

$$3\frac{3}{4}, 4, 4\frac{1}{4} \ldots$$

What is the sixth number of the sequence?

11 What is the missing number in the number sentence?

☐ × 20 + 15 = 195

MEASUREMENT AND SPACE

12 Penelope sets out to walk $6\frac{1}{2}$ km. After 30 minutes she has walked $2\frac{1}{4}$ km. How much further does Penelope need to walk, in metres?

13 A bus leaves Hanover at 1145, and four and a half hours later arrives in Bletchley. What was the 24-hour time that the bus arrived in Bletchley?

14 A vertex on a cube is cut off. How many vertices are on the new solid?

15 The point Y is shown on a grid. Agnes starts at X. She moves three units to the left, four units down and two units to the right to arrive at Y. What is the location of X?

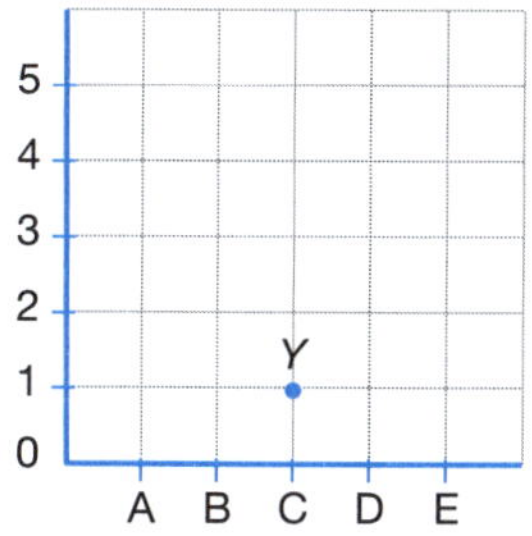

16 On an analog clock the time is 8 o'clock. If the minute hand moves 120°, what is the new time?

STATISTICS AND PROBABILITY

17 A spinner has sections which are coloured red (R), blue (B), yellow (Y) or green (G). The arrow on this spinner is spun. What is the probability it does **not** stop on blue?

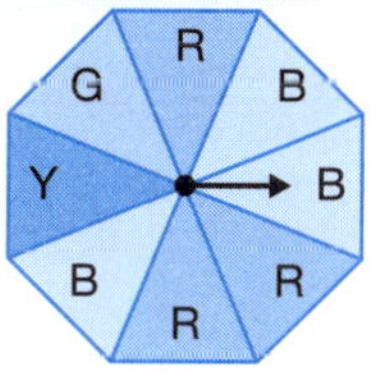

18 The graph shows the temperature in Hobart one day in September.

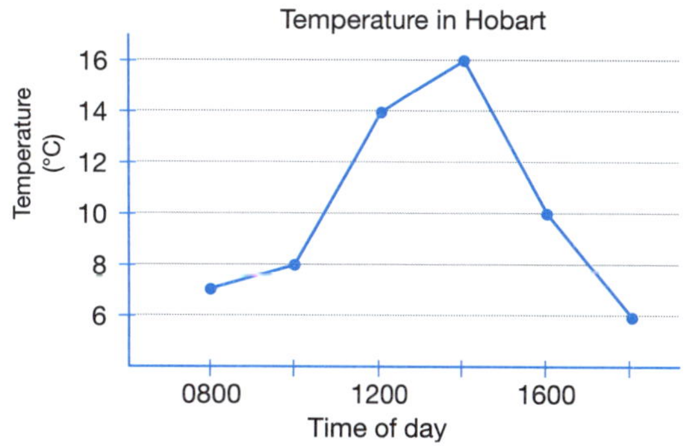

Between what two times (in 12-hour time) was the temperature falling at the fastest rate?

1 Order these numbers from largest to smallest.

1 032 406   1 216 198   1 009 999   1 136 199

largest [ ] [ ] [ ] [ ] smallest

2 Here is a shaded shape on a grid. The mirror line is used to reflect the shape.

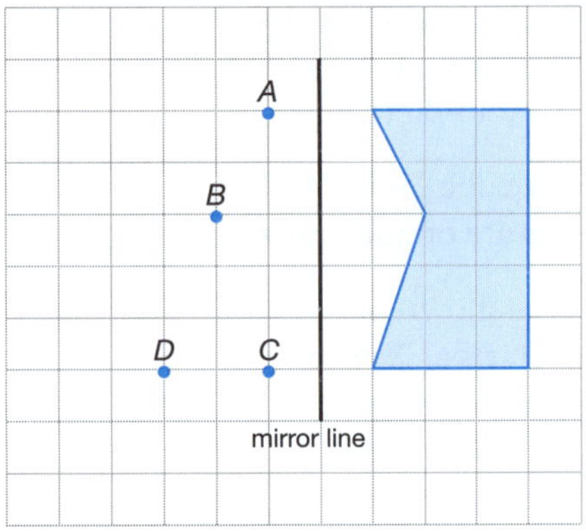

Which of these is **not** a vertex of the image?

A A

B B

C C

D D

3 Buses have been ordered to take spectators from the stadium back to the city at the end of a game.

Each bus has a capacity of 68 passengers.

If 30 buses have been ordered, how many spectators can be transported? [ ]

4 Bryson buys a bag of bird seed for $13.45. He pays for it using this note.

How much change will he receive?

A $6.55   B $6.65   C $7.55   D $7.65

5 One afternoon, Michael's farm received 26 mm of rain in a thunderstorm.

The next day another 28 mm fell.

Select **two** ways that could be used to work out the total amount of rain in the two days.

A 26 + 26 + 2   B 28 + 28 – 4   C 30 + 30 – 4   D 30 + 30 – 6

6 At midday on Tuesday, the temperature in the playground was 28.7 °C.

At midday on Wednesday, the temperature was 32 °C.

How much warmer was it on Wednesday at noon than on Tuesday at noon? ☐ °C

7 Karmala weighed her two shopping bags.

The lighter bag had a mass of 3.8 kg.

The other bag was twice as heavy.

What was the total mass of the two bags? ☐ kg

8 Lenore has read 40 pages of her novel.

She has 80 more pages to read.

Select **all** the numbers that show the fraction of her novel she has already read.

$\frac{1}{2}$	$\frac{1}{3}$	$\frac{8}{12}$	$\frac{4}{120}$	$\frac{20}{40}$	$\frac{4}{12}$
A	B	C	D	E	F

9 The graph shows the time taken by students to complete a word search.

How many students took at least 7 minutes? ☐

10 Children from second class each tossed the same number of balls into a bucket. If the total number of balls tossed into the bucket was 72, which of the following could NOT have been the number of balls tossed by each student? Select **all** correct answers.

3	5	8	12	16
A	B	C	D	E

11 If half of a number is less than 8, the number must be

3.	16.	less than 3.	greater than 16.	less than 16.
A	B	C	D	E

12 Brett goes for a run three mornings per week. On average, he runs for 36 minutes each morning. What is the total time he runs every week?

A 1 hour 8 minutes

B 1 hour 48 minutes

C 4 hours 12 minutes

D 4 hours 20 minutes

13 Nupur is eating jelly beans in the following order: one red, one orange, one white, one green, one red, one orange, and so on. What colour will be the twenty-sixth jelly bean she eats?

A red B orange C white D green

14 Four angles are named on the diagram.

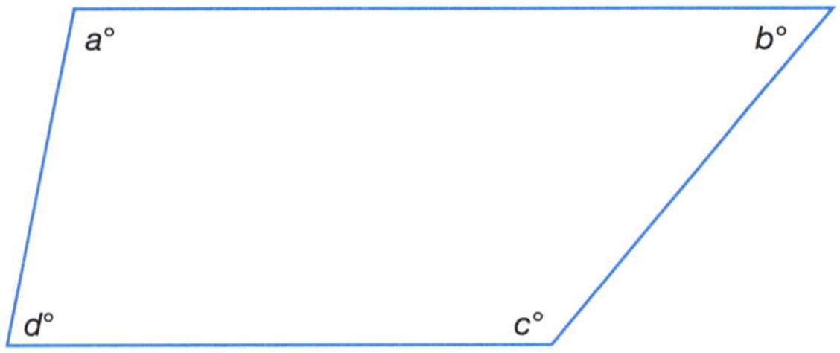

Which of these is the second largest angle?

A $a°$ B $b°$ C $c°$ D $d°$

15 The net of a cube is drawn below.

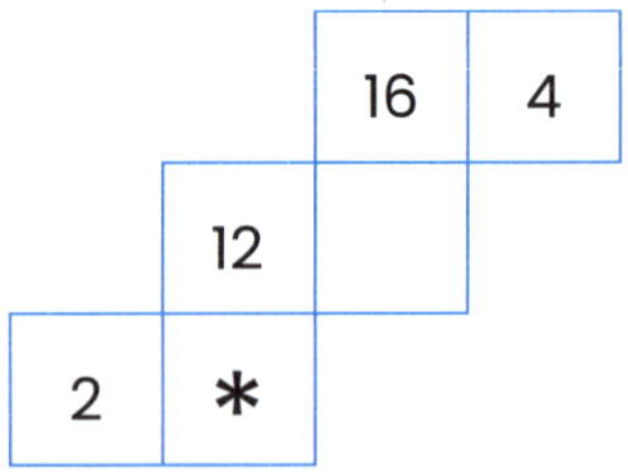

Each pair of numbers on opposite faces multiply to the same number.

What is the number represented by *?

16 The shapes in these number sentences represent numbers.

□ × 3 = 18

△ ÷ □ = 4

What number is represented by △ ?

---

17 The spinner is spun many times.

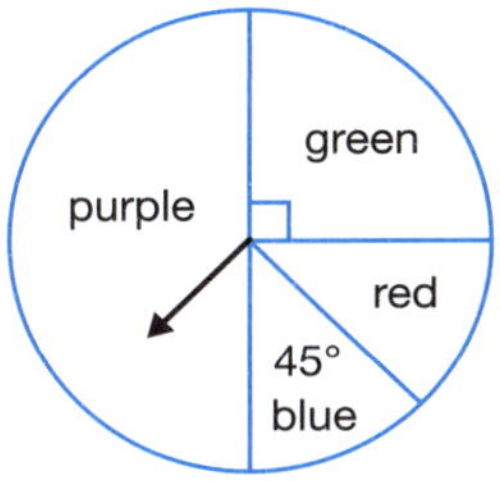

The spinner lands on red 30 times.

Which of these is the best estimate of the number of times the spinner lands on purple?

A 200 **B** 240 **C** 100 **D** 120

---

18 The first three numbers in two patterns are shown.

Pattern A: 1740, 1660, 1580 …

Pattern B: 1210, 1240, 1270 …

What number is common to both patterns?

---

19 Alma used the rule 'subtract 8 and divide by 2' to write this pattern of numbers.

400 196 94 …

What is the fifth number in the pattern?

---

20 A regular octagon and a square have the same perimeter.

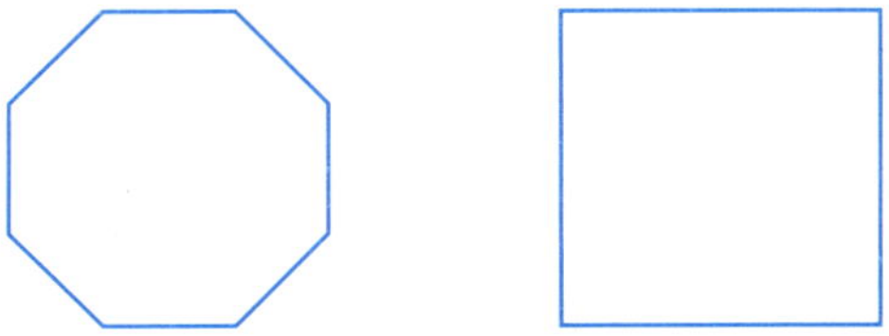

not actual size

The length of each side of the octagon is 4 cm.

What is the area of the square? cm^2

NUMBER AND ALGEBRA

1 Welbourne is calling out his 7 times tables. He made two mistakes.

21, 28, 30, 37, 42, 49

Circle his **two** mistakes.

2 What is the sum of 4821, 9789 and 7190 to the nearest thousand?

3 What is the remainder when 130 is divided by 8?

4 There are nine chocolate biscuits in a packet. If there are 120 packets in a supermarket display, what is the total number of chocolate biscuits?

5 Complete: $21 \times 14 = 21 \times 7 \times$ ☐

6 Plot and label $1\frac{1}{2}$ on the number line.

7 What is $\frac{24}{25} - \frac{7}{25} - \frac{13}{25}$?

8 What is the sum of 12.6 and 3?

9 Damon bought a pair of shoes for \$80 and two T-shirts for \$30 each. How much did Damon pay in total?

10 Here is a pattern of numbers.

32, 38, 44, 50, 56 …

Complete the statement.

The rule is 'Start with .... and .... by ....'.

11 Here is a number sentence.

$60 - \square = 24 \times 2$

What is the missing number?

MEASUREMENT AND SPACE

12 Mr Stefanovic marks out a running circuit of length 960 m around the school. Isaiah runs around the circuit twice. How far does he run, in metres?

13 Mila starts her violin practice at quarter past four in the afternoon. What is this expressed in 24-hour time?

14 Here are some 3D shapes. Circle any solid that is a hemisphere.

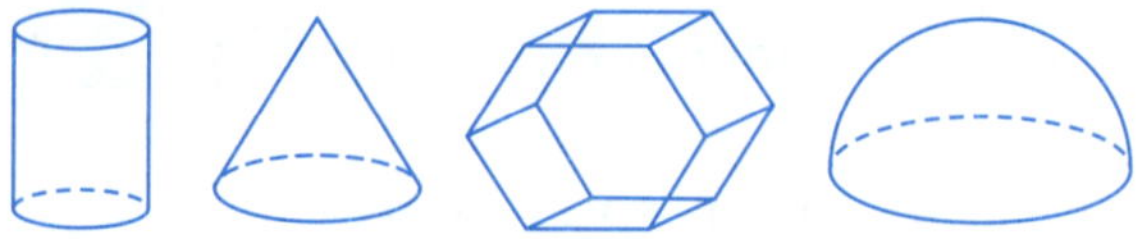

15 The grid shows the points X and Y.

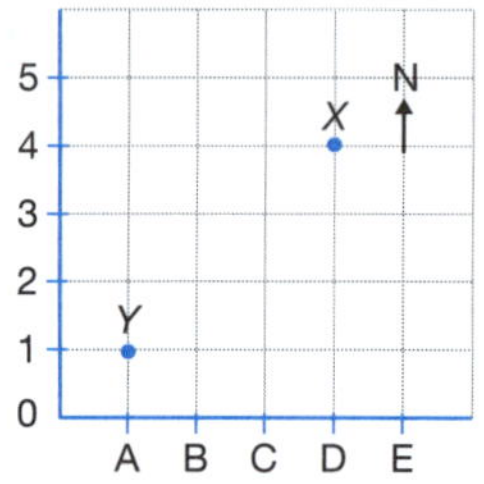

Y is .... of X. Circle the correct direction.

south-east north-east
north-west south-west

16 Complete the statement.

An obtuse angle measures more than ....° but less than ....°.

STATISTICS AND PROBABILITY

17 A regular octagon is made into a spinner. Different sections of the spinner have been numbered. The arrow on this spinner is spun.

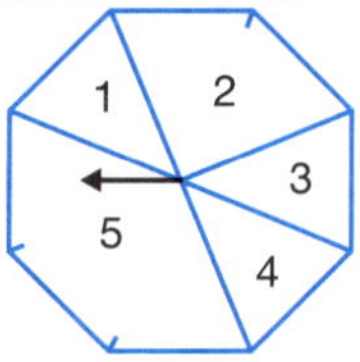

What is the probability it stops on 4?

18 The table shows the result of a survey of students' favourite colours.

Favourite colours	
Colour	**Tally**
Blue	|||
Yellow	𝍸 ||
Green	𝍸 ||||
Red	𝍸 𝍸	

How many students were surveyed?

NUMBER AND ALGEBRA

1 The 28 students in a class are each given a different number from 1 to 28. When the teacher calls out a number, all students who are a factor of that number stand up. How many students stand when 36 is called out?

2 What is the sum of 23 418, 55 920 and 9023 to the nearest thousand?

3 Charlotte's home swimming pool has a length of 12 m. She wants to swim at least 1 km. How many laps will she need to complete?

4 A local sports team had an average home game attendance of 928. If there were 13 home games in the season, what was the total attendance for the season?

5 What is 43×22?

6 Here are four points located on a number line.

Which letter is closest to $\frac{49}{5}$?

7 Aditya drives from Kalgoorlie to Albany. When he has driven three-tenths of the distance he stops for a rest. What fraction of the distance remains?

8 On three consecutive mornings Ravi cycled 32.4 km, 27.3 km and 36.1 km. What was the total distance?

9 An activity centre holds children's parties. There is a hiring fee of $60 plus a cost per child. If eight children attend, the total cost is $180.

What would the total cost be if 10 children attended?

10 Here is a sequence of numbers: 1100, 1065, 1030 …
What is the fifth number in the sequence?

11 What is the missing number in the number sentence?

$40 \times \square - 10 = 230$

MEASUREMENT AND SPACE

12 Mr Robson marks out a running circuit around the school. Paisley runs around the circuit three times. If she runs a total of 2 km 460 m, how long is the circuit?

13 Brooklyn's mother picked her up from school at 1510. She had spent six and a half hours at school. What time had Brooklyn arrived at school?

14 Two identical triangular prisms are formed using equilateral triangles. The prisms are glued together, using rectangular faces, to form a new solid. How many edges has the new solid?

15 The grid shows the point *X*. From *X*, move 3 units north. Now move east to *Y*, which is north-east of *X*.

What is the location of *Y*?

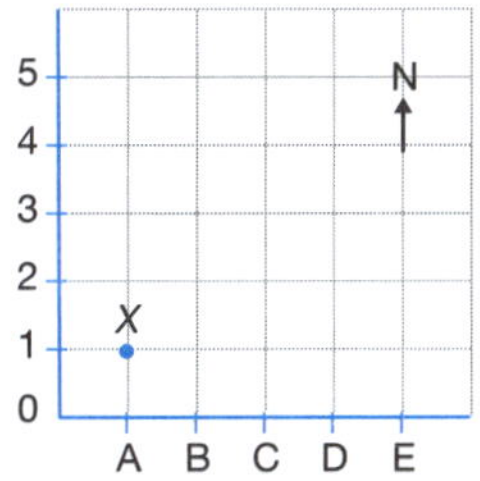

16 With a protractor, Luke measured two angles as 50° and 40°. How many degrees is the angle marked as *?

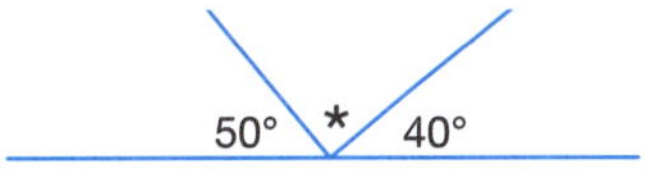

STATISTICS AND PROBABILITY

17 A regular octagon is made into a spinner. Different sections of the spinner have been numbered. The arrow on this spinner is spun.

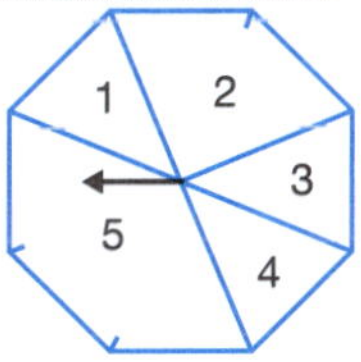

What is the probability it stops on an even number?

18 The table shows some of the results of a survey of students' favourite colours. Four times as many students chose red than blue. How many more students chose red than yellow?

Favourite colours	
Colour	**Tally**
Blue	|||
Yellow	𝍸 ||
Green	𝍸 ||||
Red	

NUMBER AND ALGEBRA

1 Lisa wrote down this list of numbers.

60, 205, 480, 270

Circle the numbers that are divisible by 20.

2 Here are the populations of three towns: 1786, 3189 and 2921. Which of these is the best estimate of the total population?

6000 7000 8000 9000

3 A multiscreen cinema complex has seven cinemas, each with 164 seats. What is the total number of seats in the complex?

4 Limes are to be sold in bags of 6. If there are 94 limes, how many bags are required?

5 What is the answer: $3 \times 2 \times 11 \times 0 \times 5$?

6 The diagram shows three rectangles.

Shade squares to represent the improper fraction $1\frac{1}{2}$.

7 What is $\frac{7}{10} - \frac{2}{10} + \frac{4}{10}$?

8 Here is a number line.

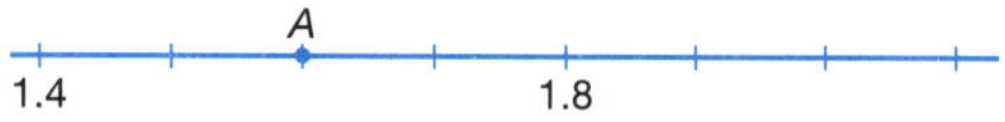

What decimal is represented by *A*?

9 Sam and Sarah took their son Tommy to the movies. An adult ticket cost $23 and a child ticket cost $16. What was the total cost?

10 Here is a pattern of numbers.

51, 44, 37, 30 …

Complete the statement.

The rule is 'Start with .... and .... by ....'.

11 Here is a number sentence.

38 – 14 = ☐ × 2

What is the missing number?

MEASUREMENT AND SPACE

12 Find the perimeter of the shape.

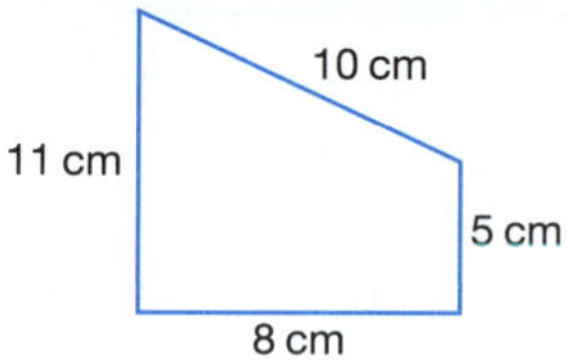

13 After-school tennis practice starts at half past three. Express this in 24-hour time.

14 Which two 3D shapes were used to construct this shape?

15 On the grid mark *P* at C3. From *P*, move 2 units south and then 1 unit west. Mark this location as *Q*.

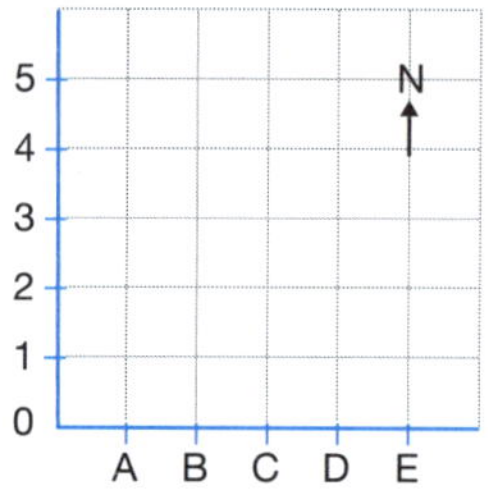

16 Complete the statement.

A reflex angle measures more than .... ° but less than .... °.

STATISTICS AND PROBABILITY

17 A regular hexagon is made into a spinner. Different sections of the spinner have been numbered. The arrow on this spinner is spun.

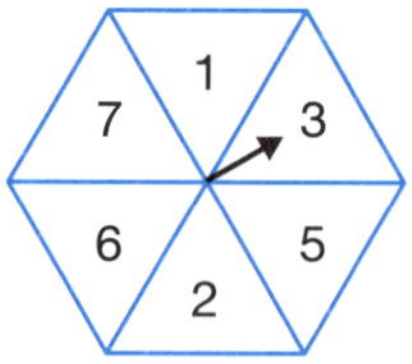

What is the probability it stops on an even number?

18 The dot plot shows the results of a survey of students' eye colours.

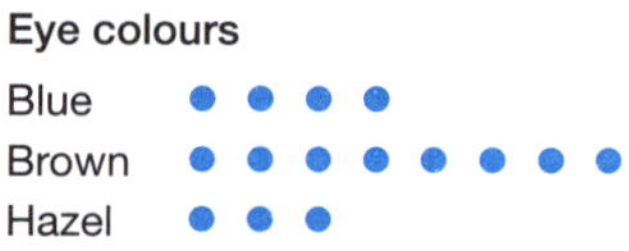

What fraction of the students surveyed had brown eyes?

NUMBER AND ALGEBRA

1 A prime is a number with only two factors. How many primes are between 40 and 60?

2 The populations of three cities are 14 889 540, 21 056 347 and 57 925 402. Estimate the total population of the cities, to the nearest million.

3 During the COVID-19 pandemic Raoul bought a 2-L container of hand sanitiser and poured it into eight smaller bottles. How much hand sanitiser was in each bottle, in millilitres?

4 Raj trains in a 25-m swimming pool. Each morning he swims 24 laps. What is the total distance he swims if he trains three mornings each week?

5 What is the answer to $29 \times 5 \times 20 \times 32 \times 0 \times 271$?

6 The diagram shows three rectangles.

Shade squares to represent the improper fraction $\frac{13}{6}$.

7 What is $2 - \frac{13}{20}$?

8 Here is a number line.

What decimal is represented by *X*?

9 A school bought 10 basketballs and eight cricket balls. A basketball costs three times as much as a cricket ball. If a basketball costs \$60, what was the total cost?

10 Here is a sequence of numbers.

34, 40, 46 …

What is the 10th number of the sequence?

11 What is the missing number in the number sentence?

100 ÷ ☐ + 8 = 28

MEASUREMENT AND SPACE

12 The perimeter of this shape is 84 cm.

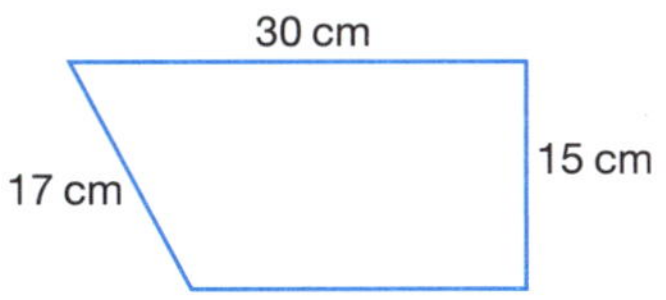

What is the length of the missing side?

13 What is the time 1 hour 40 minutes before midnight, in 24-hour time?

14 The top of a square-based pyramid is removed. How many edges has the new solid?

15 Start at *P*, which is at E1. Move north 2 units, west 4 units and then north [?] units to a location that is north-west of *P*.

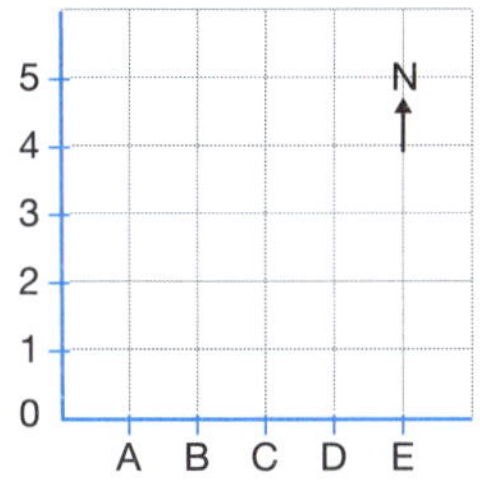

What is the missing number?

16 With a protractor, Kaylyn measured two angles as 70° and 90°. How many degrees is the angle marked as *?

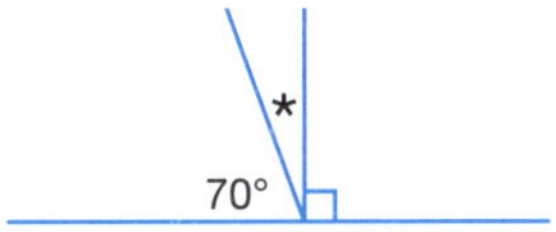

STATISTICS AND PROBABILITY

17 A regular hexagon is made into a spinner. Different sections of the spinner have been numbered. The arrow on this spinner is spun.

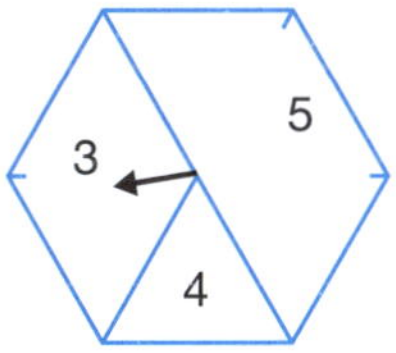

What is the probability it stops on an odd number?

18 The eye colours of 24 students are recorded. The students with hazel eyes are shown in the dot plot.

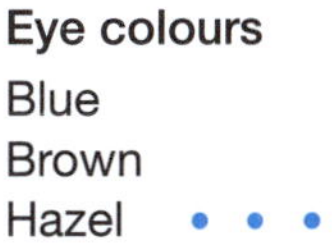

If half the students had brown eyes, how many students had blue eyes?

NUMBER AND ALGEBRA

1 Maxine's favourite number is a multiple of 7 and is **between** 60 and 70. What is her favourite number?

2 Over four consecutive days a social media clip is viewed the following number of times daily: 185, 311, 484, 603. Estimate, to the nearest hundred, the total number of views.

3 Cans of soup are transported to the supermarket in boxes of 12. If 180 cans are needed, how many boxes should be ordered by the supermarket?

4 A large group of people need to be transported to a protest rally. Buses can hold 47 people and minivans can transport nine people. The organiser hired six buses and three minivans. How many people can be transported?

5 Complete: $450 \div 15 = \square \div 30$.

6 The diagram shows three rectangles.

Shade squares to represent the improper fraction $2\frac{1}{3}$.

7 What is $\frac{5}{8} - \frac{2}{8} + \frac{1}{8}$?

8 Work out $\frac{7}{10} + \frac{6}{10}$, writing your answer as a decimal.

9 A supermarket sells a container of flour for \$3 and a bag of sugar for \$4. How much will David pay in total if he buys three containers of flour and two bags of sugar?

10 Here is a pattern of numbers.

$$4, 4\frac{1}{4}, 4\frac{2}{4}, 4\frac{3}{4}, 5, \ldots$$

Complete the statement.

The rule is 'Start with .... and .... by ....'.

11 Here is a number sentence.

$120 \div 10 = \square - 8$

What is the missing number?

MEASUREMENT AND SPACE

12 Find the perimeter of the shape.

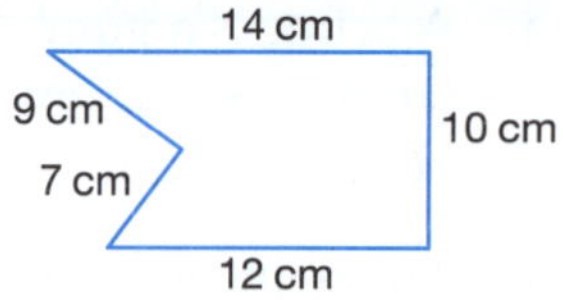

13 A timetable shows that Addison's train should arrive at 1917. What is this in 12-hour time?

14 Which two 3D shapes were used to construct this shape?

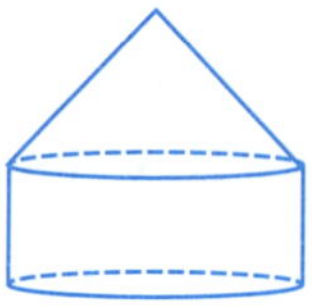

15 The grid represents a map with scale 1 unit = 2 km. George leaves *X* and travels south 2 units and then east to *Y*. How many kilometres has he travelled?

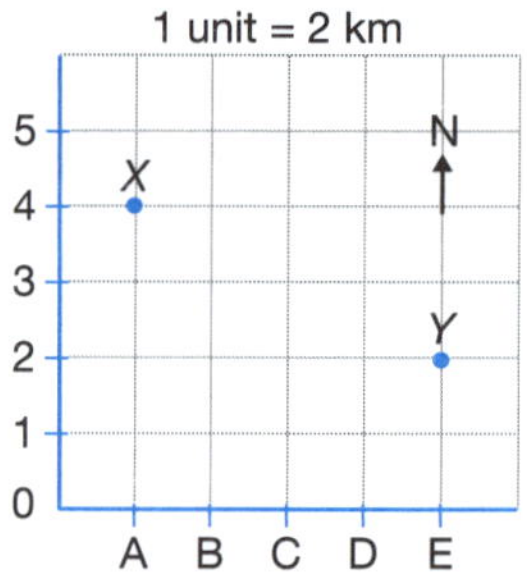

16 Violet used her protractor to measure an angle of 100°. What is the type of angle measured?

STATISTICS AND PROBABILITY

17 A regular hexagon is made into a spinner. Different sections of the spinner have been coloured red (R), blue (B) or green (G). The arrow on this spinner is spun.

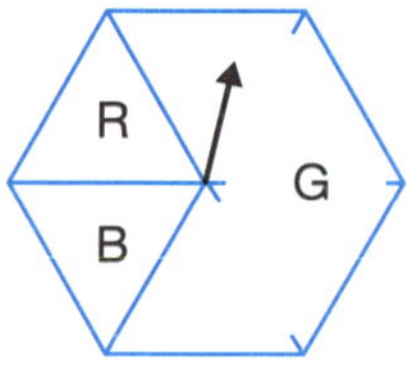

What is the probability it stops on blue?

18 The dot plot shows the ages of children at a party.

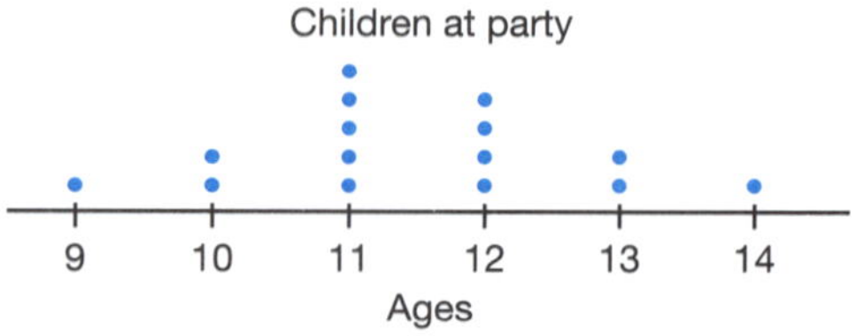

How many more 11-year-old children than 14-year-old children were at the party?

NUMBER AND ALGEBRA

1 What number is divisible by 4, a multiple of 6, less than 60 and the sum of its digits is a factor of 15?

2 A pie shop is open six days each week. Here are the sales for one week: M 409, T 278, W 227, T 492, F 305, S 411. Estimate the total sales, to the nearest hundred.

3 For an outdoor concert seats were arranged in rows and aisles. Between aisles, seats were arranged in rows of 60. If there were 2880 seats, how many rows were there?

4 Stella pays a $50 fee plus $37 per week to store her caravan. How much will it cost for 32 weeks storage?

5 Complete: $280 \div 35 = \square \div 70 = \triangle$.

6 Here are three circles. What does the shading represent?

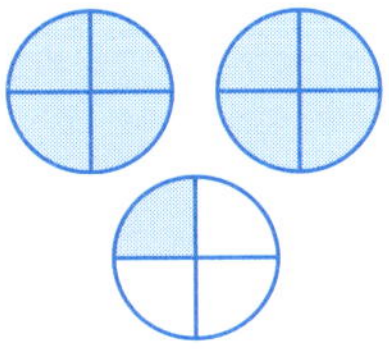

Mixed numeral = ...

Improper fraction = ...

7 What is the missing fraction? $1 - \frac{67}{1000} = \square$

8 Work out $\frac{21}{10} + \frac{34}{100} + \frac{9}{100}$, writing your answer as a decimal.

9 Hazel's parents give her a weekly allowance of $15 every Monday. If 1 July is a Friday, how much will Hazel be paid in July?

10 Here is a sequence of numbers: 187, 180, 173 …

What is the 13th number of the sequence?

11 Here is a number sentence. What is the missing number?

$12 \times 6 - \square = 65$

MEASUREMENT AND SPACE

12 The perimeter of this shape is 43 cm.

What is the length of the missing side?

13 Rey parked her car and paid for parking for 2 hours 20 minutes, which meant she could park until 1643. At what time did she arrive at the parking space?

14 A large cube is made from 27 small identical cubes. The outside of the large cube is painted. Once dry, the cube is pulled apart. How many of the small cubes have two faces painted?

15 The grid represents a map. Phoebe leaves *P* and travels east for 10 km, then north for 15 km, then west to *Q* which is north of *P*.

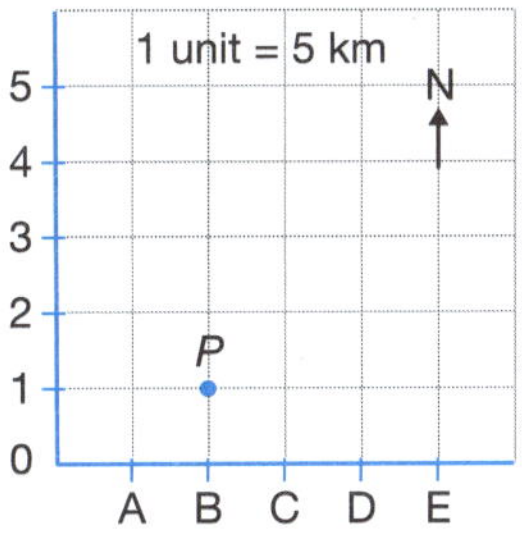

What is the total distance travelled, in kilometres?

16 With a protractor Avery measured angles as 120° and 140°. How many degrees is the angle marked as *?

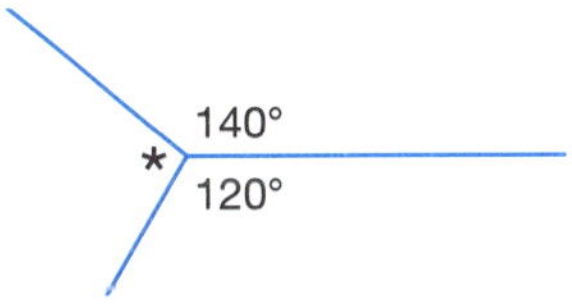

STATISTICS AND PROBABILITY

17 This spinner has sections coloured red (R) or blue (B). The arrow on this spinner is spun and it stops on blue. The arrow is spun again and stops on blue again. When the arrow is spun a third time, what is the probability it stops on red?

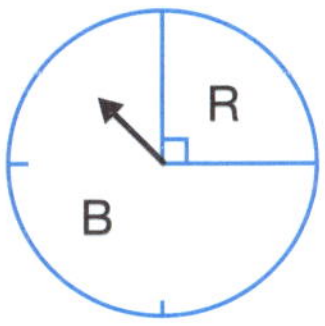

18 The dot plot shows the ages of children at a party.

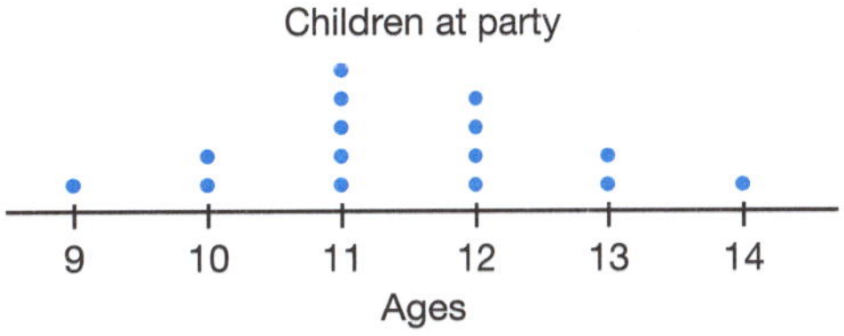

Later, two 10-year-olds arrived. How many children were then at the party?

NUMBER AND ALGEBRA

1 Here is a list of numbers.

27, 44, 63, 72, 91

What fraction of the numbers are **not** multiples of 9?

2 Which of these is the best estimate of 32×19?

450 600
900 1300

3 So far this season an English Premier League team has had an average home crowd per match of 29 600. If there have been eight matches, what has been the total attendance?

4 What is the missing number?

$136 \div 4 = 3\square$

5 What is 99×43?

6 The diagram shows three rectangles.

Shade squares to represent the improper fraction $1\frac{5}{6}$.

7 What is $\frac{9}{10} - \frac{6}{10} - \frac{1}{10} - \frac{1}{10}$?

8 Work out $\frac{440}{1000} - \frac{41}{1000}$, writing your answer as a decimal.

9 Savannah's grandmother gave her \$80 for Christmas. She bought two tops for \$38 each. How much did she have left?

10 Here is a sequence of numbers. 16, 27, 38 …

What are the next three numbers?

11 Here is a number sentence.

$10 \times 8 = 37 + \square$

What is the missing number?

MEASUREMENT AND SPACE

12 Find the perimeter of the shape.

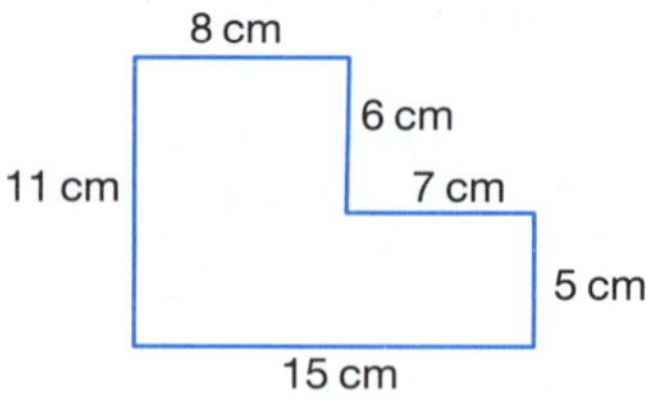

13 Nora's mother is picking her up from a friend's home at 1730. What is this in 12-hour time?

14 How many faces has an octagonal prism?

15 An object is reflected in the mirror line.

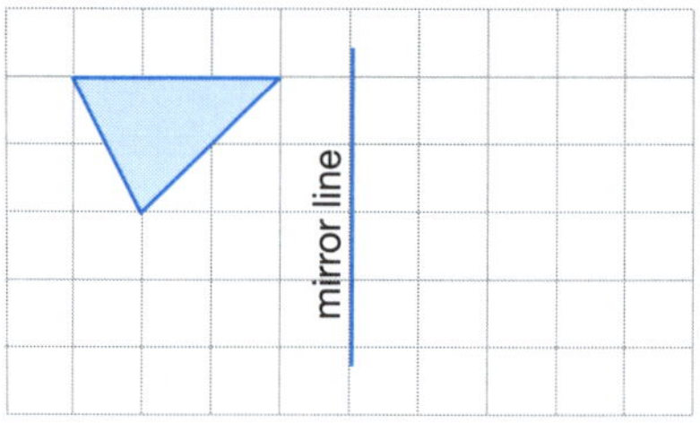

Draw the image.

16 Draw a shape with two acute angles and an obtuse angle.

STATISTICS AND PROBABILITY

17 A coin is tossed. What is the probability that it lands on tails?

18 The results of a quiz are shown.

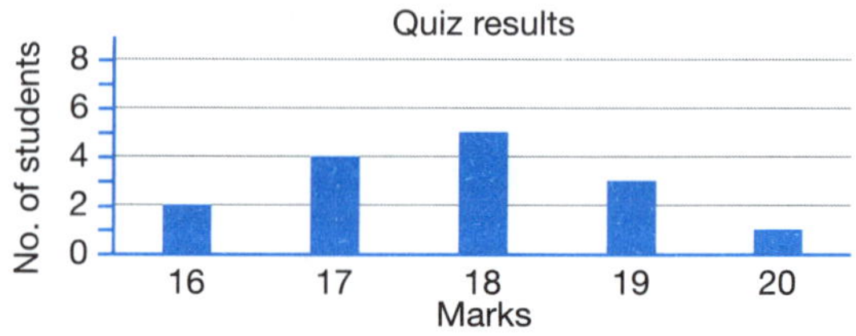

What was the highest mark scored?

NUMBER AND ALGEBRA

1 Kel has a container of balls. When he separates them into groups of 4 he has one left over and when he separates them into groups of 3 he also has one left over. What is the smallest number of balls in the container?

2 Which of these is the best estimate of 506 × 68?

28 000 31 000
34 000 41 000

3 A bus interchange had 130 bus arrivals in one day. If the average number of passengers was 19, what was the total number of passengers?

4 What is the missing number?

$$5\overline{)3485} = 6?7$$

5 What is 999 × 71?

6 Here are three circles.

What does the shading represent?

Mixed numeral = ...

Improper fraction = ...

7 What is the missing fraction? $1 - \square = \frac{19}{100}$

8 Work out $\frac{23}{10} - \frac{14}{10}$, writing your answer as a decimal.

9 Claire won a lotto prize of 8 million dollars. She decided to give $1 650 000 to charity. How much does she have left?

10 Here is a sequence of fractions.

$$\frac{3}{10}, \frac{5}{10}, \frac{7}{10}, \ldots$$

What is the 20th member of the sequence, as a mixed numeral?

11 Here is a number sentence.

$8 \times 7 + \square = 70$

What is the missing number?

MEASUREMENT AND SPACE

12 Find the perimeter of this shape.

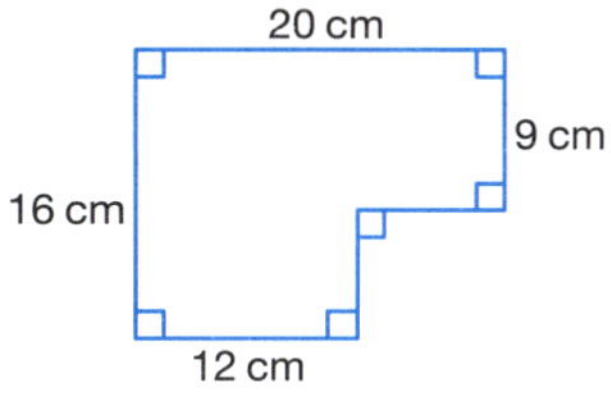

13 Julian turned on his television at 2140. He watched one program for 20 minutes before turning to another channel to watch some live sport for 2 hours 10 minutes. What time did he turn the television off, in 24-hour time?

14 In an octagonal prism, what does the number of faces plus the number of vertices minus the number of edges equal?

15 An object is reflected in the mirror line. Draw the image.

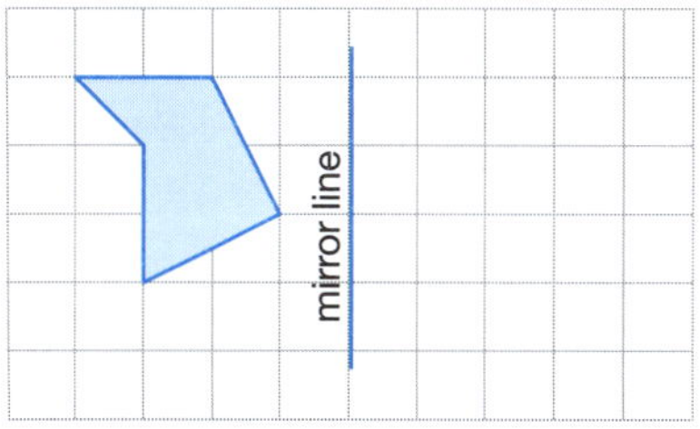

16 With a protractor, Emma measured two angles as 40° and 90°. How many degrees is the angle marked as *?

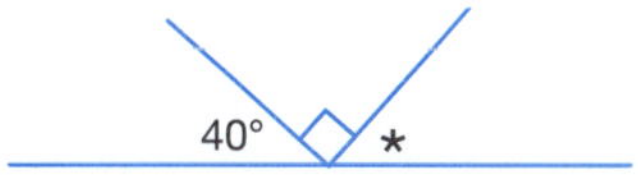

STATISTICS AND PROBABILITY

17 A coin is tossed six times and lands on heads every time. What is the probability that on the seventh toss it lands on tails?

18 The results of a quiz are shown.

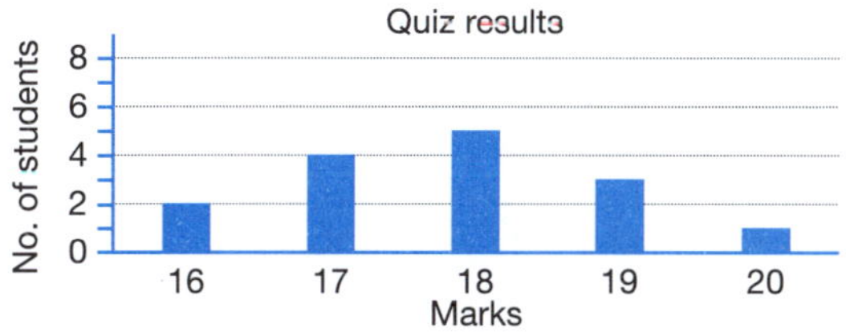

How many students scored at least 17 marks?

NUMBER AND ALGEBRA

1 Theo has 24 marbles and wants to place them in groups where he has none left over.

How many marbles can Theo put in each group? Circle the correct answers.

4, 5, 8, 10, 12

2 What is 250 less than 416?

3 What is the missing number?

625 ÷ 5 = 12☐

4 Aaron pays $15 plus an hourly rate of $12 to hire a trailer. What was the total cost for 6 hours?

5 What is the product of 99 and 85?

6 The number line has been marked in thirds.

Plot and label $\frac{2}{3}$, $\frac{4}{3}$ and $\frac{5}{3}$.

7 What is $2 - 1\frac{1}{4}$?

8 Here is a list of fractions and decimals.

$\frac{3}{10}$, 0.8, $\frac{2}{10}$, 0.5

Rewrite the list from smallest to largest.

9 An electrician charges $85 per hour. If a job takes him 3 hours, what is the total cost of the job?

10 Here is a sequence with two missing numbers.

5, ..., 19, 26, ..., 40, 47

What are the missing numbers?

11 12.8 + ☐ = 21.5

Find the missing number.

MEASUREMENT AND SPACE

12 Find the perimeter of the shape.

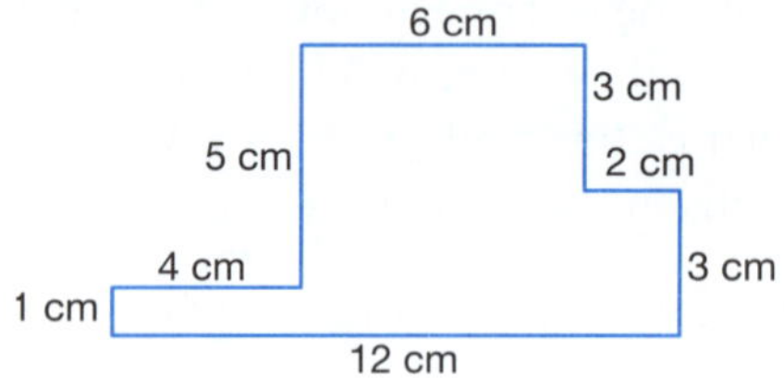

13 Elijah's watch is showing a time of 2116. He adjusts the display to 12-hour time. What will the watch now show?

14 How many edges has a hexagonal prism?

15 An object has been reflected in the mirror line and the image is shown below.

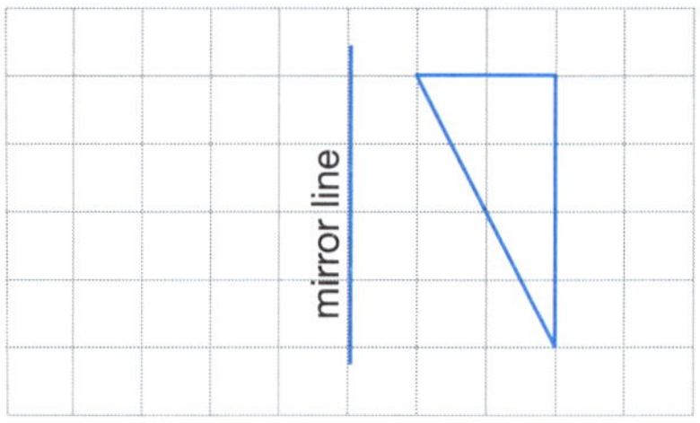

Draw the object.

16 Draw a shape with an obtuse angle, a right angle and two acute angles.

STATISTICS AND PROBABILITY

17 A normal dice is rolled. What is the probability that it lands on a 5?

18 A group of students were asked how many siblings they each had.

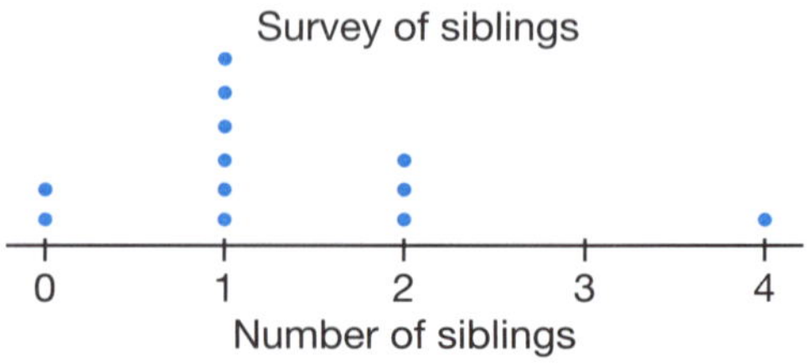

How many students were surveyed?

NUMBER AND ALGEBRA

1 Here is a list of numbers.

72, 96, 142, 240

Circle the numbers that are divisible by 2, 3, 4 and 12.

2 Caleb compared the odometers on his parents' cars. His dad's car had travelled 206 573 and his mum's car had travelled 75 896 km.
What was the difference between the two distances?

3 What is the missing number?

$9\overline{)6?7}$ = 73

4 A stadium has seating for 32 417 plus 24 VIP boxes that can hold 18 people each.
What is the maximum stadium attendance?

5 What is the product of 990 and 65?

6 

On the number line, plot and label $2\frac{1}{2}$ and $4\frac{1}{2}$.

7 What is the missing fraction? $1 - \square = \frac{87}{200}$

8 Here is a list of fractions and decimals.

$\frac{27}{100}$, 0.25, 0.31, $\frac{3}{10}$

Rewrite the list from smallest to largest.

9 Jackson runs a small business from home. In May his expenses totalled $8511 and his income was $11 308.
What was his profit for May?

10 Here is a sequence of fractions.

$8\frac{3}{4}$, 8, $7\frac{1}{4}$ …

What is the 10th member of the sequence?

11 $204 + \square = 739$

Find the missing number.

MEASUREMENT AND SPACE

12 Find the perimeter of the shape.

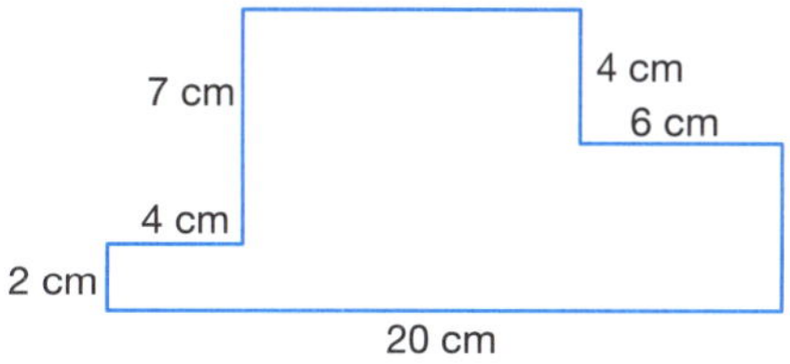

13 What is the time 2 hours 20 minutes before midday, in 24-hour time?

14 In a hexagonal prism, what does the number of faces plus the number of vertices minus the number of edges equal?

15 An object has been reflected in the mirror line and the image is shown below.

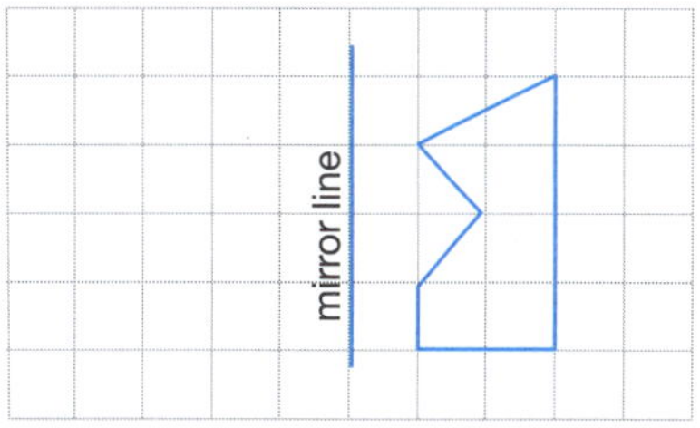

Draw the object.

16 With a protractor, Mila measured two angles as 90° and 60°.

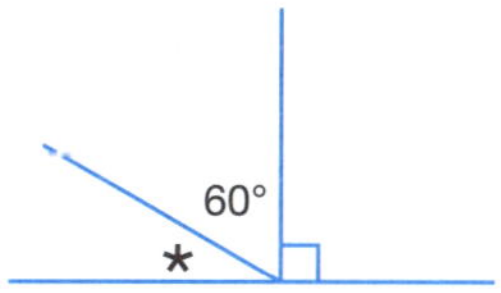

How many degrees is the angle marked as *?

STATISTICS AND PROBABILITY

17 A normal dice is rolled. What is the probability that it lands on a number less than 5?

18 A group of students were asked how many siblings they had.

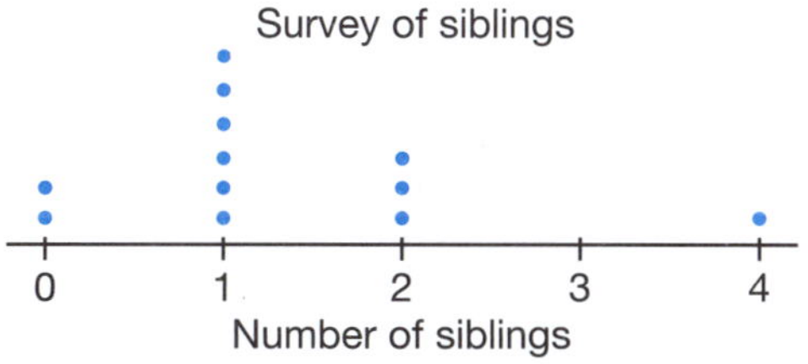

What was the total number of siblings?

NUMBER AND ALGEBRA

1 Here is a list of numbers.

24, 42, 8, 441, 48

Circle the numbers that are **not** multiples of 4.

2 817 – 388 = ☐

Circle the number closest to the answer.

300 400 460 500

3 Evelyn reads the same number of pages each night but wants to finish reading her book in a week. She has 98 pages to read. How many pages should she read each night?

4 A multi-level parking station has six levels of parking. Each of the levels has 236 car spaces. What is the total number of car spaces in the parking station?

5 Complete:
$72 \times 102 = 72 \times 100 + 72 \times$ ☐

6 The number line has been marked in quarters.

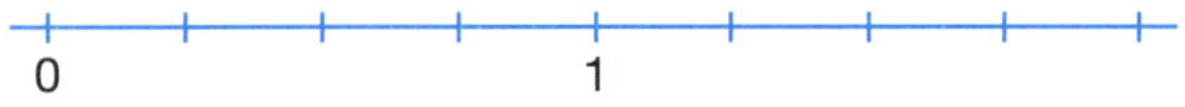

Plot and label $\frac{1}{4}$, $\frac{3}{4}$ and $\frac{7}{4}$.

7 A rectangle has been split into eighths. Shade $\frac{3}{4}$ of the rectangle.

8 Express $102\frac{71}{1000}$ as a decimal.

9 The entry prices for a safari park are \$31 for adults and \$17 for children. What would be the total cost of entry for two adults and two children?

10 Here is a sequence with two missing numbers.

33, ..., 25, 21, ..., 13, 9

What are the missing numbers?

11 Find the missing number.

16.3 – ☐ = 9.5

MEASUREMENT AND SPACE

12 Find the area of the rectangle.

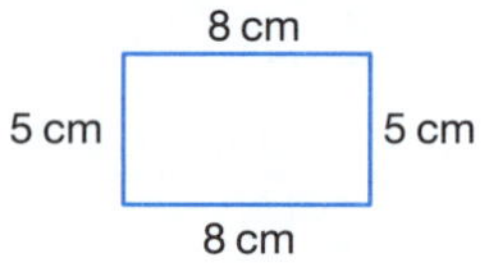

13 Camilla usually wakes at 7 am. This morning she woke up at 0815. How long was Camilla's sleep-in?

14 How many vertices has a trapezoidal prism?

15 Rotate the points *P* and *Q* 90° in a clockwise direction about *O*.

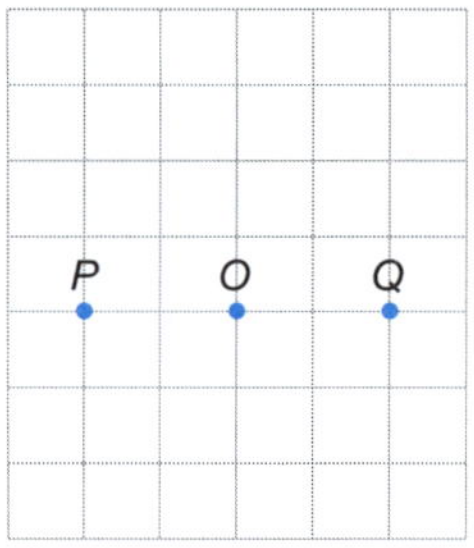

16 Draw a shape with a reflex angle, two right angles and two acute angles.

STATISTICS AND PROBABILITY

17 A bag contains identical balls numbered from 1 to 9. A ball is selected from the bag at random. What is the probability that it is numbered at least 7?

18 The temperatures in Bulli on one spring day are graphed.

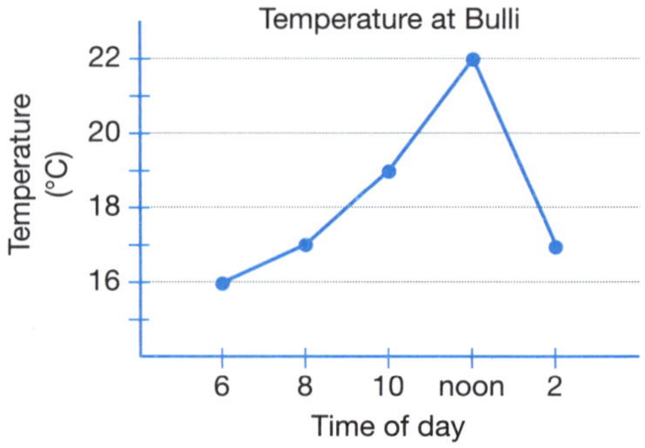

What was the difference between the highest and lowest temperature?

NUMBER AND ALGEBRA

1 A prime is a number with only two factors. How many numbers less than 100 containing the digit 9 are primes?

2 42 878 – 27 053 = ☐

Circle the number closest to the answer.

14 000 15 000 16 000

3 What are the two missing numbers?

```
   123?
6) 743?
```

4 A hospital has 16 wards. Each ward has eight rooms. Six of the rooms have four beds and the others have two beds. How many beds are in the hospital?

5 $35 \times 102 =$ ☐

6 On the number line, plot and label $3\frac{1}{2}$ and $4\frac{1}{4}$.

7 What is the missing fraction?

$1 - \frac{21}{1000} =$ ☐

8 What is the sum of $\frac{71}{100}$ and $\frac{315}{1000}$ as a decimal?

9 Mary babysits for her parents' friends. She charges $18 plus $7.50 for every hour of babysitting. How much will she charge for babysitting from 7 pm to 11 pm?

10 Here are some numbers in a pattern.

… 63, 60, 57, …

If 63 is the fifth number in the pattern, what is the first number?

11 $2.7 + 4.3 = 3.9 +$ ☐

Find the missing number.

MEASUREMENT AND SPACE

12 The perimeter of the rectangle is 42 cm. What is the area of the rectangle?

12 cm

13 Aria left her home at 0930. She drove for 2 hours, stopped for 20 minutes and then drove for another 1 hour and 30 minutes. At what time did she arrive, in 24-hour time?

14 In a trapezoidal prism, what does the number of faces plus the number of vertices minus the number of edges equal?

15 Rotate the triangle 90° in a clockwise direction about *O*.

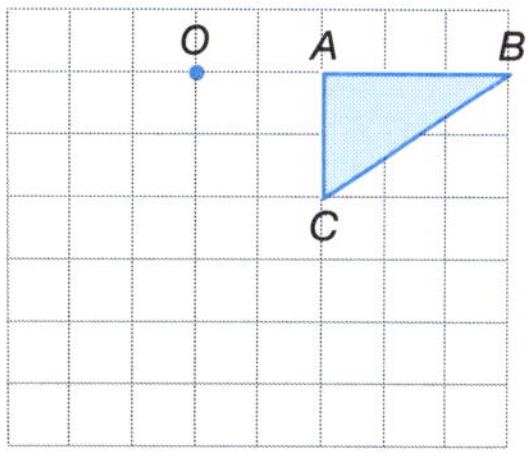

16 Three **equal** angles on the diagram are marked as *.

What is the size of each angle?

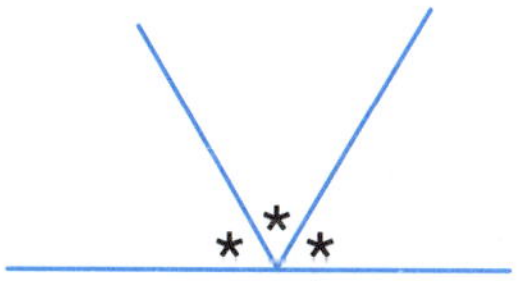

STATISTICS AND PROBABILITY

17 A bag contains identical balls numbered from 1 to 9. A ball is selected from the bag at random. What is the probability that it is an even number?

18 The temperatures in Bulli on one spring day are graphed. For how long was the temperature recorded?

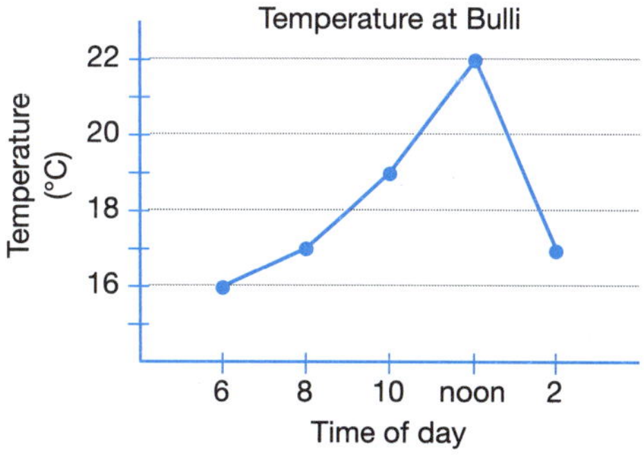

NUMBER AND ALGEBRA

1 True or false?
The number 20 has five factors.

2 The correct answer to a question is 12 650. Liam's answer was 12 628 and Aria's was 12 676. Who was closer to the correct answer?

3 A grocer has eight boxes of oranges for sale. Each box contains 144 oranges.
What is the total number of oranges?

4 $\square \times 9 = 126$
What is the missing number?

5 Complete: $4 \times 12 = 8 \times \square$

6 Here is a number line.

Plot and label $\frac{3}{5}$ and $\frac{6}{5}$ on the number line.

7 A rectangle has been split into twelfths. Shade $\frac{2}{3}$ of the rectangle.

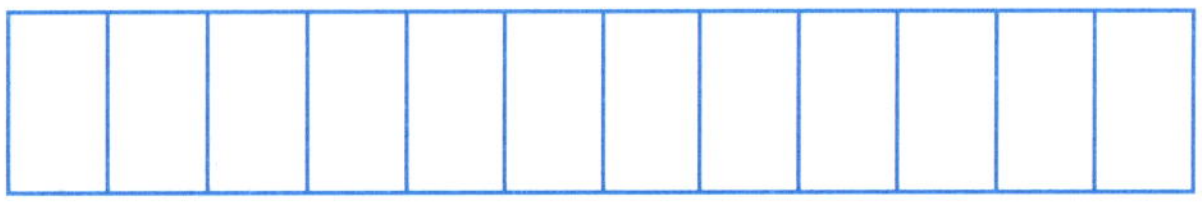

8 What is 1.6 – 0.87?

9 Levi has saved $80. His grandmother gives him $50 for his birthday and he spends $120 on a new game. How much does he have left?

10 Here is a pattern of numbers.
11, 25, 39 …
What are the next **two** numbers?

11 $\square - 17.3 = 25$
Find the missing number.

MEASUREMENT AND SPACE

12 A regular pentagon is drawn with each side 6 cm in length.
What is the perimeter?

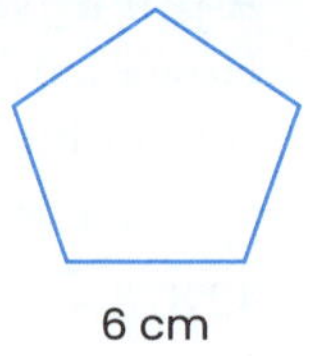

13 Write 1420 in 12-hour time.

14 How many edges has a pentagonal prism?

15 Rotate the line *AB* 90° in a clockwise direction about *O*.

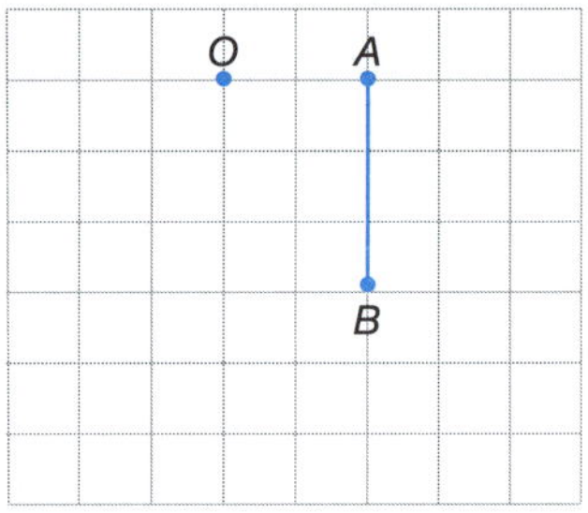

16 What is the total of the two angles marked as *a* and *b*?

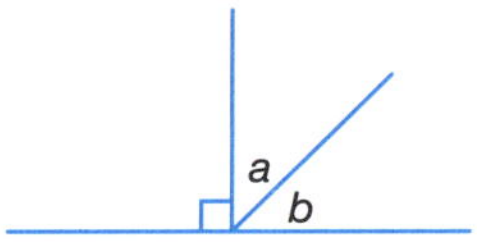

STATISTICS AND PROBABILITY

17 There are eight identical discs in a bag. The discs are either red or blue. The probability of randomly selecting a blue disc from the bag is $\frac{1}{2}$.
How many blue discs are in the bag?

18 The number of goals scored by a team over four rounds of soccer is shown in the graph.

How many goals were scored in total?

NUMBER AND ALGEBRA

1 Freda looks at the calendar for April. She crosses out all the multiples of 2, 3 and 5.

How many dates remain?

2 The correct answer to a question is 327 485. Brooklyn's answer was 327 416 and Wyatt's was 327 551. Who was closer to the correct answer?

3 Each can of soft drink contains 375 mL. How many millilitres are in a carton of 24 cans?

4 $\square \times 7 = 9499$.

What is the missing number?

5 What is $32 \times 18 = \square$

6 On the number line, plot and label $4\frac{1}{6}$, $4\frac{1}{2}$ and $4\frac{2}{3}$.

7 What is the missing fraction?

$1 - \frac{69}{1000} = \square$

8 Maddie had a 4-m long ribbon. She cut 2.67 m from the ribbon. What length of ribbon remained?

9 Last week Poppie worked for 8 hours in her casual job and was paid $136. This week she worked for 14 hours at the same pay rate.

What will she be paid for this week's work?

10 Here are some numbers in a pattern.

… 23, 17, 11 ….

If 23 is the eighth number in the pattern, what is the second number?

11 $\square + 121.7 = 345.2$

Find the missing number.

MEASUREMENT AND SPACE

12 A regular pentagon has a perimeter of 345 mm. What is the length of each side?

13 Clare and John left their home and drove in separate cars to their friend's holiday unit. John arrived at 1545 and Clare arrived three-quarters of an hour later. At what time did Clare arrive, in 24-hour time?

14 In a pentagonal prism, what does the number of faces plus the number of vertices minus the number of edges equal?

15 Rotate the triangle 90° in an anticlockwise direction about *O*.

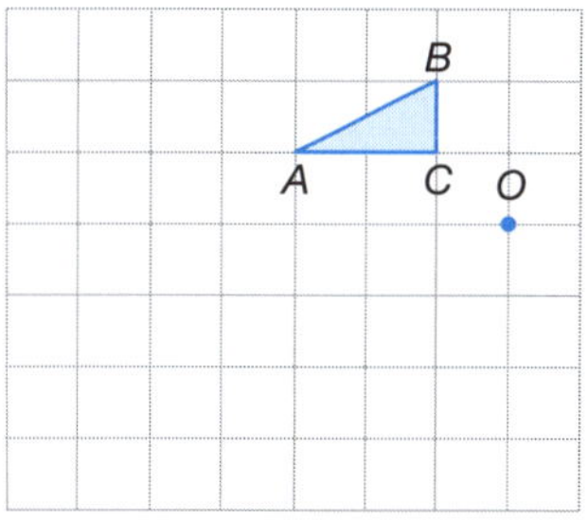

16 Four **equal** angles on the diagram are marked as *. What is the size of each angle?

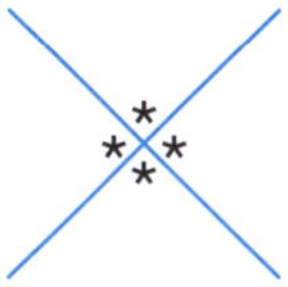

STATISTICS AND PROBABILITY

17 There are 10 identical discs in a bag. The discs are either red, blue or yellow. There are twice as many blue discs in the bag as red discs. The probability of randomly selecting a red disc from the bag is $\frac{3}{10}$.

What is the probability of selecting a yellow disc?

18 The number of goals scored by Logan's team over four rounds of soccer is shown.

The opposition teams scored two goals, three goals, four goals and two goals respectively in the four games.

How many games were won by Logan's team?

NUMBER AND ALGEBRA

1 Which of these are factors of 28? Circle all the correct numbers.

7, 24, 4, 1, 8, 56

2

$$\begin{array}{r} 5732 \\ +\ 2964 \\ \hline \end{array}$$

3 Skylar thinks of a number. She multiplies it by 5 and the answer is 280. What number did Skylar think of?

4 Over two consecutive weekends, four buses transport 48 passengers each to the ski fields. What is the total number of passengers in the two weekends?

5 What is $238 \times 10\,000$?

6 Part of a square is shaded.

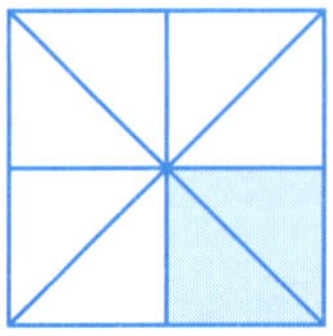

What fraction is **not** shaded?

7 What is $\frac{28}{5} - \frac{16}{5}$ as a mixed numeral?

8 Find the difference between $\frac{9}{100}$ and $\frac{2}{100}$, as a decimal.

9 Kira purchased 30 L of petrol at $1.69 per litre. What was the total cost?

10 Here is a pattern of numbers.

1.5, 2.7, 3.9 …

What are the next two numbers?

11 $\square + \frac{3}{5} = 2$

Find the missing number.

MEASUREMENT AND SPACE

12 The perimeter of an equilateral triangle is 36 cm.

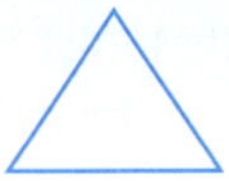

What is the length of each side?

13 Camilla's dental appointment is at 1315.

What is this in 12-hour time?

14 How many edges has a square-based pyramid?

15 Translate the shape 2 units to the right.

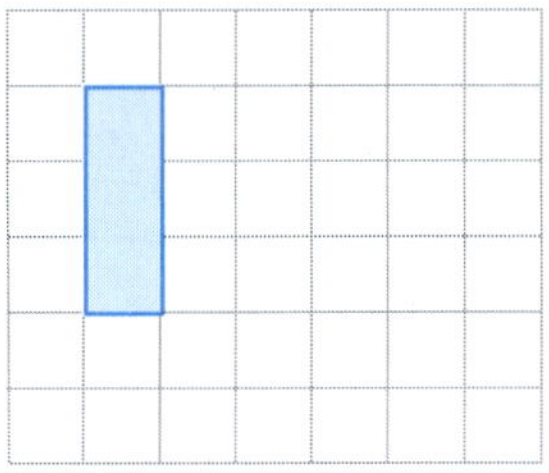

16 What is the total of the two angles marked as a and b?

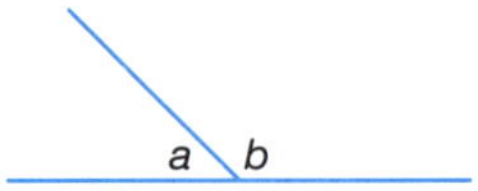

STATISTICS AND PROBABILITY

17 A spinner has sections which are coloured red (R), blue (B), yellow (Y) or green (G). Noah wins a game if he spins red.

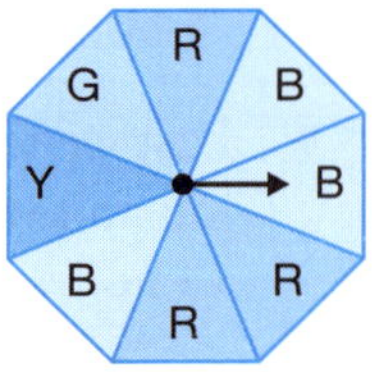

What is the probability that Noah wins?

18 Paisley has recorded the number of laps run on 5 days.

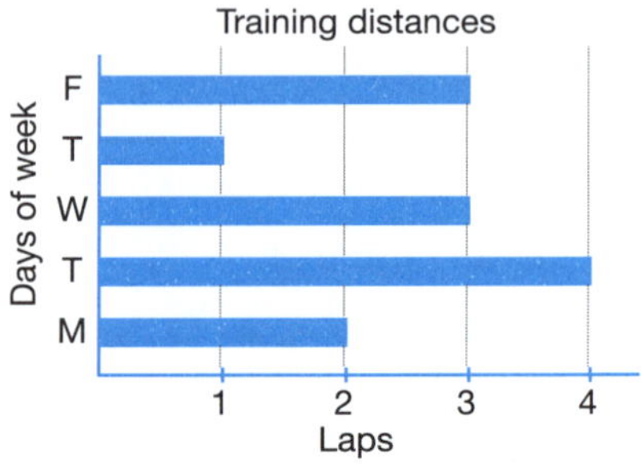

On how many days did Paisley run at least two laps?

NUMBER AND ALGEBRA

1 A kitchen tap drips every 3 seconds. In the same house, the laundry tap drips every 8 seconds. If both taps drip at the same instant, how long will it take for the taps to drip at the same instant five more times?

2 Find the sum of 72 378, 18 518, 8791 and 237 189.

3 Kenny's Chocolate Company sells Chockybites in packets of 12. How many packets are needed to buy 20 076 Chockybites?

4 Sixteen avocados are packed into each tray. A restaurant plans to use six trays each day of a seven-day week. How many avocados are used?

5 What is $46 \times 30\,000$?

6 Here are three circles. What does the shading represent?

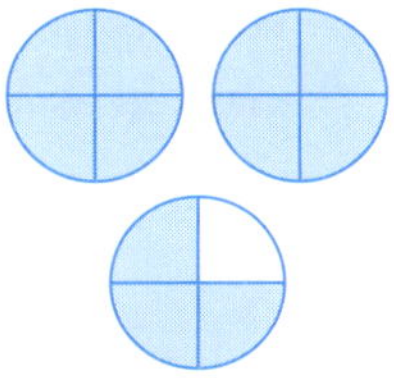

Mixed numeral = ...

Improper fraction = ...

7 Henry and William bought a pizza to share. Both boys ate $\frac{3}{8}$ of the pizza each. What fraction of the pizza remained?

8 Find the difference between $1\frac{3}{10}$ and $\frac{7}{10}$, as a decimal?

9 As a hobby, Juliet sells her handmade soap at markets. She paid $55 for a stall at a Sunday market and throughout the day sold 54 soaps at a price of $10 each. If each soap costs $4 to make, how much profit did Juliet make?

10 Here are some numbers in a pattern.

… 53, 57, 61 ….

If 53 is the 10th number in the pattern, what is the 20th number?

11 $\square + \frac{1}{4} + \frac{2}{4} = 1$

Find the missing number.

MEASUREMENT AND SPACE

12 The shape shows an equilateral triangle on top of a rectangle. The perimeter of the shape is 34 cm. What is the width of the rectangle?

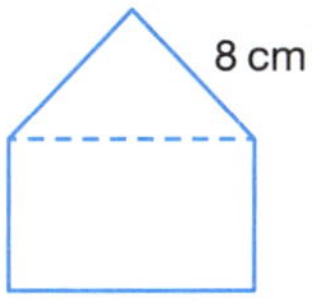

13 Madison started watching a movie at 7:45 pm. The movie ran for 115 minutes. What 24-hour time did the movie finish?

14 In a square-based pyramid, what does the number of faces plus the number of vertices minus the number of edges equal?

15 Translate the shape 3 units to the right.

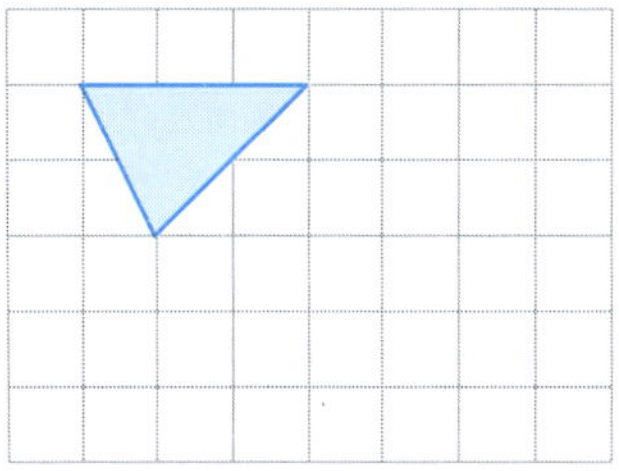

16 Kenzo is giddy after he spun around three and a half times. Through how many degrees did he rotate?

STATISTICS AND PROBABILITY

17 A spinner has sections which are coloured red (R), blue (B), yellow (Y) or green (G). Ava wins a game if she spins green or yellow.

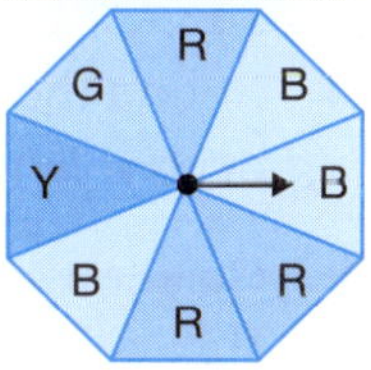

What is the probability that Ava **does not** win?

18 Paisley has recorded the number of laps run on 5 days. Paisley repeats this program for 10 weeks.

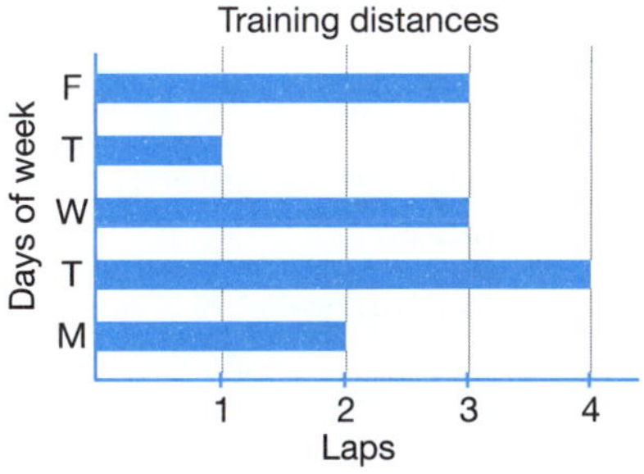

What was the total number of laps run?

NUMBER AND ALGEBRA

1 Circle the numbers that are **not** multiples of 5.

52, 15, 505, 3600, 501

2 Which of these is the best estimate for 63 761 ÷ 20 871?

2 3 20 30

3 When Addison was born, her father's height was four times Addison's length. If her dad was 184 cm tall, how long was Addison when she was born?

4 There are 12 packets of chips in a variety box. How many packets are in a carton of 16 boxes?

5 $14 \times 4 + 6 \times 4 =$ ☐

6 Part of a square is shaded.

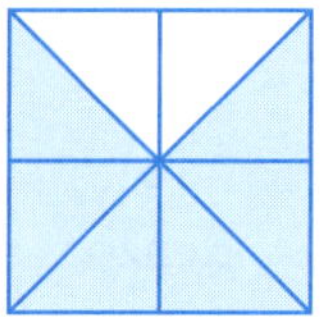

What fraction is **not** shaded?

7 What is $\frac{1}{5} + \frac{2}{5} + \frac{3}{5} + \frac{4}{5}$?

8 Round the decimal 21.683 to the nearest tenth.

9 Gershon wanted to cook spaghetti bolognaise. He bought 500 g of mince which cost \$8.50, a tin of tomatoes for \$2.10, a jar of tomato paste for \$3.85 and a packet of spaghetti for \$2.95. What was the total cost?

10 ...., ..., 58, 81, 104, 127

What are the first two numbers?

11 Here is a number sentence.

☐ + 9 = 22

Joshua thinks the missing number is 11. Is Joshua correct?

MEASUREMENT AND SPACE

12 A regular hexagon has a perimeter of 138 cm. What is the length of each of the sides?

13 Ellie drove to the shopping centre, arriving at 1030. She has 3 hours free parking. What is the latest she should leave and not pay for parking?

14 How many edges has a triangular prism?

15 Translate the shape 3 units to the left.

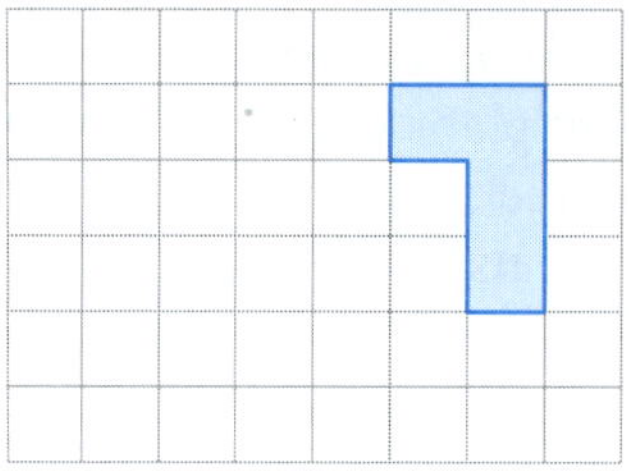

16 What is the total of the two angles marked as a and b?

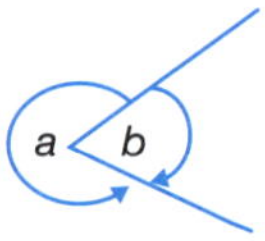

STATISTICS AND PROBABILITY

17 A bag contains an equal number of red, green and white balls. If there is a total of 12 balls, what is the probability of randomly choosing a white ball?

18 The graph shows the fundraising amounts for four classes.

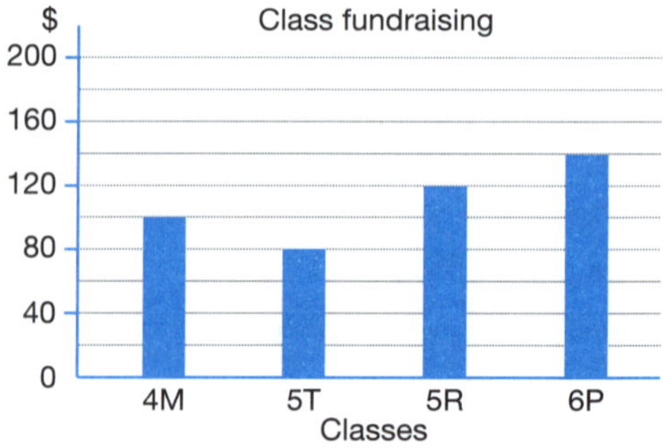

What was the total amount raised by class 4M and 5R altogether?

NUMBER AND ALGEBRA

1 How many numbers less than 20 have fewer than three factors?

2 Which of these gives the best estimate for 610 400 ÷ 18 590?

15 30 150 300

3 In this number sentence, the □ and △ are hiding numbers.

4872 ÷ 24 = □ ÷ 6 = △.

□ = ... △ = ...

4 A hotel has 24 rooms on each of its 16 floors. How many rooms are in the hotel?

5 Lillian is 11 years old and Julian is 9 years old. For Christmas, their grandpa gives them $5 for every year of their age. What is the total amount of money?

6 Find the missing number.

$4\frac{5}{8} = \frac{\square}{8}$

7 What is $\frac{2}{3} + \frac{1}{3} + \frac{2}{3}$, as a mixed numeral?

8 Round the decimal 1.0798 to the nearest hundredth.

9 Per kilogram cherries cost $6.90, lychees cost $7.90 and dates cost $19.20. Audrey bought half a kilogram of each of the three fruits. What was her change from a $20 note?

10 Stella writes a pattern of numbers.

… 106, 120, 134 …

If 106 is the seventh number in the pattern, what is the 50th number?

11 INPUT → ÷ 4 → − 3 → OUTPUT

If the OUTPUT is 17, what is the INPUT?

MEASUREMENT AND SPACE

12 A regular hexagon has each side of length 250 mm. What is the perimeter in metres and centimetres?

□ m □ cm

13 Jayden ran a fun run in 1 hour 50 minutes. If he finished the run at 1310, what time, in 12-hour time, did he start?

14 In a triangular prism, what does the number of faces plus the number of vertices minus the number of edges equal?

15 Translate the shape 3 units to the left.

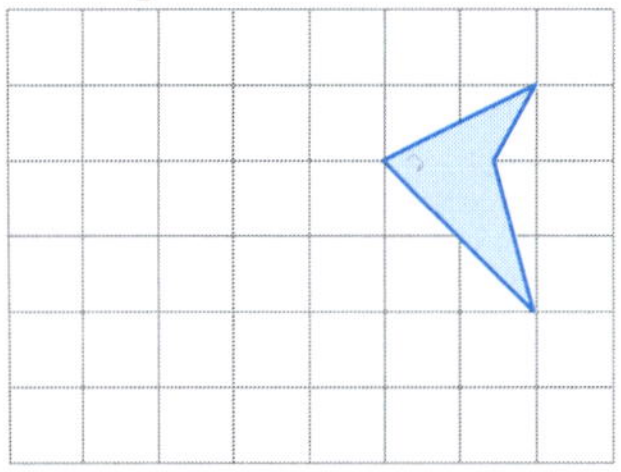

16 How many pairs of parallel sides has a regular decagon?

STATISTICS AND PROBABILITY

17 A bag contains an equal number of blue, purple, pink, white and orange marbles. What is the probability of randomly selecting a purple or a pink marble?

18 The graph shows the fundraising amounts for four classes.

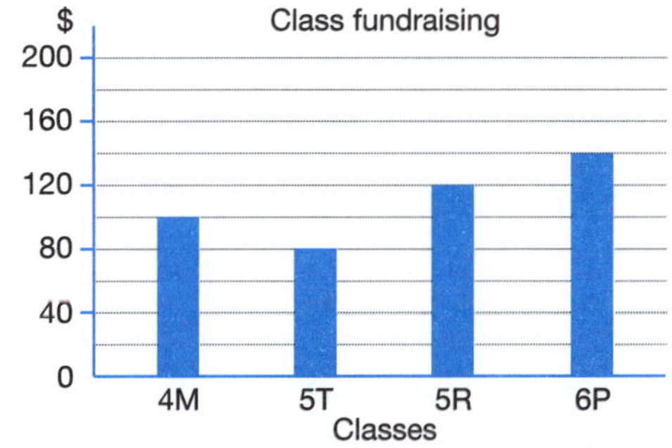

How much more was raised by 4M and 6P than 5T and 5R?

NUMBER AND ALGEBRA

1 How many multiples of 4 are between 10 and 30?

2 What is the difference between 76 and the sum of 45 and 23?

3 What is $15 \times 2 \times 8$?

4 Lexie uses her handspan to measure a table. The table is 192 cm long which is 12 handspans. What is the length of her handspan?

5 $16 + 13 - 11 + 18 - 12 =$ ☐

6 Shade $\frac{2}{3}$ of the rectangle.

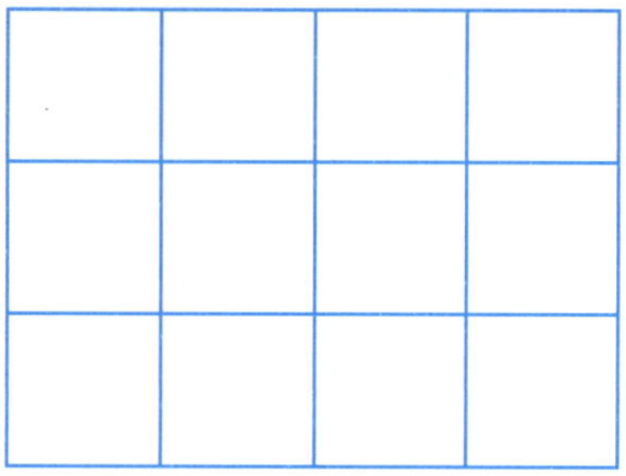

7 Aaron is flying from Singapore to Perth. After watching a movie, he calculates that he has flown two-fifths of the distance. What fraction of the flight remains?

8 Rewrite $\frac{37}{10}$ as a decimal.

9 An ice-skating rink charges adults $12 entry and children $10. What is the cost of entry for two adults and three children?

10 Here is a pattern of decimals.

☐, 3.8, 4.2, 4.6, ☐

What are the two missing decimals?

11 Here is a number sentence.

$5 \times$ ☐ $= 150$

Alexa thinks the missing number is 30. Is Alexa correct?

MEASUREMENT AND SPACE

12 A rectangle has an area of 70 cm^2. If the width of the rectangle is 7 cm, what is the length?

13 Write 10:50 pm in 24-hour time.

14 This solid is cut with a knife, shown by the dotted line.

Circle the shape that is the cut face.

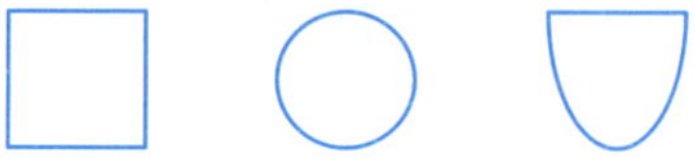

15 Enlarge the shape by a scale factor of 2.

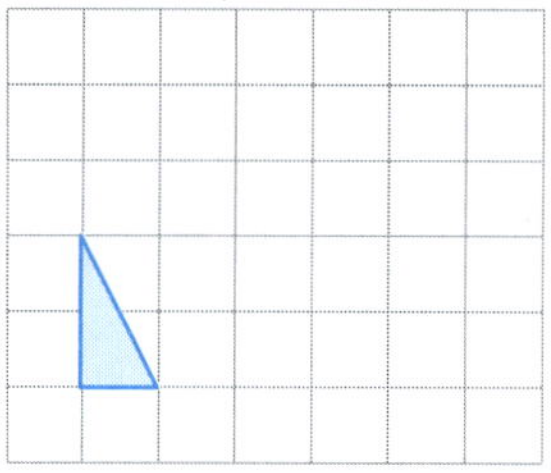

16 Here are some angles.

70° 100° 200° 5°

Circle the acute angle(s).

STATISTICS AND PROBABILITY

17 A box contains three red balls, five green balls and some blue balls. If the probability of selecting a red ball is $\frac{3}{10}$, how many blue balls are in the box?

18 A survey was conducted to find the number of home-cooked nightly meals consumed by students in a week.

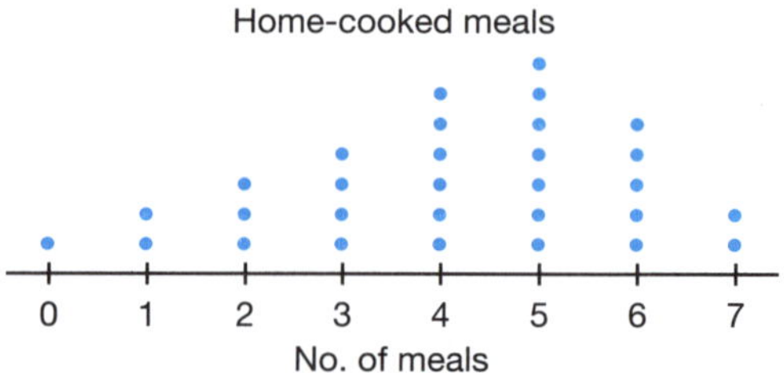

How many students had fewer than three home-cooked meals?

NUMBER AND ALGEBRA

1 Brad wrote a list of the first 20 numbers that were divisible by 3. Cassie wrote a list of the first 20 numbers that were divisible by 4. How many numbers were common to both lists?

2 What is the difference between the sum of 4156 and 9412 and the sum of 5367 and 6185?

3 Caleb rides 13 km to work each morning and rides the same route home in the evening. He rides three days every week. What is the total distance he rides?

4 When Symon walks, the average length of his stride is 80 cm. How many steps will be showing on his smartwatch if he calculates that he has walked 12 km in a day?

5 43 – 29 + 37 – 23 + 26 =

6 Shade $\frac{5}{6}$ of the rectangle.

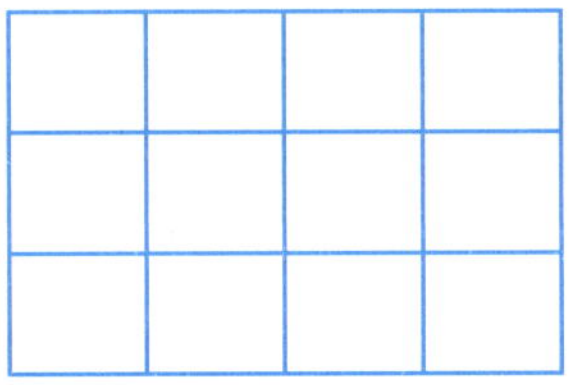

7 Pepper Tree School is fundraising for an orphanage in India. Class 5P has raised $\frac{3}{10}$ of the target amount, 6T has raised $\frac{1}{10}$ and other classes have raised another $\frac{3}{10}$ of the target amount. What fraction still needs to be raised?

8 Rewrite $\frac{209}{100}$ as a decimal.

9 Scarlett bought a T-shirt for $26.90 and a pair of shorts for $33.30. She also bought a coat that was three times the price of the pair of shorts. What was the total amount she spent?

10 Here is a sequence of mixed numerals.

$5\frac{2}{5}, 6\frac{3}{5}, 7\frac{4}{5}, \ldots$

What comes next in the sequence?

11 INPUT → + 14 → × 3 → OUTPUT

If the INPUT is 7, what is the OUTPUT?

MEASUREMENT AND SPACE

12 What are the dimensions of a rectangle with a perimeter of 24 cm and an area of 32 cm^2.

13 Owen took 12 hours 20 minutes to drive from Brisbane to Bowen. If Owen arrived at 2200, at what time did he leave Brisbane, in 12-hour time?

14 This solid is cut with a knife, shown by the dotted line.

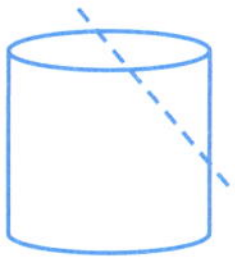

Circle the shape that is the cut face.

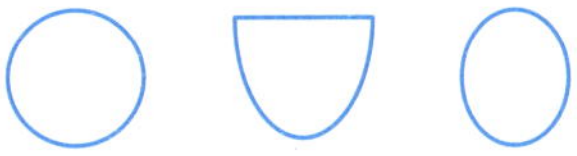

15 The rectangle is enlarged by a scale factor of 3.

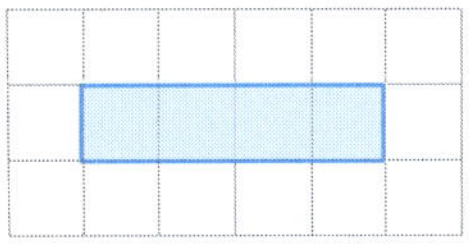

What is the perimeter of the enlarged shape?

16 Colton uses his protractor to show that the angles in a quadrilateral add to 360°. If two of the angles are right angles and another one of the angles measures 70°, what is the size of the last angle?

STATISTICS AND PROBABILITY

17 A box contains 10 red balls, four green balls and some blue balls. If the probability of selecting a green ball is $\frac{1}{5}$, what is the probability of selecting a blue ball?

18 A survey was conducted to find the number of home-cooked nightly meals consumed by students in a week.

How many students had more home-cooked meals in a week than non-home-cooked meals?

NUMBER AND ALGEBRA

1 60 is a multiple of 4. Write down the next three multiples of 4 after 60.

2 Increase 678 by the difference between 232 and 110.

3 If 65 ÷ ☐ = 5, what is the value of ☐ ?

4 Ellie uses four red balloons, three pink balloons and two white balloons to make a bunch. She wants to use 16 bunches of the balloons to decorate a hall. How many balloons does she need?

5 What is 40 – 11 – 12 – 4?

6 Shade $\frac{3}{4}$ of the rectangle.

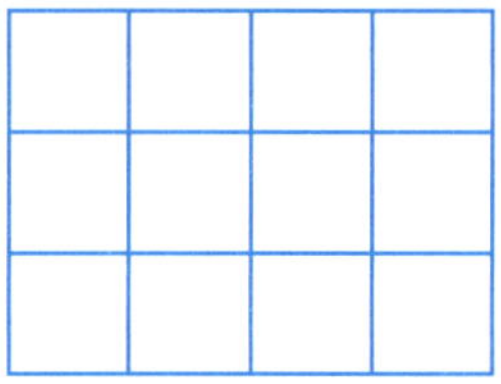

7 Ava shades $\frac{5}{12}$ of the rectangle, Ben shades $\frac{2}{12}$ and Liam shades $\frac{4}{12}$.

What fraction remains unshaded?

8 Multiply 4.67 by 8.

9 For school, Isaac bought four exercise books at $0.63 each and a packet of glue sticks for $1.92. What is the total cost, to the nearest 5 cents?

10 Here is a pattern of fractions.

$\frac{1}{5}, \frac{3}{5}, 1,$ ...., ...

What is the next two numbers in the pattern, written as mixed numerals?

11 Here is a number sentence: 140 ÷ ☐ = 7

Cathy thinks the missing number is 20. Is Cathy correct?

MEASUREMENT AND SPACE

12 Change 6 hectares into m^2.

13 Tonight's basketball game starts at twenty past seven. Write this time in 24-hour time.

14 This solid is cut with a knife, shown by the dotted line.

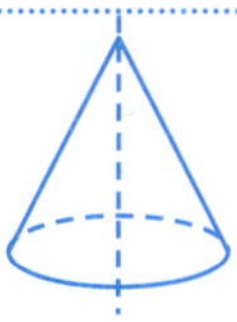

Circle the shape that is the cut face.

15 Enlarge the shape by a scale factor of 2.

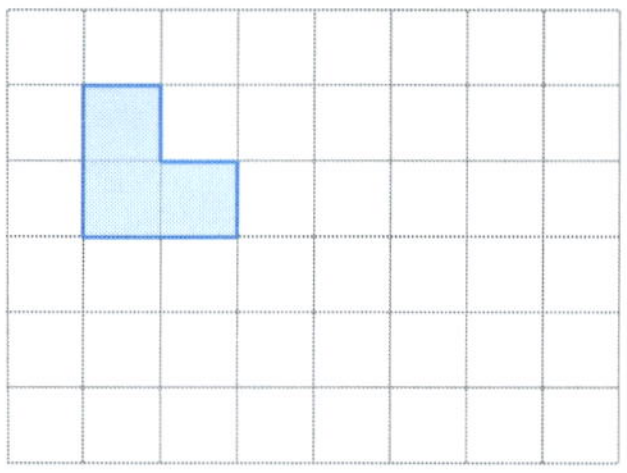

16 Here are some angles.

70° 100° 200° 175°

Circle the obtuse angle(s).

STATISTICS AND PROBABILITY

17 There is an equal number of red pens and blue pens in a pencil case. A pen is chosen at random. What is the probability of selecting a red pen?

18 The graph shows the results of a survey of gym members who attend fitness classes.

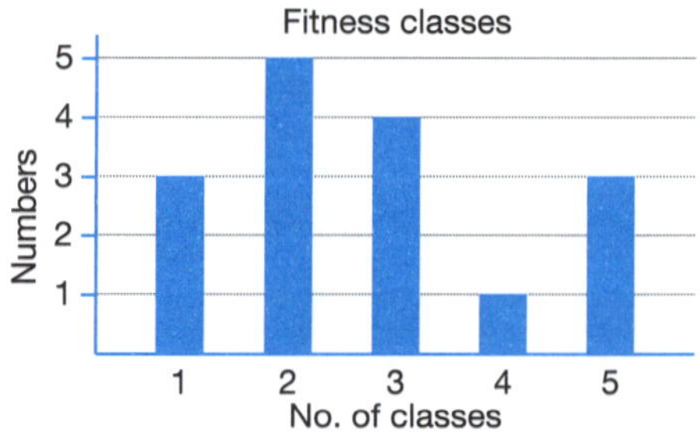

How many classes were attended by five members?

NUMBER AND ALGEBRA

1 Here is a list of numbers: 18, 24, 28, 64

Which number has the most factors?

2 Decrease 14 000 by the sum of 4569, 2781 and 4789.

3 If △ ÷ □ = ○, then what is △ ÷ ○?

4 Eight players on a basketball team have identical training plans. Three mornings every week they each run 4 km. How far do the players run in total in a fortnight?

5 Andrew has a weekly goal of cycling 100 km. On Monday he cycled 26 km, on Tuesday 18 km, on Wednesday 32 km and on Thursday 13 km. What distance does he still need to cycle?

6 Shade $\frac{3}{4}$ of the balls.

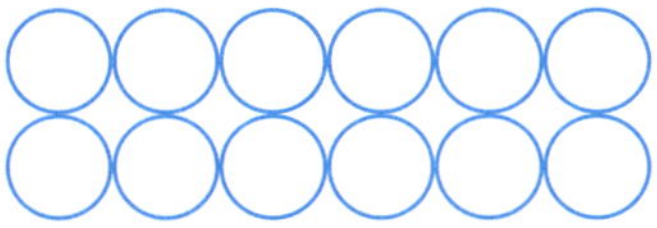

7 Anthony and Aria shade parts of the same rectangle. Anthony shades one-third and Aria shades one-half of the rectangle. What fraction is shaded?

8 What is 37.8 multiplied by 26?

9 Dylan won a $1653 lotto prize. He decided to give $165 to charity, $378 to his sister and half the remainder to his son. What amount did Dylan keep?

10 Zoe is training for a fun run. Every week she plans to run 1.5 km longer than the previous week. In week 5 she ran 7.5 km. How far does she plan to run in week 11?

11 INPUT → − 18 → ÷ 3 → OUTPUT

If the INPUT is 30, what is the OUTPUT?

MEASUREMENT AND SPACE

12 The area of a large rectangular paddock is 8.6 ha. The width of the paddock is 200 m. The paddock is to be fenced. What is the perimeter of the fence?

13 Isaac took 1 hour 20 minutes to walk between two parks. His friend Paisley rode her bike and took half the time. If both Isaac and Paisley left at 1400, at what time did Paisley arrive?

14 This solid is cut with a knife, shown by the dotted line.

Circle the shape that is the cut face.

15 The rectangle is enlarged by a scale factor of 3. What is the area of the enlarged shape?

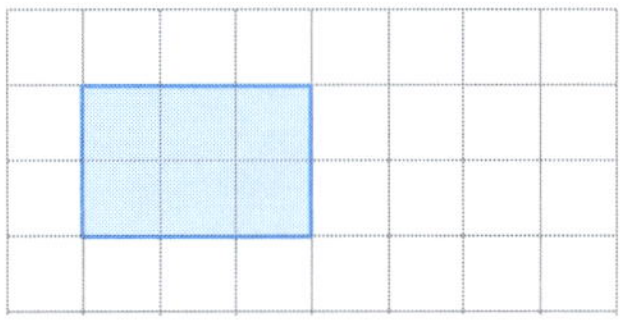

16 Dakari uses her protractor to show that the angles in a triangle add to 180°. If two of the angles measure 66° and 78°, what is the size of the other angle?

STATISTICS AND PROBABILITY

17 There are twice as many blue pens as black pens in a pencil case. A pen is chosen at random.

What is the probability of selecting a black pen?

18 The graph shows the results of a survey of gym members who attend fitness classes.

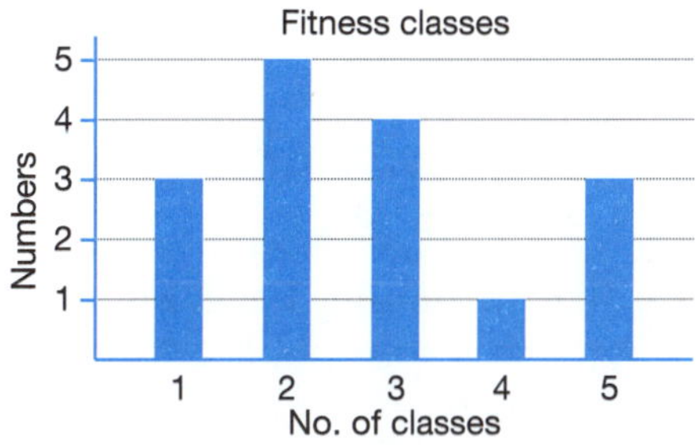

How many members attended at least three classes?

NUMBER AND ALGEBRA

1 How many factors has 25?

2 David buys a jumper for $39 and a pair of shoes for $72. Which of these is closest to the total cost?

$90 $100 $110 $120

3 Nora places 100 sheets of paper in her printer. She needs to print copies of an eight-page report. How many copies of the report can she print?

4 What is $12 \times 3 \times 8$?

5 What is $500 \div 2 - 200 \div 2$?

6 Rewrite $1\frac{3}{5}$ as an improper fraction.

7 Natalie shades $\frac{7}{12}$ of the rectangle.

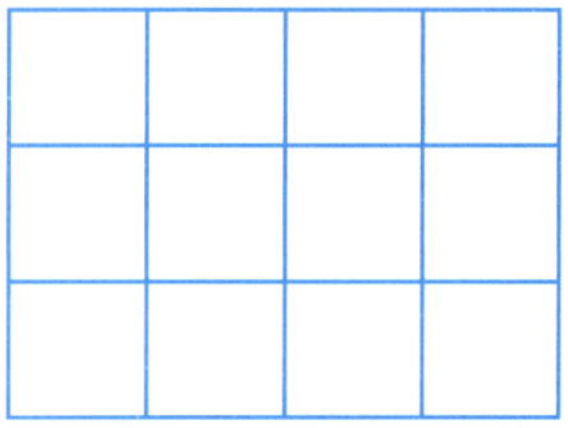

What fraction of the rectangle remains unshaded?

8 *A* and *B* have been marked on the number line.

How far apart are *A* and *B*?

9 The usual price of a pair of jeans is $79. At a sale the price is reduced by $16.65.

What is the new price?

10 Here is a pattern of decimals.

........, 7.45, 7.65, 7.85, ...

What are the two missing decimals?

11 $5 - \square = 2.74$

Find the missing number.

MEASUREMENT AND SPACE

12 How many hectares are in 180 000 m^2?

13 This morning Ethan got out of bed at half past seven. Write this time in 24-hour time.

14 This solid is cut with a knife, shown by the dotted line.

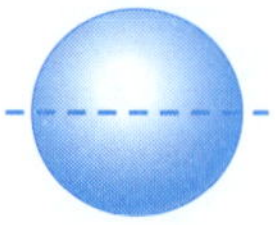

Circle the shape that is the cut face.

15 Enlarge the shape by a scale factor of 2.

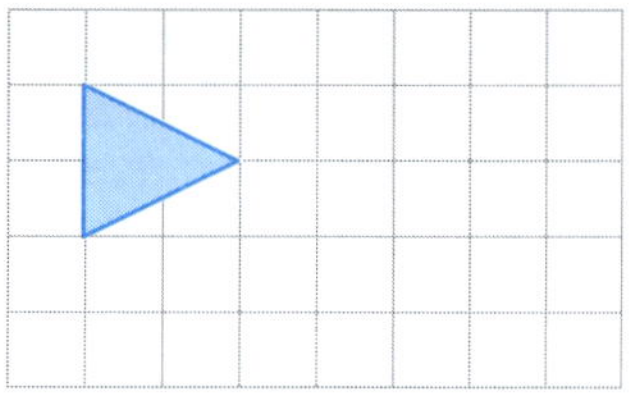

16 Here are some angles.

170° 200° 275° 300°

Circle the reflex angle(s).

STATISTICS AND PROBABILITY

17 The faces on a normal dice have been renumbered as 1, 1, 2, 3, 3, 4. The dice is rolled. What is the probability that the number on the uppermost face is a 3?

18 The number of credit cards used by a group of people is recorded.

What is the most common number of credit cards owned by people in the group?

NUMBER AND ALGEBRA

1 For fitness, Lara swims every 4 days, runs every 6 days and cycles every 16 days. If she did all activities today, in how many days will she do all three activities again on the same day?

2 Audrey wants to buy a car priced at $42 950. She adds registration costing $627, insurance of $1189, window tinting costing $712 and paint protection worth $528. Which of these is closest to the total cost?

$45 000 $45 500 $46 000

3 There are 220 people invited to a banquet. The caterer uses round tables that can seat 12 people. How many tables are needed?

4 Fiona buys a loaf of bread on Wednesdays and Sundays each week. Each loaf has 18 slices. What is the total number of slices in the loaves purchased in a year, to the nearest hundred?

5 What is 351 ÷ 5 – 336 ÷ 5?

6 How many twelfths are in $9\frac{7}{12}$?

7 Emma and Aria shade parts of the same rectangle. Emma shades one-quarter and Aria shades one-third of the rectangle. What fraction of the rectangle remains unshaded?

8 *A* and *B* have been marked on the number line.

How far apart are *A* and *B*?

9 Each week Camilla earns $1320. She pays $385 rent, and budgets $260 for food, $95 for transport, $80 for entertainment and $190 for other expenses. The remainder is saved. How much money will Camilla save in four weeks?

10 Carter uses the rule 'Start with 26 and increase by 7'. What will be the tenth number in the sequence?

11 Here is a number sentence.

25 + ☐ = 135 – 78

What is the missing number?

MEASUREMENT AND SPACE

12 What is the area, in hectares, of a rectangular park which measures 2.3 km long by 900 m wide?

13 What time is 43 minutes before 11 pm in 12-hour time?

14 This solid is cut with a knife, shown by the dotted line.

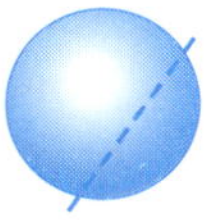

Circle the shape that is the cut face.

15 The rectangle is enlarged by a scale factor of 2. What is the area of the enlarged shape?

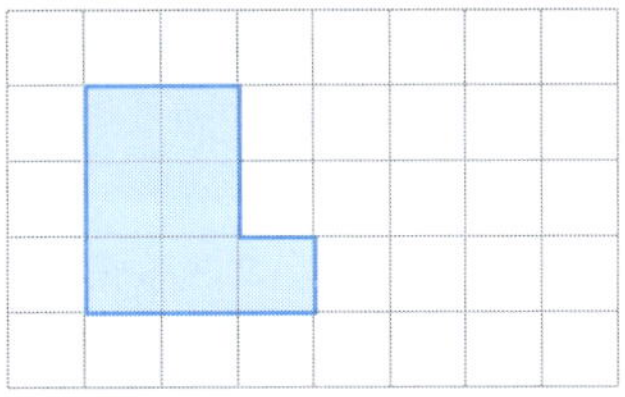

16 An analog clock shows 2:25. Aaron next checked the time at 2:55. Through what angle has the minute hand moved?

STATISTICS AND PROBABILITY

17 The faces on a normal dice have been renumbered as 1, 1, 2, 3, 3 and 4. The dice is rolled. What is the probability that the number face down on the table **is less than** 4?

18 The number of credit cards used by a group of people is recorded.

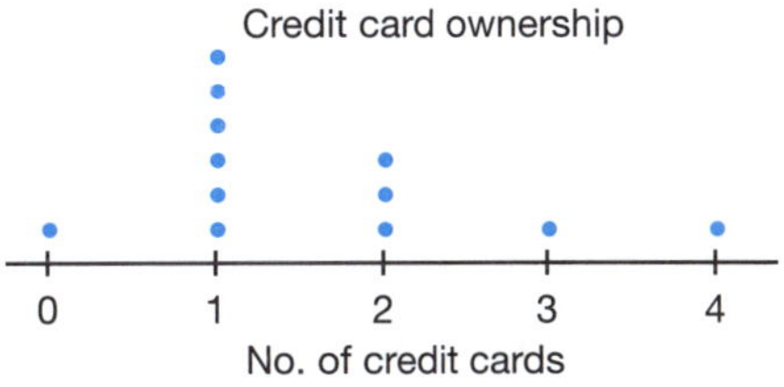

What is the total number of credit cards owned by the people in the group?

NUMBER AND ALGEBRA

1 Circle the numbers in this list that have only two factors.

9, 14, 19, 21, 23

2 Which of these rounds to 12 000, to the nearest thousand?

11.5 1201 12 678 11 541

3 An orchard has 25 rows of apple trees. Each row has 30 trees. What is the total number of trees?

4 A supermarket sells rice in 5-kg bags. How many bags are needed to have a total mass of 140 kg?

5 Complete: $16 \times 13 + 4 \times 13 = \square$

6 On the number plane, plot and label $1\frac{3}{4}$.

7 What is $\frac{2}{5} + \frac{3}{5} - \frac{1}{5}$?

8 Shade 0.6 of the rectangle.

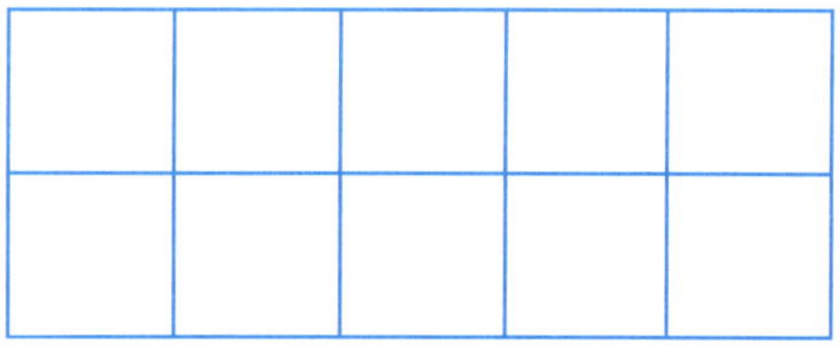

9 When Caleb works at a fast-food restaurant, he is paid $12.15 per hour. What is he paid for working 6 hours?

10 Here is a pattern of numbers.

54, 66, ..., 90, 102

Find the missing number

11 Use one of the symbols <, = or > to make a true number sentence.

$18 + 12 \square 10 + 15$

MEASUREMENT AND SPACE

12 Find the width of a rectangle with a length of 35 cm and a perimeter of 100 cm.

13 What time is 45 minutes before midnight, written in 24-hour time?

14 Here is a shape where opposite sides are the same length.

The angle *A* is a right angle. How many degrees is the angle at *C*?

15 Describe the transformation from *P* to *Q*.

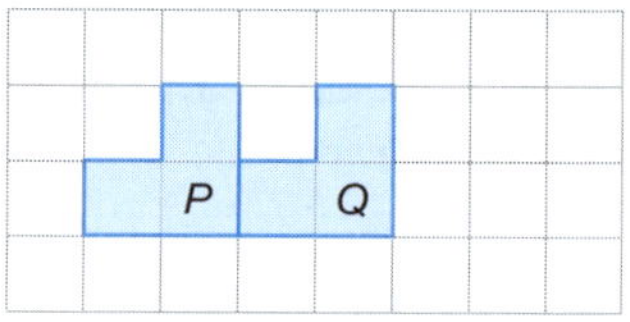

16 An analog clock shows 9:00. Allison next checked the time at 9:15. Through what angle has the minute hand moved?

STATISTICS AND PROBABILITY

17 Which of these could be the probability of an event happening? Circle the correct answer(s).

$\frac{1}{11}$ $\frac{4}{3}$ $\frac{9}{10}$ $1\frac{1}{2}$

18 The number of tickets sold for a movie is listed.

Tickets sold	
Category	**Number**
Adult	16
Child	31
Senior	13

What was the total number of tickets sold?

NUMBER AND ALGEBRA

1 Mr Jackson has to arrange 24 students in his class into different groups with an equal number of students in each. Not all students can be in one group and each group has to have more than one student. In how many ways can he form these groups?

2 Which of these is closest to 150 000?

147 683   152 321

3 A citrus farmer has 16 rows of oranges, 10 rows of mandarins and 5 rows of tangelos. If all of the rows have 36 trees, what is the total number of trees in his orchard?

4 Each team in a national sporting competition registers 30 players at the start of a season. This means a total of 480 players are registered. How many teams are in the competition?

5 Grace has a casual job and is paid $18 per hour. One week she works for 13 hours and the next week she works for 17 hours. What is her total pay for the two weeks?

6 On the number plane, plot and label $4\frac{2}{3}$.

7 What is $\frac{5}{8} + \frac{3}{8} - \frac{3}{4}$?

8 Shade 0.75 of the rectangle.

9 Abdul is given money as birthday presents from his family. He buys two games at $89.95 each and a controller for $68.50. He still has $61.60 remaining. What was the total amount of money he received for his birthday?

10 Penelope uses the rule 'Start with 500 and decrease by 12'. What is the 21st number in the sequence?

11 Here is a number sentence.

26 – ☐ = 63 ÷ 9

What is the missing number?

MEASUREMENT AND SPACE

12 The perimeter of a rectangle is 186 cm. The length of the rectangle is twice the width. What is the area of the rectangle?

13 What time is 15 minutes before 10 pm, in 24-hour time?

14 Here is a shape where two pairs of adjacent sides are the same length.

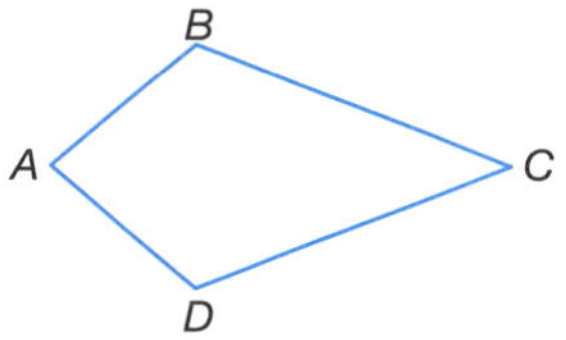

What angle is formed where the diagonals intersect?

15 Describe the transformation from *A* to *B*.

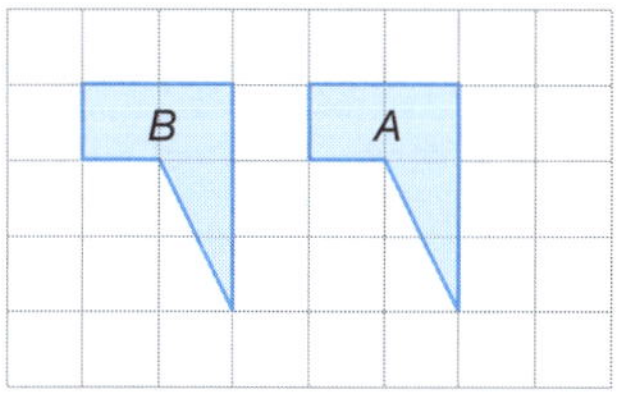

16 After Reagan cooked a pizza she sliced it into six equal slices. She measured the angle represented by each slice. What was the measurement?

STATISTICS AND PROBABILITY

17 Which of these could **not** be the probability of an event happening? Circle the correct answer(s).

$\frac{1}{11}$ 1.0001 $\frac{4}{3}$ 0.3

18 The number of tickets sold for a movie is listed.

Tickets sold	
Category	**Number**
Adult	16
Child	31
Senior	13

An adult ticket costs $12; children and seniors tickets cost $10. What was the total ticket sales?

NUMBER AND ALGEBRA

1 Circle all numbers in this list which are divisible by 5.

45, 56, 305, 1200, 55 551

2 Which of these is the closest estimate for $795 \div 4.1$?

160   200   300   600

3 Brooklyn baked 90 cakes to sell at the school market day. She sold the cakes in small boxes of four. How many boxes did she fill?

4 How many hours are in one week?

5 Find the value:
$12 \times 6 + 5 \times 6 + 3 \times 6$.

6 On the number plane, plot and label $1\frac{2}{5}$.

7 Here are two circles.

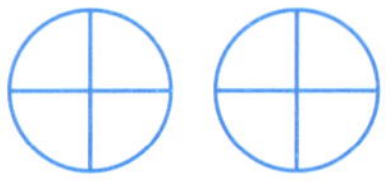

John shades three-quarters of one circle. What part is unshaded, as a mixed numeral?

8 A piece of timber is cut into three equal pieces 1.6 m long. What was the length of the original piece of timber?

9 Ryan receives 10 cents for each bottle he deposits in a recycling machine. On Wednesday he deposited 76 bottles and on Saturday another 118 bottles.

How much did he receive in total?

10 Here is a pattern of fractions.

$2\frac{1}{4}, 2\frac{2}{4}, 2\frac{3}{4}$, ..., ...

What are the **two** missing numbers?

11 Use one of the symbols <, = or > to make a true number sentence.

37 – 20 ☐ 9 × 2

MEASUREMENT AND SPACE

12 A square has a perimeter of 48 cm. What is the area of the square?

13 Sophia's school bell rings at 3:10 pm and one hour later she starts her maths tutoring. What time, in 24-hour time, does her tutoring start?

14 Here is a shape where opposite sides are the same length. What angle is the same size as angle *B*?

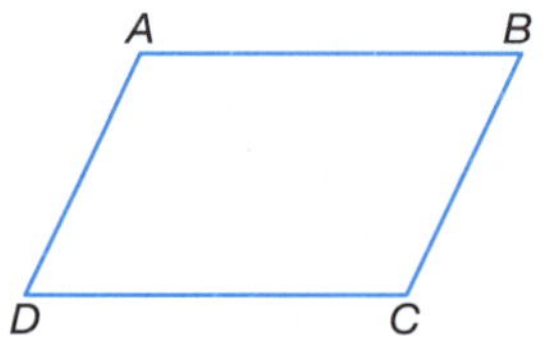

15 Describe the transformation from *S* to *T*.

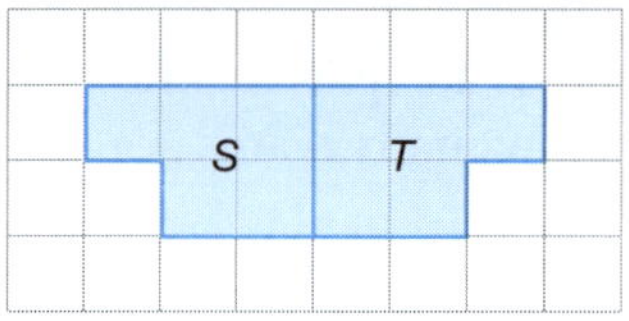

16 Hailey is facing east. She turns around and faces west. Through how many degrees has she rotated?

STATISTICS AND PROBABILITY

17 Here are three spinners. Circle the spinner which gives the highest probability of landing on 3.

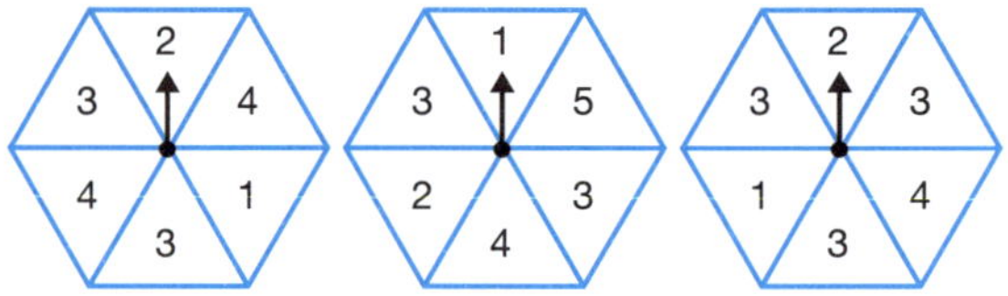

18 A group of people were surveyed regarding their favourite citrus fruit.

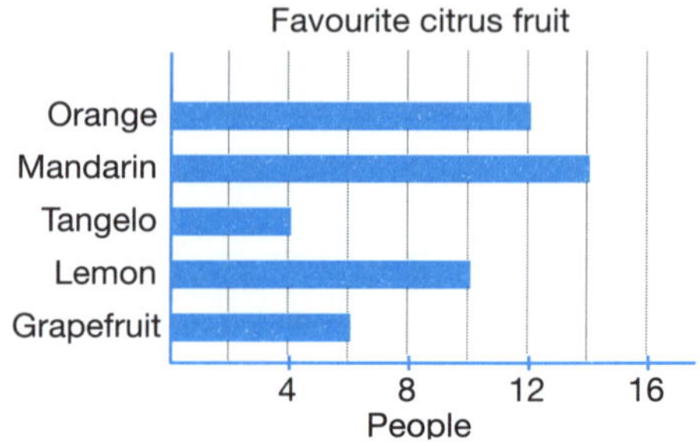

How many more people nominated mandarin than tangelo?

NUMBER AND ALGEBRA

1 Rob has two ropes. One is 60 m long and the other is 48 m long. He wants to cut them in such a way that all the pieces are equal but as long as possible. How many pieces of rope will Rob get?

2 Which of these is the closest estimate for 504 × 31?

16 000 19 000 23 000 150 000

3 A normal deck has 52 cards. A game is played with two decks of cards. All the cards are dealt out to each of the players, with every player receiving 6 cards. Two cards are left over. How many people are playing the game?

4 How many days are in the last six months of the year?

5 Steel balls with a mass of 240 g each are handed to three girls. Audrey has 12 balls, Ella has 16 balls and Mia has 22 balls. What is the total mass of the balls, in kg?

6 On the number plane, plot and label $4\frac{5}{6}$.

7 Nora uses shapes and shading to help her work out $2\frac{1}{2} - \frac{3}{4}$. What is her working and answer?

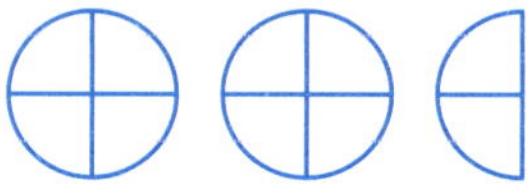

8 Write, as a decimal, the part of the rectangle that has been shaded.

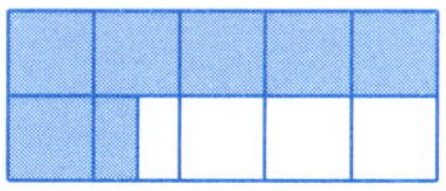

9 Coco and Jason buy their lunch from the same shop. Coco orders a wrap and an iced tea and pays $7.50. Jason orders two wraps for $9.80. What is the price of the iced tea?

10 Here is a pattern of decimals.

........, 5.898, 5.873, 5.848, ...

What are the **two** missing decimals?

11 Jack thought of a number ☐. Three times the number is the same as the sum of 12 and 18.

Using Jack's number ☐ and symbols, write a number sentence and find his number.

MEASUREMENT AND SPACE

12 A square paddock is to be fenced. The cost of fencing is $9 per metre. If the total cost of fencing is $864, what is the area of the paddock?

13 How much time is there between 1115 and 1340?

14 In the triangle, sides *AB* and *BC* are the same length.

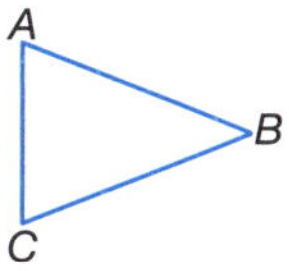

Which two angles are the same size?

15 Describe the transformation from *X* to *Y*.

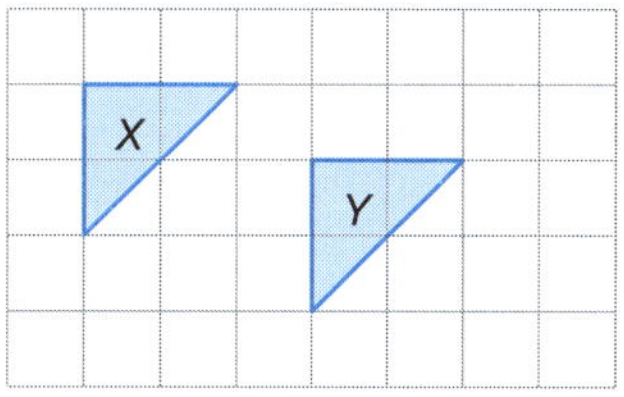

16 Jeremiah baked a circular birthday cake. He cut the cake into 12 equal slices. Three slices were removed. He measured the angle represented by the remaining cake. What was the measurement?

STATISTICS AND PROBABILITY

17 Here are three spinners. Circle the spinner which gives the highest probability of landing on a 2.

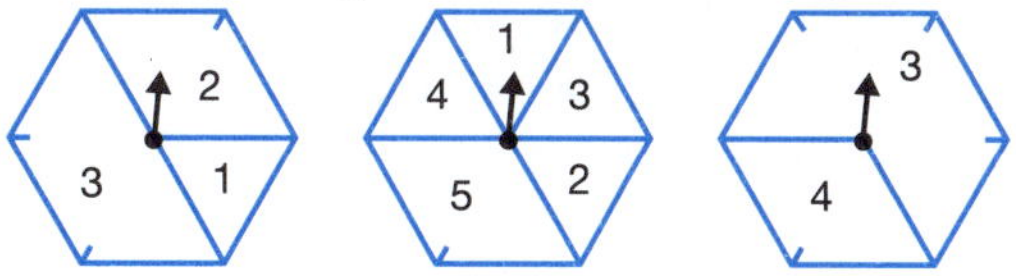

18 A group of people were surveyed regarding their favourite citrus fruit.

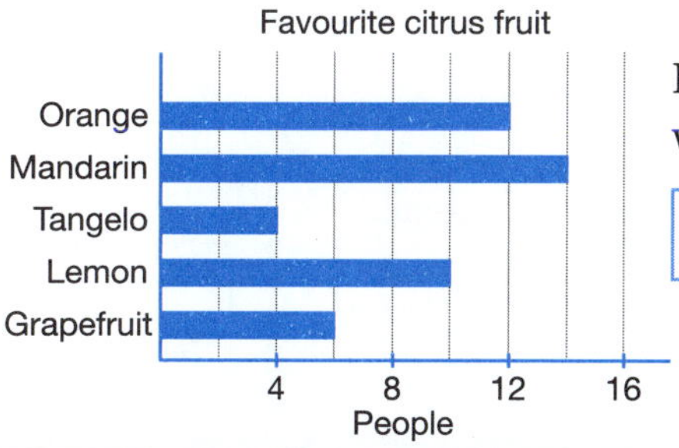

How many people were surveyed?

NUMBER AND ALGEBRA

1 What number am I? I am a multiple of 4. I am more than 10 but less than 30. My digits add up to 6.

2 Sofia recorded the distances she drove each of three days: M 176 km, T 191 km and W 207 km. What is the total distance she drove?

3 Grayson has a collection of matchbox cars. He arranges the cars in 12 rows of 16 cars. How many cars are in Grayson's collection?

4 Lucas had 115 tomato plants arranged in five equal rows. How many plants did he have in each row?

5 What is half the sum of 25 and 15?

6 Express $\frac{35}{8}$ as a mixed numeral.

7 Here are two circles.

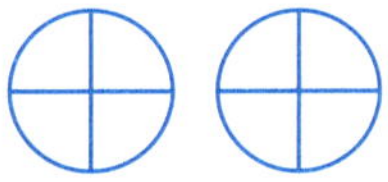

John shades $1\frac{3}{4}$ circles. What part is unshaded, as a fraction?

8 What decimal is halfway between 3.6 and 4.6?

9 Isaiah is going camping and buys a sleeping bag for $79.90, a torch for $11.25 and a backpack for $89. What was the total amount he spent?

10 Find the first four numbers in the sequence 'Starting with 170 and decreasing by 30'.

11 Use one of the symbols <, = or > to make a true number sentence.

106 – 37 ☐ 48 + 21

MEASUREMENT AND SPACE

12 Find the perimeter of the shape.

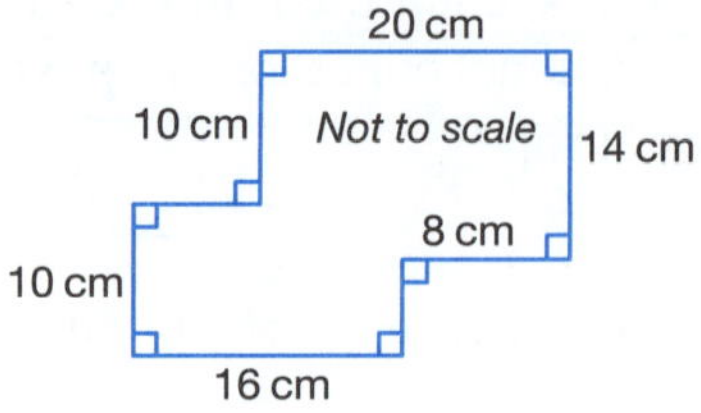

13 Last night Owen went to bed at 2121. What is this in 12-hour time?

14 The parallelogram below is not drawn to scale.

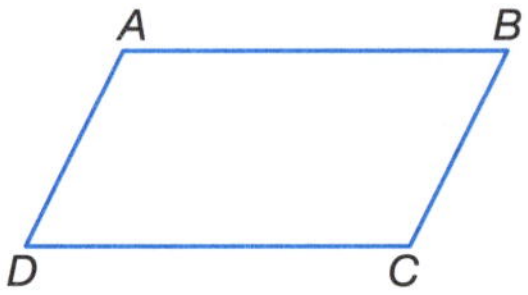

The length of side *AB* is 12 cm and the length of *BC* is 8 cm.

What is the perimeter of the parallelogram?

15 A square has a side length of 3 cm. The square is enlarged by a scale factor of 2. What is the perimeter of the new square?

16 Here are four angles. Circle any angles that measure more than 90°.

STATISTICS AND PROBABILITY

17 A spinner has four sections which are numbered.

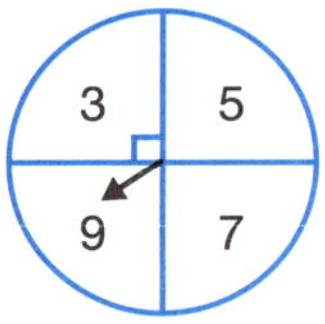

What is the probability of spinning a number less than 5?

18 The number of home streaming subscriptions of a group of people is graphed.

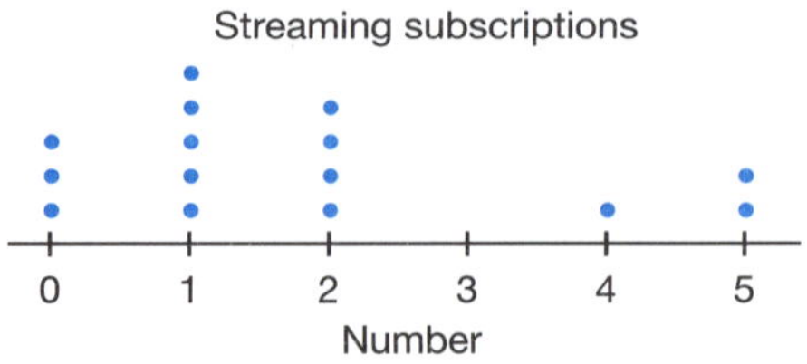

How many people have four streaming subscriptions in their home?

NUMBER AND ALGEBRA

1 For his market food stall, Sam wants to buy an equal number of hot dogs and bread rolls. Hot dogs can be purchased in packets of 15 and bread rolls are available in packets of 12. What is the smallest number of packets of hot dogs Sam will buy?

2 A car company recorded the sales of new cars over 6 months: 8910, 9167, 11 871, 16 412, 13 987 and 12 704. What is the total number of sales?

3 Levi has 16 jigsaw boxes in his cupboard. Eight of the jigsaws have 750 pieces, five have 1000 pieces and the remainder have 1500 pieces. What is the total number of jigsaw pieces?

4 During the COVID-19 pandemic, social distancing regulations meant that restaurants had a 4 m^2 rule for each seated customer. Dimmy's Restaurant has a seating area of 136 m^2. What is the maximum number of customers that could be seated?

5 What is a quarter of the sum of 36, 56 and 64?

6 Express $\frac{4372}{9}$ as a mixed numeral.

7 Nora uses shapes and shading to help her work out $2\frac{1}{3} - 1\frac{2}{3}$. What is her working and answer?

8 What decimal is halfway between 2.8 and 3.12?

9 A street vendor sells fruit. Bananas cost 80 cents each and apples 70 cents each. Stacey buys three bananas, four apples and two mandarins. She hands the vendor $10 and receives $3.60 in change. What is the cost of a mandarin?

10 Here is a pattern of numbers.

......, 356, 337, 318, ...

What are the **two** missing numbers?

11 Layla thought of a number ☐. The sum of Layla's number and 43 is the same as the difference between 82 and 11. Using Layla's number and symbols, write a number sentence and find her number.

MEASUREMENT AND SPACE

12 Find the area of the shape.

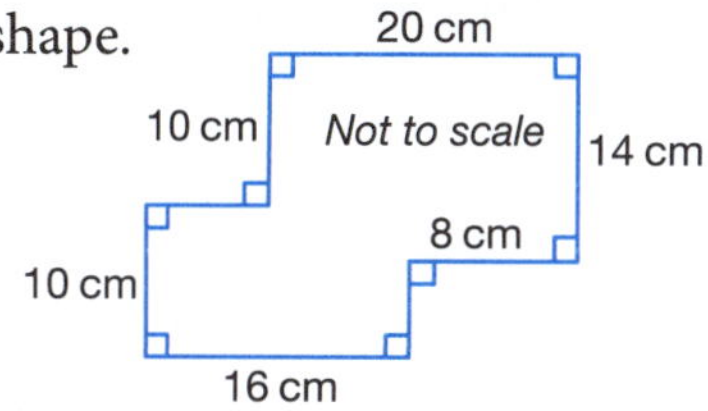

13 Amelia caught the train from Holmesville to Arcadia. The journey took 3 hours and 25 minutes. If the train arrived in Arcadia at 1310, what time had it left Holmesville?

14 The parallelogram below is not drawn to scale.

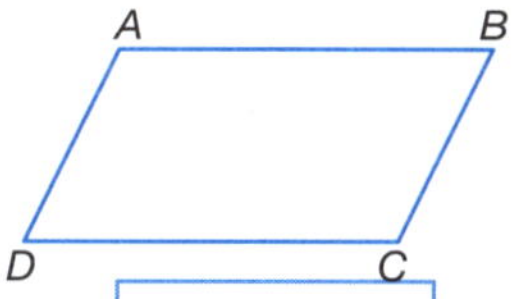

If the length of side *AB* is 12 cm and the length of *BC* is 8 cm, which of these is the best estimate for the length of diagonal *BD*?

21 cm 17 cm 11 cm 7 cm

15 A rectangle has a length of 12 cm and an area of 96 cm^2. The rectangle is to be enlarged by a factor of 5. What is the perimeter of the new rectangle, in metres?

16 Kylie faced south-east. She rotated 225° in an anticlockwise direction. What direction is she now facing?

STATISTICS AND PROBABILITY

17 A spinner has been split into three sections. What is the probability of spinning a number 3?

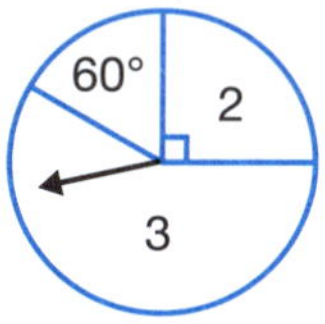

18 The number of home streaming subscriptions of a group of people is graphed. What is the total number of subscriptions?

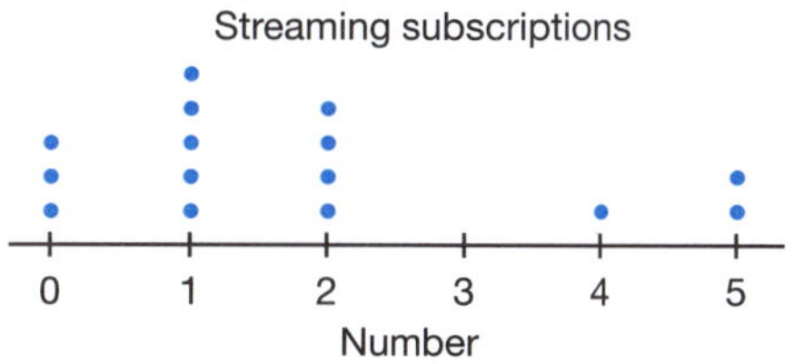

NAPLAN-STYLE TEST 2

1 Which of these shows the time at twenty to nine last night?

A 1740 B 1840 C 1940 D 2040

2 Here are four decimals written on cards.

3.4 3.28 3.047 3.36

Rearrange the cards in ascending order.

3 Arthur spent $96 on shrubs at a sale.
All the shrubs were the same price.
Which of these is a possible number of shrubs purchased?
Select **all** possible answers.

6	9	12	16	18
A	B	C	D	E

4 Hannah used this net to make a cube where opposite faces add to the same total.

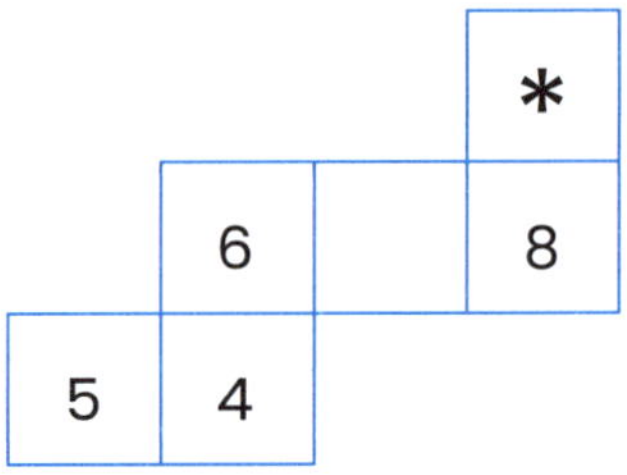

What is the number represented by *?

5 Here is a pattern of numbers.

16, 22, 28, 34 …

The pattern continues. Which of these numbers is in the pattern?
Select **all** possible numbers.

48	50	52	54	58
A	B	C	D	E

6 Here is a number sentence with a missing number.

$\square \div 6 = 12 + 18$

What is the missing number?

7 A box contains red balls and blue balls. There are twice as many blue balls as there are red balls in the box. A ball is chosen at random from the box.

What is the probability that it is red?

8 The grid below shows the location of a disc *X* at F6.

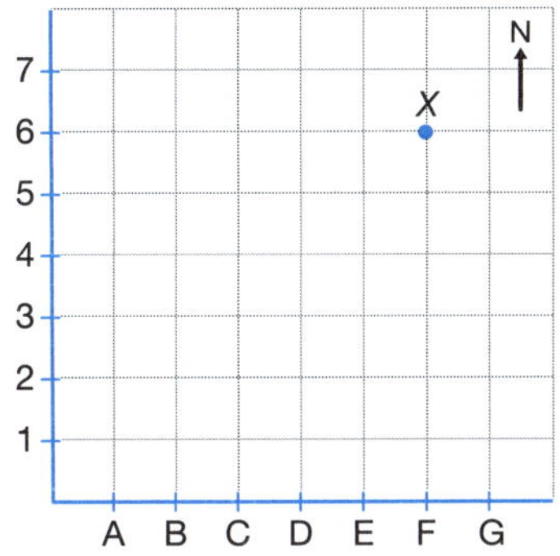

Bella moved the disc 5 units west, 4 units south, 3 units east and ☐ units north to *Y*. *Y* is south-west of *X*.

What number is represented by ☐ ?

9 What is this shape? Select **all** possible answers.

A scalene triangle

B isosceles triangle

C right-angled triangle

D equilateral triangle

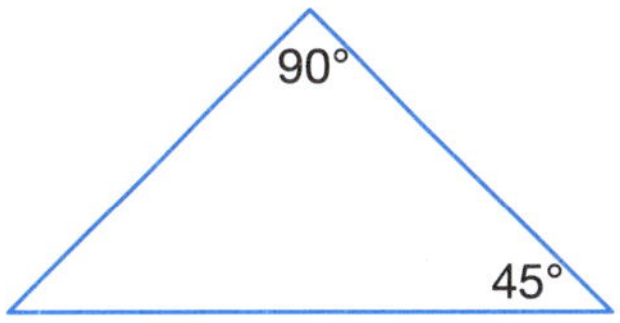

10 A primary school has four sports houses: Cyclone, Hurricane, Tornado and Typhoon. The final point score for the swimming carnival is shown below. The points for Tornado are missing.

Swimming carnival	
House	**Points**
Cyclone	384
Hurricane	397
Tornado	
Typhoon	411
Total	**1600**

Which house came second?

A Cyclone B Hurricane C Tornado D Typhoon

11 A protractor is used to measure an obtuse angle.

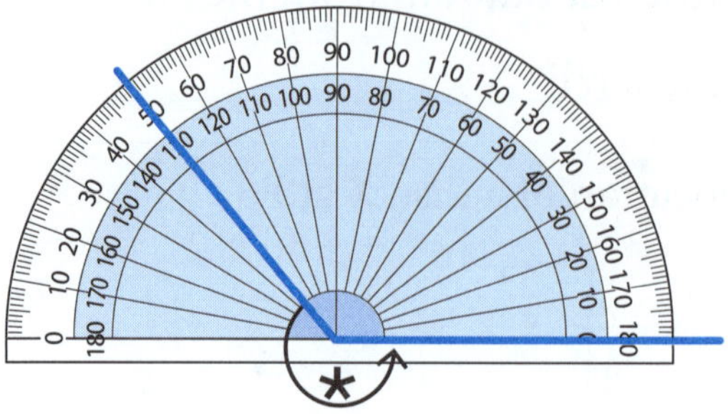

What is the size of the reflex angle marked as *? [ ] degrees

---

12 A number line is shown below.

What decimal is represented by *X*?

A 4.105 **B** 4.15 **C** 4.25 **D** 4.3

---

13 One adult ticket and two child tickets to the circus cost $62.

Two adult tickets cost $52.

What is the cost of one adult and three child tickets? $ [ ]

---

14 Simon has two identical square-based pyramids.

He glues the bases of the pyramids together to make a new solid.

How many edges has the new solid? [ ]

---

15 Stevie starts with a number.

She multiplies her number by 3 and then subtracts 25. The result is 23.

What was Stevie's starting number? [ ]

---

16 At the start of a school year Loukia buys four notebooks at $2.99 each, three pens at $2.10 each and an external hard drive at $79.95.

Which of these gives the best estimate for the total price paid?

A $85 **B** $90 **C** $95 **D** $100

17 A group of students were surveyed to find the number of pets they have at home. The results are shown on the dot plot.

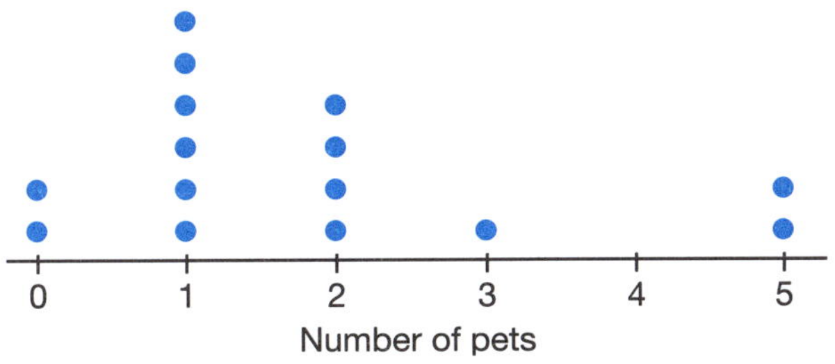

What was the total number of pets?

18 The shape is to be reflected about the mirror line. Which of these will not be hidden by the image of the reflected shape? Select **all** possible answers.

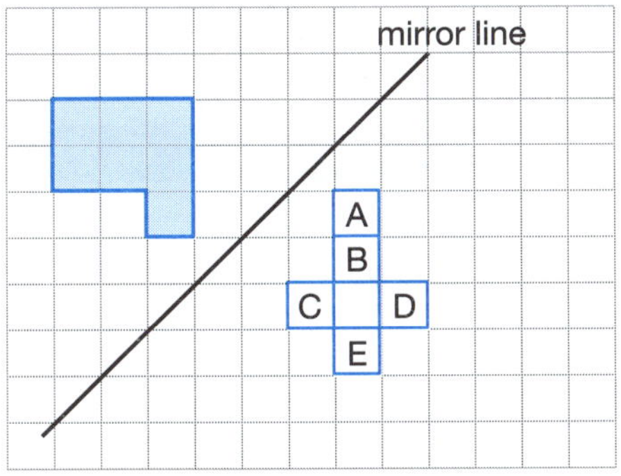

A A

B B

C C

D D

E E

19 A bag contains 10 identically sized marbles. Five of the marbles are red, two are blue and the remainder green. A marble is chosen at random.

The colour of the marble is recorded and the marble returned to the bag. This occurs a total of 50 times.

What is the expected number of times a green marble is chosen?

20 Three squares are drawn on grid paper.

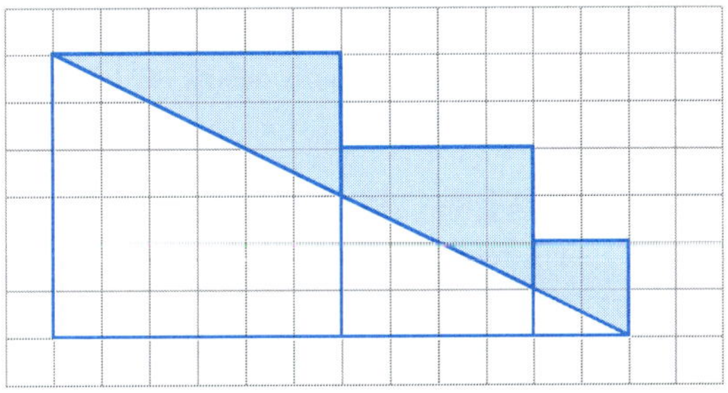

The areas of the squares are 36 units^2, 16 units^2 and 4 units^2.

A part of each square is shaded. What is the area of the shaded section? units^2

WORKED SOLUTIONS & ANSWERS

Section 1

Unit 1A PAGE 10

1. **6 thousand**
   The number is sixteen thousand and forty-three. The value of the 6 is 6 thousand, or 6000.
2. **8 ten-thousand**
   The number is three hundred and eighty-six thousand and nine. The value of the 8 is 8 ten thousand, or 80 000.
3. **4 thousand**
   Multiplying by 10 means a 0 is placed at the end of the original number. The new number is 674 520. The value of the 4 is 4 thousand, or 4000.
4. **2**
   The number is 80 402. There are 2 zeros.
5. **24, 36**
   The 6 times table gives the numbers 6, 12, 18, 24, 30, 36, 42, 48 … From the list the numbers are 24 and 36.
6. **63, 49, 7**
   The 7 times table gives the numbers 7, 14, 21, 28, 35, 42, 56, 63, 70 … From the list the numbers are 63, 49 and 7.
7. **5**
   The 4 times table gives the numbers 4, 8, 12, 16, 20, 24, 28, **32**, **36**, **40**, **44**, **48** … There are 5 multiples.
8. **128**

$$\begin{array}{r} 314 \\ -\ 186 \\ \hline 128 \end{array}$$

   Judi still has 128 pages to read.
9. **40 786**

$$\begin{array}{r} 37\,658 \\ +\ \ 3\,128 \\ \hline 40\,786 \end{array}$$

   The odometer showed 40 786 km.
10. **180**
   71 is close to 70, 48 is close to 50 and 57 is close to 60. As 70 + 50 + 60 = 180, they have about 180 friends, to the nearest 10.
11. **400**
   712 is close to 700 and 293 is close to 300. As 700 – 300 is 400, the closest number is 400.
12. **13 583**
   13 583 is 13 thousand, five hundred and eighty-three. As the number includes 'five hundred' then the number is rounded to 14 thousand.
13. **196 km**

$$\begin{array}{r} 28 \\ \times\ \ 7 \\ \hline 196 \end{array}$$

   Tobias plans to walk 196 km.
14. **68 152**

$$\begin{array}{r} 9736 \\ \times\ \ \ \ 7 \\ \hline 68\,152 \end{array}$$

15. **52 110**
   Multiply 579 by 9 and then multiply by 10 (by writing a 0 on the end).

$$\begin{array}{r} 579 \\ \times\ \ \ 9 \\ \hline 5211 \end{array}$$

   This means the answer is 52 110.
16. **223 792**

$$\begin{array}{r} 27\,974 \\ \times\ \ \ \ 8 \\ \hline 223\,792 \end{array}$$

   The total attendance was 223 792.
17. **350**
   25 × 2 is 50 and 50 × 7 is 350. This means 25 × 2 × 7 = 350.
18. **168**

$$\begin{array}{r} 14 \\ \times\ 12 \\ \hline 168 \end{array}$$

   Jasper has 168 cars in his collection.
19. **85**
   You need to work out 425 ÷ 5. 425 = 400 + 25. 400 ÷ 5 = 80 and 25 ÷ 5 = 5. This means 425 ÷ 5 = 85.
20. **123**
   369 = 300 + 60 + 9. 300 ÷ 3 is 100, 60 ÷ 3 is 20 and 9 ÷ 3 is 3 so 369 ÷ 3 = 123
21. **142**
   1420 ÷ 10 is 142. This means 142 bags will be needed.
22. **2**
   7 × 5 is 35 so 7 × 5 + 2 is 37. The remainder is 2.
23. **79**
   The missing number is 316 ÷ 4. 316 = 280 + 36. 280 ÷ 4 is 70 and 36 ÷ 4 is 9 so 316 ÷ 4 = 79. Mark's original number was 79.
24. **28**
   115 = 100 + 15. 100 ÷ 4 is 25 and 15 ÷ 4 is 3, with remainder 3. As 25 + 3 = 28, Brielle can fill 28 boxes.
25. **160**
   To get from 16 to 8 is dividing by 2. Now dividing 320 by 2 gives 160. The missing number is 160.
26. **846**
   When adding 99 it is easier to add 100 and then subtract 1. 747 + 100 – 1 is 847 – 1 = 846.
27. **3861**
   As 99 is 100 – 1, work out 100 × 39 and then subtract 39. Now 100 × 39 is 3900 and 3900 – 39 is 3861.
28. **820**
   Both 14 and 6 are being multiplied by 41. As 14 + 6 = 20, then 20 × 41, or 41 × 20 is 820.

Unit 1B PAGE 11

1. **3300**
   In 1390, the 3 is 300. In 23 891, the 3 is 3000. As 3000 + 300 is 3300, the sum is 3300.
2. **89 100**
   In 190 231, the 9 is 90 000. In 128 970, the 9 is 900. You need to subtract 900 from 90 000.

$$\begin{array}{r} {}^{89\ 1}\\ \not{9}\not{0}\,000 \\ -\ \ \ 900 \\ \hline 89\,100 \end{array}$$

3. **50 000**
   123456789 can be rewritten as 123 456 789. The place value of the 5 is 50 000, or 50 thousand.
4. **4**
   The number is 70 360 009. There are 4 zeros.
5. **30, 60, 90**
   2, 3 and 5 are factors of 30, so look for numbers divisible by 30. From the list 30, 60 and 90 are divisible by 30 and so are divisible by 2, 3 and 5.
6. **5**
   536 is divisible by 8. 536 – 8 = 528, 528 – 8 = 520, 520 – 8 = 512. Also, 536 + 8 = 544. There are 5 numbers.
7. **10**
   First 30 × 2 = 60, so look for numbers up to 60. Numbers that are divisible by 2 and 3 are divisible by 6. As 60 ÷ 6 is 10, there must be 10 common numbers.

8. **2720 km**

$$\begin{array}{r} 3556 \\ -\ 836 \\ \hline 2720 \\ \hline \end{array}$$

The difference is 2720 km.

9. **207 572**

$$\begin{array}{r} 187\,693 \\ +\ 19\,879 \\ \hline 207\,572 \\ \hline \end{array}$$

The population of the city in 2021 was 207 572.

10. **2300 m^2**

517 is close to 500, 587 is close to 600, 595 is close to 600 and 613 is close to 600. As 5 + 6 + 6 + 6 is 23, the total is close to 2300 m^2.

11. **22 000**

56 191 is close to 56 000 and 33 894 is close to 34 000. As 56 – 34 is 22, the closest answer is 22 000.

12. **238 563**

$$\begin{array}{r} 250\,000 \\ -\ 238\,563 \\ \hline 11\,437 \\ \hline \end{array} \qquad \begin{array}{r} 261\,445 \\ -250\,000 \\ \hline 11\,445 \\ \hline \end{array}$$

As 11 437 is smaller than 11 445, then 238 563 is closer.

13. **954**

$$\begin{array}{r} 53 \\ \times\ \ 18 \\ \hline 424 \\ 530 \\ \hline 954 \\ \hline \end{array}$$

The buses can transport 954 passengers.

14. **1008**

$$\begin{array}{r} 42 \\ \times\ \ 24 \\ \hline 168 \\ 840 \\ \hline 1008 \\ \hline \end{array}$$

There is a total of 1008 daffodil bulbs.

15. **167 900**

Multiply 73 by 23 and write two more 0s on the end of the answer.

$$\begin{array}{r} 73 \\ \times\ \ 23 \\ \hline 219 \\ 1460 \\ \hline 1679 \\ \hline \end{array}$$

This means the answer is 167 900.

16. **18 060**

Multiply 86 by 21 and write one zero at the end of the answer.

$$\begin{array}{r} 86 \\ \times\ \ 21 \\ \hline 86 \\ 1720 \\ \hline 1806 \\ \hline \end{array}$$

The total number of passengers was 18060, which is written as 18 060.

17. **152 km**

You need to find 19 × 2 × 4. As 19 × 2 is 38, and 38 × 4 is 152, Nolan rides 152 km.

18. **14 500**

15 – 6 – 7 is 2. This means the total number of pieces is 750 × 6 + 1000 × 7 + 1500 × 2, which is 4500 + 7000 + 3000. This is a total of 14 500 pieces.

19. **242**

$$9\overline{)2178}\ \to\ 242$$

There will be 242 bales on each truck.

20. **$570**

As 16 + 14 is 30, you need to multiply 19 by 30. As 19 × 30 is 570, her total pay is $570.

21. **3**

8 ÷ 4 is 2 so 80 ÷ 4 is 20. As 83 = 20 × 4 + 3, the remainder is 3.

22. **3627**

$$8\overline{)29\,016}\ \to\ 3627$$

There will be 3627 packets.

23. **1843**

$$4\overline{)7375}\ \to\ 1843\ \text{r}\ 3$$

The winery could make 1843 gift packs.

24. **406**

Dividing 21 by 3 gives 7. Now dividing 1218 by 3 gives 406. The missing number is 406.

Unit 2A PAGE 12

1.

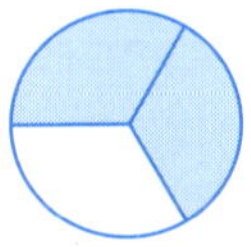

2. $\frac{1}{10}$

Each fraction has 1 as the numerator (top number). The higher the denominator (bottom number), the smaller the fraction. The smallest is $\frac{1}{10}$ and the largest is $\frac{1}{3}$.

3. $\frac{6}{6}$ **and** $\frac{3}{3}$

When the numerator (top number) is the same as the denominator (bottom number) the fraction is equal to 1 (or one whole).

4. $\frac{11}{4}$

There are 4 quarters in 1 whole.

In $2\frac{3}{4}$ there are 4 × 2 + 3 quarters.

This means there are 8 + 3 = 11 quarters, written as $\frac{11}{4}$.

5. **See below.**

Rewrite $\frac{3}{2}$ as a mixed numeral. How many 2s go into 3 … 1 and 1 left over. This means $\frac{3}{2} = 1\frac{1}{2}$. Shade 1 whole shape and $\frac{1}{2}$ of another (3 squares).

6. $\frac{5}{8}$

The square has been spilt into 8 equal triangles. Three out of 8 or $\frac{3}{8}$ of the square is shaded. This means that $\frac{5}{8}$ is not shaded.

7. ***B***

The number line from 0 to 1 is broken into eighths.

$\frac{5}{8}$ is represented by the letter *B*.

8. $\frac{7}{10}$

As 3 + 4 is 7, then $\frac{3}{10} + \frac{4}{10} = \frac{7}{10}$.

9. $\frac{11}{15}$

One whole is 15 fifteenths. 15 fifteenths minus 4 fifteenths is 11 fifteenths. This is written as $\frac{15}{15} - \frac{4}{15} = \frac{11}{15}$.

10. $\frac{2}{5}$

One whole is 5 fifths. 5 fifths minus 3 fifths is 2 fifths. This is written as $\frac{5}{5} - \frac{3}{5} = \frac{2}{5}$.

11. $\frac{3}{10}$

The missing fraction is the difference between 1 and $\frac{7}{10}$, which is $\frac{10}{10} - \frac{7}{10}$.

10 tenths minus 7 tenths is 3 tenths.

This is written as $1 - \frac{3}{10} = \frac{7}{10}$.

12. $2\frac{1}{4}$

As 3 + 3 + 3 is 9, then $\frac{3}{4} + \frac{3}{4} + \frac{3}{4} = \frac{9}{4}$.

Rewriting this improper fraction as a mixed numeral is $2\frac{1}{4}$.

13. $1\frac{3}{8}$

As $\frac{7}{8} - \frac{4}{8}$ is $\frac{3}{8}$, then $1\frac{7}{8} - \frac{4}{8}$ is $1\frac{3}{8}$.

14. 0.413

Place value is … units, decimal point, tenths, hundredths, thousandths … There will be three decimal places in $\frac{413}{1000}$. This means $\frac{413}{1000} = 0.413$.

15. 40

Four hundredths is written as 0.04. This is the same as 0.040. This means that 4 hundredths is 40 thousandths.

16. 30.21

To compare, rewrite each decimal with two decimal places: 13.29, 29.31, 29.70, 30.21. As 30.21 is only 21 hundredths from 30.00 it is the closest.

17. 3 thousandths

Both numbers are identical except the digit in the third decimal place (thousandths). The difference is 3 thousandths.

18. 4.53

You need to start with 4, followed by the decimal point, then 5 and then 3. The number is 4.53.

19. 0.51

As 14 + 37 is 51, then $\frac{14}{100} + \frac{37}{100}$ is $\frac{51}{100}$. This is written as 0.51.

20. 7.805

Rewrite the decimals with three decimal places: 7.800 and 7.810. Halfway between 800 and 810 is 805. This means the decimal is 7.805.

21. 4.309, 4.379, 4.38

Rewrite the decimals with three decimal places: 4.380, 4.309, 4.379. Now compare the last three digits in each decimal: from smallest to largest is 309, 379, 380. This means the order is 4.309, 4.379, 4.38.

22. *B*

The number line is marked in 0.2s. *B* is between 2.6 and 2.8 which can be written as 2.60 and 2.80. As 75 is between 60 and 80, then *B* is closest to 2.75.

23. 92.4

Take care with place value.

87 + 5 is 92 so 87.4 + 5 = 92.4.

24. 13.43

There is a 6 in the third decimal place. As 6 > 5, the 2 in the second decimal place increases by 1. The answer is 13.43.

25. 1.94

$$\begin{array}{r} 1.60 \\ +\,0.34 \\ \hline 1.94 \end{array}$$

26. $\frac{7}{1000}$

0.007 is 7 thousandths, which is written as $\frac{7}{1000}$.

Unit 2B PAGE 13

1.

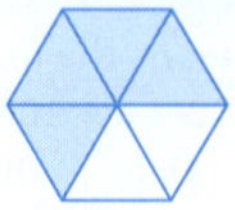

2. $\frac{1}{10}, \frac{1}{8}, \frac{1}{5}, \frac{1}{3}$

Each fraction has 1 as the numerator (top number). The higher the denominator (bottom number), the smaller the fraction. The numbers in the denominator from largest to smallest is 10, 8, 5, 3, so that the order is $\frac{1}{10}, \frac{1}{8}, \frac{1}{5}, \frac{1}{3}$.

3. $\frac{3}{5}$ and $\frac{3}{4}$

When the numerator (top number) is smaller than the denominator (bottom number), the fraction is smaller than 1.

4. 18

There are two quarters in one half. You need to change $4\frac{2}{4}$ into an improper fraction. 4 times 4 is 16 plus 2 is 18. This means 18 quarters of orange.

5. See below.

Rewrite $\frac{7}{3}$ as a mixed numeral. How many times does 3 go into 7? 2 and 1 left over. This means $\frac{7}{3} = 2\frac{1}{3}$.

Shade 2 whole shapes and $\frac{1}{3}$ of another (2 squares).

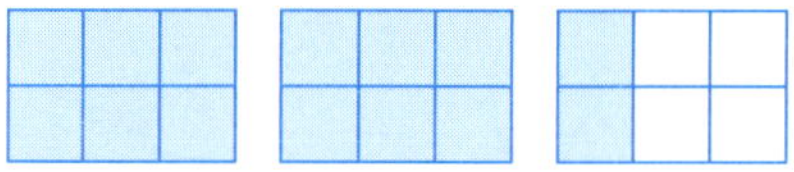

6. $\frac{7}{8}$

The square has been spilt into eight equal triangles. One out of 8 or $\frac{1}{8}$ of the square is shaded. This means that $\frac{7}{8}$ is not shaded.

7. *B*

Rewrite $\frac{18}{5}$ as a mixed numeral. How many 5s are in 18? 3 and 3 left over. This means $\frac{18}{5} = 3\frac{3}{5}$, which is represented by *B*.

8. $1\frac{5}{8}$

As 7 + 6 is 13, then $\frac{7}{8} + \frac{6}{8} = \frac{13}{8}$.

How many 8s are in 13? 1 and 5 left over. This means $\frac{13}{8} = 1\frac{5}{8}$.

9. $\frac{583}{1000}$

One whole is 1000 thousandths. As 1000 – 417 is 583, then 1000 thousandths minus 417 thousandths is 583 thousandths. This is written as $\frac{1000}{1000} - \frac{417}{1000} = \frac{583}{1000}$.

10. $\frac{9}{20}$

$\frac{7}{20} + \frac{4}{20}$ is $\frac{11}{20}$. This means she will have $1 - \frac{11}{20}$ of the book unread.

As $\frac{20}{20} - \frac{11}{20}$ is $\frac{9}{20}$, Tacoma will have $\frac{9}{20}$ of the book remaining.

11. $\frac{17}{45}$

The missing fraction is the difference between 1 and $\frac{28}{45}$, which is $\frac{45}{45} - \frac{28}{45}$.

As 45 – 28 is 17 then $\frac{45}{45} - \frac{28}{45}$ is $\frac{17}{45}$.

The missing fraction is $\frac{17}{45}$.

12. $3\frac{3}{4}$ km

$\frac{3}{4} + \frac{3}{4} + \frac{3}{4} + \frac{3}{4} + \frac{3}{4}$ is $\frac{15}{4}$. Rewriting this improper fraction as a mixed numeral is $3\frac{3}{4}$. Chloe walks a total of $3\frac{3}{4}$ km.

13. $3\frac{3}{5}$ metres

Rewrite $4\frac{1}{5}$ as an improper fraction. As 5 × 4 + 1 is 21, then $4\frac{1}{5}$ is $\frac{21}{5}$. Now, $\frac{21}{5} - \frac{3}{5}$ is $\frac{18}{5}$, which is $3\frac{3}{5}$. The length of the remaining pipe is $3\frac{3}{5}$ metres.

14. 5.009

Place value is … units, decimal point, tenths, hundredths, thousandths … There will be three decimal places in $\frac{9}{1000}$. This means $\frac{9}{1000} = 0.009$, and so $5\frac{9}{1000}$ is 5.009.

15. 5100

51 tenths is written as $5\frac{1}{10}$ or 5.1. This is the same as 5.100. This means that 51 tenths is 5100 thousandths.

16. 22.92

To compare, rewrite each decimal with three decimal places: 23.400, 23.087, 22.920, 22.908. So, 23.4 is 400 thousandths from 23, 23.087 is 87 thousandths from 23, 22.92 is 80 thousandths from 23 and 22.908 is 92 thousandths from 23. This means that 22.92 is the closest.

17. 25 thousandths

The first part of each decimal is the same but the last two digits are different. As 99 – 74 is 25, the difference is 25 thousandths.

18. **8.345**

You need to start with 8, followed by the decimal point, then the 3, then the 4 and then 5. The number is 8.345.

19. **0.551**

$\frac{5}{10}$ is the same fraction as $\frac{500}{1000}$ and $\frac{3}{100}$ is the same as $\frac{30}{1000}$. The question is $\frac{500}{1000} + \frac{21}{1000} + \frac{30}{1000}$. As 500 + 21 + 30 is 551, the answer is $\frac{551}{1000}$, which is 0.551.

20. **14.635**

The numbers can be written as 14.630 and 14.640. The middle of 630 and 640 is 635. The middle of the two numbers is 14.635.

21. **Suzy**

Rewrite the decimals with three decimal places: 13.410, 13.380, 13.357 and 13.408. Now compare the last three digits in each decimal: from smallest to largest is 357, 380, 408, 410. The winner ran the fastest time and the third fastest was Suzy in 13.408 seconds.

22. **3.005**

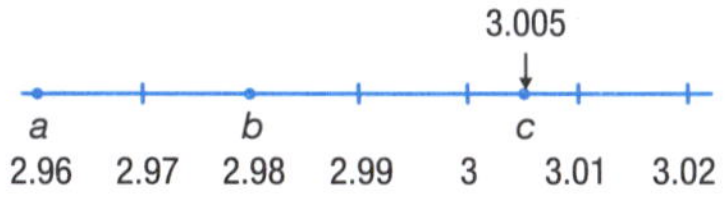

Labelling the number line means that *c* lies halfway between 3 and 3.01. Rewriting these with three decimal places gives 3.000 and 3.010. As 5 is in the middle of 0 and 10, then *c* is representing the decimal 3.005.

23. **3.70**

Look at the 7 in the third decimal place. As 7 > 5, the 9 in the second decimal place increases by 1, which means the 69 becomes 70. This means 3.697 = 3.70, correct to two decimal places.

24. **376**

As 3 times 100 is 300, you need to work out 0.76 × 100. As 0.76 is $\frac{76}{100}$, then 100 lots of 76 hundredths is 76. This means 3.76 × 100 is 376.

Unit 3A PAGE 14

1. **$62.40**

$7.80 is 780 cents.

780
× 8
6240

Eva's total savings were $62.40.

2. **$10.85**

20.00
− 9.15
10.85

Layla receives change of $10.85.

3. **$4.90**

$2\overline{)980}$ = 490

There are 980 cents in $9.80. One loaf costs 490 cents, or $4.90.

4. **$119.40**

78.90
24.55
9.20
+ 6.75
119.40

The total cost was $119.40.

5. **$27**

49
+ 24
73

100 − 73 = 27

Hayden will receive change of $27.

6. **$190**

The original price was $54.05 added to $135.95.

135.95
+ 54.05
190.00

The original price was $190.

7. **$50**

As 4 is 3 plus 1, Thea bought 3 for $35 and then 1 at $15. As 35 + 15 is 50, Thea spent $50.

8. **$680**

825
− 145
680

The new price is $680.

9. **$71.30**

44.50
+ 26.80
71.30

The cost would be $71.30.

10. **$170**

Two T-shirts at $40 each is 40 × 2 = 80. Add the cost of the shoes 90 to 80 gives a total cost of $170.

11. **$50**

Double the $19 and add $12. This means 19 × 2 + 12 = 38 + 12, which is 50. The total cost was $50.

12. **$27**

The milk costs $4 × 2 = $8 and the mince costs $9.50 × 2 = $19. As adding gives 8 + 19 = 27, the total cost is $27.

13. **$12**

29 × 2 is 58, and 70 − 58 = 12. This means Frankie had $12 remaining.

14. **$375**

75
× 5
375

The total cost was $375.

15. **$145**

Double 35 is 70 and 3 × 25 is 75. Adding 70 and 75 is 145, so the total cost would be $145.

16. **$35**

As 65 + 80 is 145, Xavier has a total of $145. As 145 − 110 is 35, Xavier will have $35 left.

17. **$59.60**

$1.49 is 149 cents.

149
× 40
5960

The petrol cost $59.60.

18. **$16.10**

6.90
2.80
3.75
+ 2.65
16.10

The total cost was $16.10.

19. **$148**

As 4 × 2 = 8, multiply $18.50 by 8. Also $18.50 is 1850 cents.

1850
× 8
14800

The total cost will be $148.

20. **$8.75**

$2.48 × 2 is $4.96.

4.96
+ 3.78
8.74

As $8.74 is close to $8.75, Max spent $8.75.

21. **$37.55**

56.00
− 18.45
37.55

The new price is $37.55.

22. **$93.25**

$18.65 is 1865 cents.

1865
× 5
9325

Michael is paid $93.25.

23. **$22.30**

96
+ 127
223

As 223 × 10 is 2230, Ryan received 2230 cents, or $22.30.

24. **$128.85**

29.90
48.95
+ 50.00
128.85

Sienna spent a total of $128.85.

Unit 3B PAGE 15

1. **$6.80**

$14.10 is 1410 cents. As $3\overline{)1410}$ = 470, one wrap costs $4.70. A hamburger costs $11.50 – $4.70.

11.50
– 4.70
6.80

The price of the hamburger is $6.80.

2. **90 cents**

The total spent on fruit was $10 – $3 = $7.

80 × 2 is 160 and 60 × 3 is 180.

160
+ 180
340

The 4 bananas cost $7 – $3.40 which is $3.60. The cost of 1 banana is 90 cents.

3. **$7**

Archer's purchase is 1 pie + 2 drinks = $10. Double Kai's purchase is 4 pies and 2 drinks = $22. Comparing these total costs using subtraction means that 3 pies cost $22 minus $10 which is $12. This means a pie costs $4, so a soft drink costs $3. A pie and a drink cost $7.

4. **$98**

Double $28 plus $42 is 28 × 2 + 42 = 56 + 42 = 98. The total cost will be $98.

5. **$17**

Double $32.50 is twice $32 + twice 50c which is $64 + $1 = $65. Double $18.50 is twice $18 + twice 50c which is $36 + $1 = $37. As 65 + 37 = 102 so the price for individual tickets would be $102. This means the saving is 102 – 85 = 102 – 82 – 3 = 20 – 3 = 17. The saving is $17.

6. **$18**

As 1 baseball costs $12, 3 baseballs cost $36. As 2 cricket balls cost $36, 1 cricket ball costs $36 ÷ 2 = $18.

7. **$83**

$2.04 minus 4 cents is $2. Now multiply 41.5 by 2. As 41 × 2 is 82 and one-half times 2 is 1, the total price is $83.

8. **8**

As 20 ÷ 5 is 4, there are four $5s in $20. As 4 × 2 is 8, Piper bought 8 bars of chocolate.

9. **3**

As an adult costs $13, the cost of the children is 40 – 13 = 27. The child cost is $9, so 27 ÷ 9 = 3 means that 3 children went to the cinema.

10. **$290**

As 200 – 50 is 150, and 150 ÷ 10 is 15, the cost for each person is $15. As 16 is 10 + 6, the additional 6 people cost $15 × 6 which is $90. The total cost will be $200 + $90 = $290.

11. **$1200**

A table costs $40. As 15 × 40 + 30 × 20 is 600 + 600 which is 1200, the total cost is $1200.

12. **$60**

3 October is a Wednesday and so are 10, 17, 24 and 31 October. This means there are 5 Wednesdays. As 12 × 5 is 60, Mackenzie is paid $60 in October.

13. **$4 425 000**

5 300 000
– 875 000
4 425 000

Kate had $4 425 000 remaining.

14. **$3776**

10 558
– 6782
3776

Adrian's profit was $3776.

15. **$45**

There are 4 hours from 6 pm to 10 pm. Leilani is paid $15 + $7.50 × 4. Now double $7.50 is $15 and double $15 is $30, and 15 + 30 is 45. Leilani is paid $45.

16. **$342**

Her hourly pay rate is 216 ÷ 12.

$12\overline{)216}$ = 18

Naomi is paid $18 per hour.

19
× 18
152
190
342

Naomi will be paid $342.

17. **$457**

As 45 – 16 is 29, Skye makes $29 for each dress sold.

29
× 18
232
290
522

Her profit for the day is 522 – 65.

522
– 65
457

Skye made a profit of $457.

18. **$2.60**

As 890 ÷ 2 is 445, the cherries cost $4.45. As 750 ÷ 2 is 375, the lychees cost $3.75. As 1840 ÷ 2 is 920, the dates cost $9.20.

4.45
3.75
+ 9.20
17.40

The cost was $17.40.

20.00
– 17.40
2.60

Leah received $2.60 in change.

19. **$187.45**

$32.50 is 3250 cents.

3250
× 4
13 000

The coat cost 13 000 cents, or $130.

32.50
24.95
+ 130.00
187.45

The total cost was $187.45.

20. **$980**

290
+ 640
930

The remainder is $2890 – $930.

2890
– 930
1960

Half of $1960 is 1960 ÷ 2.

$2\overline{)1960}$ = 980

Theodore gives his son $980 and keeps $980 for himself.

21. **$1120**

425
240
85
70
+ 260
1080

Savings is $1640 – $1080 each week.

1640
– 1080
560

As 560 × 2 is 1120, Hayley will save $1120 in two weeks.

Unit 4A PAGE 16

1. **50, 62, 74**
   As 26 – 14 is 12 and 38 – 26 is 12, the sequence starts at 14 and increases by 12. 38 adding 12 is 50, adding 12 is 62, adding 12 is 74. The next three numbers are 50, 62 and 74.
2. **39, 21**
   As 33 – 27 is 6 and 15 – 9 is 6, the rule is starting with 45 and decreasing by 6. As 45 – 6 is 39 and 27 – 6 is 21, the missing numbers are 39 and 21.
3. **56, 69**
   As 30 – 17 is 13 and 43 – 30 is 13, the pattern starts with 17 and increases by 13. 43 + 13 is 56 and 56 + 13 is 69. The next two numbers are 56 and 69.
4. **5.7, 6.9**
   3.3 – 2.1 is 1.2 and 4.5 – 3.3 is 1.2. The pattern starts with 2.1 and increases by 1.2.
   $$\begin{array}{r} 4.5 \\ +\ 1.2 \\ \hline 5.7 \end{array} \qquad \begin{array}{r} 5.7 \\ +\ 1.2 \\ \hline 6.9 \end{array}$$
   The two numbers are 5.7 and 6.9.
5. **29, 33**
   41 – 37 is 4 and 45 – 41 is 4. The pattern is increasing by 4. As 37 – 4 is 33 and 33 – 4 is 29, the first two numbers are 29 and 33.
6. **8.2, 9.8**
   9 – 8.6 is 0.4 and 9.4 – 9 is 0.4. The pattern is increasing by 0.4. As 8.6 – 0.4 is 8.2 and 9.4 + 0.4 is 9.8, the two missing numbers are 8.2 and 9.8.
7. **$1\frac{3}{4}$ and $2\frac{1}{4}$**
   The pattern is $\frac{1}{4}, \frac{3}{4}, \frac{5}{4}, \ldots$ The pattern is increasing by $\frac{2}{4}$. The next two improper fractions are $\frac{7}{4}$ and $\frac{9}{4}$, which can be written as $1\frac{3}{4}$ and $2\frac{1}{4}$.
8. **4.05, 4.85**
   Look at the last two digits. The pattern is 25, 45, 65, … The pattern is increasing by 0.20.
   $$\begin{array}{r} 4.25 \\ -\ 0.20 \\ \hline 4.05 \end{array} \qquad \begin{array}{r} 4.65 \\ +\ 0.20 \\ \hline 4.85 \end{array}$$
   The two missing numbers are 4.05 and 4.85.
9. **36**
   21 – 6 is 15 and 66 – 51 is 15. The pattern is increasing by 15. As 21 + 15 is 36, the missing number is 36.
10. **1, $1\frac{1}{5}$**
    As $\frac{3}{5} - \frac{2}{5}$ is $\frac{1}{5}$ and $\frac{4}{5} - \frac{3}{5}$ is $\frac{1}{5}$, the pattern is increasing by $\frac{1}{5}$. As $\frac{4}{5} + \frac{1}{5}$ is $\frac{5}{5}$, or 1, and $1 + \frac{1}{5}$ is $1\frac{1}{5}$, then the missing numbers are 1 and $1\frac{1}{5}$.
11. **540, 510, 480, 450**
    540, then 540 subtracting 30 is 510, subtracting 30 is 480, subtracting 30 is 450. The numbers are 540, 510, 480, 450.
12. **42 ÷ 7 = 6**
    'Quotient' means to divide. The number sentence is 42 ÷ 7 = 6.
13. **43**
    5 × 8 + 3 is 40 + 3 which is 43. The output number is 43.
14. **17**
    96 ÷ 8 is 12. The number sentence can be written as 12 = ☐ – 5.
    As 12 + 5 is 17, the missing number is 17.
15. **20**
    9 × 7 is 63. The number sentence can be written as 63 = 43 + ☐. The missing number is 63 – 43, which is 20. The missing number is 20.
16. **7.8**
    The missing number is 22.5 – 14.7.
    $$\begin{array}{r} 22.5 \\ -\ 14.7 \\ \hline 7.8 \end{array}$$
    The missing number is 7.8.
17. **7.4**
    The missing number is 15.4 – 8.
    $$\begin{array}{r} 15.4 \\ -\ 8.0 \\ \hline 7.4 \end{array}$$
    The missing number is 7.4.
18. **20.3**
    The missing number is 12 + 8.3.
    $$\begin{array}{r} 12.0 \\ +\ 8.3 \\ \hline 20.3 \end{array}$$
    The missing number is 20.3.
19. **$\frac{3}{5}$**
    The missing number is $1 - \frac{2}{5}$, which is $\frac{5}{5} - \frac{2}{5} = \frac{3}{5}$. The missing number is $\frac{3}{5}$.
20. **Yes**
    22 + 19 is 41. This means Justin is correct.
21. **No**
    As 4 × 8 is 32, then 4 × 80 is 320, not 240. This means Rachael is not correct.
22. **Yes**
    Look at 560 ÷ 70. It has the same answer as 56 ÷ 7 which is 8. This means 560 ÷ 70 = 8, so Jodie is correct.
23. **2.52**
    The number sentence can be rewritten as 4 – 1.48 = ☐
    $$\begin{array}{r} 4.00 \\ -\ 1.48 \\ \hline 2.52 \end{array}$$
    The missing number is 2.52.
24. **[>]**
    $$\begin{array}{r} 83 \\ -\ 48 \\ \hline 35 \end{array}$$
    Also, 18 + 15 is 33. As 35 > 33, then the number sentence is 83 – 48 > 18 + 15.
    Use the [>] symbol.

Unit 4B PAGE 17

1. **$3\frac{1}{8}$**
   Look at the numerators. The sequence is 3, 5, 7 … The pattern is increasing by 2. The twelfth number will be 7 plus 9 lots of 2. This is 7 + 18 which is 25, which means the twelfth member of the sequence is $\frac{25}{8}$, or $3\frac{1}{8}$.
2. **28**
   As 52 – 48 is 4 and 56 – 52 is 4, the pattern is increasing by 4. As 48 is the sixth number then the first number will be 48 minus 5 lots of 4. As 48 – 20 is 28, the first number is 28.
3. **100**
   As 65 – 58 is 7 and 58 – 51 is 7, the pattern is decreasing by 7. As 51 is the eighth number then the first number will be 51 plus 7 lots of 7. As 51 + 49 is 100, the first number is 100.
4. **84**
   As 44 – 26 is 8 and 52 – 44 is 8, the pattern is increasing by 8. As 36 is the fourth number then the tenth number will be 36 plus 6 lots of 8. As 36 + 48 is 84, the tenth number is 84.
5. **423**
   As 100 – 83 is 17 and 117 – 100 is 17, the pattern is increasing by 17. As 83 is the fifth number then the twenty-fifth number will be 83 plus 20 lots of 17. As 20 × 17 is 340, and 83 + 340 is 423, the twenty-fifth number is 423.
6. **$11\frac{1}{8}$**
   The pattern is increasing by $2\frac{2}{8}$.
   Adding $8\frac{7}{8}$ and $2\frac{2}{8}$ is $10\frac{9}{8}$. Now, $\frac{9}{8}$ is $1\frac{1}{8}$, so the next number is 10 plus $1\frac{1}{8}$ which is $11\frac{1}{8}$.

7. **14.8 km**

The sequence of distances in kilometres is 7.6, 8.8, 10 … From week 4 to week 10 is 6 weeks. The distance will be $7.6 + 1.2 \times 6$, which is $7.6 + 7.2 = 14.8$. Kelly plans to run 14.8 km.

8. **108**

The sequence is 36, 44, 52 … This means the tenth number will be $36 + 9 \times 8$. This is $36 + 72$ which is 108. The tenth number is 108.

9. **166**

The sequence is 310, 302, 294 … This means the nineteenth number will be $310 - 18 \times 8$. For 18×8, think $2 \times 9 \times 8$ which is 144.

$$\begin{array}{r} 310 \\ -\ 144 \\ \hline 166 \end{array}$$

The nineteenth number is 166.

10. **5.895, 5.847**

Look at the last two digits in each decimal. The pattern is … 83, 71, 59 … As $83 - 71$ is 12 and $71 - 59$ is 12, the pattern is decreasing by 0.012.

$$\begin{array}{r} 5.883 \\ +\ 0.012 \\ \hline 5.895 \end{array} \qquad \begin{array}{r} 5.859 \\ -\ 0.012 \\ \hline 5.847 \end{array}$$

The missing decimals are 5.895 and 5.847.

11. **1106, 1030**

All the numbers start with 10. Look at the last two digits in the numbers. $87 - 68$ is 19 and $68 - 49$ is 19. The pattern is decreasing by 19.

$$\begin{array}{r} 1087 \\ +\ \ 19 \\ \hline 1106 \end{array}$$

Also $49 - 19$ is 30 so the other number is 1030. The missing numbers are 1106 and 1030.

12. **784**

The number sentence can be rewritten as $56 \times 14 = \square$.

$$\begin{array}{r} 56 \\ \times\ \ 14 \\ \hline 224 \\ 560 \\ \hline 784 \end{array}$$

The missing number is 784.

13. **6**

Starting with 29 as the output, use inverse operations as you move to the left towards the input. $29 - 5$ is 24 and then divide by 4 to get 6. The input number is 6.

14. **24**

As 9×8 is 72, the number sentence can be written as $72 - \square = 48$. The 'missing number' can be found using $72 - 48$, which gives 24. The missing number is 24.

15. **26**

As 12×7 is 84, the number sentence can be written as $84 + \square = 110$. The 'missing number' can be found using $110 - 84$ which gives 26. The missing number is 26.

16. **248**

The missing number is $612 - 364$.

$$\begin{array}{r} 612 \\ -\ 364 \\ \hline 248 \end{array}$$

The missing number is 248.

17. **2.4**

3.5 plus 2 gives 5.5. This means the missing number is 4.4 minus 2 which is 2.4.

18. $\mathbf{\frac{2}{5}}$

1 is equal to $\frac{5}{5}$. As $\frac{2}{5} + \frac{1}{5}$ is $\frac{3}{5}$, the number sentence is $\square + \frac{3}{5} = \frac{5}{5}$.

The missing number is $\frac{2}{5}$.

19. **30**

$640 \div 8$ is 80 then $80 - 50$ is 30. The output is 30.

20. **136**

The number sentence is $10 + 14 \times 9$. As 14×9 is 126 then $10 + 126$ is 136.

21. **22**

$$\begin{array}{r} 123 \\ -\ \ 44 \\ \hline 79 \end{array}$$

The number sentence can be written as $57 + \square = 79$. The missing number is $79 - 57$ which is 22. The missing number is 22.

22. **17**

The number sentence is $\square + 16 = 44 - 11$. $44 - 11$ is 33. The number sentence can be written as $\square + 16 = 33$. Leila's number is $33 - 16$ which is 17.

Unit 5A PAGE 18

1. **24 cm**

As a square has 4 equal sides, you need to divide 96 by 4.

$$4\overline{)96}\ = 24$$

Each side is 24 cm.

2. **950 m**

There are 1000 m in one km. As Marcus has already walked 4 km 50 m you need to subtract 50 from 1000.

$$\begin{array}{r} 1000 \\ -\ \ \ 50 \\ \hline 950 \end{array}$$

Marcus needs to walk another 950 m.

3. **2340 m**

$$\begin{array}{r} 780 \\ \times\ \ \ 3 \\ \hline 2340 \end{array}$$

Greg runs 2340 m.

4. **45 cm**

Adding the lengths: $12 + 8 + 6 + 9 + 10$ is 45. The perimeter is 45 cm.

5. **50 cm**

Adding the lengths: $11 + 5 + 4 + 5 + 3 + 4 + 4 + 14$ is 50. The perimeter is 50 cm.

6. **80 cm**

An equilateral triangle has 3 sides of equal length. As $24 \div 3$ is 8, then $240 \div 3$ is 80. The sides are each 80 cm long.

7. **8 cm**

As $13 + 7 + 10$ is 30, and $38 - 30$ is 8, the missing side has a length of 8 cm.

8. **48 cm²**

The area is found by multiplying length by width. As 8×6 is 48 the area is 48 cm^2.

9. **6 cm**

The area is found by multiplying the length and the width. This means 10 times 'width' is 60. This means the width is 6 cm.

10. **12 hectares**

There are 10 000 m^2 in 1 hectare. You need to find $120\,000 \div 10\,000$, which is $120 \div 10 = 12$. There are 12 hectares.

11. **400 cm²**

In a square all sides are the same length. As $80 \div 4$ is 20, each side is 20 cm long. The area is 20×20. As 2×2 is 4, then 20×20 is 4 with 2 zeros on the end. As $20 \times 20 = 400$, the area is 400 cm^2.

12. **5 cm²**

As $20 \div 4$ is 5, the area of each triangle is 5 cm^2.

13. **4 cm²**

As $24 \div 6$ is 4, the area of each square is 4 cm^2.

14. **16 cubic centimetres**

As 4 × 2 is 8 there are 8 blocks on each layer. As there are two layers, then there are 16 blocks altogether. The volume is 16 cubic centimetres.

15. **24 kg**

As 3 × 2 is 6, there are 6 blocks in the solid. As 6 × 4 is 24, the total mass of the solid is 24 kg.

16. **90 mL**

Half of 180 is 180 ÷ 2 which is 90. There is still 90 mL of water in the glass.

17. **1250 mL**

As there are 1000 mL in 1 L, and 500 mL in half a litre, then the bottle contains 1500 mL of iced tea.
As 500 – 250 is 250, then there is still 1250 mL in the bottle.

18. **2020**

Twenty past eight at night is 8:20 pm. This time is 2020 in 24-hour time.

19. **2300**

The time is pm so add 11 on to 12. As 12 + 11 is 23, then 11:00 pm is 2300.

20. **2150**

The time is pm so add on to 12. As 12 + 9 is 21, then 9:50 pm is 2150.

21. **1615**

One hour after 3:15 pm is 4:15 pm. As the time is pm, add 4 onto 12. As 12 + 4 = 16, the time is 1615.

22. **9:48 pm**

2148 is past 1200 so it is pm. As 2100 – 1200 is 900 then 2148 – 1200 is 948. This means the time is 9:48 pm.

Unit 5B PAGE 19

1. **55 cm**

There are 100 cm in a metre, and so 200 cm in 2 m. As 200 + 20 is 220, the perimeter is 220 cm. As a square has 4 equal sides, you need to divide 220 by 4.

$$\begin{array}{r}55\\4\overline{)220}\end{array}$$

Each side is 55 cm.

2. **3750 m**

There are 1000 m in a kilometre.

As $\frac{1}{2}$ of 1000 is 500 and $\frac{3}{4}$ of 1000 is 750, you need to find 5500 – 1750.

$$\begin{array}{r}5500\\-\ 1750\\\hline 3750\end{array}$$

Henry needs to walk another 3750 m.

3. **1450 m**

As there are 1000 m in 1 km, Amelia has run 4350 m.

$$\begin{array}{r}1450\\3\overline{)4350}\end{array}$$

The length of the circuit is 1450 m.

4. **15 cm**

Adding the lengths shown: 12 + 14 + 7 + 10 is 43. As 58 – 43 is 15, the missing length is 15 cm.

5. **70 cm**

As 16 + 8 is 24, then 3 + the missing horizontal side is 24. This means the length of the missing horizontal side length is 21 cm. 6 + 5 is 11, which is the same as the missing vertical side + 3. This means the vertical side length is 8 cm.

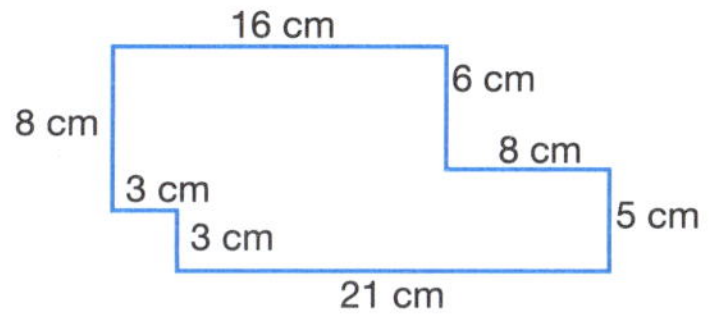

Adding the lengths: 16 + 6 + 8 + 5 + 21 + 3 + 3 + 8 is 70. The perimeter is 70 cm.

6. **10 cm**

7 + 7 + 8 + 2 × length is 42. This means 22 + 2 × length = 42, and so 2 × length is 20. This means the length of the rectangle is 10 cm.

7. **1, 920**

The regular hexagon has 6 sides each of length 320 mm. The perimeter is 6 times 320.

$$\begin{array}{r}320\\\times\quad 6\\\hline 1920\end{array}$$

As there are 1000 mm in 1 m, the perimeter is 1920 mm, or 1 m 920 mm.

8. **6 cm**

Twice the sum of the length and the width is 20. This means the sum of the length and width is 10. Find two numbers that add to give 10 and multiply to give 24. The two numbers are 6 and 4. This means the length of the rectangle is 6 cm.

9. **288 ha**

As there are 1000 m in 1 km, and 3.6 × 1000 = 3600, the length is 3600 m. The area is 3600 × 800. The answer will be 36 × 8 with 4 zeros on the end. As 36 × 8 = 288, then 3600 × 800 is 2 880 000, which is 2 880 000 m².

Dividing by 10 000 is removing 4 zeros from the end which gives 288. The area is 288 hectares.

10. **2187 m²**

As 216 ÷ 2 is 108, the sum of the length and width is 108 cm. If length is three times the width, then 3 widths + 1 width = 4 widths which equals 108. As 108 ÷ 4 is 27, the width is 27 cm. As 27 × 3 is 81, the length is 81 cm.

The area is 81 × 27.

$$\begin{array}{r}81\\\times\quad 27\\\hline 567\\1620\\\hline 2187\end{array}$$

The area is 2187 m².

11. **3600 m²**

The perimeter is found using 3840 ÷ 16. This has the same answer as 1920 ÷ 8, by dividing both numbers in the question by 2.

$$\begin{array}{r}240\\8\overline{)1920}\end{array}$$

The perimeter is 240 m, which means the side length is 240 ÷ 4 = 60 m. As 60 × 60 is 3600, the area is 3600 m².

12. **9 cm²**

As 24 ÷ 4 is 6, the side length is 6 cm. As 6 × 6 is 36, the area of the square is 36 cm². As the triangles have the same area, and 36 ÷ 4 is 9, the area of the triangle is 9 cm².

13. **60 cubic centimetres**

As 5 × 4 × 3 is 20 × 3 = 60, the volume is 60 cubic centimetres.

14. **30 g**

As 270 – 230 is 40, and 40 ÷ 2 is 20, the mass of each chocolate is 20 g. As 20 × 12 is 240, the mass of the chocolates is 240 g. As 270 – 240 is 30, the empty box has a mass of 30 g.

15. **270 g**

As 3 × 3 × 3 is 27, there are 27 blocks in the cube. As 27 × 10 is 270, the total mass is 270 g.

16. **1570 mL**

As there are 1000 mL in 1 L then there are 2000 mL in 2 L.

$$\begin{array}{r}{}^{1\,9\,1}2000\\-\ 430\\\hline 1570\end{array}$$

There is 1570 mL remaining.

17. **3000 mL**

As 1 + 2 + 3 is 6, and half of 6 is 3, there is a total of 3 L of milk. As 1000 mL is 1 L, then there is 3000 mL.

18. **7:15 am**

2015 is 8:15 pm. Adding 4 hours gives 12:15 am and then another 7 hours gets to 7:15 am. Muhammad arrives at 7:15 am.

19. **1:05 am**

As there are 60 minutes in one hour, then there are 15 minutes in a quarter of an hour. Elliot left the party 2 hours 15 minutes after 2250, or 10:50 pm. From 10:50, add 2 hours is 12:50, and then another 15 minutes is 1:05. Elliot left the party at 1:05 am.

20. **2230**

From 7:50 pm add on 2 hours which is 9:50. Now add 10 minutes, then 30 minutes. Adding 10 minutes gives 10:00 pm and then another 30 minutes is 10:30 pm. This time is 2230 in 24-hour time.

Unit 6A PAGES 20–21

1. ***E***

As *A* is opposite *C* and *D* is opposite *F*, then *E* is opposite *B*.

2. ***B***

A is opposite *C*, *F* is opposite *D* so *B* is opposite *E*.

3. ***T***

Q is opposite *S*, *R* is opposite *U* and so *T* is opposite *P*.

4. ***E***

A is opposite *D*, *C* is opposite *F* and so *E* is opposite *B*.

5. ☺

∗ is opposite ▼,
◆ is opposite ◘ and so
☺ is opposite ♥.

6. ***R***

P is opposite *S*, *Q* is opposite *U* and so *R* is opposite *T*.

7. **1**

A triangular prism has 5 faces. It has 1 pair of parallel faces.

8. **1 hexagon, 6 triangles**

The net is made from 1 hexagon and 6 triangles.

9.

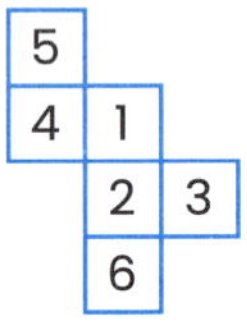

10.

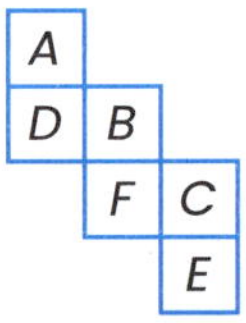

11.

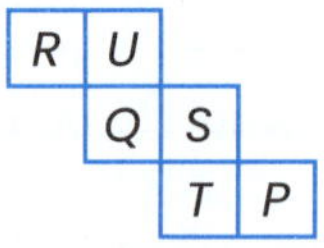

12.

13.

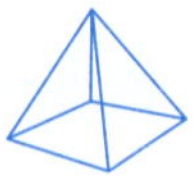

14.

15. **pyramid, rectangular prism**

A rectangular pyramid is sitting on a rectangular prism.

16. **8**

There are 8 faces.

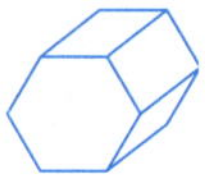

17. **10**

There are 10 vertices.

18. **5**

There are 5 vertices.

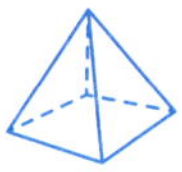

19. **5**

There are 5 faces.

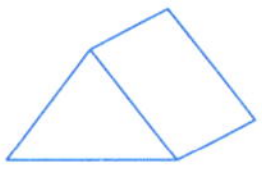

20.

21.

22.

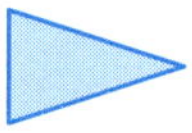

23.

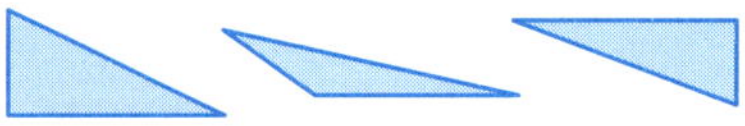

24. **decagon**

A decagon has 10 sides. A hexagon has 6 sides, a pentagon 5 sides and an octagon has 8 sides.

25.

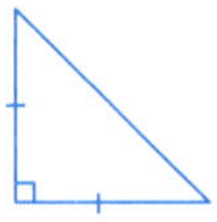

26. **All rectangles are parallelograms.**

A rectangle has two pairs of parallel sides. Not all parallelograms have a right angle.

27. **30 cm**

A parallelogram has opposite sides equal in length. The perimeter is 2 times the sum of 8 and 7. As 8 + 7 is 15, and 2 × 15 is 30, the perimeter is 30 cm.

28.

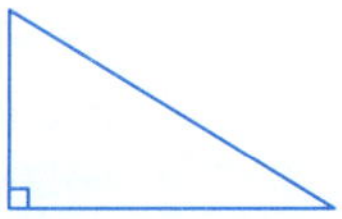

Unit 6B PAGES 22–23

1. **4**

6 and 3 are opposite faces so the total is 9. 5 and ∗ are on opposite faces, so ∗ = 9 – 5 = 4.

2. **0.7**

0.3 and ∗ are opposite faces. As 1 – 0.3 is 0.7, then ∗ = 0.7.

3. **2**

4 and 3 are opposite faces so they multiply to give 12. 6 and ∗ are on opposite faces. As 6 × ∗ gives 12, then ∗ is 2.

4. **7.5**

1.3 and 1.2 are opposite faces so the total of these two faces is 1.3 + 1.2 which is 2.5. There are 3 pairs of opposite faces. As 25 × 3 is 75, then 2.5 × 3 is 7.5. The sum of the faces is 7.5.

5. **4**

A and *D* are on opposite faces of the cube. As *A* = 6 and *D* = 8, and 6 × 8 = 48, opposite faces multiply to give 48. As *E* is the opposite face of *B*, and *B* = 12, then *E* is 48 ÷ 12 = 4. This means *E* = 4.

6. **3**

$\frac{3}{10}$ and $\frac{7}{10}$ are opposite faces and $\frac{3}{10} + \frac{7}{10} = 1$ which means that opposite faces add to 1. As there are 3 pairs of opposite faces the sum is 3.

7. **33**

36 and 17 are opposite faces and as 36 – 17 = 19, the difference will always be 19. ∗ and 14 are on opposite faces and have a difference of 19. As 14 + 19 is 33, then ∗ = 33.

8. **10**

The first cube will have a '2' opposite the '5'. The second cube will have a '10' opposite the '5. This means a 10 will be opposite the 2 on the new prism.

9. **4**

A hexagonal prism has 8 faces. It has 4 pairs of parallel faces.

10. **2 pentagons, 5 rectangles**

The net is made up of 2 pentagons and 5 rectangles.

11. 

12. 15

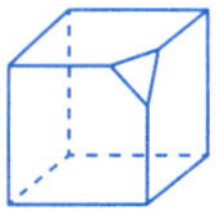

The original cube had 12 edges. If one vertex is removed, three more edges appear. This means the new solid has 15 edges.

13. 12

The solid is a rectangular prism, with 12 edges.

14. 3

The original pyramid had 5 vertices. There are 8 vertices on the new solid. There are 3 more vertices on the new solid.

15. 6

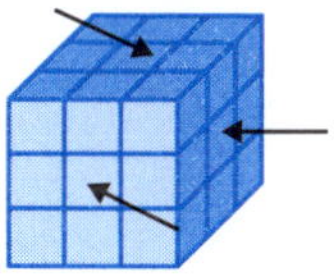

There are 6 faces, and so there are 6 cubes with only 1 painted face.

16. 2

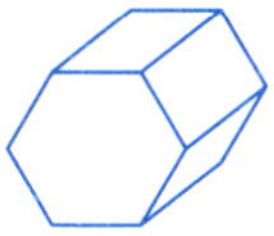

faces = 8,
vertices = 12,
edges = 18
This means 8 + 12 − 18 = 2.

17. 2

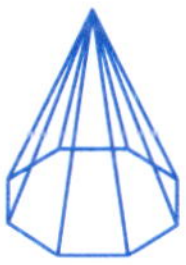

faces = 9,
vertices = 9,
edges = 16
This means 9 + 9 − 16 = 2.

18. 2

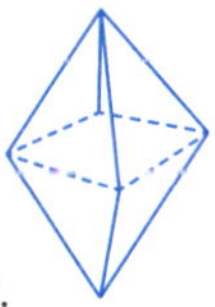

faces = 8,
vertices = 6,
edges = 12
This means 8 + 6 − 12 = 2.

19. 30

Faces + vertices − edges = 2 means 20 + 12 − edges = 2. As 20 + 12 is 32 then 32 − edges is 2. This means the number of edges is 30.

20. 

21. 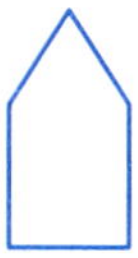

22. 

A regular polygon has equal sides and equal angles.

23. 120°

A regular hexagon has six equal angles. As 720 ÷ 6 is 120, each angle is 120°.

24. pentagon, hexagon, octagon, decagon

A hexagon has 6 sides, a decagon 10, pentagon 5 and octagon 8. The order is pentagon, hexagon, octagon, decagon.

25. square

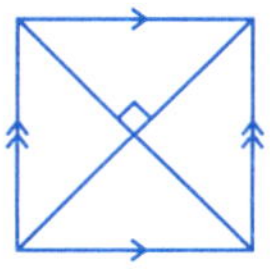

26. 80°, 100°, 100°

The opposite angle to 80° is also 80°. As 180 − 80 is 100, the other two angles are 100°.

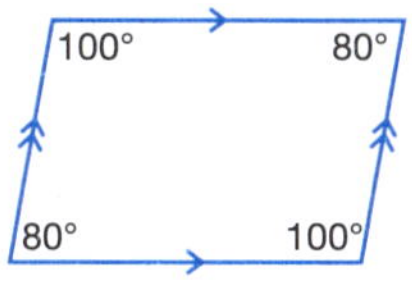

27. 96 cm²

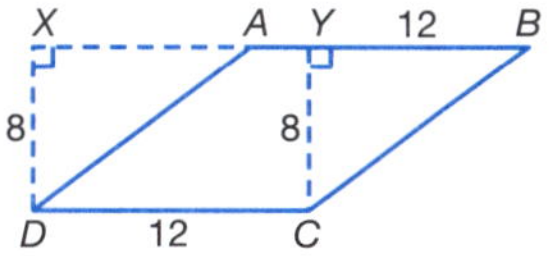

A parallelogram has its opposite sides equal in length. As 12 × 8 = 96, the area of the rectangle named *XYCD* is 96 cm². This means the parallelogram also has an area of 96 cm².

28. trapezium, kite

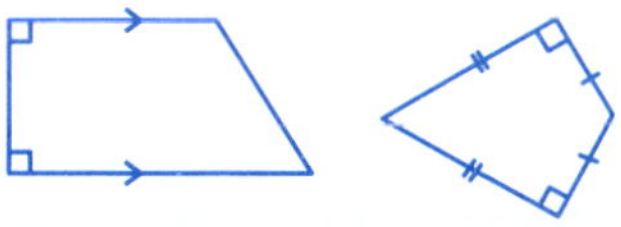

Unit 7A PAGES 24–25

1. 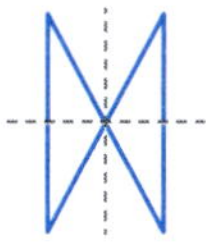

2. M, T

3. 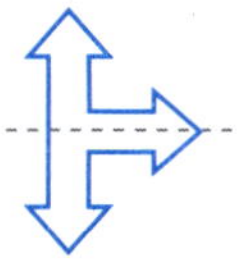

4. 

5. 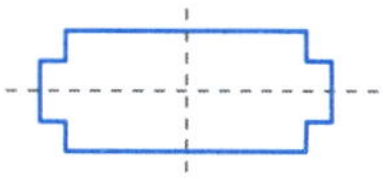

6. 

7. 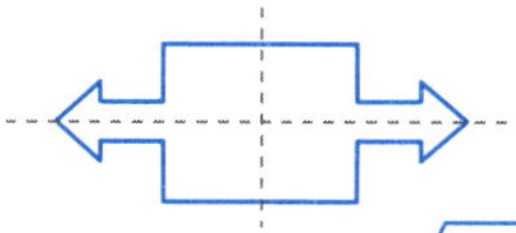

8. 0

There are no lines of symmetry.

9. 8

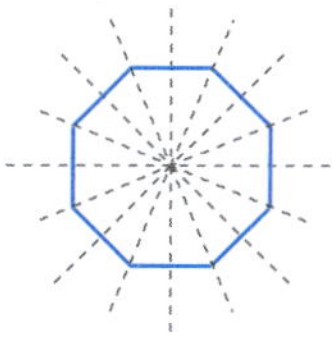

10. infinite

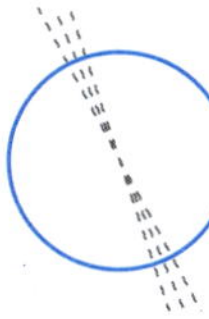

There is an infinite number of lines of symmetry.

11. 1

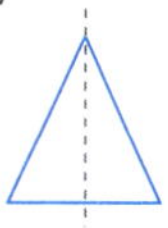

12. 

13. 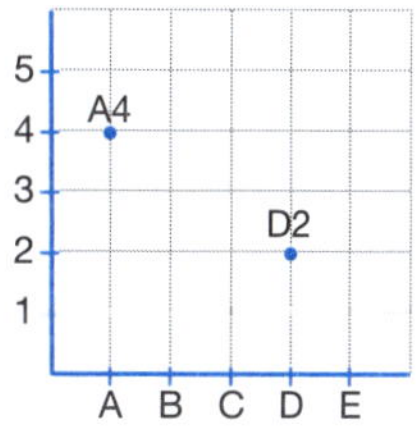

14. north-east

X is north-east of *Y*.

15. A4

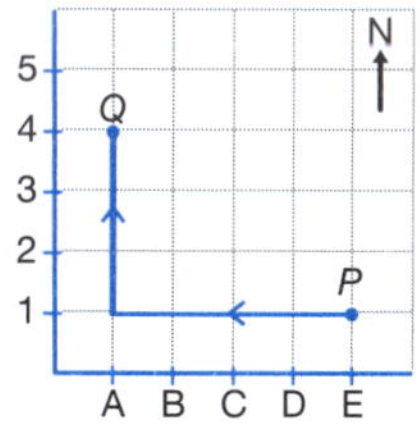

Q is at A4.

16. 14 km

As 4 + 3 is 7, Allison has travelled 7 units. Using the scale, 7 × 2 = 14 km.

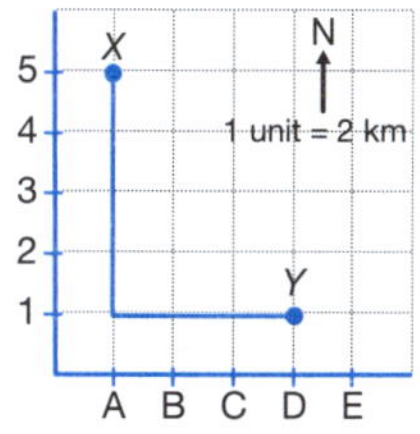

17.

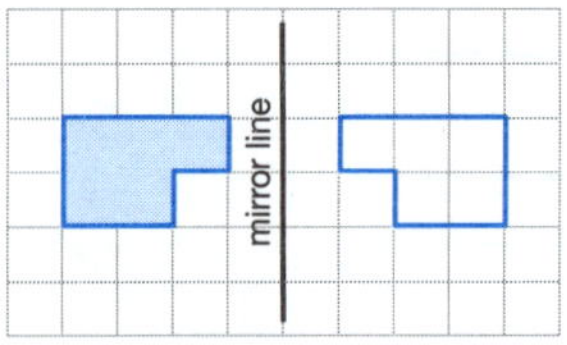

18.

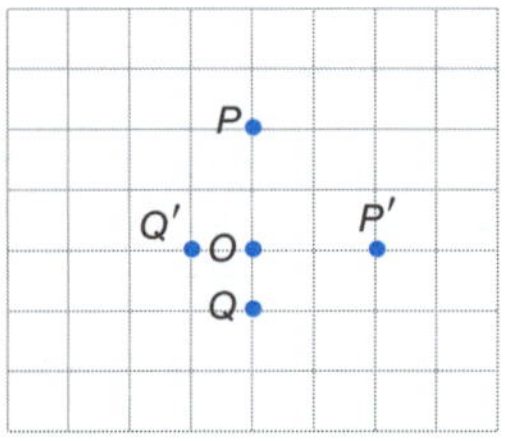

19.

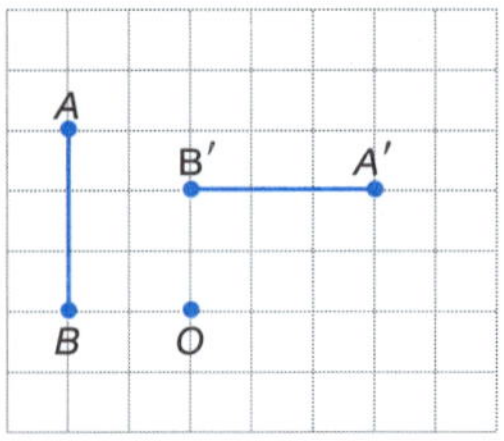

20.

21.

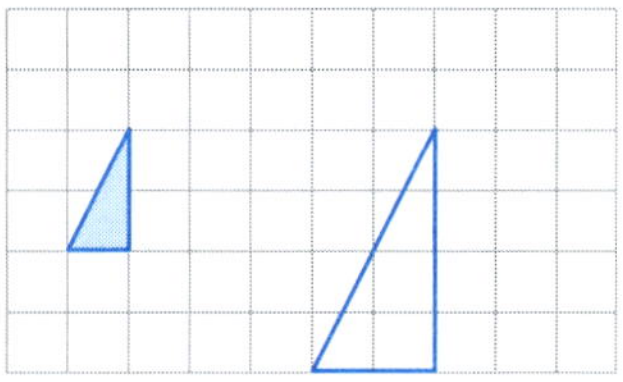

22. ***P* has been translated 3 units to the right.**

23. ***X* has been reflected in the mirror line.**

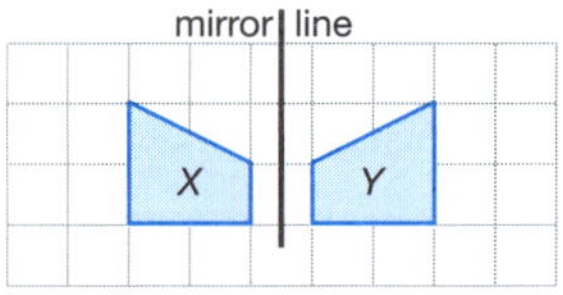

24. **32 cm**

As 4 × 2 is 8, the enlarged square has side length of 8 cm. As 4 × 8 is 32, the perimeter is 32 cm.

25.

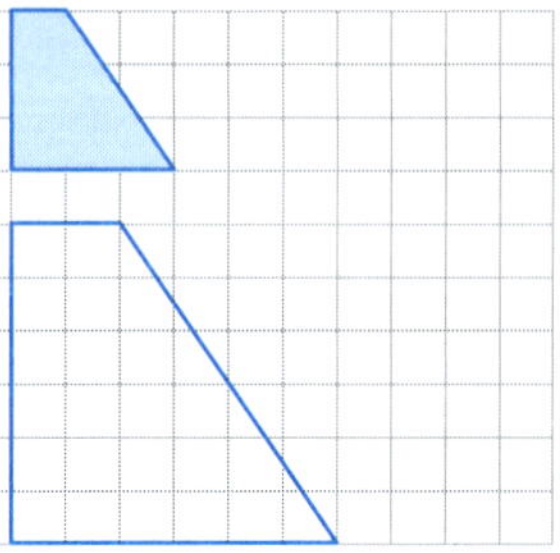

26. **16 square units**

The new square has side length 4 units. As 4 × 4 is 16, the area is 16 square units.

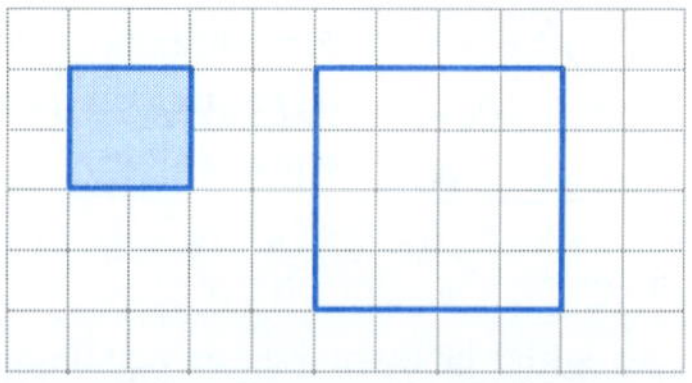

Unit 7B PAGES 26–27

1.

The first shape has a rotational symmetry of order 4. The equilateral triangle has a rotational symmetry of order 3.

2.

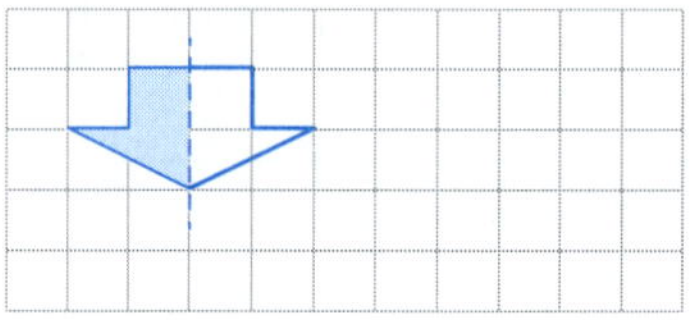

3.

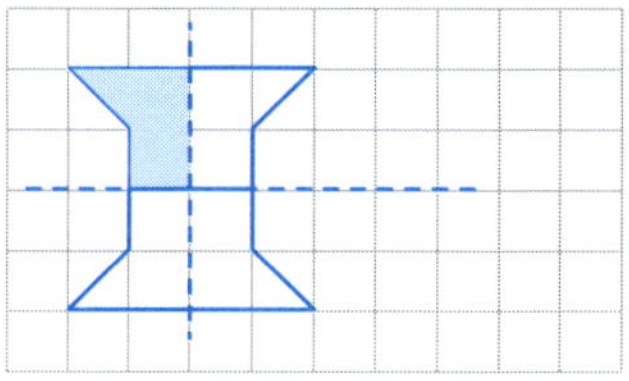

4.

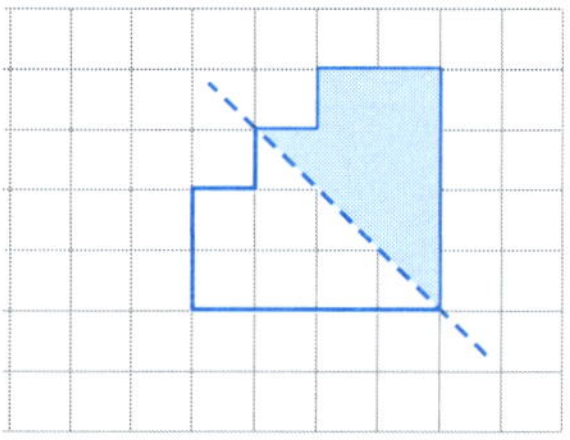

5. **2**

When it is rotated 180°, it will look the same every half turn (180°). This means it has a rotational symmetry of order 2.

6. **1**

When it is rotated 360°, it will look the same only when it has completed the rotation. This means it has a rotational symmetry of order 1.

7. **6**

When it is rotated 360°, it will look the same every sixth of a turn (60°). This means it has a rotational symmetry of order 6.

8. **2**

When it is rotated 360°, it will look the same every half turn (180°). This means it has a rotational symmetry of order 2.

9. **45°**

A full rotation is 360°. As 360 ÷ 8 is 45, the shape should rotate 45° about its centre.

10. **72°**

The shape has rotational symmetry of order 5. A full rotation is 360°. As 360 ÷ 5 is 72, the shape should rotate 72° about its centre.

11. **12**

As 360 ÷ 30 is 12, the order of rotational symmetry is 12.

12. **36°**

A regular decagon has rotational symmetry of order 10. A full rotation is 360°. As 360 ÷ 10 is 36, then the shape should rotate 36° about its centre.

13. **D2**

Q is at D2.

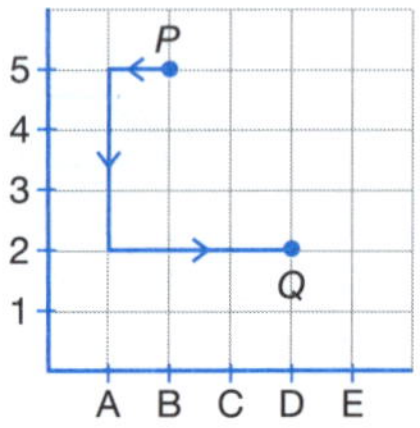

14. **A1**

Y is at A1.

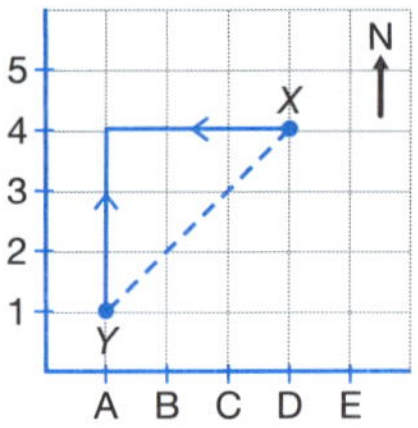

15. **1**

South-east of *X* are the locations such as B3, C2 or D1. The number of units east must equal the total number of units south.

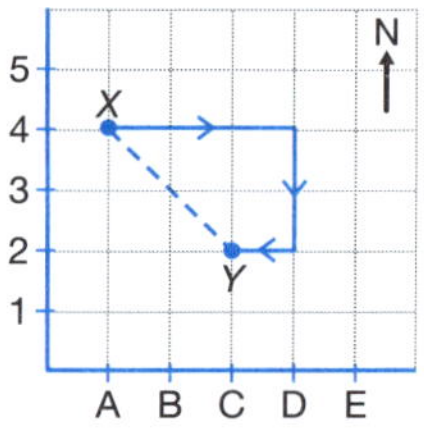

The missing number is 1.

16. **E3**

As 15 ÷ 5 is 3, 20 ÷ 5 = 4 and 10 ÷ 5 = 2, from *X* move south 3 units, east 4 units and north 2 units. *Y* is at E3.

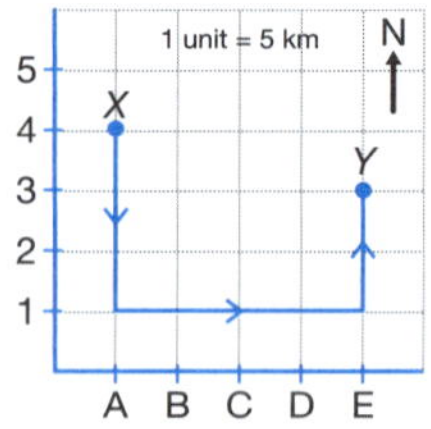

17.

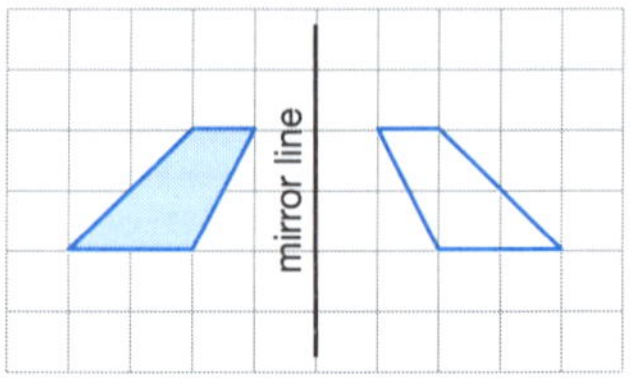

18. 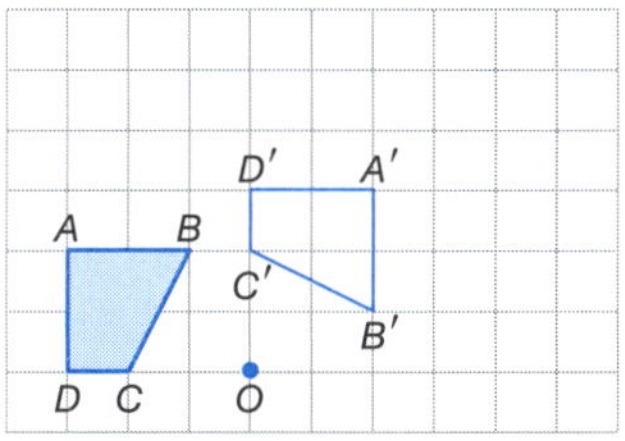

19. 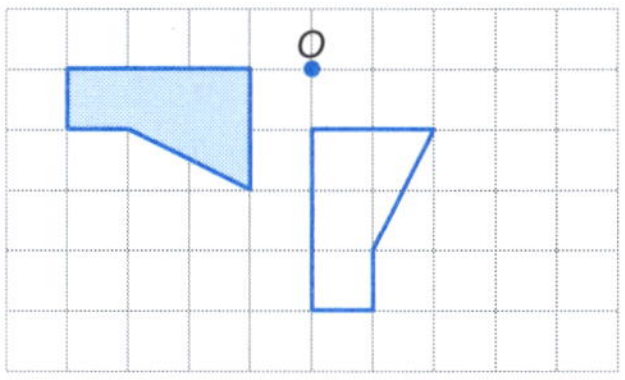

20. 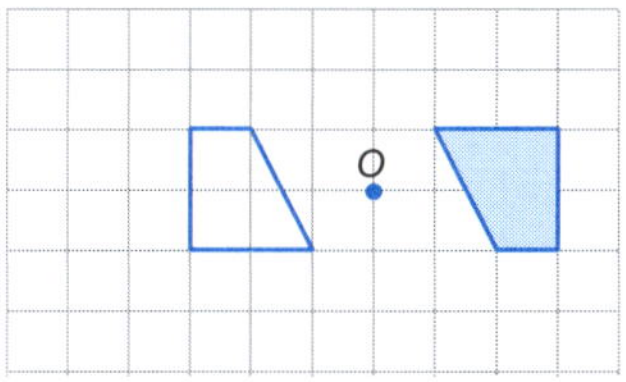

21. **54 units^2**

The dimensions have been multiplied by 3. The shape is a rectangle with new dimensions 9 units by 6 units. As 9×6 is 54, the area is 54 units^2.

22. **The triangle has been rotated 180° about *O*.**

23. **Triangle *A* has been translated 3 units to the left.**

24. **108 cm**

An area of 81 cm^2 means a side length of 9 cm. Enlargement by factor of 3 means the side length is now 27 cm. As 27×4 is 108, the perimeter of the enlarged square is 108 cm.

25. **6 units^2**

The shape covers 24 squares which means an area of 24 units^2. Enlargement by 0.5 means the dimensions have been halved. The new area is 6 units^2.

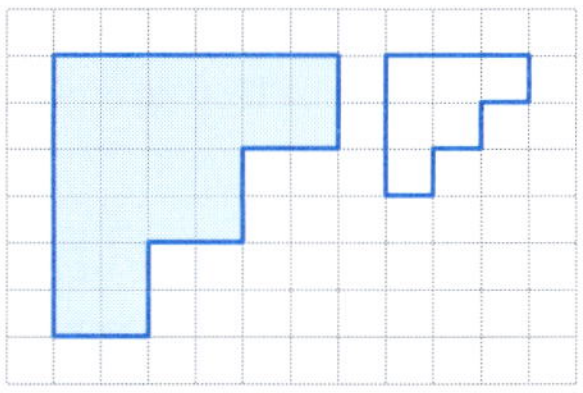

Unit 8A PAGE 28

1. **80°**

The angle is 80°.

2. 

More than 90° means more than a right angle.

3. 

4. **2**

The angles marked with a tick are larger than 90°.

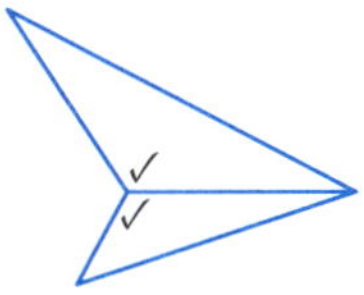

5. 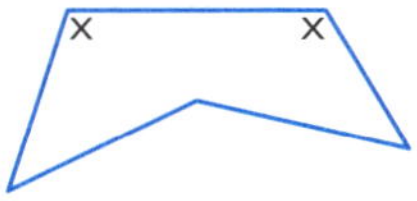

6. **half past eight, 10 o'clock**

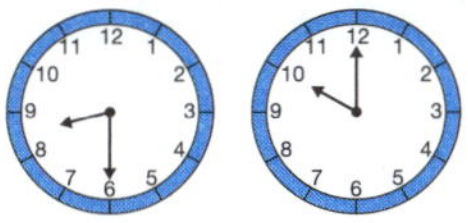

7. **6 o'clock**

8. **5 o'clock, quarter past 10**

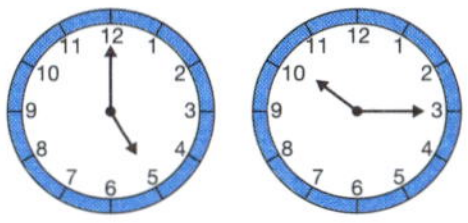

9. **9**

The 9 other angles that are less than a right angle have been marked with a cross.

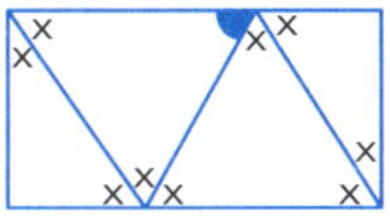

10. 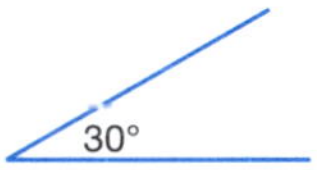

11. 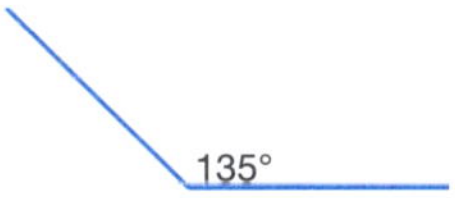

12. 

13. **120°**

The angle is 120°.

14. **half past nine**

360° is a revolution, so 720° is two revolutions. The minute hand has moved 2 hours. The time is now half past nine.

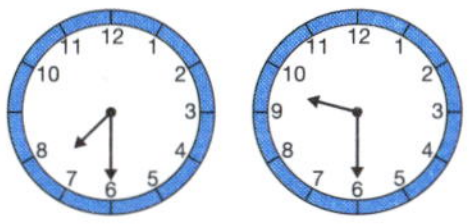

15. 

16 

17. 

18. **61°, 83°**

An acute angle measures less than 90°. This means the acute angles are 61° and 83°.

19. **101°, 178°**

An obtuse angle measures more than 90° but less than 180°. This means the obtuse angles are 101° and 178°.

20. **305°, 199°**

A reflex angle measures more than 180° but less than 360°. This means the reflex angles are 305° and 199°.

21. **180°**

The minute hand has moved through 180°.

 to 

22. **2**

A right angle measures 90°. A straight angle measures 180°. As $180 \div 90$ is 2, there are 2 right angles.

Unit 8B PAGE 29

1. **30°**

These angles add up to 180°. If one angle is 150°, then the angle on the other side is 30°.

2. **30°**

These angles add up to 180°. Two of the angles are 90° and 60° which add up to 150°. This means the other angle is 30°.

3. **35°**

These angles add up to 180°. Two of the angles are 90° and 55° which add up to 145°. This means the other angle is 35°.

4. **245°**

The two angles shown on the diagram add up to 360°. This means the unknown angle is 360° – 115°. The angle is 245°.

5. **7 o'clock**

6. **298°**

The two angles shown on the diagram add up to 360°. This means the unknown angle is 360° – 62°. The angle is 298°.

7. **210°**

The three angles shown on the diagram add up to 360°. As 70 and 80 is 150, then the unknown angle is 360° – 150°. The angle is 210°.

8. **8:45**

As 270 is three quarters of 360, then 270° is three-quarters of a revolution. This means the minute hand is pointing to 9. The time is 8:45.

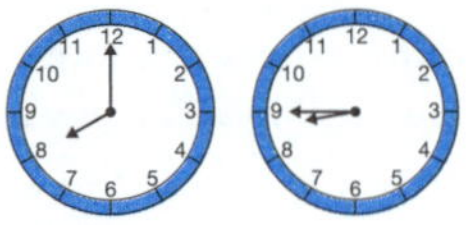

9. **11:00**

As 540 – 360 is 180, the minute hand has completed one and a half revolutions. This represents one and a half hours, so the time would be 11:00.

10. **70°**

The angles that make up a straight line add to 180°. As 180 – 40 is 140, and 140 ÷ 2 is 70, each angle is 70°.

11. **1440°**

An angle of revolution is 360°. As 360 × 4 = 1440, Lloyd rotated 1440°.

12. **104°**

A right angle measures 90°. As 90 + 110 + 56 is 256, the three angles add to 256°. As 360 – 256 is 104, the other angle measures 104°.

13. **isosceles**

As 32 + 74 is 106, and 180 – 106 is 74, the three angles measure 32°, 74° and 74°. This means it is an isosceles triangle.

14. **90°**

 to 

The hour hand has moved 3 hours out of 12 hours. This means it has travelled through 90°.

15. **45°**

An angle of revolution is 360°. As 360 ÷ 8 is 45, each slice is an angle of 45°.

16. **240°**

An angle of revolution is 360°. As 360 ÷ 6 is 60, and 2 × 60 is 120, the angle of cake removed is 120°. As 360 – 120 is 240, the angle remaining is 240°.

17. **south-west**

315 is 180 + 90 + 45. From west, rotating 180° is facing east, another 90° in a clockwise direction is south and then another 45° is facing south-west.

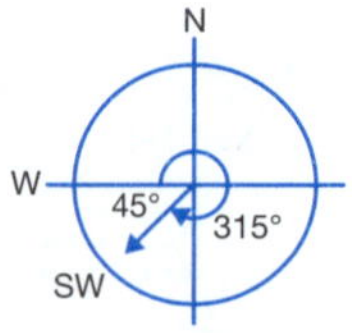

18. **7 am**

As 1800 ÷ 180 is 10, then 1800 ÷ 360 is 5. This means 5 hours has elapsed. The time is 7 am.

Unit 9A PAGE 30

1. $\frac{1}{8}$

There are eight sections on the spinner and each section is identical in size. There is one section that has the number 2. This means the probability of stopping on a 2 is $\frac{1}{8}$.

2. **0**

When an event is impossible the probability is 0.

3. $\frac{1}{6}$

There are six possible outcomes, but only one 4. This means the probability is $\frac{1}{6}$.

4. $\frac{2}{7}$

There are seven tokens in the box but only two are blue. The probability of choosing a blue token is $\frac{2}{7}$.

5. $\frac{2}{9}$

There are nine balls in the box. Two of the balls are yellow. The probability of choosing a yellow ball is 2 out of 9, or $\frac{2}{9}$.

6. $\frac{1}{8}$

There are eight balls in the box. One of the balls is numbered 4. The probability of choosing a 4 is 1 out of 8, or $\frac{1}{8}$.

7. $\frac{5}{8}$

There are eight cards in the box. Five of the cards are black. The probability of choosing a black card is 5 out of 8, or $\frac{5}{8}$.

8. $\frac{3}{5}$

There are five numbered counters in the box. Three of the numbers are odd (1, 3 and 5). The probability of choosing an odd number is 3 out of 5, or $\frac{3}{5}$.

9. $\frac{5}{10}$ **(or** $\frac{1}{2}$**)**

There are 10 balls in the bag. Five of the balls are green. The probability of choosing a green ball is 5 out of 10, or $\frac{5}{10}$, which can be written as $\frac{1}{2}$.

10. $\frac{1}{6}$

There are six possible outcomes: 1, 2, 3, 4, 5 and 6. This means the probability of it landing on a 3 is $\frac{1}{6}$.

11. **3**

There must be eight marbles in the bag. As there are five yellow marbles, there must be three green marbles.

12. $\frac{3}{4}$

There are three numbers less than 9: 3, 5, 7. The probability of spinning a number less than 9 is $\frac{3}{4}$.

13. $\frac{1}{6}$

A regular hexagon has six equal sides. There are six sections on the spinner. There is one section coloured red. This means the probability of stopping on red is $\frac{1}{6}$.

14. **6**

Half of the discs must be black. As half of 12 is 12 ÷ 2 which is 6, there must be six black discs in the bag.

15. $\frac{3}{8}$

There are eight sections on the spinner and each section is identical in size. There are three sections that are blue. This means the probability of Jonah winning is $\frac{3}{8}$.

16. **3**

There are three green balls and the probability of selecting a green ball is $\frac{3}{8}$. This means there must be eight balls in the bag. As 8 – 3 – 2 is 3, there must be three orange balls.

17. $\frac{1}{2}$

Half the children are girls. This means the probability of selecting a girl is $\frac{1}{2}$.

18. $\frac{2}{6}$ **(or** $\frac{1}{3}$**)**

There are six faces and two of them are 1s. This means the probability of rolling a 1 is $\frac{2}{6}$, which can be written as $\frac{1}{3}$.

19. $\frac{3}{8}$ **and** $\frac{4}{7}$

Probability ranges from 0 to 1. This means that an event could have a probability of $\frac{3}{8}$ or $\frac{4}{7}$.

Unit 9B PAGE 31

1. $\frac{4}{8}$ **(or** $\frac{1}{2}$**)**

There are eight sections on the spinner and each section is identical in size. The multiples of 2 on the spinner are 2, 4, 6 and 8. As there are four multiples the probability is $\frac{4}{8}$.

2. $\frac{2}{3}$

Probability ranges from 0 (which is impossible) to 1 (which is certain). If the event was likely the probability could be $\frac{2}{3}$.

3. $\frac{4}{6}$ **(or** $\frac{2}{3}$**)**

The numbers 3, 4, 5 and 6 are more than 2. This means there are four outcomes out of a possible six. The probability is $\frac{4}{6}$ which can be written as $\frac{2}{3}$.

4. $\frac{6}{9}$ **(or** $\frac{2}{3}$**)**

There are nine balls in the box. Three of the balls are red and six balls are not red. The probability of choosing a ball that is not red is 6 out of 9, or $\frac{6}{9}$, which can be written as $\frac{2}{3}$.

5. $\frac{3}{8}$

There are eight balls in the box. Three of the balls have an odd number. The probability of choosing an odd number is 3 out of 8, or $\frac{3}{8}$.

6. $\frac{5}{10}$ **(or** $\frac{1}{2}$**)**

After the two cards are added, there are 10 cards in the box. Five of the cards are white. The probability is 5 out of 10, or $\frac{5}{10}$, which can be written as $\frac{1}{2}$.

7. $\frac{4}{5}$

There are five counters in the box. The numbers in the box that are factors of 24 are 1, 3, 6 and 8. This means there are four counters that are factors of 24. The probability is 4 out of 5, or $\frac{4}{5}$.

8. $\frac{8}{10}$ **(or** $\frac{4}{5}$**)**

There are 10 balls in the bag. Two of the balls are green and so eight of the balls are not green. The probability of choosing a ball that is not green is 8 out of 10, or $\frac{8}{10}$, which can be written as $\frac{4}{5}$.

9. **15**

$\frac{2}{5}$ is the same as $\frac{10}{25}$. This means that 10 out of the 25 marbles in the bag are red. As 25 – 10 is 15, there must be 15 blue marbles.

10. $\frac{5}{8}$

A regular octagon has eight equal sides. There are eight sections on the spinner. The numbers 1 and 3 cover one section each and the number 5 covers three sections. As 1 + 1 + 3 is 5, the probability of stopping on an odd number is $\frac{5}{8}$.

11. $\frac{3}{4}$

Ignore the results from the first two spins. There are four sections on the spinner and three sections are coloured blue. This means the probability of stopping on blue is $\frac{3}{4}$.

12. $\frac{3}{6}$ **(or** $\frac{1}{2}$**)**

There are six possible outcomes: 1, 2, 3, 4, 5 and 6. There are three numbers more than 3. This means the probability of the dice landing on a number more than 3 is $\frac{3}{6}$, which can be written as $\frac{1}{2}$.

13. $\frac{2}{5}$

There is one red disc, so there must be two blue discs. As 5 – 1 – 2 is 2, there must two yellow discs. The probability of selecting a yellow disc is $\frac{2}{5}$.

14. $\frac{6}{8}$ **(or** $\frac{3}{4}$**)**

There are eight sections on the spinner and each section is identical in size. There are three sections that are red and three that are blue. This means there are six sections that are red or blue. The probability of Bridget winning is $\frac{6}{8}$, or $\frac{3}{4}$.

15. $\frac{3}{14}$

As $\frac{1}{2}$ of the balls are red there must be a total of $7 \times 2 = 14$ balls in the box. As 14 – 7 – 4 is 3, there are 3 blue balls in the box. The probability of selecting a blue ball is $\frac{3}{14}$.

16. $\frac{3}{4}$

One-quarter of the discs are blue and three-quarters are red. This means the probability of selecting a red disc is $\frac{3}{4}$.

17. $\frac{5}{6}$

There are six faces and five of them are at least 3. It does not matter whether the identified number is facedown or face up. The probability of rolling a number at least 3 is $\frac{5}{6}$.

18. $1\frac{1}{2}$ **and –0.8**

Probability ranges from 0 to 1. $1\frac{1}{2}$ is bigger than 1, and –0.8 is less than 0.

Unit 10A PAGES 32–33

1. $\frac{7}{20}$

Seven students scored less than 31 marks. The fraction is $\frac{7}{20}$.

2. **6**

As 4 + 2 is 6, there were six children who were aged 12 or 13 years old.

3. **2**

Students who have 0 siblings are the 'only child' in their family. The display shows two students have no siblings.

4. **7**

As 5 + 2 is 7, then seven students had more than five home-cooked meals.

5. **15**

There were 10 bananas and five oranges. As 10 + 5 is 15, the total is 15.

6. **18**

Five students scored 18 marks which was the most common mark as it was the tallest column.

7. **C**

In games A, B and D, or three games, there were at least two goals scored.

8. **3**

Three members attended one class, five members attended two classes, four members attended three classes and so on.

9. **11**

Three students liked tennis and eight liked netball. As 3 + 8 is 11, there is a total of 11 students.

10. **13**

3 + 1 + 3 + 4 + 2 is 13. Sidney ran a total of 13 laps.

11. **60**

As 160 – 100 = 60, Charlotte's pulse dropped by 60 beats per minute.

12. **100 cm**

From the graph, Logan was 100 cm tall.

13. **19°**

1300 is 1 pm in 24-hour time. At noon (12) the temperature was 22° and by 2 pm it was 17°. The best estimate is 19°.

14. **15**

Add 11–15 (11) and more than 15 (4) students. As 11 + 4 = 15, there were 15 students.

15. **20**

Nine students chose green and 11 students chose red. As 9 + 11 is 20, then 20 students chose green or red.

16. **more than half**

$$\begin{array}{r} 16 \\ 31 \\ +\ \ 13 \\ \hline 60 \end{array}$$

There were 60 tickets sold, and 31 were child tickets. As $\frac{31}{60} > \frac{1}{2}$, then more than half of the tickets sold were child tickets.

Unit 10B — PAGES 34–35

1. $\frac{\mathbf{15}}{\mathbf{20}}$ **(or** $\frac{3}{4}$**)**

There were 20 students and five scored at least 36. As 20 – 5 is 15, then 15 students did not win a money prize. The fraction is $\frac{15}{20}$, which can be written as $\frac{3}{4}$.

2. **5**

As 20 – 3 is 17, then a total of 17 students have either brown or blue eyes. As 12 and 5 add to 17 and their difference is 7 there must be five blue-eyed students.

3. **13**

The graph shows 15 children. As 15 – 2 is 13, there were still 13 children at the party.

4. $\frac{\mathbf{7}}{\mathbf{30}}$

As 1 + 2 + 3 + 4 + 6 + 7 + 5 + 2 is 30, and seven students had five home-cooked meals the probability is $\frac{7}{30}$.

5. $\frac{\mathbf{6}}{\mathbf{12}}$ **(or** $\frac{1}{2}$**)**

As 1 + 6 + 3 + 1 + 1 is 12, then 12 people were surveyed. As six people use only one credit card the probability is $\frac{6}{12}$, which can be written as $\frac{1}{2}$.

6. **7**

As 4 + 0 + 1 + 2 is 7, then seven people had at least two subscriptions.

7. **5**

Total number of boys is 10 + 14 = 24. Total number of girls is 12 + 7 = 19. The difference is 24 – 19 which is 5. There are five more boys than girls.

8. $\frac{\mathbf{9}}{\mathbf{15}}$ $(\frac{3}{5})$

As 5 + 3 + 1 is 9, then nine students scored at least 18 marks. As there were 15 students who sat the quiz, the probability is $\frac{9}{15}$.

9. **5**

As 3 + 2 + 1 + 3 is 9, the team scored nine goals in the first four games. As 16 – 9 – 2 is 5, Ella's team scored five goals in game 6.

10. $\frac{\mathbf{9}}{\mathbf{26}}$

The number of students per sport is basketball (6 students), tennis (3), netball (8) and football (9).

As 6 + 3 + 8 + 9 is 26, the probability that a random student's favourite sport is football is $\frac{9}{26}$.

11. **21**

Thursday plus Friday is 1 + 3 = 4. This means she ran eight laps on Saturday. As 2 + 4 + 3 + 1 + 3 + 8 is 21, Eleanor ran a total of 21 laps.

12. **10:04**

4 minutes after the race Charlotte's pulse was 80 beats per minute. This was at 10:04.

13. **12**

When he was born, Logan was 50 cm long. 50 × 3 is 150. Logan was 12 when he was 150 cm tall. This means it took 12 years.

14. **25**

The 5–10 entry has 1 added to it (8 + 1 = 9 students) and so does the 11–15 entry (11 + 1 = 12).

As 9 + 12 + 4 = 25, there were 25 students with at least five devices.

15. **32**

As 9 ÷ 3 is 3, then three students chose yellow. As 4 × 4 is 16, then 16 students chose red. As 4 + 3 + 9 + 16 is 32, then 32 students were surveyed.

Section 2

Unit 1A — PAGE 36

1. **25, 30, 55**

The last digit must be a 5 or 0. The multiples of 5 are 25, 30 and 55.

2. **700**

293 is close to 300 and 421 is close to 400. As 300 + 400 = 700, then 700 is an estimate, to the nearest 100.

3. **180**

$$\begin{array}{r} 45 \\ \times\ \ \ 4 \\ \hline 180 \end{array}$$

180 students travelled on buses.

4. **3**

28 ÷ 5 is 5 and 3 over. This means there were three students left over.

5. **350**

7 × 5 is 35 and 35 × 10 means writing a 0 on the end of 35. The answer is 350.

6.

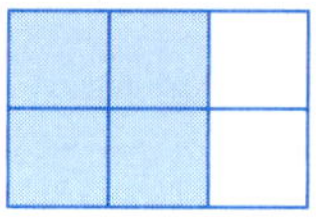

7. $\frac{\mathbf{1}}{\mathbf{3}}$

One whole is three-thirds. Three-thirds minus two-thirds is one-third. This is written as $\frac{3}{3} - \frac{2}{3} = \frac{1}{3}$.

8. **0.079**

Place value is ... units, decimal point, tenths, hundredths, thousandths ... There will be three decimal places in $\frac{79}{1000}$. This means $\frac{79}{1000} = 0.079$.

9. **$12**

As 24 ÷ 8 is 3, then Ethan needed to buy three packets. As 3 × 4 is 12, Ethan paid $12 for the bread rolls.

10. $\frac{\mathbf{7}}{\mathbf{8}}$

As 1, 3, 5 is a pattern of increasing by 2, the next number is 7. This means the next number in $\frac{1}{8}, \frac{3}{8}, \frac{5}{8}$ is $\frac{7}{8}$.

11. **70**

The question can be rewritten as 420 ÷ 6 = ☐. As 42 ÷ 6 is 7, then the missing number is 70.

12. **20 square units**

Counting the squares is 4 × 2 plus 6 × 2 which is 8 + 12 = 20. The area is 20 square units.

13. **2120**

As 12 + 9 is 21, then 9:20 pm is 2120.

14. ***F***

As B is opposite D and C is opposite E, then F is opposite A.

15.

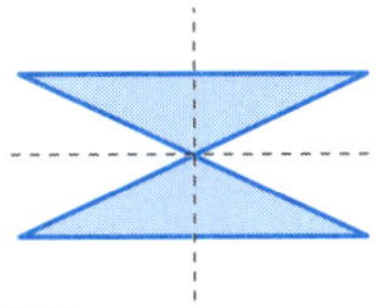

16. **110°**

The angle is 110°.

17. $\mathbf{\frac{1}{8}}$

There are eight sections on the spinner and each section is identical in size. There is one section that has the number 5. This means the probability of stopping on a 5 is $\frac{1}{8}$.

18. **13**

Thirteen students scored more than 30 marks.

Unit 1B PAGE 37

1. **30, 93, 1800**

The 3 times table gives the numbers 3, 6, 9, 12, …, 30, …, 93, … Also, as 18 is a multiple of 3, then 1800 is also a multiple of 3. The numbers are 30, 93 and 1800.

2. **$260**

$79.90 is close to $80, $48.35 is close to $50, $17.95 is close to $20 and $112.95 is close to $110. As 80 + 50 + 20 + 110 is 260, an estimate for the total cost is $260.

3. **3600**

$$\begin{array}{r} 240 \\ \times \quad 15 \\ \hline 1200 \\ 2400 \\ \hline 3600 \end{array}$$

A total of 3600 pies were produced.

4. **56**

448 = 400 + 48. 400 ÷ 8 is 50 and 48 ÷ 8 is 6 so 448 ÷ 8 = 56.

5. **160**

Both 16 × 4 and 16 × 6 are multiplying by 16. Add 4 and 6 which is 10, so the question is 16 × 10 which is 160.

6.

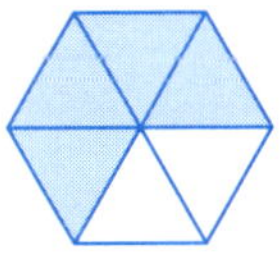

7. $\mathbf{\frac{4}{10}}$ **(or** $\mathbf{\frac{2}{5}}$**)**

$\frac{3}{10} + \frac{3}{10}$ is $\frac{6}{10}$. This means she still has $1 - \frac{6}{10}$ of the drink remaining. As $\frac{10}{10} - \frac{6}{10}$ is $\frac{4}{10}$, Alex has $\frac{4}{10}$, or $\frac{2}{5}$, of the water remaining.

8. **0.413**

$\frac{3}{10}$ is the same fraction as $\frac{300}{1000}$ and $\frac{7}{100}$ is the same as $\frac{70}{1000}$. The question is $\frac{300}{1000} + \frac{43}{1000} + \frac{70}{1000}$. As 300 + 43 + 70 is 413, the answer is $\frac{413}{1000}$, which is 0.413.

9. **$1**

As 1 orange costs 60 cents, then 5 oranges cost 300 cents, or $3. As 3 avocados cost $3, then 1 avocado is $1.

10. $\mathbf{\frac{4}{5}}$

From 2 to $1\frac{2}{5}$ is subtracting $\frac{3}{5}$. The missing number is $\frac{3}{5}$ more than $\frac{1}{5}$. Adding $\frac{3}{5}$ and $\frac{1}{5}$ is $\frac{4}{5}$.

11. **7**

98 – 42 is 56. The number sentence is 8 × ☐ = 56. This means the missing number is 56 ÷ 8 which is 7.

12. **15 cm**

The area is length × width. This means length × 8 is 120. As 120 ÷ 8 is 15, the length is 15 cm.

13. **6 pm**

1530 is 3:30 pm. Adding on 2 hours is 5:30 pm and then another half hour is 6:00 pm. The movie will finish at 6 pm.

14. **7**

6 and 4 are opposite faces so the total is 10. 3 and * are on opposite faces, so * = 7.

15.

The rectangle has a rotational symmetry of order 2. The star has a rotational symmetry of order 5.

16. **130°**

The angles on a straight line add to 180°. If one angle is 50°, then the angle on the other side is 130°.

17. $\mathbf{\frac{6}{8}}$ **(or** $\mathbf{\frac{3}{4}}$**)**

There are eight sections on the spinner and each section is identical in size. The factors of 24 that are shown on the spinner are 1, 2, 3, 4, 6, and 8. This means there are six factors and so the probability is $\frac{6}{8}$, or $\frac{3}{4}$.

18. **8**

34 minus 5 is 29. Add the number of students who scored more than 29 but less than 34. As 3 + 1 + 1 + 3 is 8, then 8 students were less than 5 marks from a money prize.

Unit 2A PAGE 38

1. **6000, 980**

The last digit must be 0. The multiples of 10 are 6000 and 980.

2. **1200**

714 is close to 700 and 479 is close to 500. As 700 + 500 = 1200, then 1200 is an estimate, to the nearest hundred.

3. **170 km**

$$\begin{array}{r} 34 \\ \times \quad 5 \\ \hline 170 \end{array}$$

Layla cycles 170 km.

4. **42**

126 = 120 + 6. 120 ÷ 3 is 40 and 6 ÷ 3 is 2 so 126 ÷ 3 = 42. Each boy receives 42 marbles.

5. **16**

Double 50 gives 100, so you need to halve 32. As 32 ÷ 2 is 16, the missing number is 16.

6. $\mathbf{\frac{1}{10}}$

Each fraction has 1 as the numerator (top number). The higher the denominator (bottom number) the smaller the fraction. The smallest is $\frac{1}{10}$ and the largest is $\frac{1}{3}$.

7. $\mathbf{\frac{3}{10}}$

The missing fraction is the difference between 1 and $\frac{7}{10}$, which is $\frac{10}{10} - \frac{7}{10}$. 10 tenths minus 7 tenths is 3 tenths. This is written as $1 - \frac{3}{10} = \frac{7}{10}$.

8. **0.413**

Place value is …, units, decimal point, tenths, hundredths, thousandths, … There will be three decimal places in $\frac{413}{1000}$. This means $\frac{413}{1000} = 0.413$.

9. **$131.20**

$$\begin{array}{r} 11.85 \\ 110.00 \\ + \quad 9.35 \\ \hline 131.20 \end{array}$$

The total is $131.20.

10. 5.39, 5.42

The pattern is adding 0.03. As 5.36 + 0.03 is 5.39, then adding 0.03 is 5.42. The next two numbers are 5.39 and 5.42.

11. 64

The missing number equals 16 × 4.

$$\begin{array}{r} 16 \\ \times \quad 4 \\ \hline 64 \\ \hline \end{array}$$

The missing number is 64.

12. 18 units

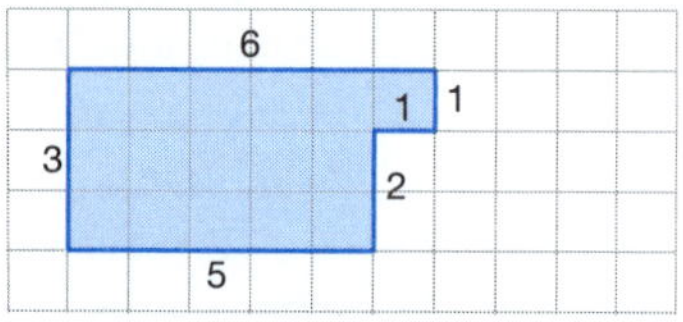

Counting the side lengths:
6 + 3 + 5 + 2 + 1 + 1 is 18.
This means the perimeter is 18 units.

13. 1755

The time is pm so add 12. As 12 + 5 is 17, then 5:55 pm is 1755.

14.

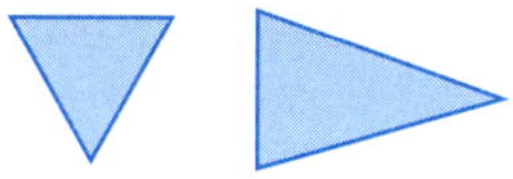

15. O

16.

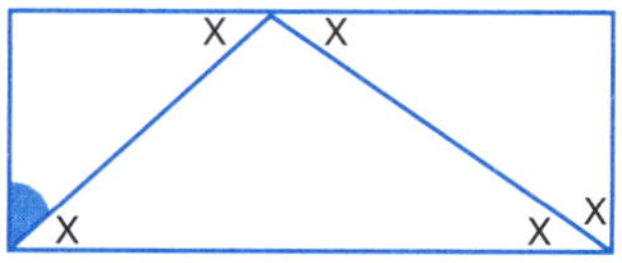

17. 1

When an event is certain the probability is 100%, or 1.

18. 20

Three students had zero siblings, eight students had one sibling, six students had two siblings, two students had three siblings and one student had four siblings.
3 + 8 + 6 + 2 + 1 is 20. This means 20 students were surveyed.

Unit 2B — PAGE 39

1. 40

Numbers with factors of 2 and 5 are multiples of 10. The only number is 40.

2. 80 000

35 768 is close to 36 000, 29 190 is close to 29 000 and 16 398 is close to 16 000. As 36 + 29 + 16 is 81, the total is close to 81 000, which is rounded off to 80 000, to the nearest ten thousand.

3. 224

$$\begin{array}{r} 16 \\ \times \quad 14 \\ \hline 64 \\ 160 \\ \hline 224 \\ \hline \end{array}$$

There were 224 seats in the library.

4. 205

1230 = 1200 + 30. 1200 ÷ 6 is 200 and 30 ÷ 6 is 5 so 1230 ÷ 6 = 205. There are 205 bales on each truck.

5. 752

Both 376 × 16 and 376 × 18 are multiplying 376. Subtract 16 from 18 which is 2, so the answer is 376 × 2 which is 752.

6. $\mathbf{\frac{2}{6}, \frac{2}{5}, \frac{2}{4}, \frac{2}{3}}$

Each fraction has 2 as the numerator (top number). The higher the denominator (bottom number), the smaller the fraction. The number in the denominator from largest to smallest is 6, 5, 4, 3, so that the order is $\frac{2}{6}, \frac{2}{5}, \frac{2}{4}, \frac{2}{3}$.

7. $\mathbf{\frac{17}{45}}$

The missing fraction is the difference between 1 and $\frac{28}{45}$, which is $\frac{45}{45} - \frac{28}{45}$.

As 45 – 28 is 17 then $\frac{45}{45} - \frac{28}{45}$ is $\frac{17}{45}$.

The missing fraction is $\frac{17}{45}$.

8. 5.009

Place value is … units, decimal point, tenths, hundredths, thousandths … There will be three decimal places in $\frac{9}{1000}$. This means $\frac{9}{1000}$ = 0.009, and so $5\frac{9}{1000}$ is 5.009.

9. 3

The cost of the children was \$54 – \$18 which is \$36. If each child ticket cost \$12, and 36 ÷ 12 is 3, then Sarah took three children with her to the park.

10. 123

The pattern is adding 22. As 57 + 22 is 79, then adding 22 is 101, adding 22 is 123. The sixth number is 123.

11. 0.21

0.79 is 79 hundredths and 1 is 100 hundredths. As 100 – 79 is 21, the missing number is 21 hundredths, or 0.21.

12. $\mathbf{13\frac{1}{2}}$ **units²**

Split the shape into a square and a triangle and count the grid squares.

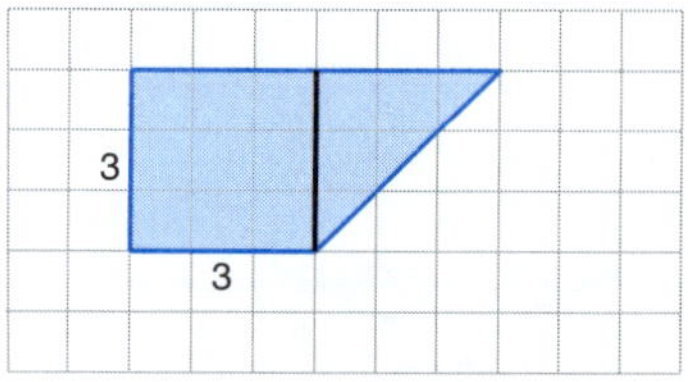

In the square there are 9 small grid squares. In the triangle there are 3 grid squares + 3 half-grid-squares which is $1\frac{1}{2}$. As 9 + 3 + $1\frac{1}{2}$ is $13\frac{1}{2}$, the area is $13\frac{1}{2}$ squares, or units².

13. 3 hours 30 minutes

As 14 to 17 is 3 then there will be 3 hours. From 20 to 50 is 30 which 30 minutes. The amount of time is 3 hours 30 minutes.

14. 6

7 and 3 are opposite faces so the total is 10. 4 and ✱ are on opposite faces, so ✱ = 6.

15. 1

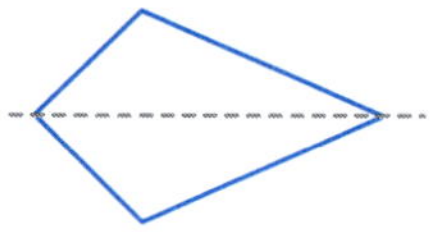

16. 110°

The angles on a straight line add to 180°. If one angle is 70°, then the angle on the other side is 110°.

17. $\mathbf{\frac{1}{3}}$

Probability ranges from 0 (which is impossible) to 1 (which is certain). If the event was likely the probability could be $\frac{2}{3}$, but it is unlikely so the probability could be $\frac{1}{3}$.

18. 30

Three students had zero siblings, eight students had one sibling, six students had two siblings, two students had three siblings and one student had four siblings. Now,
3 × 0 + 8 × 1 + 6 × 2 + 2 × 3 + 1 × 4 is 0 + 8 + 12 + 6 + 4 which is 30.
This means there are 30 siblings.

Unit 3A — PAGE 40

1. 2, 10, 20

The factors of 20 are 1, 2, 4, 5, 10, 20. From the list the numbers are 2, 10 and 20.

2. 233

$$\begin{array}{r} 85 \\ 38 \\ + \quad 110 \\ \hline 233 \\ \hline \end{array}$$

Brett scored a total of 233 runs.

3. 750

$$\begin{array}{r} 125 \\ \times \quad 6 \\ \hline 750 \end{array}$$

There were 750 tiles.

4. 1 and 2

When dividing by 4 the remainder is a number less than 4. This means 1 and 2 are possible remainders.

5. 6

Double 25 gives 50 so you need to halve 12. As 12 ÷ 2 is 6, the missing number is 6.

6. $\frac{6}{6}$ and $\frac{3}{3}$

When the numerator (top number) is the same as the denominator (bottom number) the fraction is equal to 1 (or one whole).

7. $2\frac{1}{4}$ (or $\frac{9}{4}$)

As 3 + 3 + 3 is 9, then $\frac{3}{4} + \frac{3}{4} + \frac{3}{4} = \frac{9}{4}$.
Rewriting this improper fraction as a mixed numeral gives $2\frac{1}{4}$.

8. 40

Four hundredths is written as 0.04. This is the same as 0.040. This means that 4 hundredths is 40 thousandths.

9. $27.15

$$\begin{array}{r} 40.00 \\ -\ 12.85 \\ \hline 27.15 \end{array}$$

10. 12.889, 12.895

Look at the last two digits of each decimal: 71, 77, 83 so the rule is adding 6. The next two numbers can be found by adding 83 + 6 which is 89 and another 6 gives 95. The next two decimals are 12.889 and 12.895.

11. 25

You need to work out 125 ÷ 5. 125 = 100 + 25. 100 ÷ 5 is 20 and 25 ÷ 5 is 5 so 125 ÷ 5 = 25. The missing number is 25.

12. 26 units

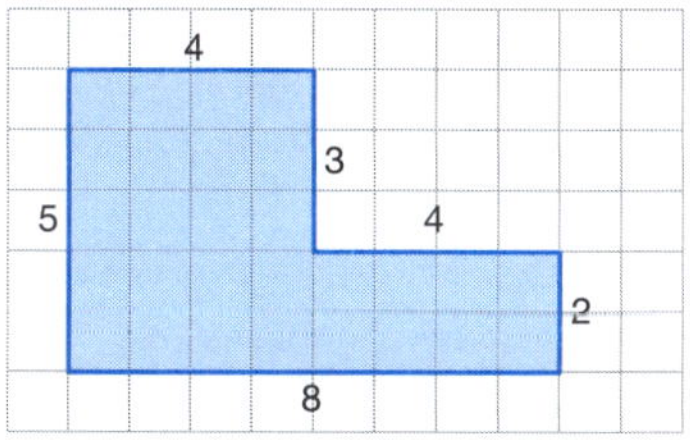

Counting the side lengths:
5 + 8 + 2 + 4 + 3 + 4 = 26.
This means the perimeter is 26 units.

13. 1:18 pm

11 am plus 2 hours is 1 pm. Add on another 18 minutes gives 1:18 pm.

14.

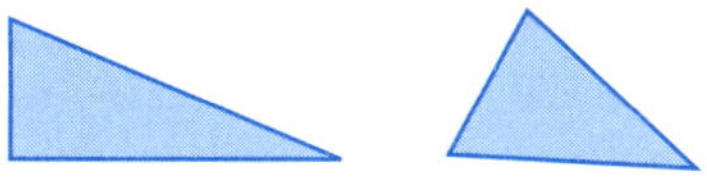

15.

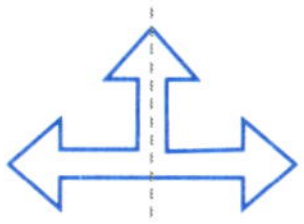

16.

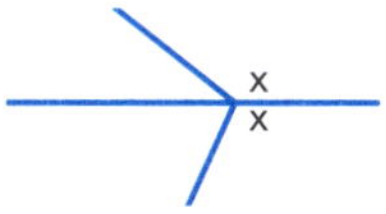

17. $\frac{1}{6}$

There are six possible outcomes, but only one 4. This means the probability is $\frac{1}{6}$.

18. 35

He counted 17 cars, six vans, 11 trucks and one motorbike. It is easier to count the number of 5s in the tally and then the other 1s. 6 × 5 + 5 is 30 plus 5 which is 35. There were 35 vehicles.

Unit 3B — PAGE 41

1. 24

Factors of 15: 1, 3, 5, 15. Factors of 18: 1, 2, 3, 6, 9, 18. Factors of 24: 1, 2, 3, 4, 6, 8, 12, 24. Factors of 28: 1, 2, 4, 7, 14, 28. This means 24 has the most factors.

2. 209 954

$$\begin{array}{r} 56\,347 \\ 53\,583 \\ +\ 100\,024 \\ \hline 209\,954 \end{array}$$

The total attendance is 209 954.

3. 988

$$\begin{array}{r} 38 \\ \times \quad 26 \\ \hline 228 \\ 760 \\ \hline 988 \end{array}$$

There are 988 seats in the theatre.

4. 39, 51

Need to find 3 more than multiples of 4. As 39 ÷ 4 is 9 remainder 3 and 51 ÷ 4 is 12 remainder 3, the possible number of balls are 39 or 51.

5. 900

Multiplying 25 by 4 gives 100. Now multiply 225 by 4, which gives 900. The missing number is 900.

6. $\frac{3}{5}$ and $\frac{3}{4}$

When the numerator (top number) is smaller than the denominator (bottom number) the fraction is smaller than 1.

7. $3\frac{3}{4}$ km

$\frac{3}{4} + \frac{3}{4} + \frac{3}{4} + \frac{3}{4} + \frac{3}{4}$ is $\frac{15}{4}$. Rewriting this improper fraction as a mixed numeral gives $3\frac{3}{4}$. Chloe walked a total of $3\frac{3}{4}$ km.

8. 5100

51 tenths is written as $5\frac{1}{10}$ or 5.1. This is the same as 5.100. This means that 51 tenths is 5100 thousandths.

9. 70 cents

As 240 ÷ 3 is 80, a banana costs 80 cents. This means that two apples cost $2.20 – $0.80 which is $1.40. As 2 apples cost $1.40, then each apple costs 70 cents.

10. 53

The pattern is adding 7. As 32 + 7 is 39, then adding 7 gives 46, and adding 7 again gives 53. The first number greater than 50 is 53.

11. $\frac{3}{5}$

The number sentence can be rewritten as $\square = 1 - \frac{2}{5}$.

As 1 is equal to $\frac{5}{5}$, and $\frac{5}{5} - \frac{2}{5} = \frac{3}{5}$, the missing number is $\frac{3}{5}$.

12. 24 units

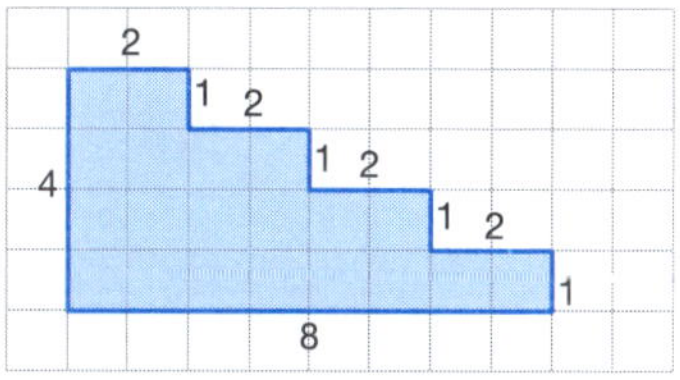

Counting the side lengths: 4 + 8 + 4 lots of 1s + 4 lots of 2s = 24. This means the perimeter is 24 units.

13. 2030

Adding 2 hours to 6:30 pm gives 8:30 pm. This is pm time so add 12 and 8 to get 20 which means Scouts finishes at 2030.

14. 4

8 and 3 are opposite faces so they multiply to give 24. 6 and ✱ are on opposite faces. As 6 × ✱ gives 24, then ✱ is 4.

15. 5

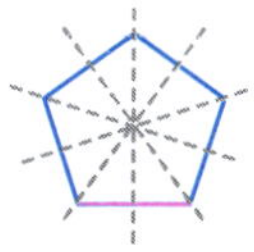

16. 120°

Angles on a straight line add to 180°. If one angle is 60°, then the other angle is 120°.

17. $\frac{3}{6}$ **(or $\frac{1}{2}$)**

The numbers 1, 2 and 3 are less than 4. This means there are three outcomes out of a possible six. The probability is $\frac{3}{6}$ which can be written as $\frac{1}{2}$.

18. **10**

There were 17 cars, six vans and one motorbike. As 6 + 1 is 7, you need to find the difference between 17 and 7. As 17 − 7 is 10, there were 10 more cars than the total of vans and motorbikes.

Unit 4A — PAGE 42

1. **32, 48**

The 8 times table gives the numbers 8, 16, 24, 32, 40, 48, 56 … From the list the numbers are 32 and 48.

2. **281 cm**

$$\begin{array}{r} 136 \\ +\ 145 \\ \hline 281 \end{array}$$

Their total height is 281 cm.

3. **143**

$$\begin{array}{r} 13 \\ \times\ 11 \\ \hline 143 \end{array}$$

There are 143 players in the club.

4. **87**

435 is 400 + 35. 400 ÷ 5 is 80 and 35 ÷ 5 is 7 so 435 ÷ 5 = 87.

5. **12 478**

In 13 478 there is 13 thousand…etc. As 13 − 1 is 12, the answer is 12 thousand…etc, or 12 478.

6. $\frac{11}{4}$

There are four quarters in one whole. In $2\frac{3}{4}$ there are 2 × 4 + 3 quarters. This means there are 8 + 3 = 11 quarters, written as $\frac{11}{4}$.

7. $1\frac{3}{8}$

As $\frac{7}{8} - \frac{4}{8}$ is $\frac{3}{8}$, then $1\frac{7}{8} - \frac{4}{8}$ is $1\frac{3}{8}$.

8. **30.21**

To compare, rewrite each decimal with two decimal places: 13.29, 29.31, 30.40, 30.21. As 30.21 is only 21 hundredths from 30.00 it is the closest.

9. **$14.60**

$$\begin{array}{r} 365 \\ \times\ 4 \\ \hline 1460 \end{array}$$

The total cost was $14.60.

10. **532.68, 532.64**

Look at the last two digits of each decimal: 80, 76, 72. The rule is subtracting 4. The next two numbers are found by subtracting: 72 − 4 = 68 and 68 − 4 = 64. The next two decimals are 532.68 and 532.64.

11. **21**

The missing number can be found from 84 ÷ 4.

$$4\overline{)84}\ \ \text{gives}\ 21$$

The missing number is 21.

12. **500**

There are 1000 metres in 1 km. As half of 1000 is 500, then there are 500 m in half a kilometre.

13. **11:45 am**

1145 is before 1200 so it is am. The time is 11:45 am.

14. ***T***

Q is opposite *S*, *R* is opposite *U* and so *T* is opposite *P*.

15.

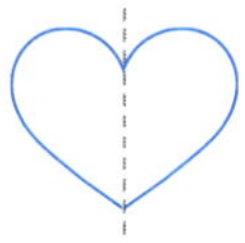

16. **2**

The angles marked with a cross are smaller than 90°.

17. $\frac{3}{7}$

There are seven tokens in the box. Three of the tokens are red. The probability of choosing a red token is 3 out of 7, or $\frac{3}{7}$.

18. **8**

There were three apples and five oranges. As 3 + 5 is 8, the total is 8.

Unit 4B — PAGE 43

1. **60, 120**

3, 4 and 5 are factors of 60. From the list, 60 and 120 are multiples of 60.

2. **519 cm**

$$\begin{array}{r} 162 \\ 181 \\ +\ 176 \\ \hline 519 \end{array}$$

The total height is 519 cm.

3. **272**

$$\begin{array}{r} 17 \\ \times\ 16 \\ \hline 102 \\ 170 \\ \hline 272 \end{array}$$

There are 272 players.

4. **3**

203 = 200 + 3. 200 ÷ 4 is 50 so 203 ÷ 4 = 50, with remainder 3.

This means 3 students travel by car.

5. **53 781**

In 63 781 there is 63 thousand … etc. As 63 − 10 is 53, the answer is 53 thousand … , etc., or 53 781.

6. **18**

There are two quarters in one half. You need to change $4\frac{2}{4}$ into an improper fraction. 4 times 4 is 16 plus 2 is 18. This means 18 quarters of orange can be cut.

7. $3\frac{3}{5}$ **metres**

Rewrite $4\frac{1}{5}$ as an improper fraction.

As 5 × 4 + 1 is 21, then $4\frac{1}{5}$ is $\frac{21}{5}$. Now, $\frac{21}{5} - \frac{3}{5}$ is $\frac{18}{5}$, which is $3\frac{3}{5}$. The length of the remaining pipe is $3\frac{3}{5}$ metres.

8. **22.92**

To compare, rewrite each decimal with three decimal places: 23.400, 23.087, 22.920, 22.908. So, 23.4 is 400 thousandths from 23, 23.087 is 87 thousandths from 23, 22.92 is 80 thousandths from 23 and 22.908 is 92 thousandths from 23. This means that 22.92 is the closest.

9. **$577**

Two games at $39 is 39 × 2 = 78. Add 499 and 78 gives
499 + 78 = 500 + 78 − 1 = 577.
The total cost was $577.

10. **19**

The pattern is subtracting 9. As 46 − 9 is 37, then subtracting 9 is 28, and subtracting 9 again is 19. The first number less than 20 is 19.

11. **18**

15 + 12 is 27, and now 27 − 9 is 18. The missing number is 18.

12. **36 cm^2**

As 24 ÷ 4 is 6, the side length is 6 cm. As 6 × 6 is 36, the area of the square is 36 cm^2.

13. **15 minutes**

As 2300 – 1200 is 1100 then 2345 – 1200 is 1145. This means the time is 11:45 pm, or a quarter to 12. As there are 60 minutes in an hour, Violet needs to wait another 15 minutes until midnight.

14. **5**

8 and 4 are opposite faces so the total is 12. 7 and ✱ are on opposite faces, so ✱ = 5.

15. **6**

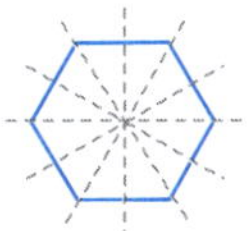

16. **40°**

Angles on a straight line add to 180°. If one angle is 140°, then the other angle is 40°.

17. $\frac{5}{7}$

There are seven tokens in the box. As there are three red tokens and two blue tokens, then five of the tokens are red or blue. The probability of choosing a red or blue token is 5 out of 7, or $\frac{5}{7}$.

18. $\frac{5}{28}$

Counting the types of fruit: 3 + 10 + 5 + 2 + 8 is 28. As five students brought an orange, the fraction is $\frac{5}{28}$.

Unit 5A PAGE 44

1. **45, 290, 15**

The last digit must be 0 or 5. The multiples of 5 are 45, 290 and 15.

2. **955**

$$\begin{array}{r} 568 \\ +\ 387 \\ \hline 955 \end{array}$$

There is a total of 955 students at both schools.

3. **$36**

9 × 4 = 36. This means the cost will be $36.

4. **4**

The missing number can be found by dividing 48 by 12. The answer is 4.

5. **356 739**

In 456 739 there is 4 hundred thousand … , etc. As 4 – 1 is 3, the answer is 3 hundred thousand … , etc., or 356 739.

6. **See below.**

Rewrite $\frac{3}{2}$ as a mixed numeral. How many 2s go into 3 … 1 and 1 left over. This means $\frac{3}{2} = 1\frac{1}{2}$. Shade 1 whole shape and $\frac{1}{2}$ of another (3 squares).

7. $\frac{3}{5}$

As 2 + 1 is 3, then $\frac{2}{5} + \frac{1}{5} = \frac{3}{5}$.

8. **3 thousandths**

Both numbers are identical except the digit in the third decimal place (thousandths). The difference is 3 thousandths.

9. **$47**

$$5\overline{)235}^{\,47}$$

Each child will receive $47.

10. **1, 21**

The pattern is adding 4. This means the last number is 17 + 4 which is 21. The first number is 5 – 4 which is 1. The two missing numbers are 1 and 21.

11. **15**

The missing number can be found by dividing 120 by 8.

$$8\overline{)120}^{\,15}$$

The missing number is 15.

12. **km**

The long distance is measured in kilometres.

13. **1615**

1415 plus 2 hours is 1615.

14. ***F***

C is opposite *E*, *A* is opposite *D* and so *F* is opposite *B*.

15.

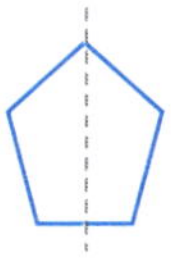

16. **See below.**

The angle marked with a cross is more than 90° but does not make a straight line.

17. $\frac{2}{5}$

There are five balls in the box. Two of the balls are black. The probability of choosing a black ball is 2 out of 5, or $\frac{2}{5}$.

18. **15**

Six students liked basketball and nine liked football. As 6 + 9 is 15, there is a total of 15 students.

Unit 5B PAGE 45

1. **24**

Multiples of 8 are 8, 16, 24, 32 … and the multiples of 12 are 12, 24, 36 … The lowest multiple of both 8 and 12 is 24.

2. **183 104**

$$\begin{array}{r} 48\,088 \\ 50\,749 \\ +\ 84\,267 \\ \hline 183\,104 \end{array}$$

The total student population is 183 104.

3. **2275 grams**

$$\begin{array}{r} 65 \\ \times\ 35 \\ \hline 325 \\ 1950 \\ \hline 2275 \end{array}$$

The total mass is 2275 grams.

4. **904**

The missing number can be found by dividing 5424 by 6.

5424 = 5400 + 24. 5400 ÷ 6 is 900 and 24 ÷ 6 is 4 so 5424 ÷ 6 = 904.

5. **10 876 083**

In 11 876 083 there is 11 million … , etc. As 11 – 1 is 10, the answer is 10 million … , etc., or 10 876 083.

6. **See below.**

Rewrite $\frac{7}{3}$ as a mixed numeral. How many 3s go into 7 … 2 and 1 left over. This means $\frac{7}{3} = 2\frac{1}{3}$. Shade 2 whole shapes and $\frac{1}{3}$ of another (2 squares).

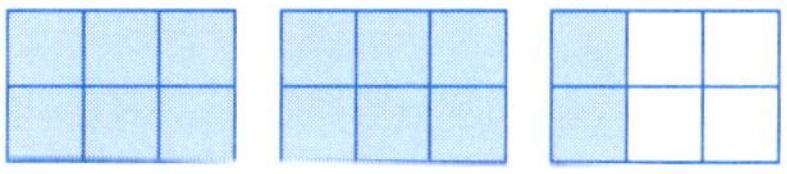

7. $\frac{4}{5}$

2 fifths plus 1 fifth plus 1 fifth is 4 fifths. This is written as $\frac{2}{5} + \frac{1}{5} + \frac{1}{5} = \frac{4}{5}$.

8. **25 thousandths**
The first part of each decimal is the same but the last two digits are different. As 99 – 74 is 25, the difference is 25 thousandths.

9. **$126**
Half of 42 is 21 so the cost of a child ticket is $21. The cost will be 42 × 2 + 21 × 2 = 84 + 42 = 126. The total cost will be $126.

10. **38.93, 38.81**
Look at the last three digits of each decimal: 929, 917, 905 so the rule is subtracting 12. The next two numbers are 905 – 12 which is 905 – 5 – 7. This is 900 – 7 which is 893 and then subtracting 12 gives 881. The next two decimals are 38.93 and 38.81.

11. **26**
53 + 37 is 90. The number sentence can be written as 116 – ☐ = 90. The missing number is 116 – 90 which is 26. The missing number is 26.

12. **16 cm**
To find the side length look for a number that multiplies itself to give 16 (square root of 16). As 4 × 4 is 16, then the side length is 4 cm. As 4 × 4 the perimeter is 16 cm.

13. **10 hours**
As 2100 is 9 pm, there are 3 hours until midnight. From midnight to 7 am is 7 hours. As 3 + 7 is 10, Jared slept for 10 hours.

14. **6**
9 and 4 are opposite faces so they multiply to give 36. As 6 and ✱ are on opposite faces, then 6 × ✱ = 36, and so ✱ = 6.

15. **1**
When it is rotated 360°, it will look the same only when it has completed the rotation. This means it has a rotational symmetry of order 1.

16. **30°**
Angles on a straight line add to 180°. If one angle is 150°, then the other angle is 30°.

17. **0**
There are five balls in the box, but none of them are green. The probability of choosing a green ball is 0 because it is impossible to choose a green ball.

18. **30**
The new numbers are basketball (6 students), tennis (3), netball (8 + 4 = 12) and football (9). As 6 + 3 + 12 + 9 is 30, there are 30 students in the class.

Unit 6A — PAGE 46

1. **4, 8, 16**
The factors of 32 are 1, 2, 4, 8, 16, 32. From the list the numbers are 4, 8 and 16.

2. **159**

```
  538
– 379
  159
```

Meghan still has 159 pages to read.

3. **168 km**

```
   24
×   7
  168
```

Henry plans to walk 168 km.

4. **209**
You need to divide 1254 by 6.
1254 = 1200 + 54. 1200 ÷ 6 is 200 and 54 ÷ 6 is 9 so 1254 ÷ 6 = 209.

5. **420**
Dividing 14 by 2 gives 7. Now dividing 840 by 2 gives 420. The missing number is 420.

6. $\mathbf{\frac{5}{8}}$
The square has been spilt into 8 equal triangles. Three out of 8 or $\frac{3}{8}$ of the square is shaded. This means that $\frac{5}{8}$ is not shaded.

7. $\mathbf{\frac{3}{4}}$
As 1 + 2 is 3, then $\frac{1}{4} + \frac{2}{4} = \frac{3}{4}$.

8. **8.32**
Need to start with 8, followed by the decimal point, then 3, and then 2. The number is 8.32.

9. **$34.75**

```
  695
×   5
 3475
```

The total cost was $34.75.

10. $\mathbf{1\frac{4}{10}}$ **(or** $\mathbf{1\frac{2}{5}}$**) and** $\mathbf{1\frac{7}{10}}$
As $1\frac{1}{10}$ is $\frac{11}{10}$, the pattern is adding $\frac{3}{10}$. This means $1\frac{1}{10} + \frac{3}{10}$ is $1\frac{4}{10}$, and then adding another $\frac{3}{10}$ is $1\frac{7}{10}$. The next two numbers are $1\frac{4}{10}$ and $1\frac{7}{10}$.

11. **31**
The missing number is 124 ÷ 4.
124 = 120 + 4. As 120 ÷ 4 is 30 and 4 ÷ 4 is 1, then 124 ÷ 4 = 31.
The missing number is 31.

12. **L**
Petrol is a liquid and so is measured in litres.

13. **1547**
The time is pm so add on 12. As 12 + 3 is 15, then 3:47 pm is 1547.

14. ***V***
U is opposite *X*, *W* is opposite *Y* and so *V* is opposite *Z*.

15.
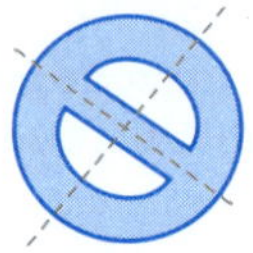

16. **11 o'clock, half past seven**

17. $\mathbf{\frac{2}{9}}$
There are nine balls in the box. Two of the balls are green. The probability of choosing a green ball is 2 out of 9, or $\frac{2}{9}$.

18. **19**
There are 12 girls in 5P and seven girls in 5R. As 12 + 7 is 19, there is a total of 19 girls in the two classes.

Unit 6B — PAGE 47

1. **45, 135, 432**
The digits will add to 9 or a multiple of 9. 45: 4 + 5 = 9, 135: 1 + 3 + 5 = 9, 432: 4 + 3 + 2 = 9. The multiples of 9 are 45, 135 and 432.

2. **2698 km**

```
  3424
–  726
  2698
```

The difference is 2698 km.

3. **1458**

```
    54
×   27
   378
  1080
  1458
```

The buses can transport 1458 passengers.

4. **209**
You need to divide 1672 by 8.
1672 = 1600 + 72. 1600 ÷ 8 is 200 and 72 ÷ 8 is 9 so 1672 ÷ 8 = 209.

5. 1120

Dividing 28 by 4 gives 7. Now dividing 4480 by 4 gives 1120. The missing number is 1120.

6. $\frac{7}{8}$

The square has been spilt into eight equal triangles. One out of 8 or $\frac{1}{8}$ of the square is shaded. This means that $\frac{7}{8}$ is not shaded.

7. $1\frac{1}{3}$

As 2 + 2 is 4, then $\frac{2}{3} + \frac{2}{3} = \frac{4}{3}$. How many 3s go into 4? … 1 and 1 left over. This means $\frac{4}{3} = 1\frac{1}{3}$.

8. 8.024

You need to start with 8, followed by the decimal point, then the 0, then the 2, and then 4. The number is 8.024.

9. $30.80

$$\begin{array}{r} 890 \\ \times \quad 3 \\ \hline 2670 \end{array} \qquad \begin{array}{r} 2670 \\ +\ 410 \\ \hline 3080 \end{array}$$

The total cost is $30.80.

10. 1.03, 0.96, 0.89

As 1.1 is 1.10, the sequence is starting at 1.24 and decreasing by 0.07. 1.10 minus 0.07 is 1.03.

$$\begin{array}{r} 1.03 \\ -\ 0.07 \\ \hline 0.96 \end{array}$$

Also, 0.96 minus 0.07 is 0.89. The next three numbers are 1.03, 0.96 and 0.89.

11. 0.47

0.53 is 53 hundredths. 1 is 100 hundredths and 100 – 53 is 47. The missing number is 47 hundredths, or 0.47.

12. 8 m by 4 m by 2.4 m

Length is 80 cm × 10 = 800 cm which is 8 m. Width is 80 cm × 5 = 400 cm which is 4 m. Height is 80 cm × 3 = 240 cm which is 2.4 m. The dimensions are 8 m by 4 m by 2.4 m.

13. 1430

The time is 2:20 pm. After another 10 minutes the time is 2:30 pm. As this is pm, add 2 on to 12 so 12 + 2 is 14 and the time the call finishes is 1430.

14. 14

8 and 12 are opposite faces so they add to give 20. As 6 and ✱ are on opposite faces, then 6 + ✱ = 20, and so ✱ = 14.

15. 1

When an isosceles triangle is rotated 360°, it will look the same only when it has completed the rotation. This means it has a rotational symmetry of order 1.

16. 50°

Angles on a straight line add to 180°. Two of the angles are 90° and 40° which add up to 130°. This means the other angle is 50°.

17. $\frac{7}{9}$

There are nine balls in the box. Two of the balls are blue and seven balls are not blue. The probability of choosing a ball that is not blue is 7 out of 9 or $\frac{7}{9}$.

18. 6

Total number of boys is 10 + 14 + 1 = 25. Total number of girls is 12 + 7 = 19. The difference is 25 – 19 which is 6. There are six more boys than girls.

Unit 7A PAGE 48

1. 14, 38

The 4 times table gives the numbers 4, 8, 12, 16, 20, 24, 28, 32, 36, 40, 44 … 80 … The numbers 14 and 38 are not on the list of multiples of 4. They will give remainders when divided by 4.

2. 13 141

$$\begin{array}{r} 29\,276 \\ -\ 16\,135 \\ \hline 13\,141 \end{array}$$

3. 96

$$\begin{array}{r} 16 \\ \times \quad 6 \\ \hline 96 \end{array}$$

Chloe will read 96 pages.

4. 63

630 ÷ 10 is 63. This means 63 bags will be needed.

5. 200

Look for pairs that add to 100. 35 + 65 = 100 and 28 + 72 = 100. This means 100 + 100 = 200.

6. *D*

The number line from 0 to 1 is broken into eighths.

$\frac{7}{8}$ is represented by the letter *D*.

7. $\frac{7}{10}$

As 3 + 4 is 7, then $\frac{3}{10} + \frac{4}{10} = \frac{7}{10}$.

8. 0.51

As 14 + 37 is 51, then $\frac{14}{100} + \frac{37}{100}$ is $\frac{51}{100}$. This is written as 0.51.

9. $51

$$\begin{array}{r} 850 \\ \times \quad 6 \\ \hline 5100 \end{array}$$

Erica's total savings was $51.00.

10. $4\frac{1}{4}$, $5\frac{1}{4}$

The pattern is adding 1. This means $3\frac{1}{4} + 1$ is $4\frac{1}{4}$, and then adding another 1 is $5\frac{1}{4}$. The next two numbers are $4\frac{1}{4}$ and $5\frac{1}{4}$.

11. 69

You need to divide 345 by 5. 345 = 300 + 45. 300 ÷ 5 is 60 and 45 ÷ 5 is 9 so 345 ÷ 5 = 69.

12. 65 cm

There are 100 cm in a metre. As 100 – 35 is 65, then there is 65 cm of ribbon remaining.

13. 2045

Quarter to nine is 8:45 pm. This is 2045 in 24-hour time.

14. ***J***

F is opposite *H*, *I* is opposite *K* and so *J* is opposite *G*.

15.

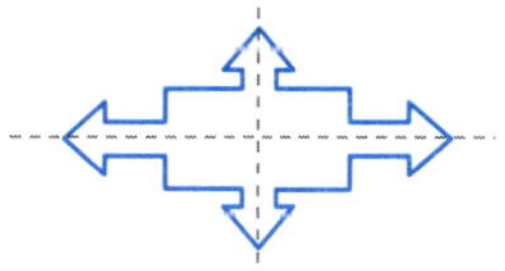

16. 9 o'clock, 3 o'clock

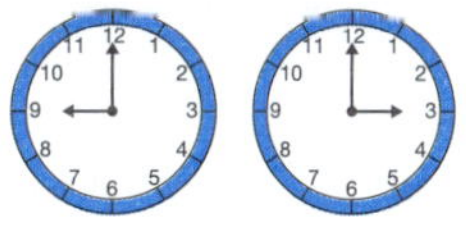

17. $\frac{3}{8}$

There are eight balls in the box. Three of the balls are numbered 2. The probability is 3 out of 8 or $\frac{3}{8}$.

18. 26

There were 38 pizzas sold on Saturday and 12 on Tuesday. As 38 – 12 = 26, there were 26 more pizzas.

Unit 7B PAGE 49

1. **320, 400**

As $2 \times 5 = 10$, the number has to be divisible by 10, or end with a 0. This means the numbers are 320 and 400.

2. **66 000**

78 294 is close to 78 000 and 11 890 is close to 12 000.
As $78\,000 - 12\,000 = 66\,000$, then 66 000 is an estimate of the crowd who had left, to the nearest thousand.

3. **775**

$$\begin{array}{r} 31 \\ \times\ 25 \\ \hline 155 \\ 620 \\ \hline 775 \end{array}$$

Nathan hopes to complete 775 sit-ups.

4. **100**

Compare 23 400 and 234. The two zeros have been removed, which happens when dividing by 100.

5. **700**

Look for pairs that add to hundreds. $123 + 77 = 200$ and $64 + 436 = 500$. This means $200 + 500 = 700$.

6. ***B***

Rewrite $\frac{18}{5}$ as a mixed numeral. How many 5s go into 18? … 3 and 3 left over. This means $\frac{18}{5} = 3\frac{3}{5}$, which is represented by *B*.

7. $1\frac{5}{8}$

As 7 + 6 is 13, then $\frac{7}{8} + \frac{6}{8} = \frac{13}{8}$. How many 8s go into 13? … 1 and 5 left over. This means $\frac{13}{8} = 1\frac{5}{8}$.

8. **0.551**

$\frac{5}{10}$ is the same fraction as $\frac{500}{1000}$ and $\frac{3}{100}$ is the same as $\frac{30}{1000}$. The question is $\frac{500}{1000} + \frac{21}{1000} + \frac{30}{1000}$. As $500 + 21 + 30$ is 551, the answer is $\frac{551}{1000}$, which is 0.551.

9. **$0.80**

As 170×3 is 510, the notebooks cost $5.10.

$$\begin{array}{r} 5.10 \\ 9.20 \\ +\ 4.90 \\ \hline 19.20 \end{array}$$

Lydia spent $19.20. The change is $20 – $19.20 = $0.80. Lydia received $0.80 in change.

10. **66**

As 27 – 14 is 13 and 40 – 27 is 13, the rule is starting with 14 and increasing by 13. As 40 + 13 is 53 and 53 + 13 is 66, the number is 66.

11. $\frac{3}{5}$

The number sentence can be rewritten as $\square = 1 - \frac{2}{5}$. As 1 is equal to $\frac{5}{5}$, and $\frac{5}{5} - \frac{2}{5} = \frac{3}{5}$, the missing number is $\frac{3}{5}$.

12. **3.2 m**

As the area is 64 cm², then the length of each side is 8 cm. This means each square requires $4 \times 8 = 32$ cm of wire. If there are 10 squares then the length of wire is $32 \times 10 = 320$ cm, or 3.2 m.

13. **8:30 am**

2230 is 10:30 pm. Adding 2 hours gives 12:30 am and then another 8 hours gets to 8:30 am. Joshua arrives at 8:30 am.

14. **8**

9 and 5 are opposite faces and as $9 - 5 = 4$, the difference will always be 4. 12 and ✱ are on opposite faces. 12 – ✱ = 4 means ✱ = 8.

15. **3**

When it is rotated 360°, it will look the same every third of a turn (120°). This means it has a rotational symmetry of order 3.

16. **2 o'clock**

17. $\frac{5}{8}$

There are eight balls in the box. Five of the balls have even numbers. The probability of choosing an even number is 5 out of 8, or $\frac{5}{8}$.

18. **114**

Monday (8), Tuesday (12), Wednesday (16), Thursday (12), Friday (28) and Saturday (38).
This is 8 + 12 + 16 + 12 + 28 + 38, which is 20 + 16 + 40 + 38 = 114.

Unit 8A PAGE 50

1. **60, 63, 66**

As 6 is a multiple of 3, then 60 is also a multiple of 3. From 60, counting on by 3s means 63 and 66 are also multiples of 3.

2. **48 000**

26 341 is close to 26 000 and 21 997 is close to 22 000.

As $26\,000 + 22\,000 = 48\,000$, then 48 000 is an estimate of the total population of the two cities, to the nearest thousand.

3. **15 048**

$$\begin{array}{r} 3762 \\ \times\ \ \ 4 \\ \hline 15\,048 \end{array}$$

4. **420**

$1260 = 1200 + 60$. As $1200 \div 3$ is 400 and $60 \div 3$ is 20, then $1260 \div 3 = 420$. There are 420 bales in each shipment.

5. **57**

As 15 + 5 + 10 is 30, the question can be rewritten as 87 – 30 which is 57.

6. $3\frac{3}{4}$

How many 4s go into 15? … 3 and 3 left over. This means $\frac{15}{4} = 3\frac{3}{4}$.

7. $\frac{7}{10}$

As 2 + 5 is 7, then $\frac{2}{10} + \frac{5}{10} = \frac{7}{10}$.

8. **7.85**

Rewrite the decimals with two decimal places: 7.80 and 7.90. Halfway between 80 and 90 is 85. This means the decimal is 7.85.

9. **$11.55**

$$\begin{array}{r} 20.00 \\ -\ 8.45 \\ \hline 11.55 \end{array}$$

Corrie receives change of $11.55.

10. **990, 960**

The pattern is subtracting 30.

$$\begin{array}{r} 1020 \\ -\ \ \ 30 \\ \hline 990 \end{array}$$

The fourth number is 990. Now, subtracting another 30 gives 960. The next two numbers are 990 and 960.

11. **108**

The missing number can be found by multiplying 18×6.

$$\begin{array}{r} 18 \\ \times\ \ 6 \\ \hline 108 \end{array}$$

The missing number is 108.

12. **935 mL**

There are 1000 mL in a litre. As 1000 – 65 is 935, then there is 935 mL of milk remaining.

13. **2230**

The time is pm so add on to 12. As 12 + 10 is 22, then 10:30 pm is 2230.

14. ***E***

C is opposite *F*, *B* is opposite *D* and so *E* is opposite *A*.

15. **1**

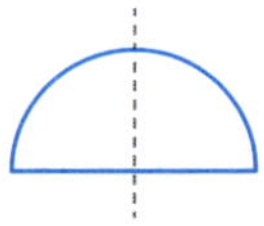

16. half past two, quarter past seven

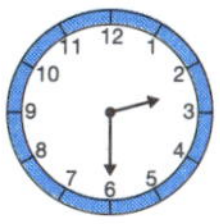
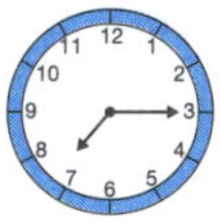

17. $\frac{1}{8}$

There are eight balls in the box. One of the balls is numbered 5. The probability of choosing a ball numbered 5 is 1 out of 8, or $\frac{1}{8}$.

18. $\frac{3}{25}$

The total number of students is $7 + 6 + 5 + 4 + 3$ which is 25. There are three students who chose PE. The fraction is $\frac{3}{25}$.

Unit 8B — PAGE 51

1. 1, 2

Factors of 6: 1, 2, 3, 6. Factors of 8: 1, 2, 4, 8. Factors of 12: 1, 2, 3, 4, 6, 12. The two common factors are 1 and 2.

2. 520 000

168 719 is close to 169 000 and 350 189 is close to 350 000. As 350 plus 169 is $350 + 150 + 19$ which is 519, then the total is close to 519 000, which rounded to the nearest ten thousand is 520 000.

3. 16 168

$$\begin{array}{r} 376 \\ \times \quad 43 \\ \hline 1128 \\ 15\,040 \\ \hline 16\,168 \end{array}$$

4. $15 000

Consider $75 \div 5$. $75 = 50 + 25$. $50 \div 5$ is 10 and $25 \div 5$ is 5 so $75 \div 5 = 15$. This means each charity receives $15 000.

5. 120

As $16 + 14 + 20 + 30$ is 80, the question can be rewritten as $200 - 80$ which is 120.

6. *D*

Rewrite $\frac{15}{4}$ as a mixed numeral. How many 4s go into 15? … 3 and 3 left over. This means $\frac{15}{4} = 3\frac{3}{4}$, which is represented by *D*.

7. $1\frac{4}{5}$

As $3 + 4 + 2$ is 9, then $\frac{3}{5} + \frac{4}{5} + \frac{2}{5} = \frac{9}{5}$. How many 5s go into 9? … 1 and 4 left over. This means $\frac{9}{5} = 1\frac{4}{5}$.

8. 14.737

Rewrite the decimals with three decimal places: 14.630 and 14.844. Halfway between 630 and 844 can be found by adding the numbers and then dividing the answer by 2. $630 + 844$ is 1474 and $1474 \div 2$ is 737. This means the decimal is 14.737.

9. $7

Cost was $450 \times 3 + 350 + 410 \times 2 + 390 \times 2$ which is $1350 + 350 + 820 + 780$.

$$\begin{array}{r} 1350 \\ 350 \\ 820 \\ + \quad 780 \\ \hline 3300 \end{array}$$

The total cost was $33. As $40 - 33$ is 7, the family have $7 left on the voucher.

10. 105

As $51 - 33$ is 18 and $69 - 51$ is 18, the rule is starting with 33 and increasing by 18. As $69 + 18$ is 87 and $87 + 18$ is 105, the number is 105.

11. 18

$15 + 12$ is 27, and now $27 - 9$ is 18. The missing number is 18.

12. 21 m

80 cm $\times$ 5 is 400 cm, or 4 metres. As $25 - 4$ is 21, then 21 metres of string remains.

13. 1400

11:30 am is written as 1130 in 24-hour time. Adding 2 hours gets to 1330. As half an hour is 30 minutes then adding 30 minutes gives 1400. Stella arrives home at 1400.

14. 4

The second cube will have a 3 opposite the 8. The first cube will have a 4 opposite the 3. This means a 4 will be opposite the 8 on the new prism.

15. 4

When it is rotated 360°, it will look the same every quarter of a turn (90°). This means it has a rotational symmetry of order 4.

16. 8 o'clock

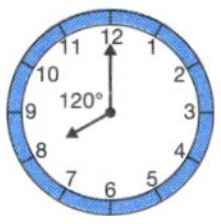

17. $\frac{5}{8}$

There are eight balls in the box. The factors of 6 are 1, 2, 3 and 6. This means five of the balls are factors of 6. The probability of choosing a factor of 6 is 5 out of 8, or $\frac{5}{8}$.

18. 2

Maths (7 students) and Science (5) is a total of 12 students. English (6) and Music (4) is a total of 10. The difference between the two totals is $12 - 10$ which is 2.

Unit 9A — PAGE 52

1. 30, 42, 60

The 6 times table gives the numbers 6, 12, 18, 24, 30 … 60 … From the list the numbers are 30, 42 and 60.

2. 61 387

$$\begin{array}{r} 58\,659 \\ + \quad 2\,728 \\ \hline 61\,387 \end{array}$$

The odometer will show 61 387 km.

3. 20 910

$$\begin{array}{r} 4182 \\ \times \quad 5 \\ \hline 20\,910 \end{array}$$

4. 60

As $24 \div 4$ is 6, then $240 \div 4 = 60$. Jack would drive 60 km.

5. 256

Change the order of the numbers to write the biggest numbers first: $200 + 50 + 6$ is 256.

6. $\frac{1}{2}$

Each fraction has 1 as the numerator (top number). The higher the denominator (bottom number) the smaller the fraction. The smallest is $\frac{1}{8}$ and the largest is $\frac{1}{2}$.

7. $\frac{5}{8}$

As $8 - 3$ is 5, then $\frac{8}{8} - \frac{3}{8} = \frac{5}{8}$.

8. 4.309, 4.379, 4.38

Rewrite the decimals with three decimal places: 4.380, 4.309, 4.379. Now compare the last three digits in each decimal: from smallest to largest is 309, 379, 380. This means the order is 4.309, 4.379, 4.38.

9. $1.30

There are 390 cents in $3.90.

$$\begin{array}{r} 130 \\ 3\overline{)390} \end{array}$$

One can costs 130 cents, or $1.30.

10. 20 075, 20 100

The pattern is adding 25. As $50 + 25$ is 75 the next number is 20 075. Adding another 25 to 75 is 100 so the next number is 20 100. The two numbers are 20 075 and 20 100.

11. **8 + 12 = 20**

'Sum' means to add. The number sentence is 8 + 12 = 20.

12. **3048**

There are 1000 mm in a metre, and so 3000 mm in 3 metres. As 3000 + 48 gives 3048, there are 3048 mm.

13. **1713**

As 12 + 5 is 17, then 5:13 pm is 1713.

14. **3**

A rectangular prism has six faces. It has three pairs of parallel faces.

15. **4**

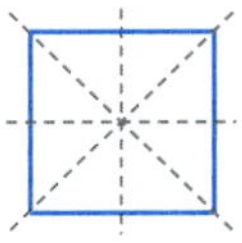

16.

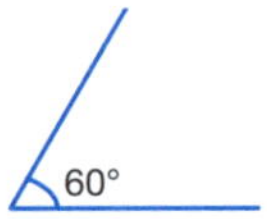

17. $\frac{3}{8}$

There are eight balls in the box. Three of the balls are numbered 2. The probability of choosing a 2 is 3 out of 8, or $\frac{3}{8}$.

18. **12**

Add the numbers that are listed: 13 + 15 + 10 is 38. If 50 people were surveyed, then the number who nominated the beach is 50 – 38 which is 12. This means 12 people nominated the beach.

Unit 9B PAGE 53

1. **12**

Factors are 1, 2, 3, 4, 5, 6, 10, 12, 15, 20, 30, 60. There are 12 factors.

2. **179 822**

```
   167 549
+   12 273
   179 822
```

The population of the city in 2021 was 179 822.

3. **3960**

```
   165
×   24
   660
  3300
  3960
```

A total of 3960 passengers rode the rollercoaster.

4. **1120**

4480 = 4000 + 480. 4000 ÷ 4 is 1000 and 480 ÷ 4 is 120.

This means 4480 ÷ 4 = 1120. The factory fills 1120 boxes each hour.

5. **2889**

Change the order of the numbers to write the biggest numbers first: 2100 + 600 + 150 + 32 + 7 is 2700 + 150 + 32 + 7, which is 2850 + 32 + 7, which is 2882 + 7, which is 2889.

6. $\frac{3}{10}, \frac{3}{8}, \frac{3}{5}, \frac{3}{4}$

Each fraction has 3 as the numerator (top number). The higher the denominator (bottom number), the smaller the fraction. In order the denominators are 10, 8, 5, 4 so that the fractions from smallest to largest are $\frac{3}{10}, \frac{3}{8}, \frac{3}{5}, \frac{3}{4}$.

7. $2\frac{1}{10}$

As 7 + 8 + 6 is 21, then $\frac{7}{10} + \frac{8}{10} + \frac{6}{10} = \frac{21}{10}$. How many 10s go into 21? … 2 and 1 left over. This means $\frac{21}{10} = 2\frac{1}{10}$.

8. **Lincoln**

Rewrite the decimals with two decimal places: 8.52, 8.09, 8.37 and 8.40. Now compare the last two digits in each decimal: from largest to smallest is 52, 40, 37, 9. The winner threw the largest distance and 40 is the second number on the list. Lincoln came second.

9. **$18**

Ryan's purchase is 2 cars + 3 trucks = $78. Double Aaron's purchase is 2 cars + 4 trucks = $96. Comparing these total costs means that a truck costs $96 – $78 = $18.

10. **401**

The numbers are increasing by 4. Each number in the sequence is 1 more than a multiple of 4. As 400 is a multiple of 4 then 400 + 1 = 401 is in the sequence.

11. **26**

53 + 37 is 90. The number sentence can be written as 116 – ☐ = 90. The missing number is 116 – 90 which is 26. The missing number is 26.

12. **18 025 192 mm**

There are 1000 mm in a metre, and 1000 m in a kilometre. This means there are 1 000 000 mm in a kilometre. 18 kilometres is 18 000 000 mm. 25 metres is 25 000 mm.

```
  18 000 000
      25 000
+        192
  18 025 192
```

13. **4:50 pm**

As 14:30 is 2:30 pm, adding 2 hours gives 4:30 pm. Adding another 20 minutes gives 4:50 pm. Hala leaves the shopping centre at 4:50 pm.

14. **1**

A pentagonal prism has five faces. It has only one pair of parallel faces.

15. **90°**

A full rotation is 360°. As 360 ÷ 4 is 90, then the shape should rotate 90° about its centre.

16. **222°**

There are two angles which add up to 360° shown on the diagram. This means the unknown angle is 360° – 138°. The angle is 222°.

17. $\frac{4}{8}$ **(or** $\frac{1}{2}$**)**

There are eight balls in the box. Four of the balls have a number at least 3. The probability is 4 out of 8, or $\frac{4}{8}$, which can be written as $\frac{1}{2}$.

18. **60**

Add the numbers that are listed: 13 + 15 + 12 is 40. This means two-thirds of the people equals 40, and so one-third will be 40 ÷ 2 = 20. The total number of people surveyed was 40 + 20 which is 60.

Unit 10A PAGE 54

1. **true**

The factors of 8 are 1, 2, 4, 8. This means it has four factors. The statement is true.

2. **512**

```
   337
+  175
   512
```

3. **11 184**

```
    1864
×      6
  11 184
```

4. **24**

You need to work out 96 ÷ 4.

96 = 80 + 16. 80 ÷ 4 is 20 and 16 ÷ 4 is 4 so 96 ÷ 4 = 24.

5. **71 400**

Mulitplying by 200 means to multiply by 2 and then multiply by 100. 357 × 2 is 714, and multiplying by 100 means writing 00 at the end of the number. The answer is 71400, which is written as 71 400.

6.

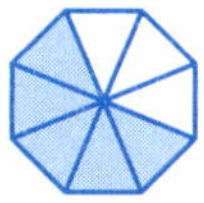

7. $\frac{11}{15}$

One whole is 15 fifteenths. 15 fifteenths minus 4 fifteenths is written as $\frac{15}{15} - \frac{4}{15} = \frac{11}{15}$.

8. ***B***

The number line is marked in 0.2s. *B* is between 2.6 and 2.8 which can be written as 2.60 and 2.80. As 75 is between 60 and 80, then *B* is closest to 2.75.

9. **$243.70**

$$\begin{array}{r} 89.00 \\ 18.95 \\ 119.00 \\ +\ \ 16.75 \\ \hline 243.70 \end{array}$$

The total cost was $243.70.

10. **10, 16, 22, 28, 34**

10, then 10 adding 6 is 16, adding 6 is 22, adding 6 is 28 and adding 6 is 34. The numbers are 10, 16, 22, 28, 34.

11. **$10 \times 9 > 65$**

'Product' means to multiply. The number sentence is $10 \times 9 > 65$.

12. **2085**

There are 1000 mL in a litre, and so 2000 mL in 2 litres. As 2000 + 85 is 2085, there are 2085 mL.

13. **4:00 pm**

1600 is past 1200 so it is pm. As 1600 – 1200 is 400 then the time is 4:00 pm.

14. **square, 4 triangles**

The net is made from 1 square and 4 triangles.

15. **3**

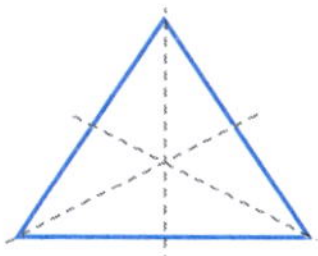

16.

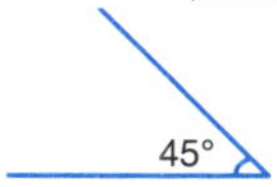

17. $\frac{3}{8}$

There are eight balls in the box. Three of the balls are white. The probability of choosing a white ball is 3 out of 8, or $\frac{3}{8}$.

18. **200**

64 + 49 + 51 + 36 can be better calculated by rewriting as 64 + 36 + 49 + 51 which is 100 + 100 = 200.

Unit 10B PAGE 55

1. **7**

All the numbers have more than two factors except 31 and 37 which have only two factors each. As there are nine numbers between 30 and 40, there must be seven numbers with more than two factors.

2. **1017**

$$\begin{array}{r} 478 \\ +\ \ 539 \\ \hline 1017 \end{array}$$

There are 1017 students.

3. **2100**

$$\begin{array}{r} 75 \\ \times\ \ 28 \\ \hline 600 \\ 1500 \\ \hline 2100 \end{array}$$

There is a total of 2100 spots.

4. **67**

You need to work out 335 ÷ 5. 335 = 300 + 35. 300 ÷ 5 is 60 and 35 ÷ 5 is 7 so 335 ÷ 5 = 67.

5. **612 000**

Multiplying by 4000 means to multiply by 4 and then multiply by 1000. 153 × 4 is 612, and multiplying by 1000 means writing 000 at the end of the number. The answer is 612000, which is written as 612 000.

6. **See below.**

Rewrite $\frac{11}{6}$ as a mixed numeral. How many 6s go into 11? … 1 and 5 left over. This means $\frac{11}{6} = 1\frac{5}{6}$. Shade one whole shape and $\frac{5}{6}$ of another (five squares).

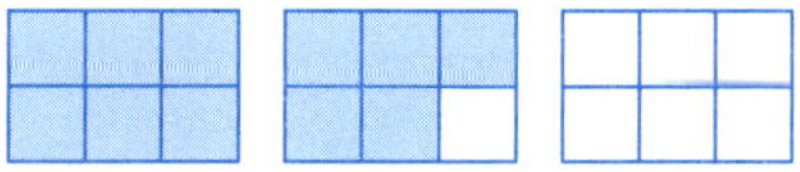

7. $\frac{583}{1000}$

One whole is 1000 thousandths. As 1000 – 417 is 583, then 1000 thousandths minus 417 thousandths is 583 thousandths. This is written as $\frac{1000}{1000} - \frac{417}{1000} = \frac{583}{1000}$.

8. **3.005**

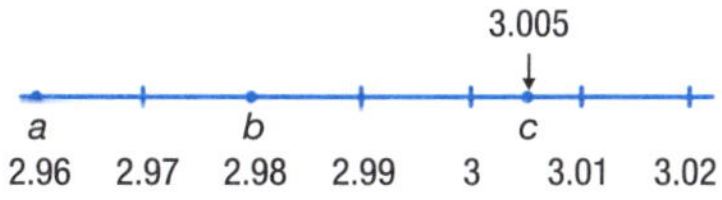

Labelling the number line means that *c* lies halfway between 3 and 3.01.

These numbers rewritten with three decimal places are 3.000 and 3.010. As 5 is in the middle of 0 and 10, then *c* is representing the decimal 3.005.

9. **$100**

Double $32 plus $36 is 32 × 2 + 36 = 64 + 36 = 100. The total cost is $100.

10. **65**

The numbers are increasing by 6. Each number in the sequence is 1 less than a multiple of 6. As 66 is a multiple of 6 then 66 – 1 = 65 is in the sequence.

11. **1575**

You need to work out 315 × 5.

$$\begin{array}{r} 315 \\ \times\ \ \ \ 5 \\ \hline 1575 \end{array}$$

The missing number is 1575.

12. **10 620 016**

There are 1000 mL in a litre, and 1000 L in a kilolitre. This means there are 1 000 000 mL in a kilolitre. 10 kilolitres is 10 000 000 mL and 620 litres is 620 000 mL.

$$\begin{array}{r} 10\,000\,000 \\ 620\,000 \\ +\ \ \ \ \ \ \ \ 16 \\ \hline 10\,620\,016 \end{array}$$

13. **25 minutes**

As 20 is 12 + 8, then 2050 is 8:50 pm. Also, 2115 is 9:15 pm. From 8:50 to 9:00 is 10 minutes and then to 9:15 pm is another 15 minutes. As 10 + 15 is 25, the video lasted 25 minutes.

14. **2 octagons, 8 rectangles**

The net is made from two octagons and eight rectangles.

15. **120°**

An equilateral triangle has rotational symmetry of order 3. A full rotation is 360°. As 360 ÷ 3 is 120, then the shape should rotate 120° about its centre.

16. **123°**

There are two angles which add up to 360° shown on the diagram. This means the unknown angle is 360° – 237°. The angle is 123°.

17. $\frac{7}{10}$

There are now 10 balls in the box. Seven of the balls are black. The probability is 7 out of 10, or $\frac{7}{10}$.

18. **26**

64 + 49 is 113. 51 + 36 is 87. The difference is 113 – 87 which is 26. There were 26 more sales in the first two days.

Unit 11A PAGE 56

1. 15, 30, 18

The 3 times table gives the numbers 3, 6, 9, 12, 15, 18, 21, 24, 27, 30 … From the list the numbers are 15, 30 and 18.

2. 4833

$$\begin{array}{r} 5000 \\ -\ \ 167 \\ \hline 4833 \end{array}$$

The store had sold 4833 boxes.

3. 31 300

$$\begin{array}{r} 7825 \\ \times\ \ \ 4 \\ \hline 31\,300 \end{array}$$

4. 24

You need to work out 147 ÷ 6. 147 = 120 + 27. 120 ÷ 6 is 20 and 27 ÷ 6 is 4 with remainder 3 so 147 ÷ 6 = 24 with remainder 3. This means 24 groups can be made.

5. 686

When adding 99 it is easier to add 100 and then subtract 1. 587 + 100 – 1 is 687 – 1 = 686.

6.

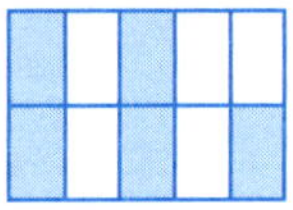

7. 1

As 2 + 3 is 5, then $\frac{2}{5} + \frac{3}{5} = \frac{5}{5}$, which is written as 1.

8. 4.682

Place value is … units, decimal point, tenths, hundredths, thousandths … This means the decimal is 4.682.

9. $12

$$\begin{array}{r} 23 \\ +\ \ 85 \\ \hline 108 \end{array}$$

120 – 108 = 12

She will receive $12 in change.

10. 44, 36, 28, 20, 12

44, then 44 subtracting 8 is 36, subtracting 8 is 28, subtracting 8 is 20, subtracting 8 is 12. The numbers are 44, 36, 28, 20, 12.

11. 35 ÷ 7 = 5

'Quotient' means to divide. The number sentence is 35 ÷ 7 = 5.

12. 2 kg 400 g

600 × 4 is 2400. As there are 1000 grams in 1 kg, divide 2400 by 1000. The answer is 2 with a remainder of 400. This means the total mass is 2 kg 400 g.

13. 1450

The time is pm so add on to 12. As 12 + 2 is 14, then 2:50 pm is 1450.

14. *U*

Q is opposite *S* and *R* is opposite *T* so *U* is opposite *P*.

15. 2

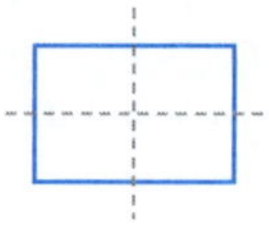

16.

17. $\frac{2}{5}$

There are five counters in the box. Two of the counters are even (6 and 8). The probability of choosing an even number is 2 out of 5, or $\frac{2}{5}$.

18. 23

The number that had more than 5 were: 5–10 (8 students), 11–15 (11) and more than 15 (4 students). As 8 + 11 + 4 = 23, there were 23 students.

Unit 11B PAGE 57

1. 60, 66, 606

Divisible by both 2 and 3 means divisible by 6. From the list, 60, 66 and 606 are divisible by 6.

2. 4437

$$\begin{array}{r} 12\,000 \\ -\ \ 7\,563 \\ \hline 4\,437 \end{array}$$

Kelsey needs another 4437 points.

3. 1344

$$\begin{array}{r} 48 \\ \times\ \ 28 \\ \hline 384 \\ 960 \\ \hline 1344 \end{array}$$

There is a total of 1344 nails.

4. 7

You need to work out 367 ÷ 8. 367 = 320 + 47. 320 ÷ 8 is 40 and 47 ÷ 8 is 5 with remainder 7 so 367 ÷ 8 = 45 with remainder 7. There will be 7 students left over.

5. 3672

When adding 990 it is easier to add 1000 and then subtract 10. 2682 + 1000 – 10 is 3682 – 10 = 3672.

6. See below.

Rewrite $\frac{5}{3}$ as a mixed numeral. How many 3s go into 5? … 1 and 2 left over. This means $\frac{5}{3} = 1\frac{2}{3}$. Shade one whole shape and $\frac{2}{3}$ of another (4 squares).

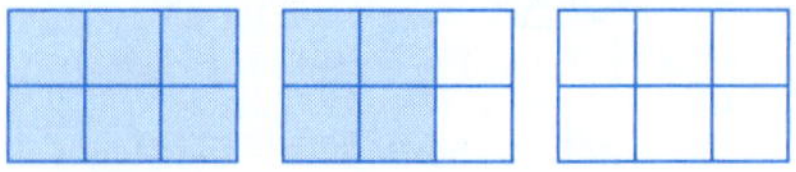

7. $\frac{2}{7}$

The missing fraction is the difference between $\frac{5}{7}$ and $\frac{3}{7}$, which is $\frac{5}{7} - \frac{3}{7}$. 5 sevenths minus 3 sevenths is 2 sevenths. This is written as $\frac{5}{7} - \frac{3}{7} = \frac{2}{7}$.

8. 0.017

Place value is … units, decimal point, tenths, hundredths, thousandths … 17 thousandths is 1 hundredth and 7 thousandths. This is written as 0.017.

9. $17

Double $29.50 is twice $29 + twice 50c which is $58 + $1 = $59. Double $16.50 is twice $16 + twice 50c which is $32 + $1 = $33. 59 + 33 = 60 + 33 – 1 = 92. The price would be $92. This means the saving is 92 – 75 = 92 – 72 – 3 = 20 – 3 = 17. The saving is $17.

10. 57

The numbers are decreasing by 11. Each number in the sequence is two more than a multiple of 11. As 55 is a multiple of 11 then 55 + 2 = 57 is in the sequence.

11. 10 580

The number sentence can be rewritten as 460 × 23 = ☐.

$$\begin{array}{r} 460 \\ \times\ \ 23 \\ \hline 1380 \\ 9200 \\ \hline 10\,580 \end{array}$$

The missing number is 10 580.

12. 11 m 20 cm

120 × 6 is 720 and 80 × 5 is 400. This means the total is 720 + 400 which is 1120. As 100 cm is 1 m, then Ruth has 11 m 20 cm.

13. 7:35 am

As 0615 is 6:15 am, adding one hour gives 7:15 am. As 15 + 20 is 35, Riley left the gym at 7:35 am.

14. See below.

A regular pentagon has 5 equal sides and 5 equal angles.

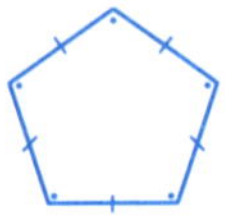

15. 72°

A regular pentagon has rotational symmetry of order 5. A full rotation is 360°. As 360 ÷ 5 is 72, then the shape should rotate 72° about its centre.

16. **220°**

There are two angles which add up to 360° shown on the diagram. This means the unknown angle is 360° – 140°. The angle is 220°.

17. $\frac{3}{5}$

There are five counters in the box. There are two counters that are multiples of 3 (3 and 6). This means there are three discs that are not multiples of 3. The probability of choosing a number that is not a multiple of 3 is 3 out of 5, or $\frac{3}{5}$.

18. **16**

The new number for 11–15 becomes 12 (11 + 1 = 12). More than 15 is 4 students. As 12 + 4 = 16, there were 16 students.

Unit 12A PAGE 58

1. **14, 35, 42**

The 7 times table gives the numbers 7, 14, 21, 28, 35, 42 ... From the list the numbers are 14, 35 and 42.

2. **49 786 km**

$$\begin{array}{r} 406\,692 \\ -\ 356\,906 \\ \hline 49\,786 \end{array}$$

The difference in the distances was 49 786 km.

3. **$1590**

$$\begin{array}{r} 265 \\ \times\quad 6 \\ \hline 1590 \end{array}$$

The students paid a total of $1590.

4. **9**

You need to work out 33 ÷ 4. 4 × 8 = 32 so 33 ÷ 4 is 8, remainder 1. The smallest number of cars is 9.

5. **1400**

Look for the easier multiplication first. 25 × 4 is 100 and so 14 × 100 means writing 00 at the end of 14. The answer is 1400.

6. $\frac{2}{9}$

Each fraction has 2 as the numerator (top number). The higher the denominator (bottom number) the smaller the fraction. The smallest is $\frac{2}{9}$ and the largest is $\frac{2}{3}$.

7. **1**

As 3 + 7 is 10, then $\frac{3}{10} + \frac{7}{10} = \frac{10}{10}$, which is written as 1.

8. **3.2**

Rewrite the decimals with three decimal places: 3.090, 3.200, 3.113, 3.140. Compare the last three digits in each decimal: from smallest to largest is 90, 113, 140, 200. As 200 is the largest of these numbers, the largest decimal is 3.2.

9. **$449.90**

The original price is $65.50 added to $384.40.

$$\begin{array}{r} 384.40 \\ +\ 65.50 \\ \hline 449.90 \end{array}$$

The original price was $449.90.

10. **2, $2\frac{1}{3}$, $2\frac{2}{3}$, 3, $3\frac{1}{3}$**

2, then 2 adding $\frac{1}{3}$ is $2\frac{1}{3}$, adding $\frac{1}{3}$ is $2\frac{2}{3}$, adding $\frac{1}{3}$ is 3, adding $\frac{1}{3}$ is $3\frac{1}{3}$.

11. **29**

4 × 6 + 5 is 24 + 5 which is 29. The output number is 29.

12. **3500**

There are 1000 m in 1 km. Half of 1000 is 1000 ÷ 2, which is 500. As there are 3000 m in 3 km, and 3000 + 500 is 3500 there are 3500 m.

13. **6:20 pm**

1820 is past 1200 so it is pm. As 1820 – 1200 is 620 then the time is 6:20 pm.

14. ***F***

B is opposite *D* and, *C* is opposite *E* so *F* is opposite *A*.

15. **5**

There are five lines of symmetry.

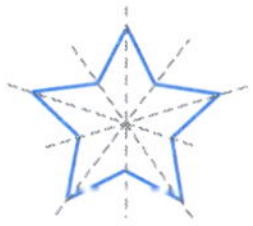

16.

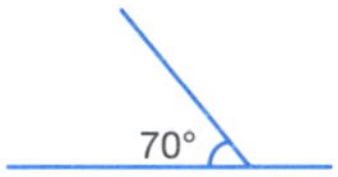

17. $\frac{3}{10}$

There are 10 marbles in the box. Three of the marbles are green. The probability of choosing a green marble is 3 out of 10, or $\frac{3}{10}$.

18. **8**

2 + 6 is 8. There are eight students who do not have a phone.

Unit 12B PAGE 59

1. **4**

434 is divisible by 7. 434 – 7 = 427, 434 + 7 = 441, 441 + 7 = 448. There are 4 numbers.

2. **562 481**

$$\begin{array}{r} 1\,000\,000 \\ -\ 437\,519 \\ \hline 562\,481 \end{array}$$

3. **82 080**

$$\begin{array}{r} 6840 \\ \times\quad 12 \\ \hline 82\,080 \end{array}$$

A total of 82 080 eggs are sold.

4. **10**

As 19 ÷ 4 is 4, and remainder 3, there needs to be five rooms for the boys. As 17 ÷ 4 is 4, and remainder 1, there needs to be five rooms for the girls as well. As 5 + 5 = 10, there needs to be 10 rooms.

5. **4200**

Look for the easier multiplications first. 25 × 4 is 100 and 6 × 7 is 42. 42 × 100 means writing 00 at the end of 42. The answer is 4200.

6. $\frac{21}{2}$ **and** $\frac{4}{8}$

When the numerator (top number) is the same as the denominator (bottom number) the fraction is equal to 1 (or one whole). This means $\frac{8}{8} = 1$ and $\frac{10}{10} = 1$, and $\frac{21}{2}$ and $\frac{4}{8}$ do not equal 1.

7. $\frac{3}{10}$

The missing fraction is the difference between $\frac{7}{10}$ and $\frac{4}{10}$, which is $\frac{7}{10} - \frac{4}{10}$. 7 tenths minus 4 tenths is 3 tenths. This is written as $\frac{7}{10} - \frac{4}{10} = \frac{3}{10}$.

8. **5.034, 5.04, 5.304, 5.34, 5.403**

Rewrite the decimals with three decimal places: 5.034, 5.340, 5.040, 5.403, 5.304. Compare the last three digits in each decimal: from smallest to largest is 034, 040, 304, 340, 403. This means the order is 5.034, 5.04, 5.304, 5.34, 5.403.

9. **$4**

As one packet of chips costs $3, then four packets cost $12. As three chocolate bars cost $12 then a chocolate bar costs $12 ÷ 3 = $4.

10. **3.9**

Look at the sequence of the last two digits: 27, 36, 45. The numbers are multiples of 9. As 3.9 is 3.90, and 90 is a multiple of 9, then 3.9 is in the sequence.

11. **3**

Starting with 15 as the output, use inverse operations as you move to the left towards the input. 15 – 3 is 12 and then divide by 4 is 3. The input number is 3.

12. **3750 m**

As there are 1000 m in 1 km, then there are 500 m in $\frac{1}{2}$ km and 250 m in $\frac{1}{4}$ km. You need to add 1500 and 2250.

$$\begin{array}{r} 1500 \\ +\ 2250 \\ \hline 3750 \end{array}$$

Abigail walked a total of 3750 metres.

13. **4:10 pm**

As 1350 is 1:50 pm, adding 2 hours gives 3:50 pm. Another 10 minutes gives 4:00 pm and the other 10 minutes gives 4:10 pm. Gabriel will arrive back at 4:10 pm.

14. **See below.**

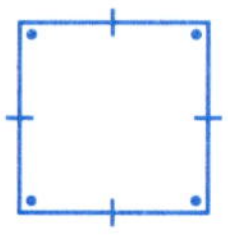

A regular quadrilateral has four equal sides and four equal angles. It is a square.

15. **60°**

A regular hexagon has rotational symmetry of order 6. A full rotation is 360°. As 360 ÷ 6 is 60, then the shape should rotate 60° about its centre.

16. **310°**

There are two angles which add up to 360° shown on the diagram. This means the unknown angle is 360° − 50°. The angle is 310°.

17. $\frac{5}{10}$ **(or** $\frac{1}{2}$**)**

There are 10 marbles in the box. Two of the marbles are red and three are green which is a total of five marbles. The probability of choosing a red or green marble is 5 out of 10, or $\frac{5}{10}$, which can be written as $\frac{1}{2}$.

18. **2**

As 12 ÷ 2 is 6 there are six boys who have a phone. Also, six boys do not have a phone. As 12 + 6 + 6 is 24, and 26 − 24 is 2, there must be two girls without a phone.

	Phone	No phone
Girls	12	2
Boys	6	6

Unit 13A PAGE 60

1. **8, 32, 48, 64**

The 4 times table gives the numbers 4, 8, 12, 16, 20, 24, 28, 32, 36, 40, 44, 48 … From the list the numbers are 8, 32, 48 and 64.

2. **156**

$$\begin{array}{r} 424 \\ -\ 268 \\ \hline 156 \end{array}$$

Angus's book has 156 more pages than Eloise's book.

3. **5696**

The missing number is 712 multiplied by 8.

$$\begin{array}{r} 712 \\ \times\ \ \ 8 \\ \hline 5696 \end{array}$$

The missing number is 5696.

4. **26**

You need to work out 208 ÷ 8. 208 = 160 + 48. 160 ÷ 8 is 20 and 48 ÷ 8 is 6 so 208 ÷ 8 = 26. There are 26 students in each class.

5. **7300**

Look for the easier multiplication first. 20 × 5 is 100 and so 73 × 100 means writing 00 at the end of 73. The answer is 7300.

6. $\frac{19}{5}$

There are 5 fifths in 1 whole. In $3\frac{4}{5}$ there are 3 × 5 + 4 fifths. This means there are 15 + 4 = 19 fifths, written as $\frac{19}{5}$.

7. **1**

As 1 + 2 + 2 is 5, then $\frac{1}{5} + \frac{2}{5} + \frac{2}{5} = \frac{5}{5}$, which is written as 1.

8. **7 hundredths**

The 7 is in the second decimal place. Place value is … units, decimal point, tenths, hundredths, thousandths … This means the place value is 7 hundredths.

9. **$70**

As 4 is 3 + 1, Anne buys 3 for $50 and then 1 at $20. As 50 + 20 is 70, Anne will spend $70.

10. $3\frac{1}{2}$**, 3,** $2\frac{1}{2}$**, 2,** $1\frac{1}{2}$

$3\frac{1}{2}$, then $3\frac{1}{2}$ subtracting $\frac{1}{2}$ is 3, subtracting $\frac{1}{2}$ is $2\frac{1}{2}$, subtracting $\frac{1}{2}$ is 2, subtracting $\frac{1}{2}$ is $1\frac{1}{2}$.

11. **51**

6 × 8 + 3 is 48 + 3 which is 51. The output number is 51.

12. **1, 400**

400 × 2 plus 300 × 2 is 800 plus 600. This answer is 1400. As there are 1000 mm in 1 m, then 1400 mm is 1 m 400 mm.

13. **2120**

The time is pm so add on to 12. As 12 + 9 is 21, then 9:20 pm is 2120.

14. ***U***

V is opposite *W* and *X* is opposite *Y* so *U* is opposite *Z*.

15. **2**

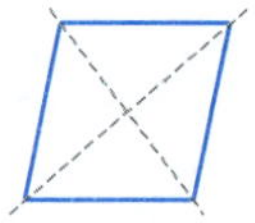

16. **150°**

The angle is 150°.

17. $\frac{3}{10}$

There are 10 balls in the bag. Three of the balls are red. The probability of choosing a red ball is 3 out of 10, or $\frac{3}{10}$.

18. **27**

As 4 + 8 + 10 + 5 is 27, there are 27 students in Mr Thompson's class.

Unit 13B PAGE 61

1. **135**

Divisible by 3 and 5 means divisible by or a multiple of 15. This means 15, 30, 45, 60, 75, 90, <u>105, 120, 135, 150, 165, 180, 195</u> … Using 135, the multiplication is 1 × 3 × 5 = 15. The number is 135.

2. **3 830 197**

$$\begin{array}{r} 27\,287\,115 \\ -\ 23\,456\,918 \\ \hline 3\,830\,197 \end{array}$$

3. **9288**

The missing number is 387 multiplied by 24.

$$\begin{array}{r} 387 \\ \times\ \ 24 \\ \hline 1548 \\ 7740 \\ \hline 9288 \end{array}$$

The missing number is 9288.

4. **19**

380 ÷ 20 is the same as 38 ÷ 2 which is 19. This means that 19 cars can park in each row.

5. **9600**

Look for the easier multiplication first. 20 × 5 is 100 and 32 × 3 is 96. 96 × 100 means writing 00 at the end of 96. The answer is 9600.

6. **67**

There are 12 twelfths in 1 whole. In $5\frac{7}{12}$ there are 12 × 5 + 7 twelfths. This means there are 60 + 7 = 67 twelfths, written as $\frac{67}{12}$. The missing number is 67.

7. $\frac{1}{4}$
The bucket is full and so is 4 quarters full. 4 quarters minus 3 quarters is 1 quarter. This is written as $\frac{4}{4} - \frac{3}{4} = \frac{1}{4}$.

8. **2 ten-thousandths**
The 2 is in the fourth decimal place. Place value is …, units, decimal point, tenths, hundredths, thousandths, ten-thousandths … This means the place value is 2 ten-thousandths.

9. **$53.64**
$1.53 minus 4 cents is $1.49, which is 149 cents.

$$\begin{array}{r} 149 \\ \times\ \ 36 \\ \hline 894 \\ 4470 \\ \hline 5364 \end{array}$$

Selena pays $53.64.

10. **13.75**
The decimals are decreasing by 0.15. As 14.00 – 0.15 is 13.85, minus 0.15 is 13.7, and so the decimal not in the sequence is 13.75.

11. **3**
Starting with 19 as the output, use inverse operations as you move to the left towards the input. 19 – 4 is 15 and then divide by 5 to get 3. The input number is 3.

12. **5, 30**
The perimeter is twice the length plus twice the width. Two times 2 m is 4 m and two times 65 cm is 130 cm. The perimeter is 4 m 130 cm. But 130 cm is 1 m 30 cm. The perimeter is 5 m 30 cm.

13. **2 hours 30 minutes**
1930 is 7:30 pm and 2200 is 10 pm. From 7:30 pm to 8:00 pm is 30 minutes. From 8:00 pm to 10 pm is 2 hours. Ellie will spend 2 hours 30 minutes at the party.

14. ***A***
The letter *A* represents the apex of the pyramid.

15. **45°**
A regular octagon has rotational symmetry of order 8. A full rotation is 360°. As 360 ÷ 8 is 45, then the shape should rotate 45° about its centre.

16. **43°**
There are two angles which add up to 360° shown on the diagram. This means the unknown angle is 360° – 317°. The angle is 43°.

17. $\frac{7}{10}$
There are 10 balls in the bag. Three of the balls are red and so seven of the balls are not red. The probability of choosing a ball that is not red is 7 out of 10, or $\frac{7}{10}$.

18. $\frac{8}{13}$
As 8 + 5 is 13, there are 13 students who do not play sport. As eight of these students are girls, the fraction is $\frac{8}{13}$.

Unit 14A PAGE 62

1. **3**
The multiples of 5 are 5, 10, **15**, **20**, **25**, 30 … This means there are three multiples.

2. **323**

$$\begin{array}{r} 236 \\ +\ \ 87 \\ \hline 323 \end{array}$$

There are 323 trees growing in the second park.

3. **74 070**

$$\begin{array}{r} 12\,345 \\ \times\ \ \ \ \ \ 6 \\ \hline 74\,070 \end{array}$$

4. **17**
You need to work out 85 ÷ 5. 85 = 50 + 35. 50 ÷ 5 is 10 and 35 ÷ 5 is 7 so 85 ÷ 5 = 17. Ella can build 17 towers.

5. **56 000**
Look for the easier multiplication first. As 25 × 4 is 100 then 250 × 4 is 1000. Now 56 × 1000 means writing 000 at the end of 56. The answer is 56 000.

6. **See below.**
The number line is labelled with 0 and 1 and halfway is $\frac{1}{2}$. Halfway between $\frac{1}{2}$ and 1 is $\frac{3}{4}$.

7. $\frac{7}{8}$
As 2 + 5 is 7, then $\frac{2}{8} + \frac{5}{8} = \frac{7}{8}$.

8. **less**
Rewrite the decimals with 3 decimal places: 32.761 and 32.800. As 761 is less than 800, then 32.761 is less than 32.8.

9. **$136.25**

$$\begin{array}{r} 165.00 \\ -\ \ 28.75 \\ \hline 136.25 \end{array}$$

The new price is $136.25.

10. **2.85, 2.95, 3.05, 3.15, 3.25**
2.85, then 2.85 adding 0.10 is 2.95.

$$\begin{array}{r} 2.95 \\ +\ 0.10 \\ \hline 3.05 \end{array}$$

3.05 adding 0.10 is 3.15, adding 0.10 is 3.25.

11. **8**
As 12 × 6 is 72, the number sentence can be written as 72 = ☐ × 9. The 'missing number' can be found using 72 ÷ 9 which is 8. The missing number is 8.

12. **22 cm**
As a square has four equal sides, you need to divide 88 by 4. 8 ÷ 4 is 2 so 88 ÷ 4 is 22. Each side is 22 cm.

13. **6:30 am**
Half past six is 6:30. The time is in the morning so it is written as 6:30 am.

14.

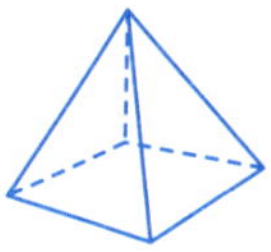

15.

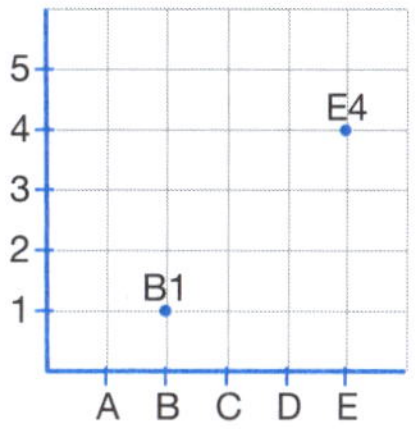

16. **90**
An acute angle measures less than 90°.

17. **5**
There must be eight marbles in the bag. As there are three red marbles, there must be five blue marbles.

18. **6**
At 3 pm the temperature was 28° and by 6 pm it was 22°. As 28 – 22 is 6, the temperature dropped 6°.

Unit 14B PAGE 63

1. **1**
34 and 28 are even and so are divisible by 2. 51 is divisible by 3. 25 is divisible by 5. This leaves only 23.

2. **101 280**

$$\begin{array}{r} 98\,232 \\ +\ \ \ 3\,048 \\ \hline 101\,280 \end{array}$$

Levi had been alive for 101 280 hours.

3. **3192**

```
   57
×  56
  342
 2850
 3192
```

4. **48**

You need to work out 288 ÷ 6. 288 = 240 + 48. 240 ÷ 6 is 40 and 48 ÷ 6 is 8 so 288 ÷ 6 = 48. There are 48 seats in each carriage.

5. **54 000**

Look for the easier multiplication first. As 25 × 4 is 100 then 250 × 4 is 1000. Also, 18 × 3 is the same as 9 × 6 which is 54. Now 54 × 1000 means writing 000 at the end of 54. The answer is 54 000.

6. ***C***

Rewrite $\frac{7}{2}$ as a mixed numeral. How many 2s go into 7? … 3 and 1 left over. This means $\frac{7}{2} = 3\frac{1}{2}$, which is represented by *C*.

7. $\frac{5}{8}$

The tank was full and so was 8 eighths full. 8 eighths minus 3 eighths is 5 eighths. This is written as $\frac{8}{8} - \frac{3}{8} = \frac{5}{8}$.

8. **greater**

Rewrite the decimals with three decimal places: 294.100 and 294.098. As 100 is greater than 98, then 294.1 is greater than 294.098.

9. **$14**

Two dozen is 24. As 24 ÷ 3 is 8, it will cost Agnes 8 × $1.75.

```
  175
×   8
 1400
```

The kiwi fruit will cost $14.

10. $6\frac{3}{5}$

The pattern is increasing by $\frac{3}{5}$.

The next number is $5\frac{2}{5} + \frac{3}{5}$ which is $5\frac{5}{5}$ or 6. Adding 6 and $\frac{3}{5}$ gives $6\frac{3}{5}$.

11. **8**

Use inverse operations. As there is '+ 31', then first subtract 31 from 231. As 231 – 31 is 200, then the 'missing number' × 25 = 200. As 4 × 25 is 100, then 8 × 25 is 200. The missing number is 8.

12. **65 cm**

There are 100 cm in a metre, and so 200 cm in 2 m. As 200 + 60 is 260, the perimeter is 260 cm. As a square has four equal sides, you need to divide 260 by 4. 260 = 240 + 20. 240 ÷ 4 is 60 and 20 ÷ 4 is 5 so 260 ÷ 4 = 65. Each side is 65 cm.

13. **3 hours 40 minutes**

1540 is 3:40 pm and 1920 is 7:20 pm. From 3:40 pm to 4:00 pm is 20 minutes. From 4:00 pm to 7 pm is 3 hours. From 7 pm to 7:20 pm is another 20 minutes. It will take 20 minutes + 3 hours + 20 minutes which is 3 hours 40 minutes.

14. ***Q***

The letter *Q* represents the apex of the cone.

15. **A5**

Y is at A5.

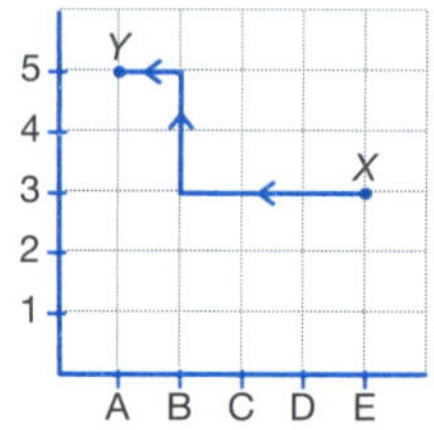

16. **152°**

There are two angles which add up to 360° shown on the diagram. This means the unknown angle is 360° – 208°. The angle is 152°.

17. **3**

$\frac{2}{3}$ is the same as $\frac{6}{9}$. This means that six out of the nine marbles in the bag are red. As 9 – 6 is 3, then there are three blue marbles in the bag.

18. **4 hours**

The highest temperature of 28° occurred at 3 pm. As 28 – 8 is 20, the temperature was 20° at 7 pm. From 3 pm to 7 pm is 4 hours.

Unit 15A PAGE 64

1. **2900, 40**

The last digit must be 0. The multiples of 10 are 2900 and 40.

2. **210**

87 is close to 90, 52 is close to 50 and 68 is close to 70. As 90 + 50 + 70 = 210, they have about 210 friends, to the nearest 10.

3. **26 920**

Multiply 673 by 4 and then multiply by 10 (by writing a 0 on the end).

```
  673
×   4
 2692
```

This means the answer is 26920, which is written as 26 920.

4. **50**

You need to work out 400 ÷ 8. 40 ÷ 8 is 5 so 400 ÷ 8 is 50. Each lap is 50 m long.

5. **320**

Dividing 32 000 by 100 means 2 zeros can be removed from the end of 32 000. This means the answer is 320.

6. **See below.**

The number line is labelled with 0 and 1 and halfway is $\frac{1}{2}$. $\frac{1}{3}$ is less than $\frac{1}{2}$.

7. $\frac{5}{8}$

As 3 + 2 is 5, then $\frac{3}{8} + \frac{2}{8} = \frac{5}{8}$.

8. **0.6**

The number line is marked in tenths (or 0.1s). A is half-way between 0.5 and 0.7. As 6 is half-way between 5 and 7, A is 0.6.

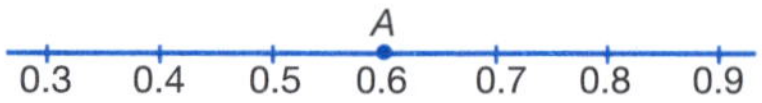

9. **$48**

Double the $18 and add $12. This means 18 × 2 + 12 = 36 + 12 = 48. The total cost will be $48.

10. **1.3, 1.1, 0.9, 0.7, 0.5**

1.3, then 1.3 subtracting 0.2 is 1.1, subtracting 0.2 is 0.9, subtracting 0.2 is 0.7, subtracting 0.2 is 0.5.

11. **6**

34 + 8 is 42. The number sentence can be written as 42 = ☐ × 7. The 'missing number' can be found using 42 ÷ 7 which is 6. The missing number is 6.

12. **850 m**

There are 1000 m in a kilometre. As Aaron has already walked 2 km 150 m subtract 150 from 1000.

```
 1000
− 150
  850
```

Aaron needs to walk another 850 m.

13. **0945**

A quarter to ten is written as 9:45 am. This is expressed as 0945 in 24-hour time.

14.

15. **B4, E2**

From each of the points, go down to the letters, then across to the numbers. *P* is B4 and *Q* is E2.

16. 10:30

As 180 is half of 360, then 180° is half of a revolution. Half of 12 is 6 which means the minute hand is pointing to 6. The time is 10:30.

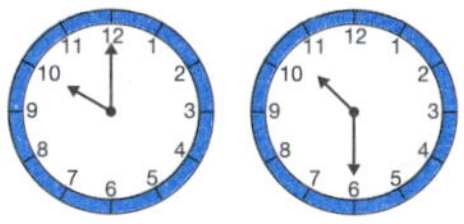

17. $\frac{3}{8}$

There are eight sections on the spinner and each section is identical in size. There are three sections that are blue. This means the probability of stopping on blue is $\frac{3}{8}$.

18. 1600

The graph shows the temperature rises until 1400 and then drops. At 1600 the temperature is 10°.

Unit 15B — PAGE 65

1. 2

Multiples of 4: 4, 8, **12**, 16, 20, **24**, 28 … Multiples of 6 are 6, **12**, 18, **24**, 30 … They will flash two more times.

2. 2600 m²

688 is close to 700, 706 is close to 700, 598 is close to 600 and 604 is close to 600. As 7 + 7 + 6 + 6 is 26, the total is close to 2600 m².

3. 360 000

Multiply 24 by 15 and write three more 0s on the end.

$$\begin{array}{r} 24 \\ \times\ 15 \\ \hline 120 \\ 240 \\ \hline 360 \end{array}$$

This means the answer is 360 000.

4. 650

You need to work out 5200 ÷ 8. 5200 = 4800 + 400. 4800 ÷ 8 is 600 and 400 ÷ 8 is 50 so 5200 ÷ 8 = 650. This means 650 boxes can be filled.

5. 94

Dividing 940 000 by 10 000 means four zeros can be removed from the end of 940 000. This means the answer is 94.

6. *D*

Rewrite $\frac{23}{3}$ as a mixed numeral. How many 3s go into 23? … 7 and 2 left over. This means $\frac{23}{3} = 7\frac{2}{3}$, which is represented by *D*.

7. $\frac{1}{4}$

3 quarters minus 2 quarters is 1 quarter. This is written as $\frac{3}{4} - \frac{2}{4} = \frac{1}{4}$.

8. 3.06

3 is 3.00 and 3.1 is 3.10. The number line is marked in 0.02s. This means *X* is 3.06.

9. 4

As an adult costs $15, then the cost of the children is 63 – 15 = 48. The child cost is $12 so 48 ÷ 12 = 4 means that four children are going ice-skating.

10. 5

The pattern is increasing by $\frac{1}{4}$. The next number is $4\frac{1}{4} + \frac{1}{4}$ is $4\frac{2}{4}$. Adding $4\frac{2}{4}$ and $\frac{1}{4}$ is $4\frac{3}{4}$. Adding $4\frac{3}{4}$ and $\frac{1}{4}$ is $4\frac{4}{4}$, or 5.

11. 9

Use inverse operations. As there is '+ 15', then first subtract 15 from 195. As 195 – 15 is 180, then the 'missing number' × 20 = 180. As 9 × 2 is 18, then 9 × 20 is 180. The missing number is 9.

12. 4250 m

There are 1000 m in a km. As $\frac{1}{2}$ of 1000 is 500 and $\frac{1}{4}$ of 1000 is 250, you need to find 6500 – 2250.

$$\begin{array}{r} 6500 \\ -\ 2250 \\ \hline 4250 \end{array}$$

Penelope needs to walk another 4250 m.

13. 1615

1145 is 11:45 am and four and a half hours is 4 hours 30 minutes. From 11:45 am add 15 minutes gives 12:00 pm. Adding 4 hours is 4:00 pm. There is still another 15 minutes to add which gives 4:15 pm. As 12 + 4 = 16, the bus arrives at 1615.

14. 10

The original cube has eight vertices. One vertex is removed but three more appear.

This means the new solid has 10 vertices.

15. D5

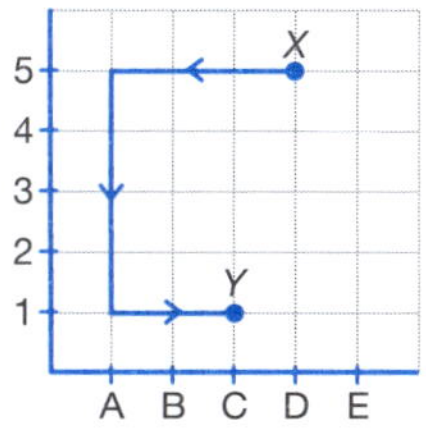

Reverse the directions. From *Y*, move two units to the left, four units up and three units to the right. *X* is at D5.

16. 8:20

As 120 is one-third of 360, then 120° is one-third of a revolution. One-third of 12 is 4 which means the minute hand is pointing to 4. The time is 8:20.

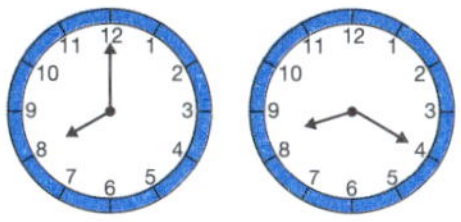

17. $\frac{5}{8}$

There are eight sections on the spinner and each section is identical in size. There are three sections that are blue, which means five sections that are not blue. This means the probability of not stopping on blue is $\frac{5}{8}$.

18. 2 pm and 4 pm

From 1400 to 1600 the temperature dropped 6 degrees. From 1600 to 1800 the temperature dropped 4 degrees. This means the temperature fell at the fastest rate from 2 pm to 4 pm.

NAPLAN-style Test 1 — PAGES 66–69

1. 1 216 198, 1 136 199, 1 032 406, 1 009 999

All numbers commence with one million so look at the hundred-thousands to make comparisons. The order is 1 216 198, 1 136 199, 1 032 406, 1 009 999.

2. *D*

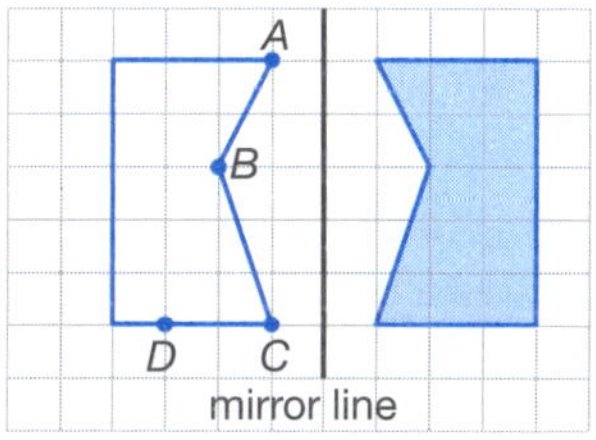

3. 2040

You need to multiply 68 by 30. As 68 × 3 is 204, then 68 × 30 is 2040. This means 2040 spectators can be transported.

4. A

$$\begin{array}{r} 20.00 \\ -\ 13.45 \\ \hline 6.55 \end{array}$$

Bryson will be given $6.55 in change.

5. A and D

As 28 is 26 + 2 then 26 + 28 = 26 + 26 + 2. Also, as 28 + 2 is 30 and 26 + 4 is 30, then 26 + 28 = 30 + 30 – 4 – 2 which is 30 + 30 – 6.

6. 3.3

$$\begin{array}{r} 32.0 \\ -\ 28.7 \\ \hline 3.3 \end{array}$$

It was 3.3 °C warmer.

7. 11.4 kg

The total mass was 3.8 × 3.

$$\begin{array}{r} 3.8 \\ 3.8 \\ +\ 3.8 \\ \hline 11.4 \end{array}$$

The total mass was 11.4 kg.

8. B and F

As 40 + 80 is 120, then Lenore has read $\frac{40}{120}$ of the novel. Now, $\frac{40}{120} = \frac{4}{12}$, which is equal to $\frac{1}{3}$.

The two fractions are $\frac{4}{12}$ and $\frac{1}{3}$.

9. 16

6 students took 7 minutes, 3 took 8, 4 took 9, 2 took 10 and 1 person took 11 minutes. As 6 + 3 + 4 + 2 + 1 is 16, then 16 students took at least 7 minutes.

10. B and E

From the list, look for factors of 72. The factors are 3, 8 and 12. This means that 5 and 16 are not factors. The children could not have used 5 or 16 balls each.

11. E

The number must be less than 2 × 8 which is 16. The number is less than 16.

12. B

As 36 × 3 = 108, Brett runs for 108 minutes each week. As there are 60 minutes in 1 hour, and 108 – 60 is 48, then Brett runs for 1 hour 48 minutes.

13. B

There are four different colours. This means the 1st, 5th, 9th and so on are red jelly beans. This is a pattern: 1, 5, 9, 13, 17, 21, 25 … As the 25th jelly bean is red so the 26th jelly bean is orange.

14. *a*°

From smallest to largest the order is *b*°, *d*°, *a*°, *c*°. The second largest angle is *a*°.

15. 3

When the cube is formed, the numbers 12 and 4 are on opposite faces. As 4 × 12 is 48, opposite faces multiply to 48. As 16 and * are on opposite faces then 16 × * = 48. This means * is 3.

16. 24

As 18 ÷ 3 is 6, then □ = 6.

As △ ÷ 6 = 4, then △ is 4 × 6, which is 24.

17. D

The angle for the red section is 45. The angle for purple is 180°. As 45 × 4 is 180, then purple is 4 times the size of red. As 30 × 4 is 120, then it is likely that purple will be spun about 120 times.

18. 1420

The numbers in pattern A are decreasing by 80. Continuing the pattern: 1500, 1420, 1340, 1260 ….

The numbers in pattern B are increasing by 30. Continuing the pattern: 1300, 1330, 1360, 1390, 1420 … The common number is 1420.

19. 17.5

As 94 – 8 is 86, and 86 ÷ 2 is 43, the fourth number is 43.

As 43 – 8 is 35, and 35 ÷ 2 is $17\frac{1}{2}$ or 17.5, the fifth number is 17.5.

20. 64

As 8 × 4 is 32, the perimeter of the octagon is 32 cm. If the perimeter of the square is 32 cm, the length of each side is 8 cm. As 8 × 8 is 64, the area is 64 cm².

Unit 16A PAGE 70

1. 30, 37

The 7 times table gives the numbers 7, 14, 21, 28, 35, 42, 49 … The mistakes in the list are 30 and 37.

2. 22 000

4821 is close to 5000, 9789 is close to 10 000 and 7190 is close to 7000. As 5 + 10 + 7 is 22, the sum is close to 22 000, to the nearest thousand.

3. 2

$$8\overline{)130} = 16 \text{ r } 2$$

The remainder is 2.

4. 1080

As 12 × 9 is 108, then 120 × 9 is 1080. There are 1080 chocolate biscuits in the display.

5. 2

As 14 = 7 × 2, the missing number is 2.

6. See below.

The number line is labelled with 1 and 2 and is marked in quarters. $1\frac{1}{2}$ is halfway between 1 and 2.

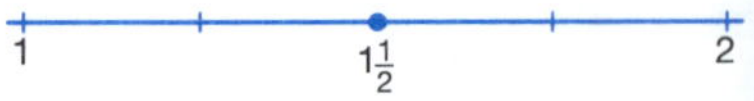

7. $\frac{4}{25}$

As 24 – 7 – 13 = 4, then $\frac{24}{25} - \frac{7}{25} - \frac{13}{25} = \frac{4}{25}$.

8. 15.6

Take care with place values. 12 + 3 is 15 so 12.6 + 3 is 15.6.

9. $140

Two T-shirts at $30 each is 30 × 2 = 60. Add 80 and 60 is 140. The total cost was $140.

10. 32, increase, 6

As 38 – 32 is 6 and 44 – 38 is 6, the rule is 'Start with 32 and increase by 6'.

11. 12

24 × 2 is 48. The number sentence can be written as 60 – □ = 48. The 'missing number' can be found using 60 – 48, which is 12. The missing number is 12.

12. 1920

$$\begin{array}{r} 960 \\ \times\ \ 2 \\ \hline 1920 \end{array}$$

Isaiah runs 1920 m.

13. 1615

A quarter past four in the afternoon is written as 4:15 pm. The time is pm so add on to 12. As 12 + 4 is 16, then 4:15 pm is 1615.

14.

15. south-west

Y is south-west of *X*.

16. 90, 180

An obtuse angle measures more than 90° but less than 180°.

17. $\frac{1}{8}$

A regular octagon has eight equal sides. There are eight sections on the spinner. There is one section numbered 4. This means the probability of stopping on a 4 is $\frac{1}{8}$.

18. 30

There are four 5s plus 3, 2, 4, and 1. 20 + 3 + 2 + 4 + 1 is 30. The survey involved 30 students.

Unit 16B PAGE 71

1. **8**

   Factors of 36 are 1, 2, 3, 4, 6, 9, 12, 18, 36. There are 8 factors less or equal to 28 so 8 students stand up.

2. **88 000**

   23 418 is close to 23 000, 55 920 is close to 56 000 and 9023 is close to 9000.

$$\begin{array}{r} 23 \\ 56 \\ +\quad 9 \\ \hline 88 \end{array}$$

   The sum is about 88 000, to the nearest thousand.

3. **84**

   1 km is 1000 m.

$$\begin{array}{r} 83 \text{ r } 4 \\ 12\overline{)1000} \end{array}$$

   Charlotte has to swim 84 laps.

4. **12 064**

$$\begin{array}{r} 928 \\ \times \quad 13 \\ \hline 2784 \\ 9280 \\ \hline 12\,064 \end{array}$$

   The total season attendance was 12 064 spectators.

5. **946**

   As 22 = 11 × 2, then 43 × 11 × 2 is 473 × 2 which is 946.

6. **B**

   Rewrite $\frac{49}{5}$ as a mixed numeral. How many 5s go into 49? … 9 and 4 left over. This means $\frac{49}{5} = 9\frac{4}{5}$, which is represented by B.

7. $\mathbf{\frac{7}{10}}$

   The whole distance is ten tenths. 10 tenths minus 3 tenths is 7 tenths. This is written as $\frac{10}{10} - \frac{3}{10} = \frac{7}{10}$.

8. **95.8 km**

$$\begin{array}{r} 32.4 \\ 27.3 \\ +\quad 36.1 \\ \hline 95.8 \end{array}$$

   Ravi cycled 95.8 km.

9. **$210**

   As 180 − 60 is 120, and 120 ÷ 8 is 15, the cost for each child is $15. As 60 + 15 × 10 is 60 + 150 which is 210, the cost is $210.

10. **960**

$$\begin{array}{r} 1100 \\ -\quad 1065 \\ \hline 35 \end{array}$$

   Also, 1065 − 1030 is 35. The pattern is decreasing by 35. The fourth number is 1030 − 35 and the fifth term is 1030 − 2 lots of 35. This is 1030 − 70 which is 960.

11. **6**

   Use inverse operations. As there is '− 10', then first add 10 to 230. As 230 + 10 is 240, then 40 × the 'missing number' = 240. As 4 × 6 is 24, then 40 × 6 is 240. The missing number is 6.

12. **820 m**

$$\begin{array}{r} 820 \\ 3\overline{)2460} \end{array}$$

   The length of the circuit is 820 m.

13. **8:40 am**

   Six and a half hours is 6 hours 30 minutes. First, subtracting the hours gives 1510 minus 600 which is 910. This is represented as 0910, or 9:10 am. As 30 = 10 + 20, subtracting 10 minutes gives 9:00 am and then another 20 minutes gives 8:40 am. Brooklyn had arrived at school at 8:40 am.

14. **12**

   The new solid has 12 edges.

15. **D4**

   After moving 3 units north, move 3 units east. *Y* is at D4.

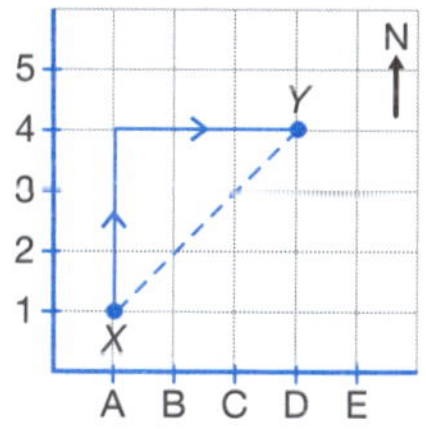

16. **90°**

   The angles that make up a straight line add to 180°. As 180 − 50 − 40 is 90, the missing angle is 90°.

17. $\mathbf{\frac{3}{8}}$

   A regular octagon has eight equal sides. There are eight sections on the spinner. The number 4 covers one section and the number 2 covers two sections. As 1 + 2 is 3, the probability of stopping on an even number is $\frac{3}{8}$.

18. **5**

   As three students chose blue, and 4 × 3 is 12, then 12 students chose red. As seven students chose yellow, and 12 − 7 is 5, then five more students chose red than yellow.

Unit 17A PAGE 72

1. **60, 480**

   Divisible by 20 means the last digit is 0 and the remaining digit(s) form an even number. This means 60 and 480.

2. **8000**

   1786 is close to 2000, 3189 is close to 3000 and 2921 is close to 3000.

3. **1148**

$$\begin{array}{r} 164 \\ \times \quad 7 \\ \hline 1148 \end{array}$$

   There are 1148 seats in the complex.

4. **15**

$$\begin{array}{r} 15 \text{ r } 4 \\ 6\overline{)94} \end{array}$$

   15 bags are required.

5. **0**

   Anything multiplied by 0 is 0.

6. **See below.**

   Shade 1 whole rectangle and $\frac{1}{2}$ of another (3 squares).

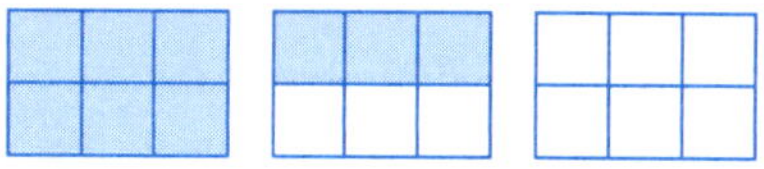

7. $\mathbf{\frac{9}{10}}$

   As 7 − 2 + 4 is 9, then $\frac{7}{10} - \frac{2}{10} + \frac{4}{10} = \frac{9}{10}$.

8. **1.6**

   The number line is marked in tenths (or 0.1s). *A* is halfway between 1.4 and 1.8. As halfway between 4 and 8 is 6, *A* must be 1.6.

9. **$62**

   Double the $23 and add $16. This means 23 × 2 + 16 = 46 + 16 which is 62. The total cost was $62.

10. **51, decrease, 7**

   As 51 − 44 is 7 and 44 − 37 is 7, the rule is 'Start with 51 and decrease by 7'.

11. **12**

   38 − 14 is 24. The number sentence can be written as 24 = ☐ × 2. As 24 ÷ 2 is 12, the missing number is 12.

12. **34 cm**

   Adding the lengths: 11 + 10 + 5 + 8 is 34. The perimeter is 34 cm.

13. **1530**

   Half past three is 3:30 pm. As the time is in the afternoon, add on to 12. This means 12 + 3 is 15 so the time is 1530.

14. **hemisphere, cylinder**

   A hemisphere is sitting on a cylinder.

15. B1

Q is at B1.

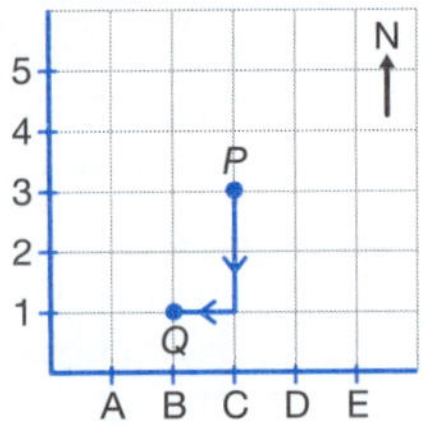

16. 180, 360

A reflex angle measures more than 180° but less than 360°.

17. $\frac{2}{6}$ **(or** $\frac{1}{3}$**)**

A regular hexagon has six equal sides. There are six sections on the spinner. The even numbers are 2 and 6. This means the probability of stopping on an even number is $\frac{2}{6}$, or $\frac{1}{3}$.

18. $\frac{8}{15}$

As 4 + 8 + 3 is 15, there were 15 students surveyed. Eight students had brown eyes. The fraction of brown-eyed students was $\frac{8}{15}$.

Unit 17B — PAGE 73

1. 5

Factors of 41 are 1 and 41. Factors of 43 are 1 and 43. Factors of 47 are 1 and 47. Factors of 53 are 1 and 53. Factors of 59 are 1 and 59. There are five primes between 40 and 60.

2. 94 000 000

14 889 540 is close to 15 000 000, 21 056 347 is close to 21 000 000 and 57 925 402 is close to 58 000 000.

$$\begin{array}{r} 15 \\ 21 \\ +\ 58 \\ \hline 94 \end{array}$$

An estimate is 94 000 000, to the nearest million.

3. 250 mL

There are 1000 mL in a litre, and so there are 2000 mL in 2 L.

$$8\overline{)2000} = 250$$

Each bottle contained 250 mL.

4. 1800 m

The total distance is 3 × 25 × 24, which is 75 × 24.

$$\begin{array}{r} 75 \\ \times\ 24 \\ \hline 300 \\ 1500 \\ \hline 1800 \end{array}$$

The total distance is 1800 m.

5. 0

Anything multiplied by 0 is 0.

6. See below.

Rewrite $\frac{13}{6}$ as a mixed numeral. How many 6s go into 13 … 2 and 1 left over. This means $\frac{13}{6} = 2\frac{1}{6}$. Shade 2 whole shapes and $\frac{1}{6}$ of another (1 square).

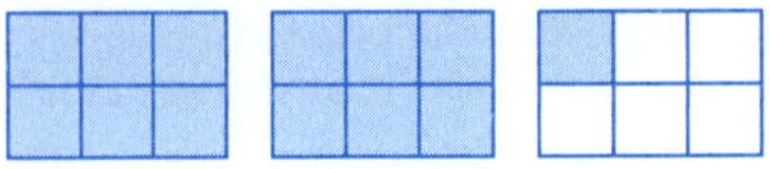

7. $1\frac{7}{20}$

One whole is 20 twentieths. 20 twentieths minus 13 twentieths is 7 twentieths. This is written as $\frac{20}{20} - \frac{13}{20} = \frac{7}{20}$. This means $2 - \frac{13}{20}$ is $1\frac{7}{20}$.

8. 1.6325

1.64 is 1.6400 and 1.65 is 1.6500. The number line is marked in 0.0025s. This means *X* is 1.6325.

9. $760

As a basketball costs $60 then a cricket ball costs $60 ÷ 3 = $20. The total cost for the school is $60 × 10 plus $20 × 8. This is $600 + $160 which is $760.

10. 88

As 40 – 34 is 6 and 46 – 40 is 6, the pattern is increasing by 6. The tenth number will be 46 plus 7 lots of 6. This is 46 + 42 which is 88.

11. 5

Use inverse operations. As there is '+ 8', then first subtract 8 from 28. As 28 – 8 is 20, then 100 ÷ the 'missing number' = 20. As 100 ÷ 5 is 20, the missing number is 5.

12. 22 cm

Add the lengths shown: 30 + 15 + 17 is 62. As 84 – 62 is 22, the missing length is 22 cm.

13. 2220

Thinking of midnight as 2400 means minus 1 hour gives 2300, which is 11:00 pm. Subtracting another 40 minutes gives 10:20 pm, or 2220 in 24-hour time.

14. 12

There are 12 edges on the new solid.

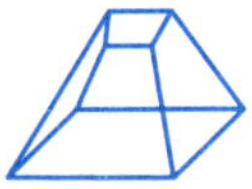

15. 2

North-west of *P* are the locations such as D2, C3, B4 or A5. The number of units west must equal the total number of units north.

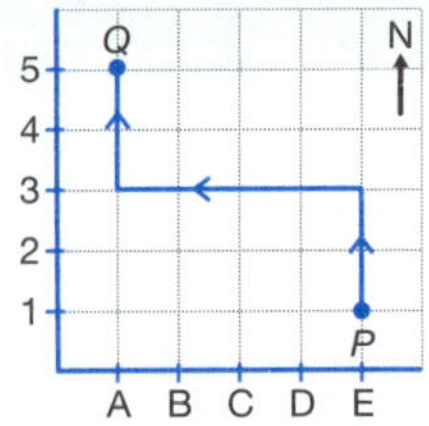

The missing number is 2.

16. 20°

The angles that make up a straight line add to 180°. As 180 – 70 – 90 is 20, the missing angle is 20°.

17. $\frac{5}{6}$

A regular hexagon has six equal sides. There are six sections on the spinner. Two sections are covered by the 3 and three sections are covered by the 5. As 2 + 3 is 5, then the probability of stopping on an odd number is $\frac{5}{6}$.

18. 9

Half of 24 is 12. This means 12 students had brown eyes. As 24 – 12 – 3 is 12 – 3 which is 9, then 9 students had blue eyes.

Unit 18A — PAGE 74

1. 63

The 7 times table gives the numbers 7, 14, 21 … 49, 56, 63, 72 … Maxine's favourite number must be 63.

2. 1600

185 is close to 200, 311 is close to 300, 484 is close to 500 and 603 is close to 600. As 2 + 3 + 5 + 6 is 16, then the clip was viewed about 1600 times.

3. 15

$$12\overline{)180} = 15$$

15 boxes should be ordered.

4. 309

47 × 6 is 282 and 9 × 3 is 27. Adding 282 and 27 gives 309. This means 309 people can be transported.

5. 900

Double 15 gives 30. This means the missing number is double 450. As 45 × 2 is 90 then 450 × 2 is 900. The missing number is 900.

6. See below.

Shade 2 whole rectangles and $\frac{1}{3}$ of another (2 squares).

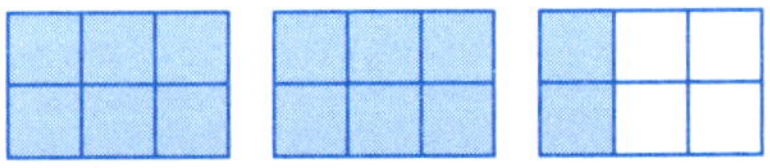

7. $\frac{4}{8}$ **(or** $\frac{1}{2}$**)**

As 5 – 2 + 1 is 4, then $\frac{5}{8} - \frac{2}{8} + \frac{1}{8} = \frac{4}{8}$ which is $\frac{1}{2}$.

8. **1.3**

As 7 + 6 is 13, then $\frac{7}{10} + \frac{6}{10}$ is $\frac{13}{10}$.

This is written as $1\frac{3}{10}$ or 1.3.

9. **$17**

The flour costs $3 × 3 = $9 and the sugar costs $4 × 2 = $8. As adding gives 9 + 8 = 17, the total cost is $17.

10. **4, increase,** $\frac{1}{4}$

From 4 to $4\frac{1}{4}$ is adding $\frac{1}{4}$. From $4\frac{1}{4}$ to $4\frac{2}{4}$ is adding $\frac{1}{4}$. The rule is 'Start with 4 and increase by $\frac{1}{4}$'.

11. **20**

120 ÷ 10 is 12. The number sentence can be written as 12 = ☐ – 8.
As 12 + 8 is 20, the missing number is 20.

12. **52 cm**

Adding the lengths: 9 + 14 + 10 + 12 + 7 is 52. The perimeter is 52 cm.

13. **7:17 pm**

1917 is past 1200 so it is pm. As 1900 – 1200 is 700 then 1917 – 1200 is 717. This means the time is 7:17 pm.

14. **cylinder, cone**

A cone is sitting on a cylinder.

15. **12 km**

As 2 + 4 is 6, George has travelled 6 units. Using the scale, 6 × 2 = 12 km.

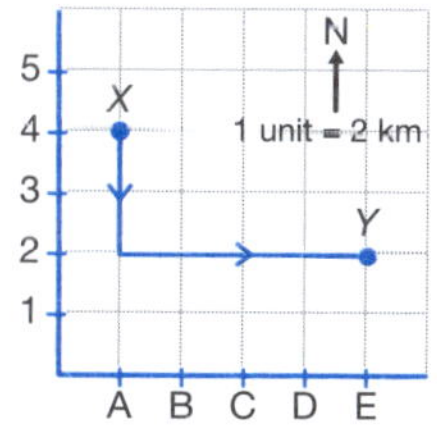

16. **obtuse**

An obtuse angle measures more than 90° but less than 180°. As 100 is between 90 and 180, it is an obtuse angle.

17. $\frac{1}{6}$

A regular hexagon has six equal sides. There are six sections on the spinner. There is one section coloured blue. This means the probability of stopping on blue is $\frac{1}{6}$.

18. **4**

There were five 11-year-olds and one 14-year-old. As 5 – 1 is 4, there were four more.

Unit 18B PAGE 75

1. **12**

Numbers which are multiples of 4 and 6 are multiples of 12. Multiples of 12 under 60 are 12, 24, 36, 48. The sum of the digits are 1 + 2 = 3, 2 + 4 = 6, 3 + 6 = 9, 4 + 8 = 12. Of these sums the only one that is a factor of 15 is 3. This means the number is 12.

2. **2100**

409 is close to 400, 278 is close to 300, 227 is close to 200, 492 is close to 500, 305 is close to 300, 411 is close to 400. As 4 + 3 + 2 + 5 + 3 + 4 is 21, an estimate of the total sales is 2100 to the nearest hundred.

3. **48**

The number of rows is 2880 ÷ 60, which is the same as 288 ÷ 6.

$$6\overline{)288}\quad = 48$$

There were 48 rows.

4. **$1234**

You need to work out 50 + 37 × 32.

$$\begin{array}{r} 37 \\ \times\ 32 \\ \hline 74 \\ 1110 \\ \hline 1184 \end{array}$$

Adding 1184 and 50 gives 1234.
The total cost is $1234.

5. **560 and 8**

Double 35 gives 70. This means ☐ is double 280. As 28 × 2 is 56 then 280 × 2 is 560. Now, 560 ÷ 70 has the same answer as 56 ÷ 7 which means △ = 8.

6. $2\frac{1}{4}$, $\frac{9}{4}$

Two whole circles are shaded plus one-quarter of the other circle. This is written as $2\frac{1}{4}$ circles. Each circle has 4 quarters so as 4 + 4 + 1 is 9, then 9 quarters, or $\frac{9}{4}$ circles are shaded.

7. $\frac{933}{1000}$

One whole is 1000 thousandths.
As 1000 – 67 is 933, then 1000 thousandths minus 67 thousandths is 933 thousandths.

This is written as $\frac{1000}{1000} - \frac{67}{1000} = \frac{933}{1000}$.

8. **2.53**

As $\frac{21}{10}$ is $2\frac{1}{10}$ or $2\frac{10}{100}$, the sum is $2 + \frac{10}{100} + \frac{34}{100} + \frac{9}{100}$, which is $2\frac{53}{100}$ or 2.53.

9. **$60**

4 July is a Monday, and so are 11, 18 and 25 July. This means there are four Mondays. As 15 × 4 is 60, Hazel is paid $60 in July.

10. **103**

As 187 – 180 is 7 and 180 – 173 is 7, the pattern is decreasing by 7. The 13th number will be 173 minus 10 lots of 7. This is 173 – 70 which is 103.

11. **7**

As 12 × 6 is 72, the number sentence can be written as 72 – ☐ = 65.
The 'missing number' can be found using 72 – 65 which is 7. The missing number is 7.

12. **14 cm**

Adding the lengths shown:
12 + 8 + 4 + 5 is 29. As 43 – 29 is 14, the missing length is 14 cm.

13. **1423**

1643 – 200 is 1443. Considering the minutes, 43 – 20 is 23. This means she arrived at 1423.

14. **12**

There are 12 cubes with two faces painted.

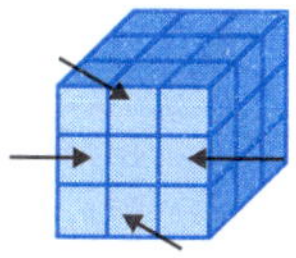

15. **35 km**

Using the map, Phoebe travelled 2 units east, 3 units north and then 2 units west to finish north of *P*.
As 2 + 3 + 2 is 7 and 7 × 5 is 35, Phoebe travelled 35 km.

16. **100°**

The angles that make up a revolution add to 360°. As 360 – 120 – 140 is 240 – 140 which is 100, the missing angle is 100°.

17. $\frac{1}{4}$

Ignore the results from the first two spins. There are four sections on the spinner and one section is coloured red. This means the probability of stopping on red is $\frac{1}{4}$.

18. **17**

The graph shows 15 children. As 15 + 2 is 17, there were then 17 children at the party.

Unit 19A PAGE 76

1. $\frac{2}{5}$

The 9 times table gives the numbers 9, 18, 27, 36, 45, 54, 63, 72, 81, 90 …
The multiples of 9 in the list are 27, 63 and 72. The two numbers that are not multiples are 44 and 91.

This means $\frac{2}{5}$ of the numbers.

2. 600

32 is close to 30 and 19 is close to 20. As 30 × 20 is 600, then the best estimate is 600.

3. 236 800

$$\begin{array}{r} 29\,600 \\ \times \quad 8 \\ \hline 236\,800 \end{array}$$

The total attendance has been 236 800.

4. 4

136 = 120 + 16. 120 ÷ 4 = 30 and 16 ÷ 4 is 4. This means 136 ÷ 4 = 34 and so the missing number is 4.

5. 4257

As 99 is 100 – 1, then work out 100 × 43 and then subtract 43. Now 100 × 43 is 4300 so 4300 – 43 is 4257.

6. See below.

Shade 1 whole rectangle and $\frac{5}{6}$ of another (5 squares).

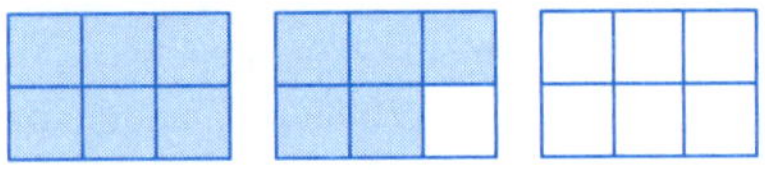

7. $\mathbf{\frac{1}{10}}$

As 9 – 6 – 1 – 1 is 1, then $\frac{9}{10} - \frac{6}{10} - \frac{16}{10} - \frac{1}{10} = \frac{1}{10}$.

8. 0.399

As 440 – 41 is 399, then $\frac{440}{1000} - \frac{41}{1000}$ is $\frac{399}{1000}$.
This is written as 0.399.

9. $4

38 × 2 is 76, and 80 – 76 = 4. This means Savannah had $4 remaining.

10. 49, 60, 71

As 27 – 16 is 11 and 38 – 27 is 11, the sequence starts at 16 and increases by 11. 38 adding 11 is 49, adding 11 is 60, adding 11 is 71. The next three numbers are 49, 60 and 71.

11. 43

10 × 8 is 80. The number sentence can be written as 80 = 37 + ☐. The missing number is 80 – 37, which is 80 – 40 + 3 = 43. The missing number is 43.

12. 52 cm

Adding the lengths: 11 + 8 + 6 + 7 + 5 + 15 is 52. The perimeter is 52 cm.

13. 5:30 pm

1730 is past 1200 so it is pm. As 1700 – 1200 is 500 then 1730 – 1200 is 530. This means the time is 5:30 pm.

14. 10

There are 10 faces.

15.

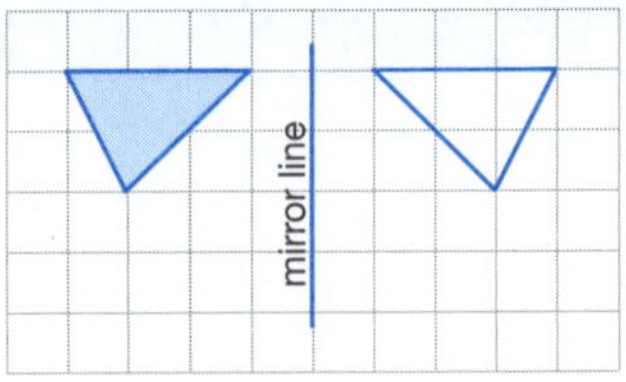

16.

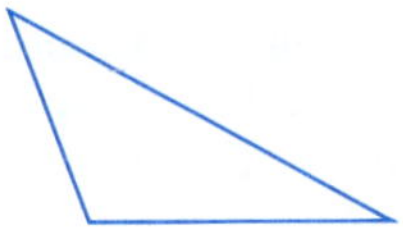

17. $\mathbf{\frac{1}{2}}$

There are two possible outcomes: heads and tails. This means the probability of it landing on tails is $\frac{1}{2}$.

18. 20

The graph shows the number of students who scored 16, 17, 18, 19 and 20. The highest mark was 20.

Unit 19B — PAGE 77

1. 13

Multiples of 4 plus 1 are 5, 9, **13**, 17, 21 … Multiples of 3 plus 1 are 4, 7, 10, **13**, 16, 19, … The first number common to both lists is 13. This means the smallest number of balls is 13.

2. 34 000

506 is close to 500 and 68 is close to 70. As 500 × 70 is 35 000, the best estimate is 34 000.

3. 2470

130 × 19 = 2470

4. 9

$$\begin{array}{r} 697 \\ 5\overline{)3485} \end{array}$$

The missing number is 9.

5. 70 929

As 999 is 1000 – 1, then work out 1000 × 71 and then subtract 71. Now 1000 × 71 is 71 000 so 71 000 – 71 is 70 929.

6. $\mathbf{2\frac{1}{3}, \frac{7}{3}}$

Two whole circles are shaded plus 1 third of the other circle. This is written as $2\frac{1}{3}$ circles. Each circle has 3 thirds so as 3 + 3 + 1 is 7, then 7 thirds, or $\frac{7}{3}$ circles are shaded.

7. $\mathbf{\frac{81}{100}}$

One whole is 100 hundredths. As 100 – 19 is 81, then 100 hundredths minus 19 hundredths is 81 hundredths. This is written as $\frac{100}{100} - \frac{19}{100} = \frac{81}{100}$.

8. 0.9

As 23 – 14 is 9, then $\frac{23}{10} - \frac{14}{10}$ is $\frac{9}{10}$.
This is written as 0.9.

9. $6 350 000

$$\begin{array}{r} 8\,000\,000 \\ -\ 1\,650\,000 \\ \hline 6\,350\,000 \end{array}$$

Claire has $6 350 000 remaining.

10. $\mathbf{4\frac{1}{10}}$

Look at the numerators. The sequence is 3, 5, 7 … The pattern is increasing by 2. The 20th numerator will be 7 plus 17 lots of 2. This is 7 + 34 which is 41, which means the 20th member of the sequence is $\frac{41}{10}$, or $4\frac{1}{10}$.

11. 14

As 8 × 7 is 56, the number sentence can be written as 56 + ☐ = 70. The 'missing number' can be found using 70 – 56 which is 14. The missing number is 14.

12. 72 cm

12 + missing horizontal side equals 20 which means the length of the missing horizontal side length is 8 cm. 9 + missing vertical side equals 16 which means the length of the missing vertical side is 7 cm.

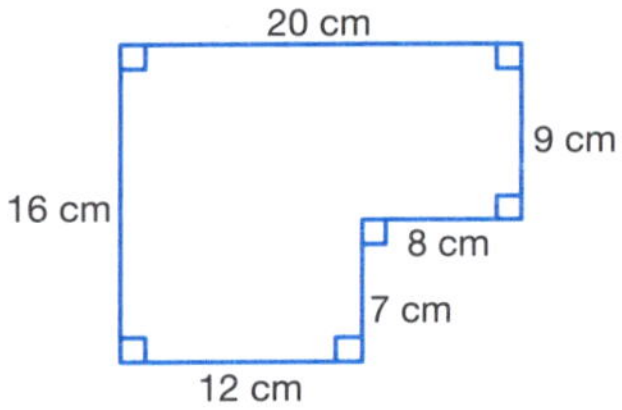

Adding the lengths shown: 20 + 16 + 12 + 7 + 8 + 9 is 72. The perimeter is 72 cm. (Also, a quicker method is 2 × 20 + 2 × 16 which is 72.)

13. 0010

2140 is 9:40 pm. Adding 20 minutes gives 10:00 pm. Another 2 hours is midnight, then adding 10 minutes gives 10 minutes after midnight. This written as 0010.

14. 2

faces = 10,
vertices = 16,
edges = 24.
This means 10 + 16 – 24 = 2.

15.

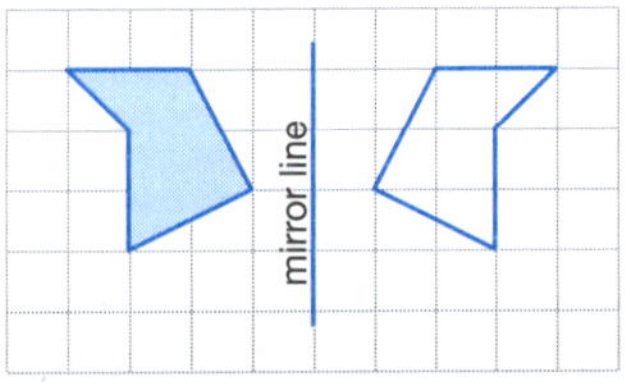

16. 50°

The angles that make up a straight line add to 180°. As 180 – 40 – 90 is 140 – 90 which is 50, the missing angle is 50°.

17. $\frac{1}{2}$

Ignore the results from the first six tosses. There are two possible outcomes: heads or tails. This means the probability of it landing on tails is $\frac{1}{2}$.

18. 13

4 + 5 + 3 + 1 is 13. This means 13 students scored at least 17 marks.

Unit 20A PAGE 78

1. 4, 8, 12

The factors of 24 are 1, 2, 3, 4, 6, 8, 12, 24. This means he can have groups of 4, 8 or 12.

2. 166

$$\begin{array}{r} 416 \\ -\ 250 \\ \hline 166 \end{array}$$

3. 5

625 = 600 + 25. 600 ÷ 5 = 120 and 25 ÷ 5 is 5. This means 625 ÷ 5 = 125 and the missing number is 5.

4. $87

As 12 × 6 is 72, then the total cost is 72 and 15 which is 87. Aaron pays $87 for the hire of the trailer.

5. 8415

As 99 is 100 – 1, then work out 100 × 85 and then subtract 85. Now 100 × 85 is 8500 so 8500 – 85 is 8415.

6.

7. $\frac{3}{4}$

$2 - 1\frac{1}{4}$ is $2 - 1 - \frac{1}{4}$, which is $1 - \frac{1}{4} = \frac{3}{4}$.

8. $\frac{2}{10}, \frac{3}{10}$, **0.5, 0.8**

$\frac{3}{10}$ is 0.3 and $\frac{2}{10}$ is 0.2. The list is 0.3, 0.8, 0.2, 0.5. From smallest to largest the order is 0.2, 0.3, 0.5, 0.8 which is $\frac{2}{10}, \frac{3}{10}$, 0.5, 0.8.

9. $255

$$\begin{array}{r} 85 \\ \times\ \ 3 \\ \hline 255 \end{array}$$

The total cost is $255.

10. 12, 33

As 26 – 19 is 7 and 47 – 40 is 7, the rule is starting with 5 and increasing by 7. As 5 + 7 is 12 and 26 + 7 is 33, the missing numbers are 12 and 33.

11. 8.7

The missing number is 21.5 – 12.8.

$$\begin{array}{r} 21.5 \\ -\ 12.8 \\ \hline 8.7 \end{array}$$

The missing number is 8.7.

12. 36 cm

Adding the lengths: 12 + 3 + 2 + 3 + 6 + 5 + 4 + 1 is 36. The perimeter is 36 cm.

13. 9:16 pm

2116 is past 1200 so it is pm. As 2100 – 1200 is 900 then 2116 – 1200 is 916. This means the time is 9:16 pm.

14. 18

There are 18 edges.

15.

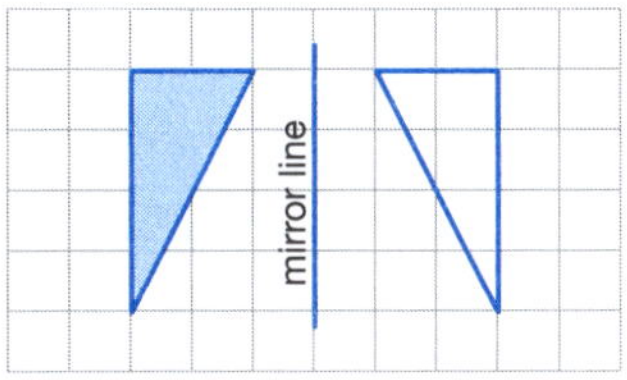

16.

17. $\frac{1}{6}$

There are six possible outcomes: 1, 2, 3, 4, 5 and 6. This means the probability of it landing on a 5 is $\frac{1}{6}$.

18. 12

2 + 6 + 3 + 0 + 1 is 12. This means 12 students were surveyed.

Unit 20B PAGE 79

1. 72, 96, 240

As 2, 3, 4 and 12 are factors of 12, then check the list for numbers that are multiples of 12. The numbers are 72 (as 6 × 12 = 72), 96 (as 8 × 12 = 96) and 240 (as 20 × 12 = 240). The numbers are 72, 96 and 240.

2. 130 677 km

$$\begin{array}{r} 206\,573 \\ -\ \ 75\,896 \\ \hline 130\,677 \end{array}$$

The difference was 130 677 km.

3. 5

Consider 73 × 9 is 657.

$$9\overline{)657}\ \ \text{quotient } 73$$

The missing number is 5.

4. 32 849

You need to add 32 417 to 24 × 18.

$$\begin{array}{r} 24 \\ \times\ \ 18 \\ \hline 192 \\ 240 \\ \hline 432 \end{array}$$

To add 32 417 and 432, just add 417 and 432 which is 849. The total is 32 849.

5. 64 350

As 990 is 1000 – 10, then work out 1000 × 65 and then subtract 10 × 65. Now 1000 × 65 is 65 000 so 65 000 – 650 is 64 350.

6.

7. $\frac{113}{200}$

One whole is 200 two-hundredths. As 200 – 87 is 113, then 200 two-hundredths minus 87 two-hundredths is 113 two-hundredths. This is written as $\frac{200}{200} - \frac{87}{200} = \frac{113}{200}$.

8. 0.25, $\frac{27}{100}, \frac{3}{10}$, **0.31**

$\frac{27}{100}$ is 0.27 and $\frac{3}{10}$ is 0.3 or 0.30. The list is 0.27, 0.25, 0.31, 0.30. From smallest to largest the order is 0.25, 0.27, 0.30, 0.31 which is 0.25, $\frac{27}{100}, \frac{3}{10}$, 0.31.

9. $2797

$$\begin{array}{r} 11\,308 \\ -\ \ 8\,511 \\ \hline 2\,797 \end{array}$$

Jackson's profit was $2797.

10. 2

Express the sequence as improper fractions. The sequence is $\frac{35}{4}, \frac{32}{4}, \frac{29}{4}$ … Look at the numerators. The sequence is 35, 32, 29 … The pattern is decreasing by 3. The 10th numerator will be 29 minus 7 lots of 3. This is 29 – 21 which is 8, which means the 10th member of the sequence is $\frac{8}{4}$, or 2.

11. 535

The missing number is 739 – 204.

$$\begin{array}{r} 739 \\ -\ 204 \\ \hline 535 \end{array}$$

The missing number is 535.

12. 58 cm

4 + 6 + missing horizontal side equals 20 which means the length of the missing horizontal side length is 10 cm.

2 + 7 is the same as 4 + missing vertical side. This means 9 is 4 + missing vertical side. The length of the missing vertical side is 5 cm.

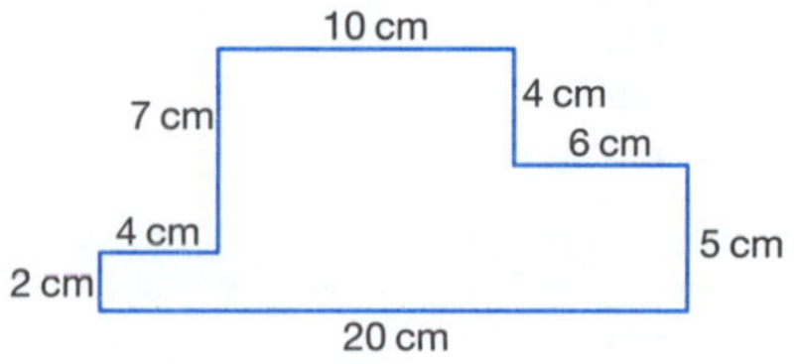

Adding the lengths: 20 + 5 + 6 + 4 + 10 + 7 + 4 + 2 is 58. The perimeter is 58 cm.

13. 0940

Midday is 12:00 pm. Subtracting 2 hours is 10:00 am. There are 60 minutes in an hour so 60 – 20 = 40. This means the time is 9:40 am, or 0940 in 24-hour time.

14. 2

faces = 8,
vertices = 12,
edges = 18.
This means 8 + 12 – 18 = 2.

15.

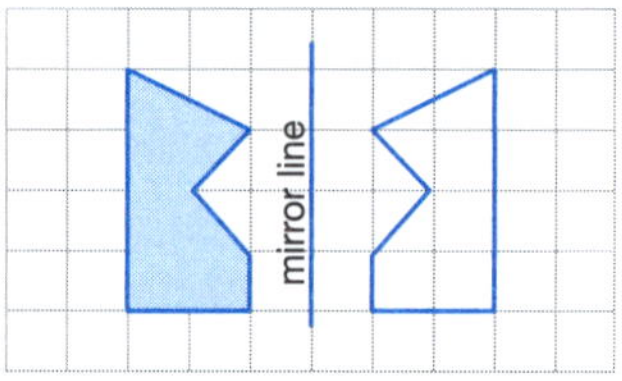

16. 30°

The angles that make up a straight line add to 180°. As 180 – 90 – 60 is 30, the missing angle is 30°.

17. $\frac{4}{6}$ (or $\frac{2}{3}$)

There are six possible outcomes: 1, 2, 3, 4, 5 and 6. There are four numbers less than 5. This means the probability of landing on a number less than 5 is $\frac{4}{6}$, which can be written as $\frac{2}{3}$.

18. 16

Two students had no siblings, 6 students had 1 sibling, 3 students had 2 siblings, no students had 3 siblings and 1 student had 4 siblings. As 2 × 0 + 6 × 1 + 3 × 2 + 0 × 3 + 1 × 4 is 0 + 6 + 6 + 0 + 4. This total is 16, which means 16 siblings.

Unit 21A PAGE 80

1. 42, 441

The 4 times table gives the numbers 4, 8, 12, 16, 20, 24, 28, 32, 36, 40, 44, 48 … Also, 441 is not a multiple of 4 as it is odd. The numbers are 42 and 441.

2. 400

817 is close to 800 and 388 is close to 400. As 800 – 400 is 400, the closest number is 400.

3. 14

$7\overline{)98}$ = 14

She needs to read 14 pages each night.

4. 1416

$$\begin{array}{r} 236 \\ \times\quad 6 \\ \hline 1416 \end{array}$$

There are 1416 car spaces.

5. 2

As 102 is 100 + 2, the missing number is 2.

6. See below.

7. See below.

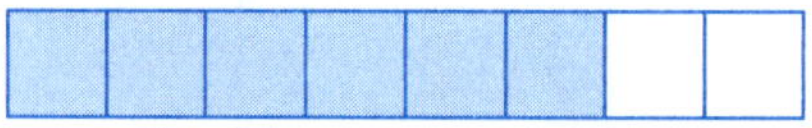

As $\frac{3}{4}$ is $\frac{6}{8}$, you need to shade 6 small rectangles.

8. 102.071

As $\frac{71}{1000}$ is 0.071, then $102\frac{71}{1000}$ is 102.071.

9. $96

Double 31 is 62. Double 17 is 34.

$$\begin{array}{r} 62 \\ +\quad 34 \\ \hline 96 \end{array}$$

The total cost would be $96.

10. 29, 17

As 25 – 21 is 4 and 13 – 9 is 4, the rule is starting with 33 and decreasing by 4. As 33 – 4 is 29 and 21 – 4 is 17, the missing numbers are 29 and 17.

11. 6.8

The missing number is 16.3 – 9.5.

$$\begin{array}{r} 16.3 \\ -\quad 9.5 \\ \hline 6.8 \end{array}$$

The missing number is 6.8.

12. 40 cm^2

The area is found by multiplying length by width. As 8 × 5 is 40 the area is 40 cm^2.

13. 1 hour 15 minutes

0815 is 8:15 am. From 7 am to 8 am is 1 hour and up to 8:15 am is another 15 minutes. This means Camilla had a 1 hour 15 minute sleep-in.

14. 8

There are eight vertices.

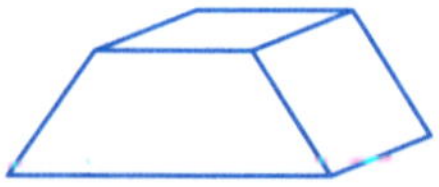

15.

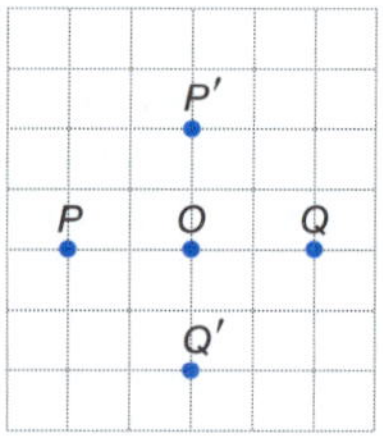

16.

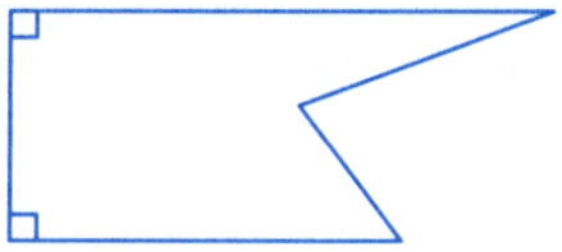

17. $\frac{3}{9}$ (or $\frac{1}{3}$)

There are nine balls in the bag. There are 3 numbers that are at least 7. This means the probability of selecting at least 7 is $\frac{3}{9}$ (or $\frac{1}{3}$).

18. 6°

The highest temperature was 22° and the lowest was 16°. As 22 – 16 is 6, the difference was 6°.

Unit 21B PAGE 81

1. 6

The primes are 19, 29, 59, 79, 89 and 97 as these only have 1 and themselves as factors. There are 6 numbers.

2. 16 000

42 878 is close to 43 000 and 27 053 is close to 27 000. As 43 – 27 is 16, the closest answer is 16 000.

3. 9 and 4

$6\overline{)7434}$ = 1239

The missing numbers are 9 and 4.

4. 448

6 × 4 + 2 × 2 is 24 + 4 which is 28. Each of the 16 wards holds 28 beds.

$$\begin{array}{r} 28 \\ \times\quad 16 \\ \hline 168 \\ 280 \\ \hline 448 \end{array}$$

There are 448 beds in the hospital.

5. 3570

As 102 is 100 + 2, then 35 × 102 is 35 × 100 + 35 × 2. This means 3500 + 70 which is 3570.

6.

7. $\frac{979}{1000}$

One whole is 1000 thousandths. As 1000 – 21 is 979, then 1000 thousandths minus 21 thousandths is 979 thousandths. This is written as $\frac{1000}{1000} - \frac{21}{1000} = \frac{979}{1000}$.

8. **1.025**

$\frac{71}{100}$ is the same as $\frac{710}{1000}$.

Now $\frac{710}{1000} + \frac{315}{1000}$ is $\frac{1025}{1000}$, which is $1\frac{25}{1000}$, or 1.025.

9. **$48**

There are 4 hours from 7 pm to 11 pm. Mary is paid $18 + $7.50 × 4. Now, double $7.50 is $15 and double $15 is $30, and 18 + 30 is 48 so Mary is paid $48.

10. **75**

As 63 – 60 is 3 and 60 – 57 is 3, the pattern is decreasing by 3. As 63 is the fifth number then the first number will be 63 plus 4 lots of 3. As 63 + 12 is 75, the first number is 75.

11. **3.1**

2.7 + 4.3 is 7.0. The number sentence can written as 7.0 – 3.9 = ☐. Now, 7.0 – 4.0 + 0.1 is 3.0 + 0.1 = 3.1. The missing number is 3.1.

12. **108 cm²**

Two times the sum of the length and the width is 42. This means the sum of the length and the width is 21. As 12 + 9 is 21, then the width is 9 cm. The dimensions are 12 cm by 9 cm.

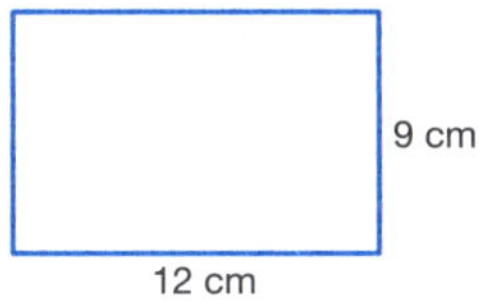

As 12 × 9 is 108, the area is 108 cm².

13. **1320**

0930 is 9:30 am. Adding 2 hours gives 11:30 am. Adding 20 minutes given 11:50 am. Adding another hour gives 12:50. As 30 is 10 + 20, first add 10 minutes to get to 1 pm and then 20 minutes gives 1:20 pm. This is written as 1320.

14. **2**

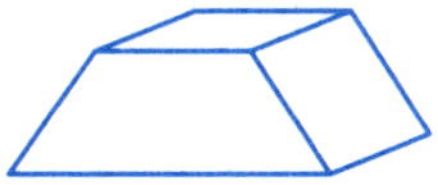

faces = 6,
vertices = 8,
edges = 12. This means 6 + 8 – 12 = 2.

15.

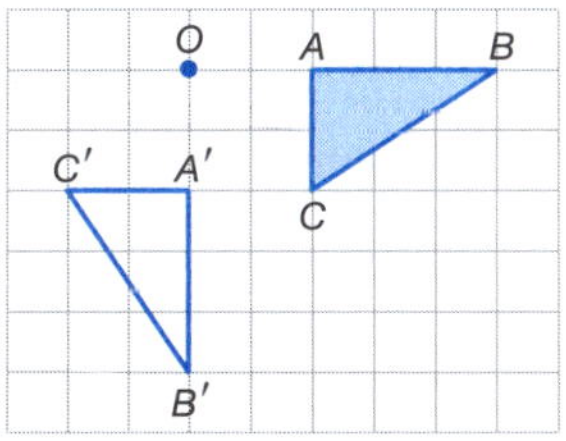

16. **60°**

The three angles make up a straight line which add to 180°. As 180 ÷ 3 is 60, each angle measures 60°.

17. $\frac{4}{9}$

There are nine balls in the bag numbered 1, 2, 3, 4, 5, 6, 7, 8 and 9. Only four of the numbers are even. This means the probability of selecting an even number is $\frac{4}{9}$.

18. **8 hours**

The graph starts at 6 am and finishes at 2 pm. From 6 am to noon is 6 hours. As 6 + 2 is 8, the graph shows the temperature over an 8-hour period.

Unit 22A PAGE 82

1. **false**

The factors of 20 are 1, 2, 4, 5, 10, 20. This means it has six factors.

2. **Liam**

As 50 – 28 is 22 then 12 628 is 22 less than 12 650. As 76 – 50 is 26 then 12 676 is 26 more than 12 650. This means Liam's answer of 12 628 was closer.

3. **1152**

$$\begin{array}{r} 144 \\ \times \quad 8 \\ \hline 1152 \end{array}$$

There is a total of 1152 oranges.

4. **14**

The missing number is 126 ÷ 9.

$$9\overline{)126} = 14$$

The missing number is 14.

5. **6**

Double the 4 and halve the 12 to give the same answer. The missing number is 6.

6.

7. **See below.**

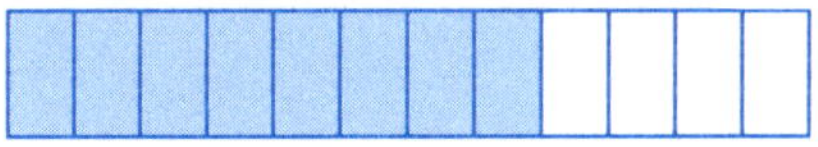

$\frac{2}{3}$ is equal to $\frac{8}{12}$.

8. **0.73**

$$\begin{array}{r} 1.60 \\ -\ 0.87 \\ \hline 0.73 \end{array}$$

9. **$10**

As 80 + 50 is 130, Levi has a total of $130. Now 130 – 120 is 10 which means Levi will have $10 left.

10. **53, 67**

As 25 – 11 is 14 and 39 – 25 is 14, the pattern starts with 11 and increases by 14. 39 + 14 is 53 and 53 + 14 is 67. The next two numbers are 53 and 67.

11. **42.3**

The missing number is 25 + 17.3.

$$\begin{array}{r} 25.0 \\ +\ 17.3 \\ \hline 42.3 \end{array}$$

The missing number is 42.3.

12. **30 cm**

A regular pentagon has five sides of equal length. As 5 × 6 is 30, then the perimeter is 30 cm.

13. **2:20 pm**

1420 is past 1200 so it is pm. As 1400 – 1200 is 200 then 1420 – 1200 is 220. This means the time is 2:20 pm.

14. **15**

There are 15 edges.

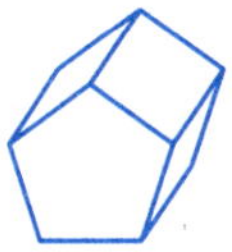

15.

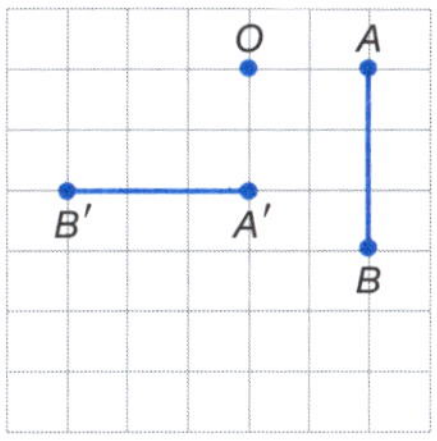

16. **90°**

The two angles add up to a right angle. This means they add to 90°.

17. **4**

Half of the discs must be blue. As half of eight is 8 ÷ 2 which is 4, there must be four blue discs in the bag.

18. **9**

As 3 + 2 + 1 + 3 is 9, a total of nine goals were scored.

Unit 22B PAGE 83

1. **8**

The dates that remain are 1, 7, 11, 13, 17, 19, 23 and 29. This means eight dates remain.

2. **Wyatt**

Brooklyn's was 85 – 16, which is 69 away from the correct answer. Wyatt's was 551 – 485, which is 66 away from the correct answer. This means Wyatt's answer of 327 551 was closer.

3. **9000 mL**

$$\begin{array}{r} 375 \\ \times \quad 24 \\ \hline 1500 \\ 7500 \\ \hline 9000 \end{array}$$

There is a total of 9000 mL (9 L).

4. 1357

The missing number is 9499 ÷ 7, which is 1357.

$7\overline{)9499}$ = 1357

5. 576

Double the 32 and halve the 18 to get the same answer. 64 × 9 is 576.

6. 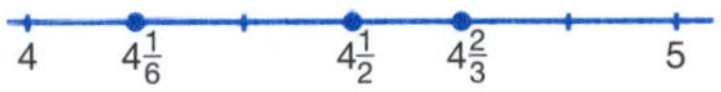

7. $\frac{931}{1000}$

One whole is 1000 thousandths. As 1000 – 69 is 931, then 1000 thousandths minus 69 thousandths is 931 thousandths. This is written as $\frac{1000}{1000} - \frac{69}{1000} = \frac{931}{1000}$.

8. 1.33 m

$$\begin{array}{r} 4.00 \\ -\ 2.67 \\ \hline 1.33 \end{array}$$

Maddie had 1.33 m of ribbon remaining.

9. $238

Her hourly pay rate is 136 ÷ 8.

$8\overline{)136}$ = 17

Poppie is paid at $17 per hour.

$$\begin{array}{r} 17 \\ 14 \\ \times\ 68 \\ 170 \\ \hline 238 \end{array}$$

Poppie will be paid $238.

10. 59

As 23 – 17 is 6 and 17 – 11 is 6, the pattern is decreasing by 6. As 23 is the eighth number then the second number will be 23 plus 6 lots of 6. As 23 + 36 is 59, the first number is 59.

11. 223.5

The missing number is 345.2 – 121.7.

$$\begin{array}{r} 345.2 \\ -\ 121.7 \\ \hline 223.5 \end{array}$$

The missing number is 223.5.

12. 69 mm

A regular pentagon has five sides of equal length. You need to find how many 5s are in 345.

$5\overline{)345}$ = 69

The length of each side is 69 mm.

13. 1630

As there are 60 minutes in one hour, then there are 45 minutes in three-quarters of an hour. Also use 45 = 15 + 30. Now, 1545 is 3:45 pm so adding 15 minutes gives 4:00 pm and then another 30 minutes is 4:30 pm which is 1630.

14. 2

faces = 7,
vertices = 10,
edges = 15.
This means 7 + 10 – 15 = 2.

15.

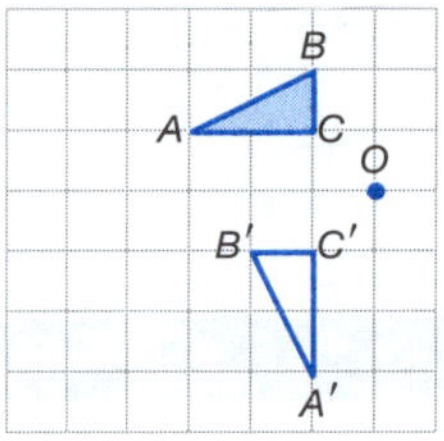

16. 90°

The four angles make up a revolution which add to 360°. As 360 ÷ 4 is 90, each angle measures 90°.

17. $\frac{1}{10}$

There are three red discs so there must be six blue discs. As 10 – 3 – 6 is 1, there must be only one yellow disc. The probability of selecting a yellow disc is $\frac{1}{10}$.

18. 2

The game scores were 3-2 win, 2-3 loss, 1-4 loss and 4-2 win. This means Logan's team won two games.

Unit 23A PAGE 84

1. 7, 4, 1

The factors of 28 are 1, 2, 4, 7, 14, 28. From the list the factors are 7, 4 and 1.

2. 8696

$$\begin{array}{r} 5732 \\ +\ 2964 \\ \hline 8696 \end{array}$$

3. 56

The missing number is 280 ÷ 5.

$5\overline{)280}$ = 56

The number is 56.

4. 384

The total number of passengers is 48 × 4 × 2, which is 48 × 8. As the answer is 384, then 384 passengers are taken to the ski fields.

5. 2 380 000

Multiplying by 10 000 means to write four zeros on the end of 238. The answer is 2380000 which is written as 2 380 000.

6. $\frac{6}{8}$ **or** $\frac{3}{4}$

The square has been spilt into eight equal triangles. Two out of 8, or $\frac{2}{8}$ of the square is shaded. This means that $\frac{6}{8}$ is not shaded. This could also be written as $\frac{3}{4}$.

7. $2\frac{2}{5}$

As 28 – 16 is 12, then $\frac{28}{5} - \frac{16}{5} = \frac{12}{5}$ or $2\frac{2}{5}$.

8. 0.07

$\frac{9}{100} - \frac{2}{100}$ is $\frac{7}{100}$, which is written as 0.07.

9. $50.70

$$\begin{array}{r} 169 \\ \times\ 30 \\ \hline 5070 \end{array}$$

The petrol cost $50.70.

10. 5.1, 6.3

2.7 – 1.5 is 1.2 and 3.9 – 2.7 is 1.2. The pattern starts with 1.5 and increases by 1.2.

$$\begin{array}{r} 3.9 \\ +\ 1.2 \\ \hline 5.1 \end{array}$$

Also, 5.1 + 1.2 is 6.3. The two numbers are 5.1 and 6.3.

11. $1\frac{2}{5}$

The missing number is $2 - \frac{3}{5}$.

As $1 - \frac{3}{5} = \frac{2}{5}$ then $2 - \frac{3}{5} = 1\frac{2}{5}$.

12. 12 cm

An equilateral triangle has three sides of equal length. As 36 ÷ 3 is 12, the sides are each 12 cm long.

13. 1:15 pm

1315 is after 1200 so it is pm. The time is 1:15 pm.

14. 8

There are eight edges.

15.

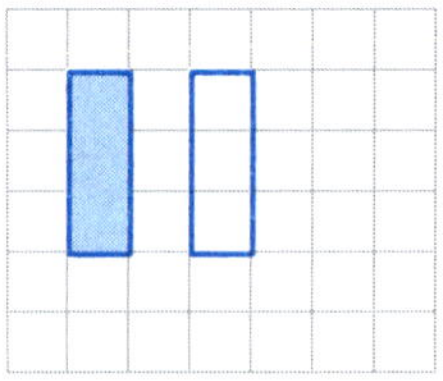

16. 180°

The two angles add up to a straight angle. This means they add to 180°.

17. $\frac{3}{8}$

There are eight sections on the spinner and each section is identical in size. There are three sections that are red. This means the probability of Noah winning is $\frac{3}{8}$.

18. **4**

Paisley ran at least two laps on Monday, Tuesday, Wednesday and Friday, which is four days.

Unit 23B PAGE 85

1. **2 minutes**

Multiples of 3 are 3, 6, 9, 12, 15, 18, 21, 24 … Multiples of 8 are 8, 16, 24, … This means they will drip after multiples of 24. As 24 × 5 is 120, it will take 120 seconds, or 2 minutes until they have dripped five more times together.

2. **336 876**

$$\begin{array}{r} 72\,378 \\ 18\,518 \\ 8\,791 \\ +\,237\,189 \\ \hline 336\,876 \end{array}$$

3. **1673**

$$12\overline{)20076} = 1673$$

There are 1673 packets.

4. **672**

The total number of avocados is 16 × 6 × 7. As 16 × 6 is 96 and 96 × 7 is 672, the restaurant plans to use 672 avocados.

5. **1 380 000**

Multiplying by 30 000 is multiplying 46 by 3, and then writing four zeros on the end. 46 × 3 is 138, and then multiplying by 10 000 gives 1380000, which is written as 1 380 000.

6. $2\frac{3}{4}$, $\frac{11}{4}$

Two whole circles are shaded plus 3 quarters of the other circle. This is written as $2\frac{3}{4}$ circles. Each circle has 4 quarters so as 4 + 4 + 3 is 11, then 11 quarters, or $\frac{11}{4}$ circles are shaded.

7. $\frac{2}{8}$ **(or** $\frac{1}{4}$**)**

As 3 + 3 is 6, then $\frac{3}{8} + \frac{3}{8}$ is $\frac{6}{8}$. The remaining fraction is $1 - \frac{6}{8}$, which is $\frac{8}{8} - \frac{6}{8}$. This is $\frac{2}{8}$, which can also be written as $\frac{1}{4}$.

8. **0.6**

Rewrite $1\frac{3}{10}$ as $\frac{13}{10}$. Now $\frac{13}{10} - \frac{7}{10}$ is $\frac{6}{10}$, which is written as 0.6.

9. **$269**

As 10 − 4 is 6, Juliet makes $6 for each soap sold.

$$\begin{array}{r} 54 \\ \times\ \ 6 \\ \hline 324 \end{array}$$

Her profit for the day was 324 − 55.

$$\begin{array}{r} 324 \\ -\ \ 55 \\ \hline 269 \end{array}$$

Juliet made a profit of $269.

10. **93**

As 57 − 53 is 4 and 61 − 57 is 4, the pattern is increasing by 4. As 53 is the 10th number then the 20th number is 53 plus 10 lots of 4. As 53 + 40 is 93, the 20th number is 93.

11. $\frac{1}{4}$

1 is equal to $\frac{4}{4}$. As $\frac{1}{4} + \frac{2}{4}$ is $\frac{3}{4}$, the number sentence is $\square + \frac{3}{4} = \frac{4}{4}$.

The missing number is $\frac{4}{4}$.

12. **5 cm**

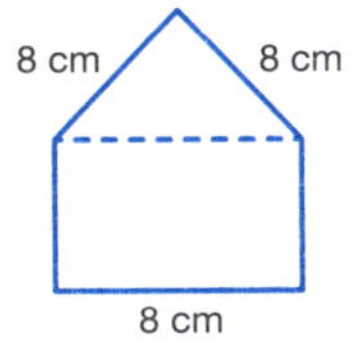

8 + 8 + 8 + 2 × width is 34. This means 24 + 2 × width is 34, and so 2 × width is 10. This means the width of the rectangle is 5 cm.

13. **2140**

There are 120 minutes in 2 hours so 115 minutes is 5 minutes short of 2 hours. Add 2 hours on to 7:45 pm which is 9:45 pm and then subtract 5 minutes which is 9:40 pm. As 1200 + 900 is 2100 this time is 2140

14. **2**

faces = 5,
vertices = 5,
edges = 8.
This means 5 + 5 − 8 = 2.

15.

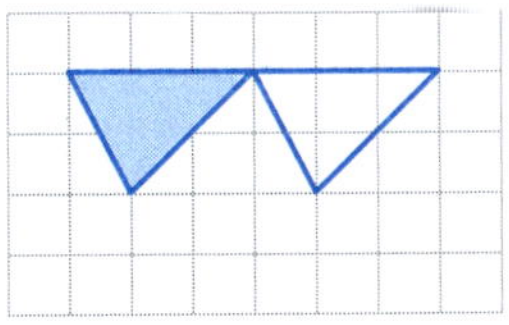

16. **1260°**

An angle of revolution is 360°, and half of a revolution is 180°. As 360 × 3 + 180 is 1080 + 180 which is 1260, Kenzo rotated 1260°.

17. $\frac{6}{8}$ **(or** $\frac{3}{4}$**)**

There are eight sections on the spinner and each section is identical in size. There is one section that is green and one that is yellow. This means there are six sections that are not green or yellow. The probability of Ava not winning is $\frac{6}{8}$, or $\frac{3}{4}$.

18. **130**

2 + 4 + 3 + 1 + 3 is 13. As 13 × 10 is 130, Paisley ran a total of 130 laps in the 10 weeks.

Unit 24A PAGE 86

1. **52, 501**

The last digit of multiples of 5 must be 0 or 5. The multiples of 5 are 15, 505 and 3600. The numbers that are not multiples of 5 are 52 and 501.

2. **3**

63 761 is close to 60 000 and 20 871 is close to 20 000. Consider 60 000 ÷ 20 000 which has the same answer as 6 ÷ 2 which is 3. The best estimate is 3.

3. **46 cm**

Addison's length was 184 ÷ 4.

$$4\overline{)184} = 46$$

Addison was 46 cm long.

4. **192**

16 × 12 = 192. There are 192 packets of chips in the carton.

5. **80**

Both 14 and 6 are being multiplied by 4. As 14 + 6 is 20, then multiplying 20 by 4 is 80.

6. $\frac{2}{8}$ **or** $\frac{1}{4}$

The square has been spilt into eight equal triangles. Six out of eight, or $\frac{6}{8}$ of the square is shaded. This means that $\frac{2}{8}$ is not shaded. This could also be written as $\frac{1}{4}$.

7. **2**

As 1 + 2 + 3 + 4 is 10, then $\frac{1}{5} + \frac{2}{5} + \frac{3}{5} + \frac{4}{5}$ is $\frac{10}{5}$, or 2.

8. **21.7**

Place value is … units, decimal point, tenths, hundredths, thousandths … Look at the 8 in the hundredths place. It is more than 5 which means the 6 in the tenths place goes to 7. 21 683 is rounded to 21.7.

9. **$17.40**

$$\begin{array}{r} 8.50 \\ 2.10 \\ 3.85 \\ +\ \ 2.95 \\ \hline 17.40 \end{array}$$

The total cost was $17.40.

10. 12, 35

81 – 58 is 23 and 104 – 81 is 23. The pattern is increasing by 23. As 58 – 23 is 35 and 35 – 23 is 12, the first two numbers are 35 and 12.

11. no

11 + 9 is 20, not 22. This means Joshua is not correct.

12. 23 cm

A regular hexagon has six sides of equal length. The length of each side is 138 ÷ 6.

$$6\overline{)138}\quad = 23$$

The length of each side is 23 cm.

13. 1330

Adding 1030 and 300 gives 1330. This means she should leave by 1330.

14. 9

There are nine edges.

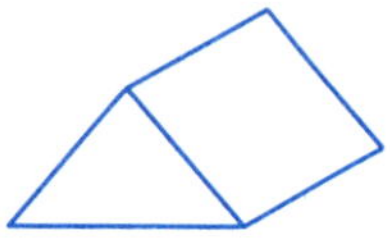

15.

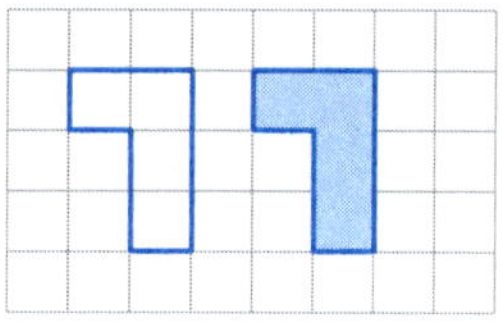

16. 360°

The two angles add up to a revolution. This means they add to 360°.

17. $\frac{4}{12}$ **(or** $\frac{1}{3}$**)**

There are four red, four green and four white balls. The probability of selecting a white ball is $\frac{4}{12}$, which can be written as $\frac{1}{3}$.

18. $220

As 100 + 120 = 220, the total was $220.

Unit 24B — PAGE 87

1. 9

You need to find the numbers with 1 or 2 factors. These numbers are 1, 2, 3, 5, 7, 11, 13, 17 and 19. This means there are nine numbers.

2. 30

610 400 is close to 600 000 and 18 590 is close to 20 000. As 600 000 ÷ 20 000 has the same answer as 600 ÷ 20, or 60 ÷ 2 which is 30, the best estimate is 30.

3. 1218 and 203

Dividing 24 by 4 gives 6. This means  is 4872 divided by 4 which is 1218.

Now, you need to find 1218 ÷ 6.

$$6\overline{)1218}\quad = 203$$

 = 1218 and  = 203.

4. 384

```
    24
×   16
   144
   240
   384
```

There are 384 rooms in the hotel.

5. $100

You need to work out 11 × 5 + 9 × 5. As 11 + 9 is 20, then the answer is found using 20 × 5 which is 100. It will cost Grandpa $100.

6. 37

There are 8 eighths in 1 whole. In $4\frac{5}{8}$ there are 8 × 4 + 5 eighths. This means there are 32 + 5 = 37 eighths, written as $\frac{37}{8}$. The missing number is 37.

7. $1\frac{2}{3}$

As 2 + 1 + 2 is 5, then $\frac{2}{3} + \frac{1}{3} + \frac{2}{3}$ is $\frac{5}{3}$. As 3 into 5 goes 1 and 2 left over, then $\frac{5}{3} = 1\frac{2}{3}$.

8. 1.08

Place value is … units, decimal point, tenths, hundredths, thousandths … Look at the 9 in the thousandths place. It is more than 5 which means the 7 in the tenths place goes to 8. 1.0798 is rounded to 1.08.

9. $3

As 690 ÷ 2 is 345, the cherries cost $3.45. As 790 ÷ 2 is 395, the lychees cost $3.95. As 1920 ÷ 2 is 960, the dates cost $9.60.

```
   3.45
   3.95
+  9.60
  17.00
```

As 20 – 17 is 3, Audrey received $3 in change.

10. 708

As 120 – 106 is 14 and 134 – 120 is 14, the pattern is increasing by 14. As 106 is the seventh number then the 50th number will be 106 plus 43 lots of 14.

```
   43
×  14
  172
  430
  602
```

The 50th number is 106 + 602 which is 708.

11. 80

Starting with 17, add 3 to give 20, then multiply 20 by 4. As 20 × 4 is 80, the input was 80.

12. 1, 50

The regular hexagon has six sides each of length 250 mm. The perimeter is 6 × 250.

```
   250
×    6
  1500
```

The perimeter is 1500 mm, or 150 cm, or 1 m 50 cm.

13. 11:20 am

As there are 60 minutes in an hour, 1 hour 50 minutes is 10 minutes less than 2 hours. Subtracting 2 hours from 1310 gives 1110. Now add the 10 minutes gives 1120 which is 11:20 am.

14. 2

faces = 5,
vertices = 6,
edges = 9. This means 5 + 6 – 9 = 2.

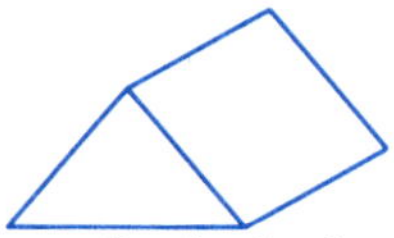

15.

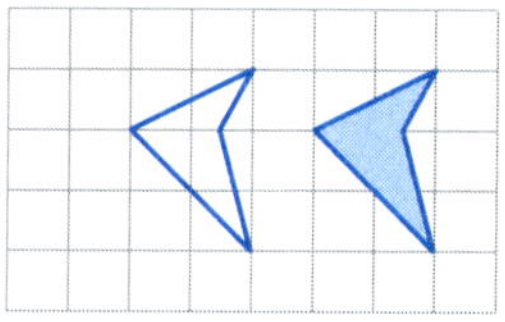

16. 5

A regular decagon has 10 equal sides and 10 equal angles.
It has five pairs of parallel sides.

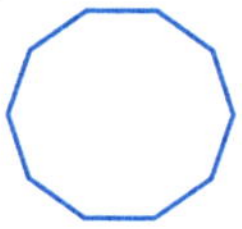

17. $\frac{2}{5}$

There are two colours out of five. The probability of selecting a purple marble or a pink marble is $\frac{2}{5}$.

18. $40

For 4M and 6P: $100 + $140 = $240.
For 5T and 5R: $80 + $120 = $200.
As 240 – 200 = 40, 4M and 6P raised $40 more.

Unit 25A — PAGE 88

1. 5

The 4 times table gives the numbers 4, 8, **12**, **16**, **20**, **24**, **28**, 32 … There are five multiples between 10 and 30.

2. 8

First, add 45 and 23 which is 68. Now the difference between 76 and 68 is 8.

3. **240**

15×2 is 30 and 30×8 is 240. This means $15 \times 2 \times 8 = 240$.

4. **16 cm**

$$12\overline{)192}\quad 16$$

Lexie's handspan is 16 cm.

5. **24**

Work out the sum of those numbers being added and then the sum of those numbers being subtracted. $16 + 13 + 18$ is $29 + 18$ which is 47. Also, $11 + 12$ is 23. Now work out $47 - 23$ which is 24.

6.

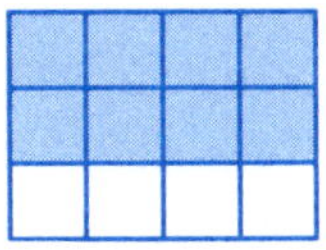

7. $\frac{3}{5}$

One whole is 5 fifths, which is $\frac{5}{5}$.

As $5 - 2$ is 3, then $\frac{5}{5} - \frac{2}{5}$ is $\frac{3}{5}$. Aaron still has $\frac{3}{5}$ of the flight to go.

8. **3.7**

First, rewrite $\frac{37}{10}$ as a mixed numeral.

You need to find how many 10s in 37, which is 3 and 7 left over.

This means $\frac{37}{10} = 3\frac{7}{10}$ which is 3.7.

9. **$54**

$12 \times 2 = 24$ and $10 \times 3 = 30$. Adding gives $24 + 30 = 54$. It will cost a total of $54.

10. **3.4, 5**

$4.2 - 3.8$ is 0.4 and $4.6 - 4.2$ is 0.4. The pattern is increasing by 0.4. As $3.8 - 0.4$ is 3.4 and $4.6 + 0.4$ is 5.0, or 5, the two missing numbers are 3.4 and 5.

11. **yes**

The missing number is $150 \div 5$. As $15 \div 5$ is 3, then $150 \div 5$ is 30. Alexa is correct.

12. **10 cm**

The area is found by multiplying the length and the width. This means 'length' times 7 is 70. This means the length is 10 cm.

13. **2250**

The time is pm so add 12 onto 10. As $12 + 10$ is 22, then 10:50 pm is 2250.

14.

15.

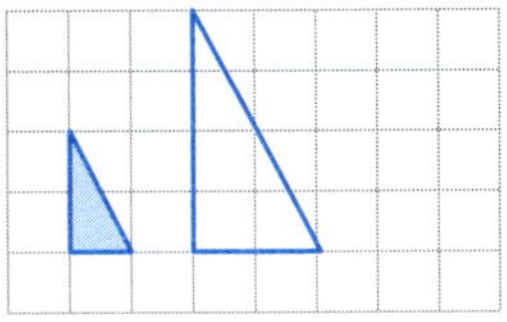

16. **70°, 5°**

An acute angle measures less than 90°. This means the acute angles are 70° and 5°.

17. **2**

As there are three red balls and the probability of choosing a red ball is $\frac{3}{10}$, there must be 10 balls in the box. As $10 - 3 - 5$ is 2, there must be two balls.

18. **6**

As $1 + 2 + 3$ is 6, six students had fewer than three home-cooked meals.

Unit 25B PAGE 89

1. **5**

First, $20 \times 3 = 60$ so look for numbers up to 60. As $3 \times 4 = 12$, the numbers will be factors of 12 up to and including 60. These numbers are 12, 24, 36, 48 and 60. There are five numbers.

2. **2016**

$$\begin{array}{r} 4\,156 \\ +\ 9\,412 \\ \hline 13\,568 \end{array}\qquad \begin{array}{r} 5\,367 \\ +\ 6\,185 \\ \hline 11\,552 \end{array}\qquad \begin{array}{r} 13\,568 \\ -\ 11\,552 \\ \hline 2\,016 \end{array}$$

3. **78 km**

You need to find $13 \times 2 \times 3$.
As 13×6 is 78, Caleb rides 78 km.

4. **15 000**

12 km is 12 000 metres which is 1 200 000 cm.

Now, $1\,200\,000 \div 80$ is $120\,000 \div 8$

$$8\overline{)120\,000}\quad 15\,000$$

He has walked 15 000 steps.

5. **54**

Work out the sum of those numbers being added and then the sum of those numbers being subtracted. $43 + 37 + 26$ is $80 + 26$ which is 106. Also, $29 + 23$ is 52. Now work out $106 - 52$ which is 54.

6.

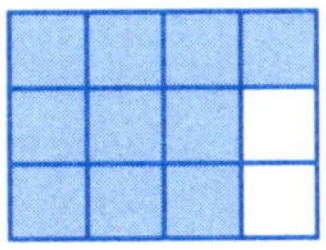

7. $\frac{3}{10}$

As $3 + 1 + 3$ is 7, then $\frac{3}{10} + \frac{1}{10} + \frac{3}{10}$ is $\frac{7}{10}$. The remaining fraction is $1 - \frac{7}{10}$, which is $\frac{10}{10} - \frac{7}{10} = \frac{3}{10}$.

8. **2.09**

First, rewrite $\frac{209}{100}$ as a mixed numeral. You need to find how many 100s are in 209, which is 2 and 9 left over.

This means $\frac{209}{100} = 2\frac{9}{100}$ which is 2.09.

9. **$160.10**

$33.30 is 3330 cents.

$$\begin{array}{r} 3330 \\ \times\ \ \ \ 3 \\ \hline 9990 \end{array}$$

The coat costs 9990 cents, or $99.90.

$$\begin{array}{r} 26.90 \\ 33.30 \\ +\ 99.90 \\ \hline 160.10 \end{array}$$

The total cost was $160.10.

10. **9**

The pattern is increasing by $1\frac{1}{5}$.

Adding $7\frac{4}{5}$ and $1\frac{1}{5}$ is $8\frac{5}{5}$, which is $8 + 1 = 9$. The next number in the sequence is 9.

11. **49**

The number sentence is $7 + 14 \times 3$. As 14×3 is 42, then $7 + 42$ is 49.

12. **8 cm × 4 cm**

Twice the sum of the length and the width is 24. This means the sum of the length and width is 12. You need to find two numbers that add to give 12 and multiply to give 32. The two numbers are 8 and 4. This means the rectangle measures 8 cm by 4 cm.

13. **9:40 am**

2200 minus 1200 is 1000, which is 10:00 am. There are 60 minutes in an hour. As $60 - 20$ is 40, then 20 minutes before 10:00 am is 9:40 am.

14.

15. **30 units**

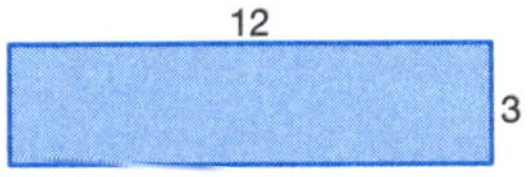

The dimensions were 4 units by 1 unit, so the enlarged rectangle has dimensions 12 units by 3 units. The perimeter is twice the sum of 12 and 3. This means 2×15 which is 30 units.

16. **110°**

A right angle measures 90°. As 90 + 90 + 70 is 250, the three angles add to 250°. As 360 − 250 is 110, the other angle measures 110°.

17. $\frac{6}{20}$ **(or** $\frac{3}{10}$**)**

As $\frac{1}{5}$ of the balls are green there must be a total of 4 × 5 = 20 balls in the box. As 20 − 10 − 4 is 6, there are six blue balls in the box. The probability of selecting a blue ball is $\frac{6}{20}$, which is equal to $\frac{3}{10}$.

18. **20**

Consider the students who had at least 4 home-cooked meals. As 6 + 7 + 5 + 2 is 20, then 20 students had a majority of home-cooked meals.

Unit 26A — PAGE 90

1. **64, 68, 72**

60 + 4 = 64, 64 + 4 = 68, 68 + 4 = 72. The next three multiples are 64, 68 and 72.

2. **800**

$$\begin{array}{r} 232 \\ -\ 110 \\ \hline 122 \end{array} \qquad \begin{array}{r} 678 \\ +\ 122 \\ \hline 800 \end{array}$$

3. **13**

$$5\overline{)65}\ \ (13)$$

□ = 13

4. **144**

As 4 + 3 + 2 is 9, you need to multiply 16 × 9. This is 144, so Ellie needs 144 balloons.

5. **13**

First, 11 + 12 + 4 is 23 + 4 which is 27. Now 40 − 27 is 13.

6.

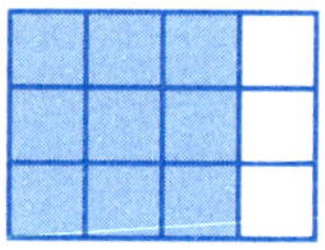

7. $\frac{1}{12}$

There are 12 squares on the rectangle, so shade 5 squares, then 2 squares and then 4 squares. One square remains unshaded, which means $\frac{1}{12}$ of the rectangle remains unshaded.

8. **37.36**

Work out 467 times 8, and insert the decimal point later.

$$\begin{array}{r} 467 \\ \times\quad 8 \\ \hline 3736 \end{array}$$

This means 4.67 × 8 is 37.36.

9. **$4.45**

$$\begin{array}{r} 63 \\ \times\quad 4 \\ \hline 252 \end{array}$$

The books cost $2.52.

$$\begin{array}{r} 2.52 \\ +\ 1.92 \\ \hline 4.44 \end{array}$$

As $4.44 is close to $4.45, Isaac spent $4.45 to the nearest 5 cents.

10. $1\frac{2}{5}$, $1\frac{4}{5}$

The pattern is $\frac{1}{5}, \frac{3}{5}, \frac{5}{5}$ … The pattern is increasing by $\frac{2}{5}$. The next two improper fractions are $\frac{7}{5}$ and $\frac{9}{5}$, which can be written as $1\frac{2}{5}$ and $1\frac{4}{5}$.

11. **yes**

Look at 140 ÷ 20. It has the same answer as 14 ÷ 2, which is 7. This means 140 ÷ 20 = 7, so Cathy is correct.

12. **60 000 m^2**

There are 10 000 m^2 in 1 hectare. As 6 × 10 000 is 60 000, there are 60 000 m^2.

13. **1920**

Twenty past seven tonight is written as 7:20 pm. Add 12 onto 7 to get 19, so the time is 1920.

14.

15.

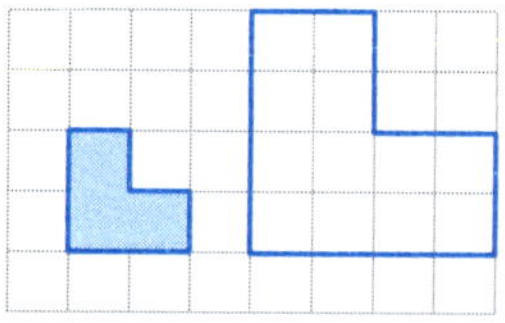

16. **100°, 175°**

An obtuse angle measures more than 90° but less than 180°. This means the obtuse angles are 100° and 175°.

17. $\frac{1}{2}$

Half the pens in the pencil case are red pens. This means the probability of selecting a red pen is $\frac{1}{2}$.

18. **2**

Three members attended one class, five members attended two classes, and so on.

Unit 26B — PAGE 91

1. **24**

Factors of 18 are 1, 2, 3, 6, 9, 18. Factors of 24 are 1, 2, 3, 4, 6, 8, 12, 24. Factors of 28 are 1, 2, 4, 7, 14, 28. Factors of 64 are 1, 2, 4, 8, 16, 32, 64. As 24 has eight factors, it is the number with the highest number of factors.

2. **1861**

$$\begin{array}{r} 4\,569 \\ 2\,781 \\ +\ 4\,789 \\ \hline 12\,139 \end{array} \qquad \begin{array}{r} 14\,000 \\ -\ 12\,139 \\ \hline 1\,861 \end{array}$$

3. □

Try some numbers: As 12 ÷ 4 = 3, then 12 ÷ 3 = 4. This means the answer is □.

4. **192 km**

There are two weeks in a fortnight. You need to find 8 × 3 × 4 × 2 which is 8 × 12 × 2. As 8 × 12 is 96 and 96 × 2 is 192, the players run a total of 192 km every fortnight.

5. **11 km**

To work out 100 − 26 − 18 − 32 − 13, first sum those numbers being subtracted. 26 + 18 + 32 + 13 is 89. Now 100 − 89 is 11, which means Andrew still has 11 km to cycle.

6. **See below.**

$\frac{3}{4}$ is 3 out of 4 which is the same as 9 out of 12. You need to shade 9 squares.

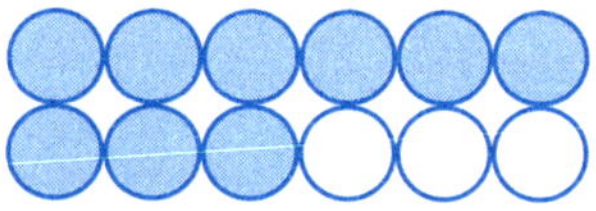

7. $\frac{10}{12}$ **(or** $\frac{5}{6}$**)**

$\frac{1}{3}$ of the rectangle is 4 squares and $\frac{1}{2}$ of the rectangle is 6 squares. As 4 + 6 is 10, then $\frac{10}{12}$, or $\frac{5}{6}$, of the rectangle is shaded.

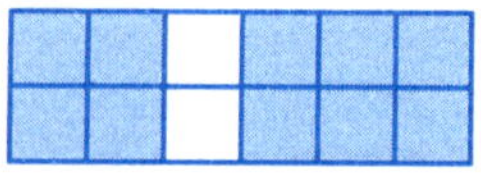

8. **982.8**

First, multiply 378 by 26 and then insert the decimal point.

$$\begin{array}{r} 378 \\ \times \quad 26 \\ \hline 2268 \\ 7560 \\ \hline 9828 \\ \hline \end{array}$$

The answer is 982.8.

9. **\$555**

$$\begin{array}{r} 165 \\ +\ 378 \\ \hline 543 \\ \hline \end{array}$$

The remainder is \$1653 – \$543.

$$\begin{array}{r} 1653 \\ -\ 543 \\ \hline 1110 \\ \hline \end{array}$$

Half of \$1110 is 1110 ÷ 2.

$$2\overline{)1110} = 555$$

Dylan gives his son \$555 and keeps \$555 himself.

10. **16.5 km**

The sequence of distances in kilometres is 7.5, 9, 10.5 … From week 5 to week 11 is 6 weeks. The distance will be 7.5 + 1.5 × 6, which is 7.5 + 1.5 × 2 × 3. This is 7.5 + 9 which is 16.5 km.

11. **24**

The number sentence is 30 – 18 ÷ 3. As 18 ÷ 3 is 6, then 30 – 6 is 24.

12. **1260 m**

There are 10 000 m^2 in 1 hectare. As 8.6 × 10 000 is 86 000, the area is 86 000 m^2. To find the length, use 86 000 ÷ 200 which is 860 ÷ 2 = 430. The length of the paddock is 430 m. As the dimensions are 430 m × 200 m, the perimeter is twice the sum of the length and width. As 430 + 200 is 630 then the perimeter is 1260 m.

13. **1440**

There are 60 minutes in an hour. 60 + 20 is 80 which means it took Isaac 80 minutes. Half of 80 is 40 so it took 40 minutes for Paisley to ride. Paisley arrived at 1440.

14.

15. **54 units²**

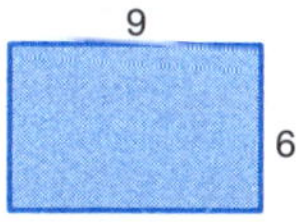

The dimensions were 3 units by 2 units, so the enlarged rectangle has dimensions 9 units by 6 units. As 9 × 6 = 54, the area is 54 units².

16. **36°**

As 66 + 78 is 144, and 180 – 144 is 36, the other angle measures 36°.

17. $\mathbf{\frac{1}{3}}$

One-third of the pens in the pencil case are black. This means the probability of selecting a black pen is $\frac{1}{3}$.

18. **8**

Four members attended three classes, one member attended four classes, and three members attended five classes. As 4 + 1 + 3 is 8, then eight members attended at least three classes.

Unit 27A PAGE 92

1. **3**

The factors of 25 are 1, 5, 25. There are three factors.

2. **\$110**

39 is close to 40 and 72 is close to 70. As 40 + 70 is 110, then the closest total is \$110.

3. **12**

$$8\overline{)100} = 12 \text{ r } 4$$

Nora can print 12 copies of the report.

4. **288**

As 12 × 3 is 36 and 36 × 8 is 288, so 12 × 3 × 8 is 288.

5. **150**

Both 500 and 200 are being divided by 2. As 500 – 200 is 300 then 300 ÷ 2 is 150.

6. $\mathbf{\frac{8}{5}}$

There are 5 fifths in 1 whole. In $1\frac{3}{5}$ there are 5 × 1 + 3 fifths. This means there are 5 + 3 = 8 fifths, written as $\frac{8}{5}$.

7. $\mathbf{\frac{5}{12}}$

There are 12 squares on the rectangle, so shading 7 squares leaves 5 squares unshaded. This means $\frac{5}{12}$ of the rectangle remains unshaded.

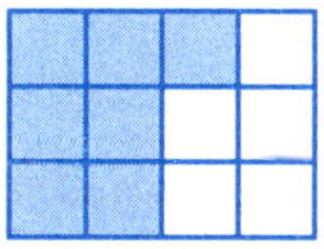

8. **0.2**

A is halfway between 2.4 and 2.6. This means *A* is 2.5 and *B* is 2.7. From 2.5 to 2.7 is 0.2. *A* and *B* are 0.2 apart.

9. **\$62.35**

$$\begin{array}{r} 79.00 \\ -\ 16.65 \\ \hline 62.35 \\ \hline \end{array}$$

The new price is \$62.35.

10. **7.25, 8.05**

Look at the last two digits. The pattern is 45, 65, 85 … The pattern is increasing by 0.20.

$$\begin{array}{r} 7.45 \\ -\ 0.20 \\ \hline 7.25 \\ \hline \end{array} \qquad \begin{array}{r} 7.85 \\ +\ 0.20 \\ \hline 8.05 \\ \hline \end{array}$$

The two missing numbers are 7.25 and 8.05.

11. **2.26**

The number sentence can be rewritten as 5 – 2.74 = □.

$$\begin{array}{r} 5.00 \\ -\ 2.74 \\ \hline 2.26 \\ \hline \end{array}$$

The missing number is 2.26.

12. **18 ha**

There are 10 000 m^2 in 1 ha. You need to find 180 000 ÷ 10 000, which is 180 ÷ 10 = 18. There are 18 ha.

13. **0730**

Half past seven this morning is written as 7:30 am, which is 0730.

14.

15.

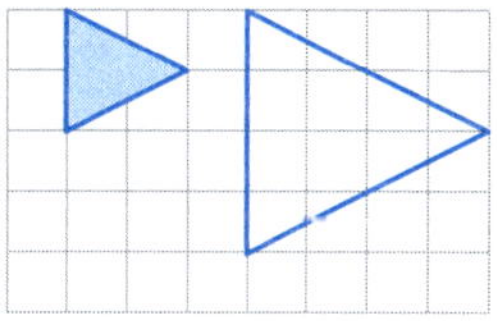

16. **200°, 275°, 300°**

A reflex angle measures more than 180° but less than 360°. This means the reflex angles are 200°, 275° and 300°.

17. $\mathbf{\frac{2}{6}}$ **(or** $\mathbf{\frac{1}{3}}$**)**

There are six faces and two of them are 3s. This means the probability of rolling a 3 is $\frac{2}{6}$, which can be written as $\frac{1}{3}$.

18. **1**

As there are six people who owned one credit card, it is the most common number of cards.

Unit 27B PAGE 93

1. **48**

Multiples of 4 are 4, 8, 12, 16, 20 … 48 … Multiples of 6 are 6, 12, 18, 24 … 48 … Multiples of 16 are 16, 32, 48 … The lowest common multiple is 48. It will take Lara another 48 days before she does all three activities on the same day again.

2. **$46 000**

42 950 is close to 43 000, 627 is close to 600, 1189 is close to 1200, 712 is close to 700 and 528 is close to 500. As 600 + 1200 + 700 + 500 is 3000 and 43 000 + 3000 is 46 000 the nearest answer is $46 000.

3. **19**

$$12\overline{)220}\quad 18 \text{ r } 4$$

As 220 ÷ 12 is 18 and remainder 4, the caterer will need 19 tables.

4. **1900**

There are 52 weeks in a year. You need to find 18 × 2 × 52, which is 36 × 52.

```
   52
×  36
  312
 1560
 1872
```

As 1872 is close to 1900, Fiona buys about 1900 slices of bread.

5. **3**

Both 351 and 336 are being divided by 5. As 351 – 336 is 15 then 15 ÷ 5 is 3.

6. **115**

There are 12 twelfths in 1 whole. In $9\frac{7}{12}$ there are 12 × 9 + 7 twelfths. This means there are 108 + 7 = 115 twelfths.

7. $\frac{5}{12}$

$\frac{1}{4}$ of the rectangle is 3 squares and $\frac{1}{3}$ of the rectangle is 4 squares. As 3 + 4 is 7, and 12 – 7 is 5, there are 5 squares unshaded. This means $\frac{5}{12}$ of the rectangle is unshaded.

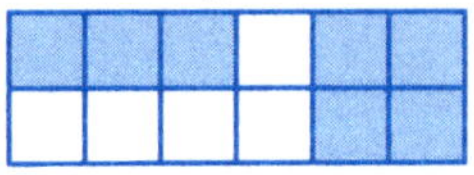

8. **0.075**

The number line has been marked in 0.025s. *A* and *B* are 3 lots of 0.025s apart. This means they are 0.075 apart.

9. **$1240**

```
   385
   260
    95
    80
+  190
  1010
```

Savings is $1320 – $1010 each week.

```
  1320
– 1010
   310
```

As 310 × 4 is 1240, Camilla saves $1240 in four weeks.

10. **89**

The sequence is 26, 33, 40 … This means the 10th number is 26 + 9 × 7. This is 26 + 63 which is 89. The 10th number is 89.

11. **32**

```
  135
–  78
   57
```

The number sentence can be written as 25 + ☐ = 57. The missing number is 57 – 25 which is 32. The missing number is 32.

12. **207 ha**

As there are 1000 m in 1 km, and 2.3 × 1000 = 2300, the length is 2300 m. The area is 2300 × 900. The answer will be 23 × 9 with four zeros on the end. As 23 × 9 = 207, then 2300 × 900 is 2070000, which is 2 070 000 m^2. Dividing by 10 000 is removing four zeros from the end which is 207. The area is 207 hectares.

13. **10:17 pm**

As 60 – 43 is 17, then 43 minutes before 11 pm is 10:17.

14.

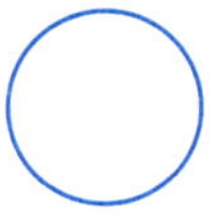

15. **28 units^2**

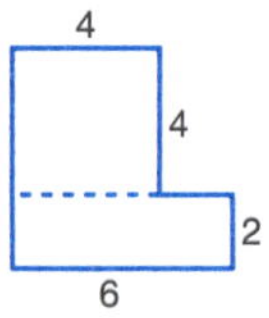

The dimensions have been mulltiplied by 2. The shape is a square and a rectangle. 4 × 4 + 6 × 2 is 16 + 12 which is 28. The area is 28 units^2.

16. **180°**

 to 

The minute hand has moved through 180°.

17. $\frac{5}{6}$

There are six faces and five of them are less than 4. It does not matter whether the identified number is face down or face up. The probability of rolling a number less than 4 is $\frac{5}{6}$.

18. **19**

One person owned zero cards, six people owned one card, three people owned two cards, one person owned three cards and one person owned four cards. 1 × 0 + 6 × 1 + 3 × 2 + 1 × 3 + 1 × 4 is 0 + 6 + 6 + 3 + 4 which is 19. The group owned a total of 19 cards.

Unit 28A PAGE 94

1. **19, 23**

19 has factors 1 and 19; 23 has factors 1 and 23. The other numbers have more than two factors.

2. **11 541**

11 541 is 11 thousand, 5 hundred and 41. As the number includes '5 hundred' then the number is rounded to 12 thousand.

3. **750**

As 25 × 3 is 75 then 25 × 30 is 750. There are 750 apple trees.

4. **28**

$$5\overline{)140}\quad 28$$

There are 28 bags of rice.

5. **260**

Both 16 and 4 are being multiplied by 13. As 16 + 4 = 20, then 20 × 13, or 13 × 20 is 260.

6. **See below.**

The number line is marked in quarters: $\frac{3}{4}, \frac{4}{4}, \frac{5}{4}, \frac{6}{4}, \frac{7}{4}$ (which is $1\frac{3}{4}$).

7. $\frac{4}{5}$

As 2 + 3 – 1 is 4, then $\frac{2}{5} + \frac{3}{5} - \frac{1}{5}$ is $\frac{4}{5}$.

8. **See below.**

As 0.6 is $\frac{6}{10}$, there must be 6 squares out of 10 shaded.

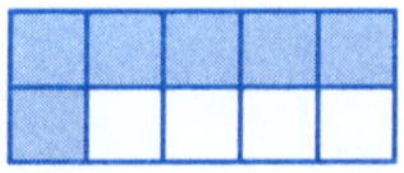

9. $72.90

1215
× 6
7290

Caleb is paid $72.90.

10. 78

66 – 54 is 12. 102 – 90 is 12. The pattern is increasing by 12. As 66 + 12 is 78, the missing number is 78.

11. >

18 + 12 is 30. 10 + 15 is 25. As 30 is greater than 25, then the number sentence is 18 + 12 > 10 + 15. Use the symbol >.

12. 15 cm

If the perimeter is 100 cm, the sum of the length and the width is 50 cm. As 50 – 35 is 15, the width is 15 cm.

13. 2315

There are 60 minutes in one hour and 60 – 45 = 15. This means the time is 11:15 pm. As the time is pm, add 11 onto 12. As 12 + 11 = 23, the time is 2315.

14. 90°

The shape is a rectangle which has four right angles. Angle *C* measures 90°.

15. *P* has been translated 2 units to the right.

16. 90°

 to 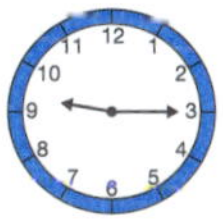

The minute hand has moved through 90°.

17. $\frac{1}{11}$ and $\frac{9}{10}$

Probability ranges from 0 to 1. This means that an event could have a probability of $\frac{1}{11}$ or $\frac{9}{10}$.

18. 60

16
31
+ 13
60

There were 60 tickets sold.

Unit 28B PAGE 95

1. 6

Factors of 24 are 1, 2, 3, 4, 6, 8, 12, 24. Ignore 1 and 24 so there are six possible groups.

2. 147 683

150 000 − 147 683 = 2 317

152 321 − 150 000 = 2 321

2317 is smaller than 2321, so 147 683 is closer.

3. 1116

First, 16 + 10 + 5 is 31. Now multiply 36 by 31.

36
× 31
36
1080
1116

There are 1116 trees in the orchard.

4. 16

480 ÷ 30 has the same answer as 48 ÷ 3.

3)48 = 16

There are 16 teams in the competition.

5. $540

As 13 + 17 is 30, you need to multiply 18 by 30. As 18 × 30 is 540, her total pay is $540.

6. See below.

The number line is marked in thirds: $2\frac{1}{3}$, $2\frac{2}{3}$, 3, $3\frac{1}{3}$, $3\frac{2}{3}$, 4, $4\frac{1}{3}$, $4\frac{2}{3}$.

7. $\frac{1}{4}$

First, $\frac{5}{8} + \frac{3}{8}$ is $\frac{8}{8}$, or 1 whole.

Now $1 - \frac{3}{4}$ is $\frac{4}{4} - \frac{3}{4}$ which is $\frac{1}{4}$.

8. See below.

As 0.75 is $\frac{75}{100}$, which is the same as $\frac{7\frac{1}{2}}{10}$. This means there must be $7\frac{1}{2}$ squares out of 10 shaded.

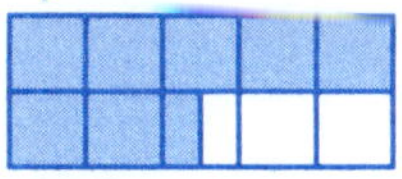

9. $310

$89.95 is 8995 cents.

8 995
× 2
17 990

The amount spent is $179.90 + $68.50.

179.90
+ 68.50
248.40

The total amount of birthday money is $248.40 + $61.60.

248.40
+ 61.60
310.00

Wong received a total of $310 for his birthday.

10. 260

The sequence is 500, 488, 476 … This means the 21st number is 500 – 20 × 12. This is 500 – 240 which is 260. The 20th number is 260.

11. 19

63 ÷ 9 is 7. The number sentence can be written as 26 – ☐ = 7. The missing number is 26 – 7 which is 19. The missing number is 19.

12. 1922 m²

As 186 ÷ 2 is 93, the sum of the length and width is 93 cm. If length is twice the width, then 2 widths + 1 width is 3 widths which equals 93. As 93 ÷ 3 is 31, the width is 31 cm, and the length is 62 cm.

The area is 62 × 31.

62
× 31
62
1860
1922

The area is 1922 m².

13. 2145

As there are 60 minutes in an hour use 60 – 15 = 45. The time is 9:45 pm, or 2145.

14. right angle

The shape is a kite. The diagonals intersect at right angles.

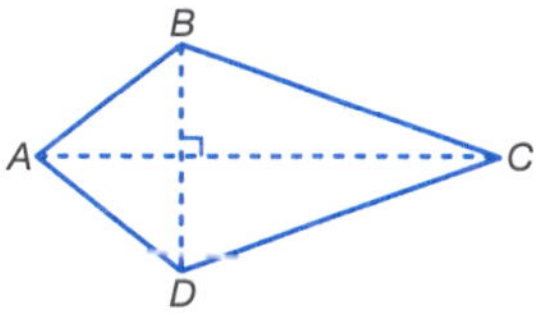

15. See below.

A has been translated 3 units to the left.

16. 60°

An angle of revolution is 360°. As 360 ÷ 6 is 60, each slice is an angle of 60°.

17. 1.0001 and $\frac{4}{3}$

Probability ranges from 0 to 1. 1.0001 and $\frac{4}{3}$, which is $1\frac{1}{3}$, are both bigger than 1.

18. $632

16 people paid $12 each. As 31 + 13 is 44, then 44 people paid $10 each. 16 × 12 is 192 and 44 × 10 is 440.

440
+ 192
632

The total is $632.

Unit 29A PAGE 96

1. 45, 305, 1200

The last digit must be 0 or 5. The multiples of 5 are 45, 305 and 1200.

2. 200

795 is about 800 and 4.1 is about 4. As 800 ÷ 4 is 200, the best estimate is 200.

3. 22

$$4\overline{)90}^{\;22 \text{ r } 2}$$

Brooklyn can fill 22 boxes.

4. 168

There are 24 hours in a day and 7 days in a week.

$$\begin{array}{r} 24 \\ \times \quad 7 \\ \hline 168 \end{array}$$

There are 168 hours in a week.

5. 120

Each number is being multiplied by 6. Add the three numbers: 12 + 5 + 3 is 20. This means the question is 20 × 6 which is 120.

6. See below.

The number line is marked in fifths: $\frac{3}{5}, \frac{4}{5}, \frac{5}{5}, \frac{6}{5}, \frac{7}{5}$ (which is $1\frac{2}{5}$).

7. $1\frac{1}{4}$

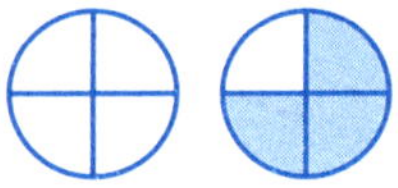

There are 5 quarters, or one-and-a-quarter circles unshaded. This is written as $1\frac{1}{4}$.

8. 4.8 m

$$\begin{array}{r} 1.6 \\ 1.6 \\ + \quad 1.6 \\ \hline 4.8 \end{array}$$

The timber was 4.8 m long.

9. $19.40

$$\begin{array}{r} 76 \\ + \quad 118 \\ \hline 194 \end{array}$$

As 194 × 10 is 1940, Ryan received 1940 cents, or $19.40.

10. 3, $3\frac{1}{4}$

As $2\frac{2}{4} - 2\frac{1}{4}$ is $\frac{1}{4}$ and $2\frac{3}{4} - 2\frac{2}{4}$ is $\frac{1}{4}$, the pattern is increasing by $\frac{1}{4}$. As $2\frac{3}{4} + \frac{1}{4}$ is 3 and $3 + \frac{1}{4}$ is $3\frac{1}{4}$, the missing numbers are 3 and $3\frac{1}{4}$.

11. <

37 – 20 is 17. 9 × 2 is 18. As 17 is less than 18, then the number sentence is 37 – 20 < 9 × 2. Use the symbol <.

12. 144 cm²

In a square all sides are the same length. As 48 ÷ 4 is 12 each side is 12 cm long. As 12 × 12 is 144, the area is 144 cm².

13. 1610

One hour after 3:10 pm is 4:10 pm. As the time is pm, add 4 onto 12. As 12 + 4 = 16, the time is 1610.

14. *D*

The shape is a parallelogram. Opposite angles are the same size. This means angle *D* is the same size as angle *B*.

15. *S* has been reflected in the mirror line.

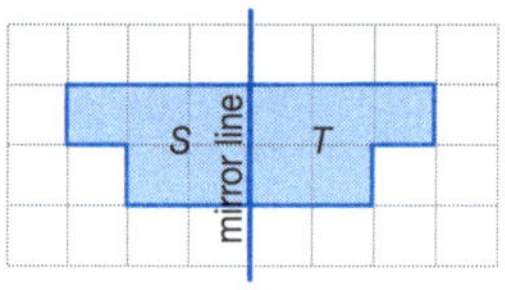

16. 180°

East and west are opposite each other on a compass rose. This means there is a rotation of 180° between east and west.

17.

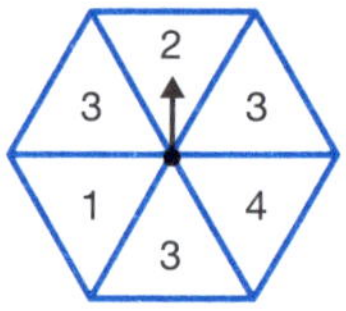

The probability of spinning a 3 is $\frac{3}{6}$ on the third spinner, which is higher than the probability on the other two spinners, which is $\frac{2}{6}$.

18. 10

14 – 4 is 10. This means 10 more people nominated mandarin.

Unit 29B PAGE 97

1. 9

Factors of 60 are 1, 2, 3, 4, 5, 6, 10, 12, 15, 20, 30, 60. Factors of 48 are 1, 2, 3, 4, 6, 8, 12, 16, 24, 48. The highest common factor is 12. Rob should cut the ropes in 12-m-long pieces. As 60 ÷ 12 = 5 and 48 ÷ 12 = 4 and 5 + 4 = 9, Rob will have nine pieces.

2. 16 000

504 is about 500 and 31 is about 30. 500 × 30 is 15 000 which is close to 16 000.

3. 17

52 × 2 is 104. The game uses 104 cards.

$$6\overline{)104}^{\;17 \text{ r } 2}$$

There are 17 people playing the game.

4. 184

July, August, October and December have 31 days. September and November have 30 days. As 31 × 4 is 124 and 30 × 2 is 60, the total number of days is 124 + 60 which is 184.

5. 12 kg

The total mass in grams is 240 × 12 + 240 × 16 + 240 × 22. Each number is being multiplied by 240. Add the three numbers: 12 + 16 + 22 is 50. This means the question is 240 × 50, which is the same as 120 × 100, which equals 12 000. The total mass is 12 000 grams (or 12 kg).

6. See below.

$\frac{2}{3}$ is the same as $\frac{4}{6}$. The number line is marked in sixths: $3\frac{4}{6}, 3\frac{5}{6}, 4, 4\frac{1}{6}, 4\frac{2}{6}, 4\frac{3}{6}, 4\frac{4}{6}, 4\frac{5}{6}$.

7. $1\frac{3}{4}$

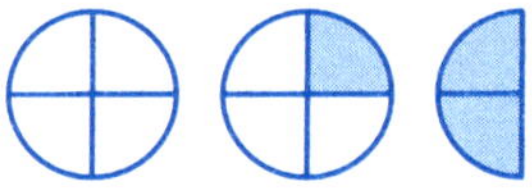

There is one whole, and three quarters remaining. This means $2\frac{1}{2} - \frac{3}{4}$ is $1\frac{3}{4}$.

8. 0.65

There are $6\frac{1}{2}$ squares out of 10 that have been shaded. This means $\frac{6.5}{10}$ of the rectangle is shaded, which is the same as $\frac{65}{100}$, or 0.65.

9. $2.60

The cost of a wrap is $9.80 ÷ 2.

As $2\overline{)980}^{\;490}$, one wrap costs $4.90.

An iced tea costs $7.50 – $4.90.

$$\begin{array}{r} 7.50 \\ - \quad 4.90 \\ \hline 2.60 \end{array}$$

The price of an iced tea is $2.60.

10. 5.923, 5.823

Look at the last two digits in each decimal. The pattern is … 98, 73, 48 … As 98 – 73 is 25 and 73 – 48 is 25, the pattern is decreasing by 0.025.

$$\begin{array}{r} 5.898 \\ + \quad 0.025 \\ \hline 5.923 \end{array} \qquad \begin{array}{r} 5.848 \\ - \quad 0.025 \\ \hline 5.823 \end{array}$$

The missing decimals are 5.923 and 5.823.

11. **10**

The number sentence is:

$3 \times \square = 12 + 18$. 12 + 18 is 30.

The number sentence can be written as $3 \times \square = 30$. Jack's number is 30 ÷ 3 which is 10.

12. **576 m²**

$$9\overline{)864}\ \ 96$$

The perimeter is 96 m, which means the side length is 96 ÷ 4 = 24 m.

$$\begin{array}{r} 24 \\ \times\ 24 \\ \hline 96 \\ 480 \\ \hline 576 \end{array}$$

The area is 576 m².

13. **2 hours 25 minutes**

1115 is 11:15 am and 1340 is 1:40 pm. From 11:15 am to 1:15 pm is 2 hours. As 40 – 15 = 25 there are 25 minutes from 1:15 pm to 1:40 pm. There is 2 hours 25 minutes between the two times.

14. ***A* and *C***

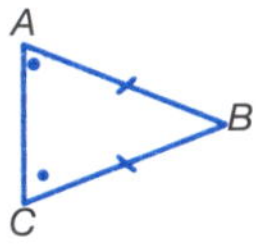

The triangle is isosceles. Angles that are opposite equal sides are equal.

15. **3 right, 1 down**

X has been translated 3 units to the right and then 1 unit down.

16. **270°**

An angle of revolution is 360°. As 360 ÷ 12 is 30, and 3 × 30 is 90, the angle of cake removed was 90°. As 360 – 90 is 270, the angle remaining was 270°.

17. **See below.**

The probability of spinning a 2 is $\frac{2}{6}$ on the first spinner, which is higher than the second spinner's probability of $\frac{1}{6}$ and the third spinner's of 0.

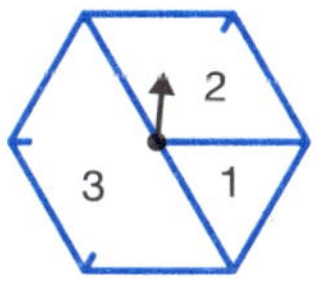

18. **46**

12 + 14 + 4 + 10 + 6 = 46. This means 46 people were surveyed.

Unit 30A PAGE 98

1. **24**

The 4 times table gives the numbers 4, 8, 12, 16, 20, 24, 28, 32 … For 24, 2 + 4 = 6, so the number is 24.

2. **574 km**

$$\begin{array}{r} 176 \\ 191 \\ +\ 207 \\ \hline 574 \end{array}$$

Sofia drove 574 km.

3. **192**

$$\begin{array}{r} 16 \\ \times\ 12 \\ \hline 192 \end{array}$$

Grayson has 192 cars in his collection.

4. **23**

$$5\overline{)115}\ \ 23$$

There were 23 plants in each row.

5. **20**

Adding 25 and 15 gives 40. Finding half of 40 is dividing 40 by 2. This means 40 ÷ 2 is 20.

6. $\mathbf{4\frac{3}{8}}$

How many 8s go into 35? … 4 and 3 left over. This means $\frac{35}{8} = 4\frac{3}{8}$.

7. $\mathbf{\frac{1}{4}}$

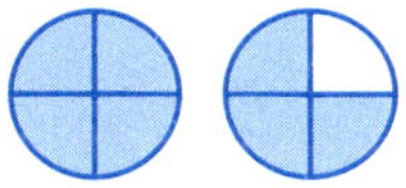

As $1\frac{3}{4} = \frac{7}{4}$, and $\frac{8}{4} - \frac{7}{4}$ is $\frac{1}{4}$, then the fraction unshaded is $\frac{1}{4}$ of a circle.

8. **4.1**

Look for the number halfway between 36 and 46. As 46 – 36 is 10, and half of 10 is 5, the middle number is 36 + 5 = 41. This means the decimal is 4.1.

9. **$180.15**

$$\begin{array}{r} 79.90 \\ 11.25 \\ +\ 89.00 \\ \hline 180.15 \end{array}$$

Isaiah spent a total of $180.15.

10. **170, 140, 110, 80**

170, then 170 subtracting 30 is 140, subtracting 30 is 110, subtracting 30 is 80. The numbers are 170, 140, 110, 80.

11. $\boxed{=}$

$$\begin{array}{r} 106 \\ -\ 37 \\ \hline 69 \end{array}$$

48 + 21 is 69. As 69 = 69, then the number sentence is 106 – 37 = 48 + 21. Use the symbol $\boxed{=}$.

12. **88 cm**

As 16 + 8 is 24 the missing horizontal side is 24 – 20 which is 4 cm. As 10 + 10 is 20, the missing vertical side is 20 – 14 which is 6 cm. As 20 + 10 + 4 + 10 + 16 + 6 + 8 + 14 is 88, the perimeter is 88 cm.

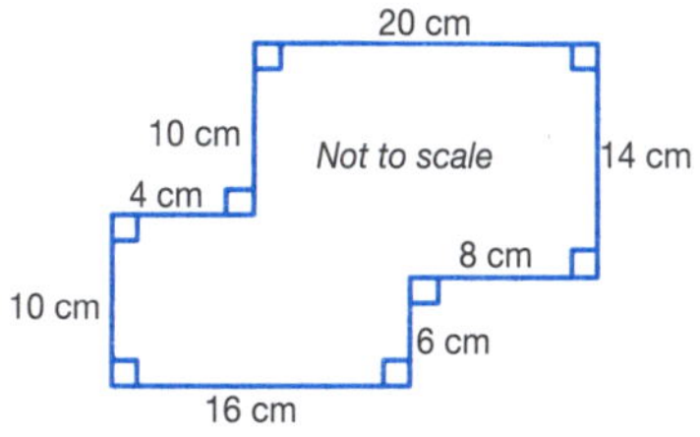

13. **9:21 pm**

2121 is past 1200 so it is pm. As 2100 – 1200 is 900 then 2121 – 1200 is 921. This means the time is 9:21 pm.

14. **40 cm**

A parallelogram has opposite sides equal in length. The perimeter is two times the sum of 12 and 8. As 12 + 8 is 20, and 2 × 20 is 40, the perimeter is 40 cm.

15. **24 cm**

As 3 × 2 is 6, the enlarged square has side length of 6 cm. As 4 × 6 is 24, the perimeter is 24 cm.

16. **See below.**

More than 90° means more than a right angle.

17. $\mathbf{\frac{1}{4}}$

Only the 3 is less than 5. It takes up one out of the four sections. This means the probability of spinning a number less than 5 is $\frac{1}{4}$.

18. **1**

The graph shows one person had four subscriptions.

Unit 30B PAGE 99

1. **4**

The multiples of 15 are 15, 30, 45, 60 … and the multiples of 12 are 12, 24, 36, 48, 60 … The first multiple common to both 15 and 12 is 60. This means Sam should buy 60 hotdogs, which means four packets.

2. 73 051

$$\begin{array}{r} 8\,910 \\ 9\,167 \\ 11\,871 \\ 16\,412 \\ 13\,987 \\ +12\,704 \\ \hline 73\,051 \end{array}$$

There was a total of 73 051 sales.

3. 15 500

As 16 – 8 – 5 is 3, there are 3 boxes of 1500 pieces (4500 pieces). Also, 750 × 8 is 1500 × 4 = 6000. As 6000 + 5000 + 4500 is 15 500, there is a total number of 15 500 pieces.

4. 34

$$4\overline{)136}\quad 34$$

The maximum number of customers is 34.

5. 39

As 36 + 64 + 56 is 156, and 156 ÷ 4 is 39, then a quarter is 39.

6. $485\frac{7}{9}$

$$9\overline{)4372}\quad 485\tfrac{7}{9}$$

7. $\frac{2}{3}$

There are 2 thirds remaining.

8. 2.96

As 2.8 is 2.80, look for the number halfway between 280 and 312. This is a total of 592, and half of 592 is 296. The decimal is 2.96.

9. 60 cents

As 80 × 3 is 240, the bananas cost $2.40. As 70 × 4 is 280, the apples cost $2.80. As $2.40 + $2.80 is $5.20, and adding $3.60 is $8.80, the mandarins cost a total of $1.20. This means the mandarins cost 60 cents each.

10. 375 and 299

As 356 – 337 is 19, the pattern is subtracting 19. As 356 + 19 is 356 + 20 – 1 = 375 and 318 – 19 is 299, the missing numbers are 375 and 299.

11. ☐ + 43 = 82 – 11. The number is 28.

As 82 – 11 is 71, then ☐ + 43 is 71. As 71 – 43 is 28, Layla's number is 28. The number sentence is ☐ + 43 = 82 – 11.

12. 392 cm²

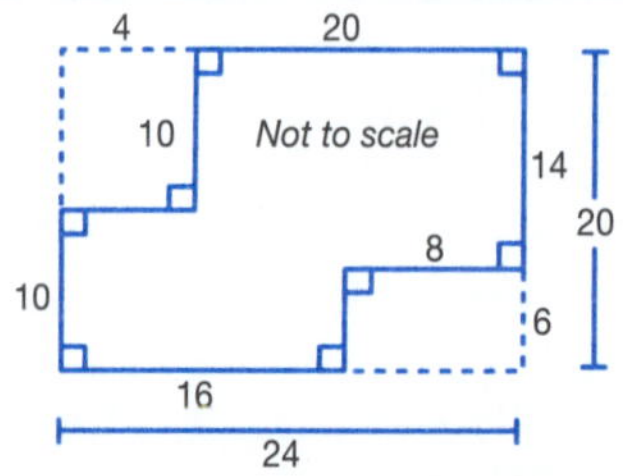

The shape is a large rectangle with two smaller rectangles removed. The area is 24 × 20 – 10 × 4 – 8 × 6. As 480 – 40 – 48 is 392, the area is 392 cm².

13. 0945

From 1310 minus 3 h is 1010. Now subtract another 25 min is 0945. The train had left at 0945.

14. 17 cm

As 12 + 8 is 20, the length of the diagonal will be between 12 cm and 20 cm. From the list of options, the best estimate is 17 cm.

15. 200 cm

As length × width is area, then 12 × width is 96. This means the width is 96 ÷ 12 = 8. The dimensions of the original rectangle are 12 cm by 8 cm, which has a perimeter of 40 cm. Muliplying by 5, the new perimeter is 200 cm.

16. west

Rotating 45° in an anticlockwise direction has Kylie facing east. Another 180° means she is facing west.

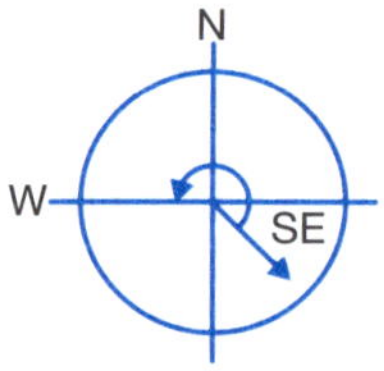

17. $\frac{7}{12}$

The angle for 1 is 60° and the angle for 2 is 90° angle. The angle for 3 is the remainder of the circle. As there is 360° around a circle, and 360 – 60 – 90 is 210, the angle for 3 is 210°. This means the probability is $\frac{210}{360}$, which is $\frac{21}{36}$, or $\frac{7}{12}$.

18. 27

5 people have 1, 2 have 4, 4 have 1 and 5 have 2. As 5 × 1 + 2 × 4 + 4 × 1 + 5 × 2 is 27, there is a total of 27 subscriptions.

NAPLAN-style Test 2 PAGES 100–103

1. D

Twenty to nine is 40 minutes past 8. This is written as 8:40 pm. As 12 + 8 is 20, the time is 2040.

2. 3.047, 3.28, 3.36, 3.4

Place zeros on the ends so that each has three decimal places: 3.400, 3.280, 3.047, 3.360. Now arrange the three digits: 47, 280, 360, 400. The order is 3.047, 3.28, 3.36, 3.4.

3. A, C, D

Look for those that are factors of 96. As 96 ÷ 6 = 16, 96 ÷ 12 = 8 and 96 ÷ 16 = 6, Arthur could have bought 6, 12 or 16 shrubs.

4. 10

6 is opposite 8, and 6 + 8 = 14, so opposite faces add to 14. As ✱ is opposite 4, and 14 – 4 is 10, then 10 is represented by ✱.

5. C, E

The pattern is increasing by 6. 34 + 6 is 40, 40 + 6 is 46, 46 + 6 is 52, 52 + 6 is 58, and so on. From the list 52 and 58 will be in the pattern.

6. 180

As 12 + 18 is 30 the number sentence is ☐ ÷ 6 = 30. Now 30 × 6 is 180 so the missing number is 180.

7. $\frac{1}{3}$

Suppose there are 10 red balls. Then, as twice 10 is 20, there must be 20 blue balls. As 10 + 20 = 30, there are 30 balls. The probability of choosing a red ball is $\frac{10}{30}$, or $\frac{1}{3}$.

8. 2

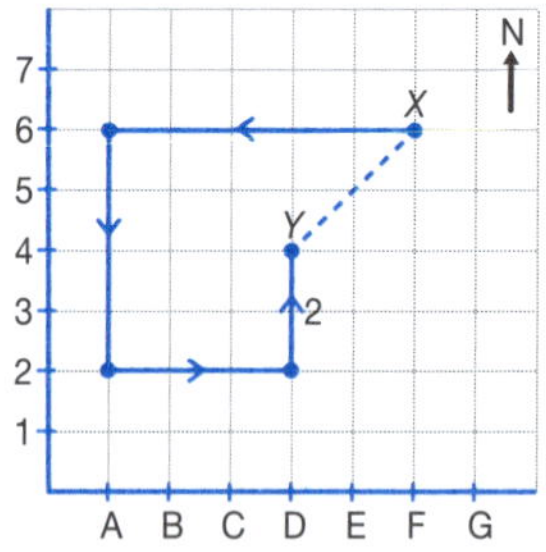

9. B, C

The missing angle is 45°. As the triangle has two angles the same size then it is an isosceles triangle. The triangle has a 90° angle, which is a right angle. The shape is also a right-angled triangle.

10. C

384
397
+ 411
1192

Now subtract the total from 1600:

1600
− 1192
408

Tornado scored 408 which placed it second.

11. 230

The protractor measures 130°. As 360 − 130 is 230, the reflex angle is 230°.

12. D

The number line is marked in 0.2s. *X* is in the middle of 4.2 and 4.4 and so is 4.3.

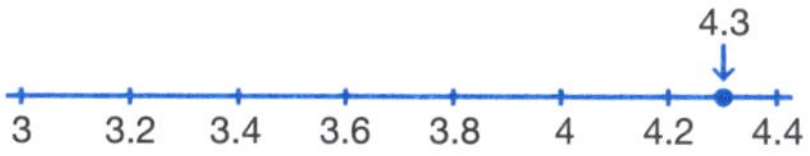

13. 80

As 52 ÷ 2 = 26, the cost of one adult ticket is $26.

62
− 26
36

The cost of two child tickets is $36. As 36 ÷ 2 is 18, the cost of a child's ticket is $18. As 26 + 3 × 18 is 26 plus 54 which is 80, the cost of 1 adult and 3 children will be $80.

14. 12

Each pyramid has eight edges, which means the two pyramids have a total of 16 edges. Once they are glued, four of the edges are shared. As 16 − 4 is 12, the new solid has 12 edges.

15. 16

Write a number sentence for Stevie.

☐ × 3 − 25 = 23. As 23 + 25 is 48, the missing number times 3 is 48. As 48 ÷ 3 is 16, Stevie starts with 16.

16. D

As $2.99 is close to $3 the notebooks will cost about $12. As $2.10 is close to $2 the pens will cost about $6. The external hard drive costs about $80. Now, 80 + 12 + 6 is 98 which is about 100. The total price is about $100.

17. 27

Two students have no pets (2 × 0), six students have one pet (6 × 1), four students have two pets (4 × 2), one student has three pets (1 × 3) and two students have five pets (2 × 5). As 0 + 6 + 8 + 3 + 10 is 27, there is a total of 27 pets.

18. A, B, D

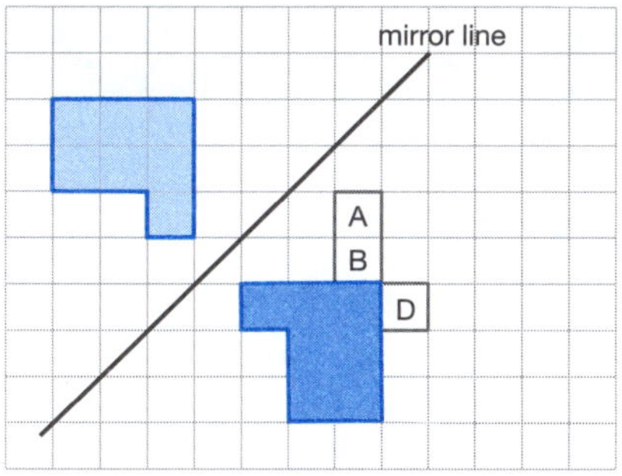

19. 15

As 10 − 5 − 2 is 3, there are three green marbles. This means the probability of choosing a green marble is $\frac{3}{10}$. Multiplying the numerator and denominator by 5 gives the identical fraction of $\frac{15}{50}$. This means that a green marble is expected to be chosen 15 times out of 50 selections.

20. 20

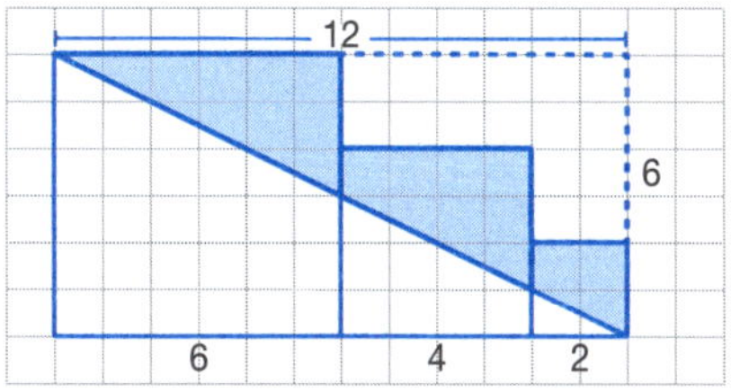

The squares have side lengths 6 units, 4 units and 2 units. The diagram shows a rectangle with sides 12 units by 6 units. As 12 × 6 is 72, the rectangle has an area of 72 units^2. The triangle is half the rectangle and so has an area of 36 units^2. Now look at the three squares. As 36 + 16 + 4 is 56, the three squares have a total area of 56 units. The shaded area is the difference between 56 units^2 and 36 units^2. As 56 − 36 = 20, the shaded area is 20 units^2.

NOTES